P9-DOH-018

3 1502 00855 9864

WITHDRAWN

15.79

DEC 2018

QUARTERBACK

Also by John Feinstein

The First Major
The Legends Club
Where Nobody Knows Your Name
The Classic Palmer
One on One
Moment of Glory
Are You Kidding Me?
Living on the Black
Tales from Q School
Last Dance
Next Man Up
Let Me Tell You a Story
Caddy for Life
The Punch
Open
The Last Amateurs
The Majors
A March to Madness
The First Coming
A Civil War
Winter Games
A Good Walk Spoiled
Play Ball
Hard Courts
Running Mates
Forever's Team
A Season Inside
A Season on the Brink

QUARTERBACK

INSIDE THE MOST IMPORTANT POSITION IN
THE NATIONAL FOOTBALL LEAGUE

JOHN FEINSTEIN

DOUBLEDAY • NEW YORK

HELEN M. PLUM MEMORIAL LIBRARY
LOMBARD, ILLINOIS

Copyright © 2018 by John Feinstein

All rights reserved. Published in the United States by Doubleday,
a division of Penguin Random House LLC, New York, and
distributed in Canada by Random House of Canada, a division
of Penguin Random House Canada Limited, Toronto.

www.doubleday.com

DOUBLEDAY and the portrayal of an anchor with a dolphin are
registered trademarks of Penguin Random House LLC.

Book design by Michael Collica
Jacket photograph by Dan Thornberg / Eye Em / Getty Images
Jacket design Michael J. Windsor

Library of Congress Control Number: 2018031266

ISBN: 9780385543033 (hardcover)
ISBN: 9780385543040 (ebook)

MANUFACTURED IN THE UNITED STATES OF AMERICA

1 3 5 7 9 10 8 6 4 2

First Edition

3 1502 00855 9864

This is for three men who helped make *A Civil War* possible twenty-two years ago and have remained close friends ever since: Bob Sutton . . . Tim Kelly . . . Dick Hall . . . I cherish their friendship.

QUARTERBACK

INTRODUCTION

On the afternoon of October 1, 2017, the Pittsburgh Steelers and Baltimore Ravens met in Baltimore, in what was billed by the media as a "battle for first place," in the National Football League's AFC North Division.

Both teams were 2-1, but the Ravens' record was deceiving. They had opened the season by beating the decidedly mediocre Cincinnati Bengals and then had beaten the historically bad Cleveland Browns in week two before traveling to London to get pounded 44–7 by a surprisingly good Jacksonville team.

The Steelers had also beaten the Browns and had then beaten the Minnesota Vikings before losing—stunningly—to the Chicago Bears on the road.

In short, people were still trying to figure out how good the two teams were, and this game would certainly provide some clues.

The Ravens had not had a good off-season. Their most reliable receiver, Dennis Pitta, had suffered a career-ending hip injury during one of their mini-camps—or as they're now called in NFL vernacular, "OTAs—Organized Team Activities." The team's 2015 first-round draft pick, wide receiver Breshaud Perriman, had blazing speed; his 4.29 40-yard dash had wowed Baltimore's scouts. He had just one weakness: an inability to actually *catch* a football on a regular basis, a glaring issue given that his job was to *catch* footballs.

Both starting guards, including Pro Bowler Marshal Yanda, were out for the season. There was no consistent running back, unless you counted Alex Collins, a talented rookie with a penchant for fumbling. Danny Woodhead, an excellent third-down receiver acquired during the off-season was—you guessed it—injured.

Joe Flacco had been the Ravens' starting quarterback for ten years—having been drafted in 2008 out of the University of Delaware. His arrival had ended a search for a solid quarterback that had started when the team first moved from Cleveland prior to the 1996 season. The Ravens had actually won a Super Bowl after the 2000 season with Trent Dilfer playing quarterback, largely because they had put together one of the great defenses in league history.

General manager Ozzie Newsome had taken Flacco with the eighteenth pick in the '08 draft at the urging of scouting director Eric DeCosta, who had gone to see Delaware play at Navy the previous October and had left the game at halftime with stars in his eyes.

"I was supposed to go to a game at Maryland [twenty-eight miles away from Navy–Marine Corps Memorial Stadium] later that afternoon," he said. "I was so excited about Flacco, I went back to the office and began digging out any tape of him I could find."

Flacco was six feet six, weighed 240 pounds, and had a cannon for an arm. He looked effortless throwing the ball downfield, and, even though Navy's defense that year wasn't very good, DeCosta watched in awe as Flacco made difficult throws look easy.

Ten years later, Flacco had won a Super Bowl and had been, for a while, the highest-paid player in the NFL. Even though other quarterbacks had surpassed him in total dollars, Flacco was still doing just fine. He was in the second year of a six-year contract worth $120.6 million. At thirty-two, he was, without question, the face of the Ravens franchise.

Which meant—as with almost every starting quarterback in the NFL—he often went from toast-of-the-town to roasted-by-the-town from week to week. Most of the time the criticism rolled off Flacco's broad back. He had acquired the nickname of "Cool Joe" early on because his demeanor almost always stayed the same. If you were going strictly off facial expressions or body language, it was difficult to tell if Flacco had just thrown a touchdown pass or an interception.

"The criticism comes with the territory," he said with a smile. "If you're going to accept being put on a pedestal when you play well, you better be ready to accept getting chopped down when you don't play well."

"Even when it's not your fault?" I asked one day.

"It's *always* my fault," he said.

On that warm October afternoon on their home turf against the Steelers, it was Flacco's fault. Even if he had plenty of help.

The Ravens were bad. They trailed 19–0 at halftime and lost 26–9 in a game that really wasn't that close. Flacco threw two fourth-quarter interceptions—one a deflection—and Collins had a critical first-half fumble. The defense, which had caused ten turnovers in the first two games, couldn't get Ben Roethlisberger and the Steelers off the field.

In all, it was a long day for all the Ravens. It began with the team kneeling as one prior to the playing of the national anthem. This was a week after Donald Trump's rant about players not standing for the anthem, and the Ravens had decided to take a knee together before the anthem. Even though the song hadn't yet begun and the entire team was standing when the music started, many fans booed the gesture.

The boos would have been quickly forgotten had the team played better. But it didn't, and the boos were heard frequently during the second half—except for a brief period when the Ravens rallied to close the deficit to 19–9.

After the game ended with the stands half empty and the Steelers walking away with a 26–9 victory, Flacco was brought into the interview room by the Ravens' public relations staff.

Every NFL quarterback comes into the interview room postgame. Most wait as long as possible before going in. They chat with teammates, shower, dress, and, as their final act before leaving the stadium to meet their families, come in to talk to the media. They can take as long as they want to, because there are two people the media must listen to after a game: the head coach and the quarterback. The coach usually goes in as soon as the locker room is opened to the media. The quarterback almost always goes last—often forty-five minutes to an hour after the game has ended.

Not Flacco.

If Ravens coach John Harbaugh doesn't go in quickly, Flacco is apt to be the first one in, still in uniform—except for his helmet.

"You have to do it, you might as well get it over with," he said with a smile. "I don't mind it. I usually know what the questions are going to be. So I go in, get it done, and then get ready to go home."

Flacco has five kids, so when the team plays at home, he doesn't linger in the locker room the way some players do. On rare occasions, to give him a break from the interview room questions, Kevin Byrne—who has run public relations for the Ravens since 1986, when they were still in Cleveland—will tell Flacco not to come to the interview room.

When that happens, he stands in front of his locker and answers the same questions he would have gotten in the interview room.

Following the Steelers loss, Flacco came in right after Harbaugh. After he had answered a general question about the game, someone said, "Joe, how would you assess your play today?"

Flacco smiled for a moment, shrugged, and said, "I sucked. We sucked as an offense, and I'm the quarterback, so I'm responsible. It's pretty simple."

The real answer to the question would have been something like this: "Look, my most reliable receiver went down in June. I threw a perfect deep ball early to Mike Wallace and he dropped it. Our first-round draft pick from 2015 couldn't catch a cold, much less a football. Our offensive line is a mess, and we've got no running game. There's only so much I can do."

Of course, there was no way Flacco was going to say any of that. "You never throw your teammates under the bus," he said. "Anything you say that's critical of anyone but yourself is going to look like you're making excuses—and, to some degree, it *is* making excuses. If I whined that way, fans wouldn't buy it, but more important than that, I couldn't go home and look my father in the eye. You take the credit when it's all good, you take the blame when it's bad.

"And when you're the quarterback, the blame, ultimately, *should* always fall on you."

—

Not long after Flacco had finished talking to the media, I got in my car to drive home. I turned on the Ravens postgame show on WBAL radio. Keith Mills, the host, was just starting to take phone calls.

The first caller was wound up and upset. "Keith," he said, "when is Joe Flacco going to stand up and take responsibility for the failures of this offense?"

Mills didn't really know what to say. Politely, on air, he said, "I thought he did." Later, off air, he said, "Beyond saying, 'I sucked,' what else was he supposed to say?"

Exactly right.

—

That caller represents the heart and soul of what this book is about.

There is no position in sports that is more glamorous, more lucrative, more visible, more high-risk than being a starting NFL quarterback. In thirty-two cities, the quarterback carries the hopes and dreams of millions of fans and is the centerpiece for the media that covers every NFL team.

The NFL—even with all the issues that have beset it in recent years—remains the colossus of professional sports in the United States. It dominates the sports media twelve months a year. An off day by a starting quarterback *during off-season workouts in May* can cause all-out panic among those covering a team.

Billion-dollar franchises may rise or fall on the shoulders of one twentysomething athlete. Aaron Rodgers is carted off a football field in Minnesota and the entire state of Wisconsin goes into mourning. The most controversial and talked-about figure in Washington, D.C., in 2017 might have been Donald Trump, but Kirk Cousins wasn't far behind.

Quarterback is a dependent position. Linemen must block, receivers must run precise patterns and make catches while being crushed by defenders. But if it all goes right, the quarterback becomes the most popular man in that city. If it goes wrong—no matter how razor-thin the margin, and—even if he's standing on the sideline when the decisive plays are being made—he becomes the fall guy.

The line between being rich, famous, and beloved—or rich, famous, and excoriated—is almost invisible at times. Quarterbacks make the most money; they receive the most endorsements; and they are the subject of the most publicity.

They know that eight months of preparing to play sixteen games can go down the drain in a heartbeat—and, ultimately, the finger will be pointed at them.

Doug Williams, the first African American quarterback to start and win a Super Bowl, talks about "seeing colors." The reference is to a quarterback who feels the pressure of huge men bearing down on him and releases the ball or sprints from the pocket a split second too soon rather than hanging in there, knowing a painful hit is coming, and making the play.

The great ones don't see colors. It is easier said than done.

No one is ever neutral on a quarterback's performance—including the quarterback.

———

Flacco's case is a prime example. He signed a new contract shortly after leading the Ravens to a victory in the 2013 Super Bowl. He had turned down a long-term offer from the Ravens the previous spring because he believed if he had a good year, he would be paid a lot more than what the team was offering. He was praised for "betting on himself" when the bet paid off, and he signed for six years at about $20 million a year. He never saw it quite that way.

"Unless I got seriously hurt, someone was going to pay me good money at the end of my contract," he said. "I was going to be twenty-eight, presumably going into the prime years of my career. I knew if I produced, [Ravens owner] Steve Bisciotti would pay me fairly because he's that kind of guy. And if he didn't, someone else would. I didn't see it as that much of a gamble."

Quarterbacks are almost always the highest-paid players on their teams. They are also the most visible because they touch the ball on every offensive play. They get credit for touchdown passes—even if they toss the ball 5 yards to someone who then runs 90 yards through the defense—and blame for interceptions—even if they throw a perfect pass and it bounces off their receiver's hands.

Most are like Flacco: they get it. They know that the fans and media will rip them for the failures of their teammates and canonize them for the success of the team.

Or, as in the case of the Kansas City Chiefs' Alex Smith in 2017, they know they can go from being an MVP candidate to hearing media members ask the coach if he's thinking about benching him—*in six weeks*.

The best quarterbacks understand that the mood of an entire city is often on their shoulders. When Aaron Rodgers broke his collarbone in the sixth week of the 2017 season, virtually everyone in Wisconsin woke up the next day in a bad mood. You almost expected the Green Bay Packers to show up the next Sunday wearing black patches on their uniforms that said "Aaron," as if he had died.

Fortunately, Rodgers was very much alive, just hurt. It was the Packers' season that had died. They were 4-1 when Rodgers went down.

They went 3-8 the rest of the way, Rodgers coming back for one late-season game. Clearly rusty and looking nowhere close to healthy, he threw three interceptions (and three touchdown passes) in a 31–24 loss to a good Carolina Panthers team.

Rodgers was not, by any stretch, the only quarterback who suffered a major injury that destroyed his team's season.

Andrew Luck missed the entire season in Indianapolis. Predictably, the Colts finished 4-12.

Luck landed in Indianapolis in 2012 after being the number one pick in the NFL draft coming out of Stanford. The Colts were in the number one spot because Peyton Manning had missed all of the 2011 season after neck surgery. As the Colts' losses piled up that fall, many Indianapolis fans began to root for their team to keep losing so it could draft Luck. The slogan "Suck for Luck" was born. The Colts finished 2-14.

Luck was a golden child most of his life. He was the son of a former NFL quarterback who went on to become athletic director at West Virginia, his alma mater, and was then hired by the NCAA.

After retiring, Oliver Luck was the general manager of two teams in the World League of American Football—one in London and the other in Frankfurt. As a result, Andrew grew up at least as much a soccer fan as a football fan. But he had his father's gift for the game, and was a bigger (six-foot-four, 240-pound), more athletic version of his dad, who was listed at six-two, 196 pounds. He chose Stanford because it was a great place to go to school and because he would be playing for Jim Harbaugh, also a former NFL quarterback.

By the time he was a redshirt junior, it was almost a given that Luck would be the number one pick in the NFL draft. He almost certainly would have been the number one pick a year earlier, but he chose to return to Stanford because he liked college and wanted to graduate.

A year later, after Luck led Stanford to an 11-2 record and finished second in the Heisman Trophy voting behind Baylor's Robert Griffin III, the Colts took him with the number one pick. Washington took Griffin after giving up a bevy of draft picks to get up to number two.

Both starred as rookies, leading their teams to the playoffs. The Colts went from 2-14 in the YAP (Year After Peyton) to 11-5 in the first year AAA—After Andrew Arrived. Both teams lost in the opening round of the playoffs. Washington lost at home to Seattle in a game that changed

Griffin's life and the arc of the franchise. Griffin tore up his knee, was kept on the field by Coach Mike Shanahan after he'd gotten hurt in the first quarter, and was never the same player after that afternoon.

That same day, Luck played well while the Colts were losing on the road to the Baltimore Ravens—who would go on to win the Super Bowl.

Luck's star continued to glow brighter the next two seasons. The Colts were 11-5 again in both seasons, winning one playoff game in 2013 and two in 2014 before losing (badly) to the Patriots in the AFC Championship in the infamous "Deflategate" game.

It was during his fourth season—2015—that injuries began to become an issue for Luck. He missed two early-season games after feeling pain in his throwing shoulder. He came back and played the next five weeks before a lacerated kidney and a torn abdominal muscle forced him out for the rest of the season.

Frustrating as it was, Luck knew—as every football player knows—that injuries are almost inevitable if you have a lengthy career. Even Tom Brady, who seems invincible, missed an entire season after tearing an ACL in week one of the 2008 season.

The Colts certainly weren't worried about the long-term future of their franchise quarterback. On June 29, 2016, a few weeks prior to the start of his fifth training camp, Luck signed a six-year, $140 million contract with the Colts, with $87 million guaranteed. That made him the highest-paid player in the history of the NFL.

"Didn't make me the *best* player in the history of the NFL," he said one night with a smile. "It just meant that I was next in line."

In fact, Derek Carr, Matthew Stafford, Jimmy Garoppolo, and Kirk Cousins have since surpassed Luck's contract in annual value, with Aaron Rodgers and Drew Brees likely to go past them in the near future.

But the upward arc of Luck's career came to a halt in 2016.

The shoulder pain that had kept him out of two games the previous season never completely went away, even after he sat out the last six weeks because of the kidney problem. It didn't hurt enough to keep him out of the lineup, but it wasn't getting better. Making deep throws became more difficult. Then, pushing his way through a revolving door or shaking hands or reaching for a spoon began to hurt.

He had hoped to avoid surgery, but in January 2017, after the Colts had gone 8-8 for a second straight season, he decided it was time to get the injury behind him once and for all and had labrum surgery. He wasn't worried about being ready for OTAs—most veterans need OTAs like a hockey player needs time to practice his skating—but planned to be ready to go at 100 percent when training camp began in July.

Only, it didn't happen. In fact, Luck never took a snap all season. He returned to light practice briefly in October, then flew to the Netherlands in late October to seek treatment. Without Luck, the Colts' season was destroyed: they went 4-12.

It isn't as if a team can't survive an injury to the starting quarterback. Carson Wentz was on his way to winning the MVP Award when he tore his ACL in week fourteen of the Philadelphia Eagles' 2017 season. Nick Foles, who had been a starter previously in the NFL, stepped in and took the Eagles to a Super Bowl championship. It was a wonderful story, but it is worth remembering that the Eagles had already clinched their division when Wentz got hurt, and they got to play both their NFL playoff games at home. If Wentz had been hurt in, say, week seven, it might have been a different story.

There was also Case Keenum, who stepped in for Sam Bradford and took the Minnesota Vikings to the NFC Championship game that same season. Another feel-good story. Except Bradford isn't exactly Luck—or Brady or Drew Brees or Aaron Rodgers. The drop-off at quarterback wasn't that great.

Rodgers, ironically, was hurt in a game against the Vikings—in week six. The Packers were 4-1 when he was carted off with a broken collarbone. By the time he returned, the Packers were 7-6, having barely beaten the winless Browns to avoid being 6-7. They went from Super Bowl contenders to, ultimately, out of the playoffs.

If you lose a good quarterback, you might be able to survive, usually short term. Lose a great one and, almost always, your season is done unless your backup is Tom Brady, who stepped in when Drew Bledsoe was injured the second week of the 2000 season and went on to become, well, Tom Brady.

Perhaps Jimmy Garoppolo, who took over for Brady during his Deflategate suspension and is now in San Francisco, will be the closest thing we've seen to Brady since then.

Playing quarterback isn't like playing any other position in professional sports. The quarterback runs every one of his team's offensive plays. He is the glamour guy; the rich guy; the face of the franchise; and, when things go wrong, the guy who takes the fall. And quarterbacks take a physical beating.

"There's a difference between being injured and being hurt," Alex Smith, who played his thirteenth NFL season a year ago, said. "Most games you come into the locker room, take off your uniform, and sort of check around to make sure nothing hurts too badly. *Something always hurts, it's just a matter of how much.*"

The quarterback—along with the head coach—is also the team spokesman. He is expected to speak to the media after every game, more often than not in the interview room with all the cameras clicking and whirring.

What I set out to do in this book is try to get inside the head of a number of quarterbacks who have played in the NFL for a while; who have experienced the best and worst of playing the position; who have dealt with injuries and fans and the media ready to point a finger at them, first and foremost when their team doesn't win the Super Bowl.

I didn't go looking for the five or six *best* quarterbacks in the NFL, I went looking for a cross-section of *smart* quarterbacks—knowing full well that only the smartest guys would understand what I was hoping to accomplish in writing this book largely through their eyes.

I ended up with what I think was an eclectic list of five very bright, very accomplished (and very patient) men: Alex Smith, Andrew Luck, Joe Flacco, Ryan Fitzpatrick, and Doug Williams.

Williams is different from the other four in that he's retired and he's African American. I needed an African American voice in the book because the experience—even now—is very different than it is for white quarterbacks. Williams was the first African American quarterback to win a Super Bowl and can vividly remember when the mere notion of a black quarterback in the NFL was worthy of headlines.

Plus, he's willing to speak his mind. Williams is now director of player personnel in Washington. When I asked him where Deshaun Watson, the superb Houston rookie whose season was ended by an ACL injury, would have gone in the 2017 draft had he been white, he smiled and said: "Before [Mitchell] Trubisky."

"Trubisky went number two," I said. Watson had been picked twelfth.

"I know," Williams said.

There is great hope in Houston right now because of what Texans fans have seen of Watson. In Chicago, there's hope too—but questions still—about Trubisky. That's pretty much the way it is in the NFL. If you think you've got your franchise quarterback, the feeling is that everything else will fall into place.

If not, well, you're the Cleveland Browns.

PART ONE

1

As he trotted back onto the field at Arrowhead Stadium on the evening of January 6, 2018, Alex Smith knew exactly what was at stake at that moment.

Having led 21–3 at halftime, the Kansas City Chiefs now trailed the Tennessee Titans 22–21 with 2:18 left to play in the AFC wildcard game. A little more than three hours earlier, when the game kicked off just after 3:30 Central time, the temperature had been thirty degrees, though it felt colder because of the swirling winds whipping through the stadium. Now, with the sun down, it was considerably colder.

The last thing on Smith's mind was the weather.

"Once you get into a game, you stop thinking about whether it's hot or cold or windy or rainy," he said. "If there's a lot of wind or if the ball's wet, you have to think about that because that affects the way you play. But you really don't feel the cold, especially at that point in the season. You're way beyond that. What's happening on the field is way too important."

What was happening as Smith stepped into the huddle was pretty simple: the Chiefs' entire season was at stake. All the off-season work; the springtime OTAs; training camp in the brutal Midwestern summer heat; and sixteen enervating regular season games essentially came down to one play.

"There was a chance we might get the ball back," Smith said. "But even if we did, it would have taken something miraculous to save us by then. This was our best chance. That's why we knew we had to go for it."

Their chance came with the ball on the Tennessee 44-yard line. The Chiefs had driven the ball to that point from their own 27 after the Titans had scored to go ahead with 6:06 left in the game. Plenty of time. Except the Chiefs hadn't scored in the second half, while the Titans found the end zone on all three of their possessions.

The Chiefs had one last chance to save their season. Smith, one of the National Football League's more nimble quarterbacks even at age thirty-three, had picked up 18 yards to the Tennessee 42 on the second play of the drive, only to have the play called back by a holding penalty on tight end Demetrius Harris. The hold wasn't the most egregious call—or non-call—made that evening by referee Jeff Triplette and his crew, but it was questionable.

Harris made up for his mistake by catching a third-and-4 pass from Smith to set the Chiefs up at the Tennessee 45 with a first down. One more first down and they would probably be in field goal kicker Harrison Butker's range.

But the offense had bogged down there. Kareem Hunt, the NFL's leading rusher as a rookie, picked up a yard on first down. A short Smith-to-Harris pass was broken up. Then, with nobody open, Smith had been forced to scramble and had barely made it back to the line of scrimmage.

Suddenly, it was fourth-and-9, the two-minute warning was approaching, and the Chiefs had to take their second time-out. Smith came to the sideline and consulted with head coach Andy Reid and offensive coordinator Matt Nagy. Six weeks earlier, in the midst of a skid during which the Chiefs had lost six of seven games, Reid had handed the play-calling duties to Nagy.

"Sometimes when things go wrong you have to look at yourself," Reid had said in announcing the change.

For Smith, the only real change had been logistical. Nagy had been at Reid's side for four years and thought very much the way Reid did. He had also been the voice Smith heard inside his helmet when plays were relayed in.

"The only real difference was that Matt didn't have to relay Andy's calls," he said. "That probably saved five to ten seconds on each snap. Gave me more time if I wanted to check off [change the play] at the line or if I wanted to change a protection."

When you see a quarterback step to the line and point at someone on the defensive side, it is usually to let his offensive line know that someone is in a different spot than expected. That can mean that who blocks whom is being changed.

Reid and Nagy were in agreement that the best play call was "twenty-two on three set—skat-red-right, personnel." In English that reflected Smith's receiving options, the line protections, and the personnel on the field. He could also audible.

That meant Albert Wilson, a fourth-year wide receiver, would be the primary target running down the middle of the field. If Travis Kelce had been in the game, he would have been the primary receiver. Kelce was the Chiefs' leading receiver, Smith's go-to guy on big plays. He had caught eighty-three balls in the regular season and had made his fourth catch of the game late in the first half on a short crossing route.

Kelce was hit as soon as he caught the ball by the Titans' Zach Brown. As Kelce was going down, Tennessee safety Johnathan Cyprien dove at him and hit him helmet-to-helmet. For all its talk about player safety, the NFL still hasn't figured it out. According to the league's apologists, Cyprien's hit did not merit a penalty because Kelce was "a runner," as opposed to being "helpless"—trying to make a catch. Kelce was on his way down because of Brown's tackle, and pretty helpless. Finally, for the 2018 season, the NFL tightened the rule.

Whether Cyprien intended to hurt him or not didn't matter. He did. When Kelce attempted to stand up, it was clear he had been knocked silly, and he fell into the arms of teammates. Watching Kelce being led off the field, Smith knew he was done for the night.

"You could see it in his eyes," he said later. "At that moment, I don't think he knew where he was."

The lack of a flag and the absence of Kelce didn't matter for the next few minutes. Kelce's catch had set up a third-and-6 at the Chiefs' 25. Seven plays later, Smith threw a perfect 14-yard scoring strike to Demarcus Robinson with three seconds left in the half, and Kansas City's halftime lead was 21–3.

Thoughts of a trip to New England—back to the place where the season had started—danced through the minds of most in the sold-out stands of Arrowhead Stadium.

Except the lead didn't last. The Titans scored touchdowns on their first three second-half series—the first coming when quarterback Marcus Mariota tried to throw a pass into the end zone on third-and-goal from the 6-yard line, only to have it knocked away by nickelback Darrelle Revis. The ball ricocheted right back to Mariota, who caught it and dove into the end zone. It was the first time in NFL playoff history that a quarterback threw and caught a touchdown pass on the same play.

Mariota-to-Mariota was a key play, since it closed the gap to 21–10 after a drive that lasted eight minutes, but it also turned out to be a harbinger. The Chiefs had one great chance to perhaps put the game away when they recovered a fumbled punt at the Tennessee 30-yard line. But the offense wasn't the same without Kelce and didn't move the ball. Butker, who had been remarkably reliable all season, came in for a 48-yard field goal attempt, but the ball clanged off the right upright. And so, Mariota's 22-yard touchdown pass to Eric Decker with 6:06 left had put the Titans in the lead, 22–21.

On the ensuing two-point conversion attempt, Chiefs safety Daniel Sorensen blitzed, spun Mariota around, and appeared to force a fumble, which he picked up and took the other way for what would have been a two-point play for the Chiefs, giving them the lead back.

But referee Jeff Triplette, working his last NFL game, decided that Mariota's forward progress had been stopped and ruled him down. That left the Chiefs trailing.

Which is why the game, and Smith's five seasons in Kansas City, suddenly came down to one play.

That wasn't on Smith's mind as he came to the line and waited for the snap. Looking at the Tennessee defense, he thought the coaches had made the correct call, so he didn't audible.

The shotgun snap from center Zach Fulton was true, and Smith took a couple of quick steps back, saw that Wilson had come open for a moment, and zinged the ball down the middle in his direction. But the Titans had safety help coming from deep, and Wilson was hit as he reached for the ball. It hit off his fingers and bounced away harmlessly.

The game wasn't over. The Chiefs had all time-outs and the two-minute warning still left. But Titans running back Derrick Henry ran the ball once for 12 yards and then for 22 yards. The second first down eliminated any doubt. Mariota knelt twice and Kansas City's season, which had started with so much promise, was over.

The Chiefs trudged silently into their locker room. There really wasn't much to say. "You can talk about it all you want," Smith said. "You can talk about the missed calls—and they were huge—no doubt. You can talk about Kels [Kelce] getting hurt and what that meant. You can second-guess yourself—that's sort of natural.

"In the end, none of it matters. Your first goal every season is to get to postseason. Once you do that, anything can happen. You can win on the road, you can lose at home. You can be the sixth seed and win the Super Bowl. It happens. But there are no second chances once you get to January. We had our chance. We had the big lead at halftime.

"Bottom line is always the bottom line: the final score. We just didn't get it done."

Statistically, Smith had just completed his best season in the NFL. He had led his team to a second straight AFC Western division title—the first time in the Chiefs' fifty-eight-year history that had happened. He had thrown for more than 4,000 yards in spite of sitting out the regular season finale after the Chiefs had clinched the division title a week earlier.

And yet, almost from the instant Smith's last pass fell incomplete, the biggest question in Kansas City was who would be under center when the 2018 season started the following September.

"Nothing is forever," Smith said. "Especially in football."

Especially when you're a quarterback.

—

Ryan Fitzpatrick had been in the NFL for the same thirteen seasons as Smith. His career arc, however, could not have been more different.

Several years earlier, Smith and Fitzpatrick had both played in the annual celebrity golf tournament held each July (shortly before the start of training camp) in Lake Tahoe. As luck would have it, the two were paired together on the first day.

The introductions in Tahoe tend to be fairly lavish, if only to remind the crowd just how important each celebrity golfer is in his own world.

And so, it wasn't surprising that when Smith stepped up onto the tee, the starter grandly announced, "Please welcome the *number one* pick in the 2005 NFL draft, from the Kansas City Chiefs . . . Alex Smith!"

A moment later, it was Fitzpatrick's turn to be introduced. He had asked that the starter not mention his Harvard education, whom he was playing for, or any success he'd had in his career. Instead, the starter followed Fitzpatrick's request and said, "Please welcome the *two-hundred-and-fiftieth* pick in the 2005 NFL draft . . . Ryan Fitzpatrick."

Smith had been drafted ahead of the other 255 players chosen in that draft. Fitzpatrick had been drafted ahead of the last six.

"And happy to be chosen there," he said with a laugh.

In a twist, Smith and Fitzpatrick had almost been teammates—in college.

Both were excellent students in high school: Fitzpatrick growing up near Phoenix; Smith in San Diego. Neither was recruited very much—if at all—by the so-called big-time schools. Fitzpatrick, after being ardently pursued by Coach Tim Murphy, decided to go to Harvard.

"I was figuring I'd get a chance to start, play on a good team [Harvard was always at or near the top of the Ivy League], and I'd leave with a Harvard degree. Anything in football after that would just be gravy. I certainly wasn't counting on it."

Smith felt much the same way. "When I dreamed about football as a kid, it was about college football," he said. "It was about being in a packed stadium on a Saturday and getting to play in a bowl game when the season was over. The thought of the NFL never crossed my mind. It was always about college football for me."

Even though Smith's Helix High School won a state championship in Smith's senior year, most of the credit went to his teammate Reggie Bush, who would go on to win the Heisman Trophy at USC in 2005. (Helix also produced NBA star Bill Walton.) Smith was rated as a "two-star" prospect by the various scouting services, meaning he was considered a marginal Division I prospect.

Smith's uncle, John L. Smith, was the head coach at Louisville in the fall of 2001, when Smith was a senior at Helix. Louisville recruited him, but Smith thought there might be some nepotism involved and wasn't sure he wanted to go someplace where people would think he got his scholarship only because his uncle was the coach.

Utah had also shown some interest, and Smith was familiar with the Salt Lake City area, largely because he and his family often skied in Utah, so he was intrigued.

And then there was Harvard.

"I was interested in the Ivy League in general. We made a trip east the summer before my senior year and visited Harvard, Yale, Princeton, and Penn. I liked them all, but I really liked Coach Murphy and, well, Harvard was Harvard. My mom was completely sold on Harvard.

"I honestly think I would have ended up there if not for the postseason thing. It wasn't as if Utah was telling me they were dying to have me. In fact, the thought was that I'd redshirt as a freshman, which was fine. But I had always thought of college football as ending with your team playing in a bowl game—any bowl game. I wanted that to be part of my college experience.

"The Ivy League doesn't let its champion play postseason. I had trouble understanding that, and it really was kind of a downer for me when making my decision."

For some reason that can only be explained, no doubt, by those smart enough to be Ivy League presidents, the conference allows teams from every other sport—including basketball—to take part in postseason play. Two Ivy League teams have made basketball's Final Four: Bill Bradley's famous Princeton team in 1965 and Pennsylvania in 1979. In recent years, both Harvard and Yale have pulled first-round upsets that brought the schools and the league a good deal of attention—not to mention revenue. In 2010 Cornell reached the Sweet Sixteen.

Smith finally chose Utah, a solid Division I program that had gone to a bowl game in 2001. He knew he would be asked to redshirt (not play as a freshman in order to gain eligibility for a fifth fall) at Utah, which was not a problem with him, even though he would be entering college as a junior since he had received nine AP credits in high school.

Had he chosen to go to Harvard, Smith would not have redshirted—the Ivy League doesn't allow it—but wouldn't have started there as a freshman since the Crimson returned Neil Rose, who was a senior, and Fitzpatrick, a sophomore, at quarterback.

"Ryan was perfect for us to come in and back Neil up and then take over," Harvard coach Tim Murphy said. "He was an excellent student, so we knew he could get into school and I knew he'd learn fast, so he'd be ready when Neil graduated. As it turned out, he was ready to play before Neil was done. We had to find ways to get him on the field."

Like Smith, Fitzpatrick harbored no thoughts about an NFL career. He was an economics major at Harvard and almost certainly would have gone to grad school if he hadn't been given the chance to play football after graduation. In his senior season, Fitzpatrick led Harvard to a 10-0 record and began to get attention from NFL scouts.

In those days, the draft was held over two days—as opposed to now, when it drags out over three—and Fitzpatrick knew he wasn't going to be taken during the first three rounds on day one. By the time the seventh and final round started the next day, he had resigned himself to the possibility that he wouldn't be drafted at all.

Minutes before the draft ended, the St. Louis Rams took him with pick number 250. Fitzpatrick was delighted. "I wanted to be drafted," he said. "Teams will always give someone they drafted a shot as opposed to someone they sign as a free agent. I knew I'd have a shot to make the team."

He made the Rams and started three games after coming off the bench in week eleven to lead them to a 33–27 overtime win over the Titans in a game his team had trailed 24–3 at halftime. When he started a week later, he became the first Harvard graduate to start an NFL game at quarterback.

Two years later, his odyssey began. He was traded to Cincinnati, where he stayed for two seasons before moving to Buffalo to play for the Bills for four seasons; to Tennessee to play one year for the Titans; to Houston and then to the Jets for two seasons. He started for most of two seasons in Buffalo and often spelled starters in Cincinnati, Tennessee, and Houston.

In his first season in New York, he had a career year, starting all season and leading the Jets to a 10-6 record, missing the playoffs on the final Sunday by losing to his former team, the Bills, and the Jets' former coach Rex Ryan.

"That one hurt," he said. "Our fate was completely in our hands, and we let it get away. I felt responsible."

The quarterback is always responsible.

A year later, he lost his starting job, then got it back during a miserable 5-11 season. New York fans have short memories, and Fitzpatrick was booed as the season unraveled. Getting his job back and a win in the season finale was small consolation.

"I honestly thought my career might be over," he said. "I thought maybe it should be over, it was time. I'd played twelve years, a lot longer than I ever expected to play. I'd made a lot more money than I ever expected to make and had a lot more success than I think people ever thought I had. I remember when I went past twenty-five thousand yards [in career passing yardage], my dad was so proud. So, if it was over, I was okay with it, although it certainly wasn't the exit I'd hoped for."

Then came May and an offer to go to Tampa Bay to back up and mentor Jameis Winston. The Bucs appeared to be on the verge of a breakthrough, and there was no doubt that Winston, the oft-controversial 2013 Heisman Trophy winner from Florida State, was the centerpiece of the renaissance.

Even though it meant moving his family—six children, the oldest eleven—yet again, Fitzpatrick decided to go back for one more year. The money wasn't close to what he had made in New York—$12 million in 2016—but $3 million to back up Winston was a pretty fair deal.

So, as the old song from *The Beverly Hillbillies* went, he and his wife, Liza, loaded up the truck and moved to Tampa . . . Bay, that is. Swimming pools, a rising football team.

In the meantime, Andrew Luck was contemplating his comeback in Indianapolis. He'd finally had the shoulder surgery he'd wanted to avoid in January and expected to be back in plenty of time to get ready for the 2017 season. Little did he know that he would never see the field.

Joe Flacco was also on the mend, slowly recovering from an injury he suffered lifting weights during the off-season. In an ideal world, he would have played in one preseason game, but, as it turned out, everyone including Flacco decided not to take any risks in a game that ultimately didn't count. Unlike Luck, though, he was on the practice field and knew he'd be ready to go for the opener in Cincinnati.

As for Doug Williams, he hadn't taken an NFL snap since 1989, when he had retired at the age of thirty-four after losing his job as Washington's starter to Mark Rypien. Less than two years earlier, Williams had become the first African American to start in the Super Bowl at quarterback. He had thrown for 340 yards in the game and had thrown four touchdown passes in the *second quarter,* leading Washington from a 10–0 first-quarter deficit to a 35–10 halftime lead on the Denver Broncos. The final was 42–10.

Williams had been a coach and a scout after retiring and, finally, in the spring of 2017 had been named Washington's director of player personnel. Much like Ozzie Newsome in Baltimore in 1996, he wasn't given the title of general manager even though he had the responsibilities of one.

His attitude was much the same as Newsome's had been. "When I prove to them I can do the job, they'll give me the title," he said. "I don't need the title. I want the job. I want the chance to prove myself."

He smiled. "That's all I've ever asked my entire life."

2

Doug Williams never wanted to be a football player. His first loves growing up in Zachary, Louisiana, were baseball and basketball.

"I thought I was the second coming of Pete Maravich or Don Drysdale or both," he said, laughing in his deep baritone at the memory. "I had no desire to play football. I didn't want to get hit. I didn't want any part of contact."

When he got to the eighth grade, he was informed that he didn't have a choice anymore about football. The informer was Robert, his oldest brother. Doug was the sixth of Robert and Laura Williams's eight children. Robert, the oldest, was fifteen years older than Doug. He had played football and baseball at Grambling and had gone to training camp with the Cleveland Indians in 1964. But he tore his rotator cuff that spring. In those days, the injury was career-ending. Robert Williams came home to Zachary to coach basketball at Chaneyville High School, assist with the football team, and coach the junior high school football team.

His little brother was *going* to play football.

"Actually he gave me a choice," Doug said. "He said I could play football or fight him, and if I won the fight, I didn't have to play. So I played. No sense wasting time getting beaten up."

Doug Williams was five feet four and weighed "about nothing" as an eighth-grader. A year later, he was five-six and still weighed close to nothing when he enrolled at Chaneyville, the all-black high school in still-segregated Zachary. Back then, the town, which is about fifteen miles north of Baton Rouge, had a population of just over 5,000. It has grown since then to a population of just under 15,000 in the 2010 census.

Chaneyville's coach was Bernard Lucas, a no-nonsense former player at Southern. Doug told him that he was a quarterback, even though "I could barely see over the line when I lined up to take a snap." Since he wasn't going to see much time behind more experienced (and bigger) quarterbacks, Lucas played Williams at safety.

That didn't last very long. Early in the season, Chaneyville faced Second Ward High School. The Ward quarterback was a talented freshman named Terry Robiskie, who would go on to be one of the first African American players at LSU and then play five years in the NFL.

"We were both ninth-graders," Williams remembered. "I hadn't grown yet. Terry was already the same size he was when he went to LSU [six-one, 210 pounds, according to his bio]. Terry ran a play right at me. I tried to go low to tackle him, and he just ran right over me. I went over to Coach Lucas and said, 'Do whatever you want to me, but I'm not playing defense anymore.'"

When Robiskie got to LSU in 1973, he was converted to running back. That's what coaches did with black quarterbacks in those days.

Williams continued to play baseball and basketball in high school—he was all-district in basketball—but he blossomed as a football player in his junior year. By then, he'd had a major growth spurt to reach six feet two and could throw a football a mile. Since his brother had gone to Grambling, he was recruited early by legendary coach Eddie Robinson, who coached at Grambling for fifty-five seasons and won a (then) record 408 games. Joe Paterno surpassed him in 2011 with 409, had 111 victories stripped in 2012 in the Jerry Sandusky scandal, but then had them restored two years later.

"I wanted to play football and baseball in college," Williams said. "Coach Rob said, 'I don't let my quarterbacks play baseball. They need to be in spring ball to learn.' It was Eddie Robinson. If he said I wasn't playing baseball, I wasn't playing baseball. At that point in time you did *not* turn down the chance to play football at Grambling."

In those days, Grambling was known as "the black Notre Dame." Very few Division I schools were willing to play the Tigers. The Southeastern Conference had just started to integrate in football. Kentucky had recruited the first black football player in 1967. LSU and Mississippi, in 1972, were the last teams in the league to desegregate.

That same fall, Tennessee's Condredge Holloway became the SEC's first black quarterback. Holloway had also been recruited by Alabama but had decided on Tennessee after Coach Bear Bryant told him he wouldn't be able to play quarterback because "Alabama's not ready for a black quarterback yet."

"I appreciated his honesty," Holloway said in a later interview.

It wasn't until 1980, when Walter Lewis was a freshman, that Bryant started a black quarterback.

None of this really mattered to Williams. The only SEC school that recruited him as a high school senior in 1973 was LSU—and that was for baseball.

"I played in an American Legion Tournament after my senior year," he said. "A coach from LSU was there, and he said they might be interested in giving me a scholarship to play baseball. I'd already committed to Coach Rob, so it was a moot point. I was going to Grambling."

There were eight quarterbacks taking snaps at preseason practice that summer, and Robinson told Williams he was going to be redshirted so he could spend the season learning the position and getting his feet on the ground academically. A year later, he was the starter and embarked on one of the most prolific college careers in history.

Grambling was 39-8 during Williams's four seasons as a starter. In all, he threw for more than 9,000 yards running Robinson's old-fashioned winged-T offense. As a senior, he led the nation in passing with 3,286 yards and thirty-two touchdown passes. That fall, he finished fourth in the Heisman Trophy voting behind Earl Campbell, Terry Miller, and Ken MacAfee.

"I never thought about the Heisman at all," he said. "The summer before my senior year I was playing in a softball tournament and I got a message to call the SID [sports information director] at Grambling. He said, 'We're going to push you for the Heisman this season.' I said, 'Sounds good,' and went back to playing softball."

The NFL was another story. Williams wanted very much to follow in the footsteps of another great Grambling quarterback, James Harris. Like Williams, Harris, who was six feet four, had a strong arm and had quarterbacked excellent teams at Grambling.

But he had graduated in 1969. At that point only one black quarterback had ever been an NFL or AFL starter. Marlin Briscoe had been drafted in the fourteenth round by the AFL's Denver Broncos in 1968, coming out of Nebraska-Omaha. He'd been converted to defensive back in training camp, but injuries had forced Coach Lou Saban to play him at quarterback. He started five games that season and played well—throwing fourteen touchdown passes in his five starts.

But Saban had decided to go with the immortal Pete Liske as his starter for the 1969 season, and Briscoe asked for his release. He signed with Buffalo and was—naturally—converted to wide receiver. He went on to have an excellent career as a pass catcher in Buffalo, Miami, and New England. One of the quarterbacks he caught passes from was Harris, who had been taken by the Bills in the 1969 draft with the 192nd pick—which in those days was in the eighth round.

The AFL and NFL were getting ready to merge in 1970 and had started holding a common draft two years earlier. The ten AFL teams tended to be more willing to think outside the box than the sixteen NFL teams. In those days, giving a black quarterback a chance to play was considered outside the box.

Harris was a hero and role model for Williams. He was proof that you *could* start at quarterback in the NFL if someone was willing to give you a chance. Williams had a superb senior season, leading to his fourth-place finish in the Heisman Trophy voting. There wasn't any doubt, at least in his mind, that he'd get a chance to play quarterback at the next level.

But a black quarterback in the NFL was still a novelty and, for many teams, considered a risk. There was no combine in those days, so it was up to teams to scout players individually when the season ended.

The one team that showed a keen interest in Williams was the Tampa Bay Buccaneers, then a third-year expansion franchise that had gone 0-14 and 2-12 in its first two seasons. During that winless 1976 season, Bucs coach John McKay, a hugely successful college coach at USC (four national titles), was asked, "Coach, what do you think about your team's execution?" According to legend, McKay replied, "I'm in favor of it."

McKay's running backs coach back then was thirty-seven-year-old Joe Gibbs. McKay sent Gibbs to Grambling to check Williams out.

"He spent two days with me," Williams remembered. "He sat in on the class I was student-teaching to get my degree [in education]; he watched me throw and we talked—for hours. I know the reason I got drafted in the first round was Joe."

Gibbs would go on to become such an icon in Washington, leading the team to three Super Bowl wins, that most people there believe his first name is actually "Coach," because no one would dare call him Joe. Back then, though, he was just a young assistant coach learning his trade.

And he was willing to push his chips into the middle of the table to support taking a quarterback from an all-black college in the first round. Which, in those days, was unheard-of in the NFL.

The Bucs took Williams with the seventeenth pick in the draft. He was the only quarterback taken in the first round. In fact, the second quarterback picked was Matt Cavanaugh, who went to the Patriots in the second round with the fiftieth pick.

Even though he was a first-round pick, the Bucs offered him considerably less money than Williams and his agent, Jimmy Walsh (also Joe Namath's agent), felt a quarterback taken seventeenth should be paid.

"We held out," Williams said. "Finally, we signed a week into training camp for more than they'd offered but less than I thought I should get. But I wanted to get going."

Williams signed a five-year contract that paid him $565,000. "I knew it was relatively low for a first-round quarterback," he said. "But at the time, I didn't care. I just wanted the chance to play."

On his first day in camp, still not knowing the playbook at all, he made a mistake on a play call. Bill Nelsen was the quarterbacks coach, and he didn't have a lot of patience for young quarterbacks—especially one who had missed a week of camp by holding out.

"I don't remember exactly what happened, but there's no doubt I did something wrong," Williams said. "Nelsen started screaming at me, up and down. Wouldn't stop. Finally, Joe [Gibbs], who was at the other end of the field, just ran in and told him to stop. He kept saying, 'You have to give him time to learn. Don't talk to him like that.' I heard later that the two of them got into it again when the coaches met after practice.

"From that day on, I went to Joe's house almost every night. I'd have dinner with him and his family, and then we went over the playbook until I had to get back to camp for curfew. By the time we were finished with the sessions, I knew the playbook cold. I'm not sure where my career might have gone if not for him. He and Coach McKay both believed in me and let me know that. I needed that support."

He needed it, because his life off the field wasn't always easy. He was married with a young child and bought a house in a virtually all-white neighborhood. The neighborhood felt safe. The areas around it, not so much.

"When I drove out of the neighborhood toward Dale Mabry Drive to get to I-4, I went past a corner bar," Williams remembered. "One night, two black guys were leaving there with two white women. They were both shot and killed. When the killers were arrested, they said they'd done it because black guys shouldn't be with white women. Tampa was a *Southern* town. I learned that pretty quickly."

He often learned it when he went to his mailbox or, more often, when the team passed mail on to him. "It wasn't as if there weren't some people pulling for me," he said. "There were. But a lot of the mail was the hate variety. 'Get out of town you n——'; 'We don't want you here n——.'

"I opened one envelope and there was rotting watermelon inside. The note said, 'Try throwing this to your n—— friends. See if they can catch it.'"

He smiled. "After a while I learned that if there was no return address on the envelope, I didn't need to open it."

Fortunately, he had support from Gibbs and McKay.

"When I first got to camp, the guys told me you could tell if McKay liked you if he put an 'ie' on the end of your name. A couple weeks in, during practice he said, 'Dougie, come over here a minute.' After that, it was always 'Dougie.' As long as he called me that, I figured I was okay."

McKay didn't start Williams right away. The Bucs quarterbacks during their 2-12 second season had been Gary Huff, Jeb Blount, and Randy Hedberg. McKay, not wanting to be completely dependent on a rookie, had signed two veteran quarterbacks, Mike Boryla and Mike Rae. Both had enjoyed some success in the NFL: Boryla had started for most of two seasons with the Eagles and had even made the Pro Bowl in 1975. Rae had played for McKay at USC, leading the Trojans to an undefeated season and the national title in 1972, and had been a backup quarterback for the Raiders when they won Super Bowl XI following the 1976 season.

At the end of training camp, McKay decided to go with "Dougie," with Huff, still around, as his backup for the opener against the New York Giants. Williams's debut was brief and painful. He completed two passes—one to a teammate, one to the Giants' Terry Jackson, who returned it for a touchdown. Always blunt, McKay called the pass, "a terrible blunder" after the game.

Williams didn't get a chance to redeem himself because near the end of the first quarter, he was hit late by the Giants' Gary Jeter while going out-of-bounds and came down on his shoulder. He could feel it pop, but ran back to the huddle and called a play. As he came to the line and tried to move the shoulder, he felt a searing pain and fell over in agony.

"As I was lying on the ground, I heard a voice from the stands," Williams said with a laugh, years later. "It was a woman, and she said, 'Lord, they done shot him!'"

Williams sat out the next week with the shoulder injury, and Boryla got the start against the Detroit Lions. He too left injured, a reoccurrence of a knee injury from the previous season, and, as in the opener, Huff came on in relief. The result was the same: the Lions won, 15–7.

A week later, Williams made a triumphant return in Minneapolis, throwing a touchdown pass and leading the Bucs to a 16–10 victory, making the franchise's overall record 3-28. He started eight straight weeks, and the team was a more-than-respectable 4-5 going into Los Angeles to play the Rams. But Jack Youngblood broke Williams's jaw on a blitz in the first half. This time Rae replaced him, and the Rams won, 26–23.

Williams didn't play again until the finale against the Saints, when he started even though his jaw was still wired shut. He didn't get much chance to make anything happen that day because New Orleans controlled the ball for forty-one minutes and won the game, 17–10. The Bucs finished 5-11, a marked improvement from their first two seasons. They were 4-6 in the games Williams started—two of the losses coming when Williams had to leave early with an injury.

"All I wanted was a fair shot to play that year, and Coach McKay gave it to me," Williams said. "When I look back, I realize that if not for him and for Joe [Gibbs] I probably never would have gotten that chance. There were still plenty of people back then who didn't think blacks were smart enough to play quarterback. I mean, Warren Moon had to go to Canada for six years before he got a chance. All he did was have a Hall of Fame career. There are plenty of other examples."

One was Tony Dungy, the Hall of Fame coach who led the Big Ten in passing during his senior year at Minnesota. Dungy went undrafted in 1977 and was brought to training camp that summer by the Pittsburgh Steelers—as a defensive back. When NBC aired a piece on Super Bowl Sunday in 2018 about Gibbs's relationship with Williams, Dungy got choked up the first time he viewed the piece.

"It meant a lot to me," he said on the air, "because it brought back memories of a different time. I'm very glad we've made so much progress since then."

Progress, yes. But anyone who thinks that there is no racial prejudice involved in judging quarterbacks *even today* is naive.

"If you're a star, a first-round pick, a guy who is considered a lock starter, it's not a problem anymore—most of the time," Williams said. "Guys like Jameis Winston, Cam Newton, Deshaun Watson—the no-brainer talents, they don't have a problem. But there are guys who get taken lower because they aren't considered locks. Where did Russell Wilson go? [third round] Dak Prescott? [fourth] The other problem is guys don't get a chance very often to come in as backups, to maybe get a chance to learn holding a clipboard. Backup quarterback is still, more often than not, a white position. There are exceptions, but not that many."

There are also players drafted lower than they should be drafted for reasons other than race. Tom Brady, the all-time "miss," was passed on 198 times in 2000 before the Patriots took him to back up starter Drew Bledsoe because he hadn't started until his senior year at Michigan and was judged a poor athlete after the combine, where he ran a snail-like 5.28 40-yard dash. Wilson was overlooked because of a different sort of bias: he's only five feet eleven.

But there is still a tendency for many teams and scouts to give the benefit of the doubt to the white quarterback. In 2017, the Chicago Bears took Mitchell Trubisky with the second pick in the draft after he had been North Carolina's starting quarterback for one season. Trubisky checked all the scouting boxes for a quarterback: six feet three, 220 pounds, with a strong arm.

Deshaun Watson went ten picks later to the Houston Texans after leading Clemson to a 14-1 record and a national championship. In his two full seasons as a starter, Clemson was 28-2.

Watson is six-two, 215 pounds, and also has a strong arm. But he's far more mobile than Trubisky, a trait that many scouts saw as a drawback. A quarterback who can run is also a quarterback who can get hurt. That's the rationale anyway.

Watson was actually the third quarterback chosen. Patrick Mahomes, also an African American, was taken by Kansas City, whose coach Andy Reid had made Donovan McNabb the number two pick in the draft when McNabb came out of Syracuse in 1999. Reid, in his first year as a head coach, was glad to have the chance to grab McNabb after the Cleveland Browns used their first pick as an expansion team to take Tim Couch.

Houston took Watson two picks after Mahomes went to Kansas City. Williams was a big fan of Watson's because after the scouts had done all the breakdowns on hand size, arm strength, 40-yard speed, and muscle mass, there was one thing he noticed about Watson that he thought invaluable: he won games.

"There are times you have to look past a kid's won-lost record in college," Williams said. "I loved the way the kid competed—in addition to having all the physical attributes."

Year two in Tampa Bay went considerably better for Williams than year one. It helped that the team was markedly better. The defense had steadily improved and had a genuine star in Lee Roy Selmon. Plus, the starting quarterback had a year under his belt and felt a good deal more confident.

"I knew it was my team, for better or worse, in the second year. Coach McKay always had faith in me, but that first year because of the injuries, I didn't improve as much as I thought I should. The second year, you could see we were becoming a good team and I was becoming a good quarterback."

There were still racial slurs tossed at him when the team lost, but they happened less and less often. If anyone in the media questioned "Dougie," McKay quickly backed them down. The team went 10-6 and won the NFC Central division. They played Dick Vermeil's Philadelphia Eagles in the first round of the playoffs and beat them handily, 24–9. That put them in the NFC Championship game—one step from the Super Bowl.

The day was a lost one from the start. The Rams had a defense as good as—or better than—the Bucs', and they shut the offense down in the first half. Then, early in the third quarter, Williams got hit on a blitz and was knocked out of the game. Rae took over but had no more luck than Williams. The final was 9–0.

The Bucs made the playoffs again in 1981 and 1982—the strike-shortened season in which teams played only nine regular season games. Williams started sixty-two straight games, dating to the last game of his rookie season and including the Bucs' four postseason games.

But while his football career was going in the right direction, his personal life was not. His father had to have a leg amputated during the 1982 season, and then, soon after their first child, Ashley, had been born, Doug and Janice Williams learned that Janice, only twenty-six years old, had a brain tumor.

Doctors performed what they hoped would be lifesaving surgery on March 31, 1983, and the initial signs were hopeful. The hope turned out to be false. On April 7, Janice Williams died, leaving Doug to raise their three-month-old daughter alone.

If Williams's personal tragedies mattered to Tampa Bay owner Hugh Culverhouse, he didn't show it in his contract negotiations.

Williams recalled, "I can remember walking down the hall one day with [general manager] Phil Krueger, and him saying to me, 'Mr. C. told me not to make friends with *his* money.' In 1982, my fifth year as a starting quarterback in the league, I was the fifty-fourth-highest-paid quarterback. My backup, Mike Rae, was making more than me.

"I wanted $600,000 a year, which in that market was more than reasonable. Phil told me they were willing to pay me $400,000—$375,000 plus incentives to get to $400,000. That still wouldn't have put me close to market value, much less the value they should have been paying a quarterback who'd been a starter for five years and taken them to postseason in three years out of the last four.

"I'd have taken $500,000 because I didn't really want to leave and I had other things going on in my life. But they wouldn't budge. Not a nickel.

"I remember thinking to myself, 'You know what, I don't *have* to play football. I have a degree in education and I need to be home with my little girl.' So I quit."

For a twenty-seven-year-old starting quarterback in the NFL to just walk out was unheard-of then—just as it is now. There was no real free agency in those days. If a team put you on its "protected list" of thirty-seven players, any team that signed you had to compensate the team you had left—making it more a trade than a free agent signing.

Williams went back home to Zachary and taught middle school for considerably less than he would have made playing for the Bucs. "I worked as a sub, filling in wherever I was needed," he said. "Got paid about fifty dollars a day."

He also helped out with the football team. As far as he was concerned, playing football was over.

A year later, the United States Football League entered his life. The USFL had been founded in 1983 as a spring football league with some big-bucks owners behind it—among them Donald Trump. It signed a number of college stars and NFL stars, and William Tatham Sr., the owner of the expansion (in 1984) Oklahoma Outlaws, decided he wanted Williams to be his quarterback.

He asked Williams to go to dinner with him and sold him on the idea of playing in the USFL. Williams can't remember now exactly how much he was paid, but it was considerably more than $50 a day. More important, he wanted to play football again.

"I liked teaching, but I missed playing," he said. "I was too young to never play again. And Mr. Tatham clearly wanted me. That was appealing."

The Outlaws started out 6-2 in the spring of 1984 before losing their last ten games. Two years in, the league was already hurting financially, and the Outlaws were merged with the virtually bankrupt Arizona Wranglers and moved operations to Phoenix. Even in a much larger stadium, the team's attendance actually went *down*—from 21,000 a game to 17,000 a game. Williams threw for a lot of yards again, but the team went 8-10 and missed the playoffs.

By the end of 1985, the USFL was clinging to life. The owners had decided to move their season to the fall for 1986 but were counting on winning an antitrust lawsuit from the NFL to stay afloat financially. The league *did* win the lawsuit—and was awarded $1 in damages, which became $3 after it was trebled under antitrust law. The league "suspended" operations, never to return.

Which left Williams out of a job. He was ready to return to Zachary when his phone rang. On the other end of the line was Joe Gibbs, who had become the head coach in Washington in 1981 and had won the Super Bowl after the strike-shortened 1982 season.

Joe Theismann's career had ended on a Monday night in October when he suffered one of the most gruesome leg injuries ever seen on a football field after being tackled by the Giants' Lawrence Taylor.

Jay Schroeder had stepped in as the starter and played well.

"Doug," Gibbs said on the phone, "do you think you can handle being a backup?"

Williams laughed retelling the story more than thirty years later. "Joe Gibbs to the rescue," he said. "Again."

3

To say that Joe Flacco grew up in a jock household would be an understatement. His father, Steve, was a two-sport athlete at Penn; his mother, Karen, played softball at the College of New Jersey; and he and his four brothers and one sister were all athletes.

Joe, born in January 1985, was the oldest and the biggest: growing to a little more than six feet six while easily carrying 240 pounds. Mike, the fourth brother, is just about as big, at six feet five, but John, Brian, and Tom are all closer to six feet, much like their dad, who is five-eleven, and their mom, who is five-six.

Knowing football as he did, Steve Flacco didn't allow his boys to play the game until they were twelve. Joe was a good baseball player with a strong arm and might have succeeded as a baseball player had he stuck with it. But by the time he got to Audubon High School, it was clear his future was in football.

"Even before I grew I always had a very strong arm," he said. "I liked playing quarterback, even though I didn't get to start until I was a junior. There were older guys ahead of me, so I had to wait my turn. But I feel like I was always meant to be a quarterback."

Flacco had to wait—again—in college. Once he grew, he was recruited by a number of Division I schools, including in-state Rutgers, the University of South Florida (tempting for the weather), and Pittsburgh. Eventually, he chose Pitt because it wasn't too far from home and the school had known national success in the past. Coach Walt Harris told him he'd be redshirted as a freshman because he had a fifth-year senior, Rob Rutherford, who would be the starter, and he would save a year of eligibility by sitting out. "I was fine with that," he said. "I figured my chance to play would come the next year."

Only it didn't. Harris had rebuilt a fallen Pitt program into a solid Big East team, but hadn't won a championship or sniffed a major bowl.

There was some pressure on him beginning in 2004 to take the next step. As a result, Harris went with the slightly more experienced Tyler Palko—a redshirt sophomore—as his starter, and, though in uniform and ready to play, Flacco was an observer for virtually the entire season.

Palko played well, leading Pitt to an 8-3 record, the Big East title, and a berth in the Fiesta Bowl. There, they were routed, 35–7, by Utah—the first team not from one of the so-called BCS leagues to receive a bid to a BCS bowl game. The Utes were 12-0 that season, led by a quarterback named Alex Smith.

After going 8-4 and winning the Big East title, Harris left Pitt at season's end to become the coach at Stanford. Palko wasn't going anywhere, and Flacco knew it. He had hardly played at all during the season, completing one pass for 11 yards—total.

Dave Wannstedt, the new coach, wanted Flacco to stay. He could see Flacco's potential, as could Matt Cavanaugh, the ex-Pitt quarterback whom Wannstedt had hired as his offensive coordinator. Flacco knew there was no guarantee he would play and that Palko, after a full season as the starter, would have the advantages of incumbency.

"I didn't really want to face the idea of sitting for two more years until Tyler graduated," he said. "I basically hadn't played for two years already. I wanted to get on the field."

He decided to transfer. He knew if he transferred a level down to I-AA, he wouldn't have to sit out a transfer season. What he didn't know was that rule applied only if the school he was leaving granted him a release. Wannstedt wouldn't release him, figuring if he had to sit out a year, he'd stick around.

Flacco left anyway, transferring to Delaware, which had long been a Division I-AA power under legendary coach Tubby Raymond, who won three hundred games and three national titles there in thirty-six seasons. Raymond was replaced in 2002 by K. C. Keeler, a Delaware grad who'd had great success at Division III Rowan.

In Keeler's second season, the Blue Hens won another national title, going 15-1. Quarterback Andy Hall, who'd had great success after transferring from Division I Georgia Tech, graduated (and played two seasons in the NFL) and was replaced by Sonny Riccio—another D-I transfer. Riccio would be a senior in 2005, and Keeler had Flacco penciled in to back him up and then be the starter the next two seasons.

It worked out that way . . . sort of . . . Flacco had to sit out the 2005 season because Pitt wouldn't release him. He spent the 2005 season quarterbacking Delaware's scout team to prepare the defense for each week's opponent.

Finally, Flacco became the starter at Delaware in 2006 after having played almost no football for three seasons. He played reasonably well and drew some attention from pro scouts because of his arm strength, but he wasn't high on any draft boards when the 2007 season began. Delaware was coming off a 5-6 season, Keeler's worst since taking over from Raymond.

One team that was aware of Flacco was the Baltimore Ravens. The Ravens needed a quarterback—and had needed one almost from the day they moved to Baltimore from Cleveland in 1996. Vinny Testaverde had put up impressive numbers but hadn't won many games. Then Trent Dilfer won a Super Bowl at the end of the 2000 season, only to be summarily dumped because the feeling was that the Ravens' extraordinary defense had been responsible for the title—not Dilfer. There was truth in that, even though Dilfer had done everything he'd been asked to do once he became the starter midway through the season.

The team signed Elvis Grbac to replace Dilfer and an aging Randall Cunningham as his backup. A year later both were gone, and journeymen Jeff Blake and Chris Redman shared the job during a 7-9 season. General manager Ozzie Newsome and Coach Brian Billick were desperate to find a quarterback in the 2003 draft.

During the NFL draft combine, they fell in love with Kyle Boller, who'd had a good senior season at California after playing on bad teams prior to that. Boller was six feet four and had a strong arm, but he won the Ravens over when they interviewed him during the annual NFL combine in Indianapolis. Boller was smart, funny, and charming. He came from a family of firefighters and figured to fit in on what was a "blue-collar" type of team.

The Ravens had to give up their second-round pick in 2003 *and* their first-round pick in 2004 to the New England Patriots in order to move up to the nineteenth spot in the draft so they could draft Boller. Four quarterbacks went in the first round that year: Carson Palmer at number one to Cincinnati; Byron Leftwich at number seven to Jacksonville; Boller; and Rex Grossman at number twenty-two to Chicago.

Only Palmer became a star. No other quarterback in that year's draft had any real impact on his team or the league. A year later, in 2004, Eli Manning, Philip Rivers, and Ben Roethlisberger went at number one, four, and eleven, respectively. Manning and Roethlisberger have won two Super Bowls apiece, and Rivers has been a star for most of fourteen seasons. All are still playing and all may end up in the Hall of Fame.

That's how hit-and-miss drafting quarterbacks can be. Boller became the Ravens' quarterback at the start of his 2003 rookie season, and even though he missed seven games with injuries—replaced by Anthony Wright—the Ravens went 10-6 and made the playoffs.

A year later, Billick brought in Jim Fassel—a close friend who had coached the New York Giants to the Super Bowl only to lose to the Ravens four seasons earlier—to be Boller's personal tutor. Boller started all sixteen games and the Ravens went 9-7. He wasn't terrible, but he wasn't great. A year later, in 2005, after the Ravens had gone 6-10, they traded for thirty-three-year-old Steve McNair.

McNair had a superb season in 2006, and the team was 13-3 before losing in the first round of the playoffs to the Indianapolis Colts. A year later, McNair was oft hurt and clearly showing his age. By then, Eric DeCosta had become the Ravens' director of college scouting. It was his job to bring to Newsome the best quarterbacks who would be available in the 2008 draft.

DeCosta was thirty-seven and had played Division III college football at Colby. He had worked as a graduate assistant at Trinity in Connecticut—archrivals of Wesleyan, the school that produced Bill Belichick—and was hired by the Ravens in 1996 as a scout when the team moved to Baltimore and Newsome was put in charge of player personnel.

DeCosta had moved up the Ravens' ladder and had become Newsome's number two man in 2005 when Phil Savage left to become the general manager in Cleveland. He loved scouting, loved the adrenaline rush of seeing a player he thought could help the team.

Flacco had first come onto his radar during the 2006 season when Joe Douglas, now the personnel director for the Eagles but then a college scout for the Ravens, had seen Flacco play in a game at Richmond. Delaware had upset the tenth-ranked (in Division I-AA) Spiders, 28–24, and Douglas had been impressed by Flacco.

"He called me on the phone en route home," DeCosta said. "I could tell by his voice that he was excited, that he thought we were on to something down the road."

At that point, McNair was still playing well and there was no reason to think about drafting a quarterback. By the following fall, with McNair injured (he would retire at season's end) and the team floundering, the situation had become desperate.

Looking at the schedule prior to the season, DeCosta saw a unique opportunity on October 27: Delaware was scheduled to play at Navy at noon, and Clemson was playing at Maryland, thirty miles away in College Park, at 3:30.

"It wasn't as if I couldn't drive to Delaware to see Flacco," he said. "But they were playing a Division I-A team in Navy. They might not have been ranked or anything, but it was a step up for Delaware, plus I could go watch three quarters in Annapolis, beat the traffic there, and probably get to College Park right around kickoff. I remember Clemson had several players I wanted to see."

DeCosta never made it to College Park. He went down onto the field to watch Flacco warm up and liked what he saw from up close: Flacco had size, had huge hands, and threw the ball with an effortless motion.

"He had the look," DeCosta said. "The physical attributes were all there, but so was the attitude. Not cocky, but confident."

DeCosta went upstairs to eat some pregame pizza and ran into Ron Wolf, the former Packers general manager who had retired to Annapolis. Wolf knew exactly why DeCosta was there.

"Looking for your trigger-man, Eric?" he asked rhetorically.

By halftime, DeCosta was sold, especially after Flacco took his team the length of the field in the final two minutes to tie the game at 28–28.

"He was like a surgeon during that drive," DeCosta said, his eyes widening in retelling the story more than ten years later. "Every pass was right there, he knew just what he was doing with the clock. They didn't have any time-outs left, but it didn't matter. He made it look easy."

DeCosta ended up leaving before the end of the third quarter. But instead of driving west down Route 50 to the Washington Beltway, he drove north on I-97 back to the Ravens' offices.

"I was too excited about Flacco for it to be worth my time to go to College Park," he said. "Even if I had gone, I wouldn't have been focused the way I needed to be. I wanted to go back right then and look at whatever tape we had on Flacco."

The Ravens had started the season with a list of four quarterbacks they liked: Matt Ryan of Boston College; Brian Brohm of Louisville; Chad Henne of Michigan; and Flacco. By season's end, the list was down to two: Ryan and Flacco.

"We liked Ryan a little more than we liked Joe," DeCosta said. "Ryan had played well in a big-time program and had been a consistent winner. If we'd had the chance to draft Ryan, we'd have taken him."

Flacco had also proven himself a winner during that final season at Delaware. The Blue Hens made the NCAA playoffs and won three games—against Delaware State, top-seeded Northern Iowa, and fourth-seeded Southern Illinois—to reach the championship game. There, they lost to an Appalachian State team that had started the season by winning *at* Michigan—a victory so historic it later spawned a book—and ended it by beating Delaware for a third straight national title.

The Ravens had finished the season by beating the Pittsburgh Steelers in a meaningless game to finish at 5-11. That turned out to be crucial. Had they lost to the Steelers and finished 4-12, they would have moved up several spots in the draft. Instead, the 4-12 Atlanta Falcons, picking third, drafted Ryan.

That was no surprise to the Ravens. They were locked in on picking Flacco if, in fact, Ryan was off the board. DeCosta had little trouble convincing Newsome that Flacco was worth a first-round pick.

"I liked what I saw of him and I had no hesitation taking an FCS [I-AA] player," Newsome said. "Steve McNair had come out of Alcorn State, which was also an FCS school, and had become a star. If you're good enough, you're good enough."

———

In fact, McNair had been the last quarterback from an FCS school taken in the first round when the Houston Oilers had drafted him with the third overall pick in 1995.

Newsome wasn't the only one DeCosta had to convince. The Ravens had a new coaching staff. Brian Billick had been fired and replaced by John Harbaugh. Because Harbaugh was tied up hiring a staff and putting together a playbook, he made Cam Cameron, the new offensive coordinator, and Hue Jackson, the quarterbacks coach, his representatives on the quarterback search.

When DeCosta first brought Flacco up to Cameron, he was skeptical. "I wouldn't say he pooh-poohed the idea," DeCosta said. "I'd just say he was less than sure."

Flacco was invited to the Senior Bowl, which has become a weeklong tryout camp for college players. The practices are actually more important than the game because the players—with NFL coaching staffs in charge—are asked to do things that give scouts a chance to judge their skills.

Many scouting staffs don't even stay for the game. The Ravens were scheduled to fly out of Mobile, Alabama, site of the game, on Thursday afternoon. On Thursday morning, they went to one last workout and watched all the quarterbacks throw.

"The weather was miserable," DeCosta said. "I remember we went upstairs to find cover. You could see though that the wind and the rain didn't affect Joe's ball. His passes didn't wobble, they didn't miss their targets. I remember thinking, 'This guy is an AFC North quarterback.'"

Meaning he'd be able to perform in bad weather in Baltimore, Pittsburgh, Cincinnati, and Cleveland in December and January.

Next came the combine with all its various tests: height, weight, hand size, arm strength, 40-yard dash, shuttle run. There is also an (alleged) intelligence test that consists of fifty questions. Some of the smartest quarterbacks ever to play the game haven't done that well on what is called the Wonderlic test—invented by a man named E. F. Wonderlic.

It consists of fifty multiple-choice questions that have to be answered in twelve minutes. Only one player, Harvard punter Pat McInally, ever scored a 50. Ryan Fitzpatrick, who finished in nine minutes and left one question blank intentionally, scored a 48. Thirteen of the twenty-one players who have scored 40 or higher are quarterbacks.

For the record, Tom Brady scored a 33 and Flacco scored a 27. Matt Ryan had a 32 at the same combine as Flacco. "Disappointing," Flacco said, laughing, years later. "Thought I'd do better."

The average score is 20. The Wonderlic can be vastly overrated. The only player to ever score 49 on a Wonderlic was Boston College defensive end Mike Mamula. He so impressed the Eagles' scouting staff with his overall performance at the combine that they traded up from the twelfth spot to the seventh—giving the Tampa Bay Buccaneers their twelfth pick and two second-round picks—to get Mamula. The Bucs swung another trade and ended up drafting Warren Sapp and Derrick Brooks with the picks they got from Philadelphia. Both are in the Hall of Fame. Mamula had a decent five-year career in Philadelphia—nothing more.

The lesson: beware the Wonderlic. Teams have learned that. A. J. Green scored a 10 coming out of Georgia in 2010, was still taken with the fourth overall pick by the Bengals, and is one of the best receivers in the game.

—

After the combine, DeCosta was convinced of two things: Ryan wasn't going to be on the board when the Ravens drafted, and Flacco was their man. He still had to convince the coaches, who would certainly have input with Newsome before a final decision was made.

After the annual combine, high-profile players are often asked to perform for any scouts interested in them in what's called a "pro day." Some players skip the combine and hold a pro day instead of the combine. Teams are invited to their college campus on one specific day, and the player performs for all of them at once.

Other players who may not be in quite so much demand will do individual workouts for teams that request them. The Ravens asked Flacco for an individual workout and scheduled it for the ides of March.

"It was cold and rainy, I remember that," DeCosta said. "We drove to Newark [Delaware] in two cars: Joe Douglas, Joe Hortiz [another scout], and I were in one car. Cam and Hue were in the other."

Flacco met the group on an unlined practice field, carrying a bag of footballs with two of his teammates in tow.

Cameron was in charge of the workout. He asked Flacco to make different throws, asked him how he would read certain formations, and about how he might handle different protections.

"What I remember most is that it was—sort of like that day in Mobile at the Senior Bowl—lousy conditions," DeCosta said. "Cam kept picking up the pace—barking at Joe. The field we were on wasn't in great shape, and the receivers he was working with weren't guys who were going to play at the next level by any stretch. But he handled everything, never seemed to get rattled no matter how fast Cam was going.

"When we were finished, we thanked Joe and Cam said to me, 'I get it now.' Assuming we weren't going to get Ryan, we were all in agreement that Joe was the guy we wanted; the guy we really needed to get."

That didn't mean DeCosta and Newsome weren't willing to make a couple of moves to strengthen other positions before getting their quarterback.

———

The Ravens were slated to draft eighth, and they certainly wanted to pick Ryan. DeCosta believed, however, that eight was too high to take Flacco, and that the team should "trade back"—get other picks to move out of the eighth slot—to strengthen their overall draft board.

They made a deal with Jacksonville to move all the way down to twenty-sixth, picking up two later-round picks to let the Jaguars move up.

"We couldn't take Flacco at eight," DeCosta said. "That's just the way the NFL is. People would have laughed at us if we had taken Joe that high, and we were a little sensitive anyway because of what had happened with Boller. But I knew no one else would take him that high, so I wasn't uncomfortable with moving back."

The Ravens got two picks—a third and a fourth from the Jaguars—to move back to twenty-sixth. DeCosta was comfortable that Flacco would still be there at that spot. But as the first round wore on, Newsome and team owner Steve Bisciotti began to get a little nervous. With Ryan gone, Flacco was the only quarterback they coveted, and they worried someone might make a trade, jump in front of them, and grab him.

Finally, with the Houston Texans about to pick, Newsome decided it was time to stop hoping: he traded a third-round pick to the Texans to move up to the eighteenth spot, and the Ravens grabbed Flacco.

There was jubilation in the draft room—except for one problem. Like most NFL teams, the Ravens planned to allow their public relations people, along with the team's video crew, into the room as the pick was being made.

DeCosta was supposed to notify Kevin Byrne, the Ravens' vice president of public relations, when the pick was about to be made. But when the trade happened, there was almost no time to give Byrne a heads-up, and DeCosta, still thinking the pick was coming at twenty-six, had told Byrne it was okay to take a bathroom break. By the time Byrne returned, the pick had been made.

"Kevin said, 'We have to reenact it,'" DeCosta remembered, laughing. "We had to have the camera crew come into the room first, and then I had to burst into the hallway and scream to Cam, who was down the hall in the coaches room, 'We got our guy!' Then we ran down the hall and hugged. I remember Cam saying to me, 'Let's not ever do *that* again.'"

Regardless of the reenactment, the Ravens *had* gotten their man. The question now was whether he would become *the* man. Realistically, they figured it would take a while to find out.

They were wrong.

4

Alex Smith and Ryan Fitzpatrick are friends, even though they don't see each other that often. They have played together in the annual celebrity golf tournament in Lake Tahoe, and they often text each other to keep up with families and to offer congratulations or condolences on wins and losses during the course of a football season.

As each enters his fourteenth season in the NFL, their pro careers have followed very different paths: Smith came into the NFL as the number one pick in the entire draft. Fitzpatrick, as he likes to point out, was taken a mere 249 picks later.

Fitzpatrick is with his seventh team; Smith his third. Smith has started for most of his career; Fitzpatrick has frequently been the guy who starts because someone gets hurt or because he has surprised his coaches by outplaying the guy who was supposed to be the starter.

But their beginnings were similar—in fact, they might well have been college teammates at Harvard. "I don't think my mother has ever completely forgiven me," Smith likes to say about his college decision. "She wanted me to go to Harvard for the simple reason that it's *Harvard.*"

Fitzpatrick did go to Harvard, in part because it's Harvard but also because he didn't have any scholarship offers from Division I-A schools. Harvard plays one level down in Division I-AA, the same level as Eastern Washington, the other school that showed interest in him.

Smith had one solid Division I-A offer—from Utah. He was considered a two-star recruit (out of a possible five by college scouting services).

"If I'd been rated at all, they'd have had to create a half-star category for me," Fitzpatrick often jokes.

A two-star prospect is considered a marginal Division I-A prospect. (Division I-A is now called "the Football Bowl Subdivision" by the

NCAA, and Division I-AA is called "the Football Championship Subdivision" because the NCAA doesn't like to imply that any level is superior to another.)

When Smith arrived at Utah in the summer of 2002, he expected to redshirt as a freshman—which was fine with him. Academically, he was a junior because he had nine AP credits coming out of high school. That meant his academic workload would be considerably heavier than a typical first-year football player, so not having to worry about playing in games was actually something of a relief.

"It wasn't that big a deal," he said. "But not having to worry about playing in games didn't seem like a bad idea."

He had been recruited by Ron McBride, who was entering his thirteenth season at Utah. McBride had turned around a fallen program when he'd taken over in 1990, and Utah had gone to six bowl games in his twelve years—including 2001, when it had bounced back from a 4-7 season to go 8-4, with a victory in the Las Vegas Bowl.

Smith was slated to sit behind Brett Elliott and Lance Rice, two experienced quarterbacks, and then be given a chance to play the following season. The Utes won their first two games, then went into a six-game nosedive, which meant they wouldn't play postseason, and put McBride's job in jeopardy, since it would be the team's second losing season in three years.

Seven games in, with the team floundering at 2-5, offensive coordinator Craig Ver Steeg came to see Smith. The coaches had decided to abandon the redshirt for him and play him that week against New Mexico. Smith was more confused than anything else.

"It didn't seem to make much sense," he said. "The season was already pretty much lost, and it wasn't as if Brett and Lance had been awful and that playing a freshman was going to suddenly turn things around. I think they were all thinking that if we didn't at least play better, they were going to lose their jobs, so maybe a new voice in the huddle might give the team a boost."

He didn't get to say much, playing briefly in two games and completing two of four passes, one of the incompletes being an interception returned for a touchdown. He also took a couple of sacks, so his rushing total was two rushes for minus-11 yards.

"It didn't go well, to put it mildly," he said. "I never really understood why I was in there if they were only going to play me a couple of series."

After the two cameos, it was back to the bench, his redshirt blown because he had played. If he had been injured, he could have played as many as three games and not lost his redshirt. But since his coaches had been holding him out even though he was healthy, his redshirt was gone as soon as he stepped onto the field.

"I was pretty upset about it at the time," he said. "It made no sense to begin with and even less sense when they played me for a few minutes and then I never played again. At that point, I certainly wasn't thinking that the NFL draft was going to be a possibility after my third season."

McBride was fired at the end of the season. The new coach was thirty-eight-year-old Urban Meyer, who had drawn the attention of Utah by going 17-6 in two seasons at Bowling Green.

"Urban's reputation was that he was a little bit crazy," Smith said. "He ran this wide-open offense, all shotgun, and he also wanted every single session in the weight room, every single thing you did, to be all-out. He was full of intensity. Which, in the long run, worked out very well. But it was a little overwhelming at first."

Elliott was still the starting quarterback when the 2003 season started. The Utes beat Utah State in their opener, then lost 28–26 at Texas A&M a week later. Late in that game, Elliott broke his wrist diving for the pylon. Smith took his place, and Utah's version of Wally Pipp/Lou Gehrig was born. Smith started the last ten games of that season and all twelve games the next.

His first start came in a Thursday night, nationally televised game against California whose quarterback was Aaron Rodgers. Smith completed 18 of 26 passes; Rodgers was 15-of-25 and the Utes won, 31–24. The Utes won five in a row and climbed to number twenty-three in the AP poll, before losing a 47–35 donnybrook to New Mexico. Smith was 18-of-32 for 220 yards and four touchdowns, but it wasn't enough.

Utah then capped its season by beating archrival Brigham Young, 3–0, in a snowstorm and then pitched another shutout in a 17–0 Liberty Bowl win over Southern Mississippi, to finish 10-2; 9-1 with Smith as the starter.

Still, the NFL was the furthest thing from his mind when the 2004 season began. In fact, all he was really thinking about was beating Texas A&M, one of the two teams Utah had lost to the previous season. The Utes pounded the Aggies, 41–21, and went from there to have one of the most dominant seasons in college football history. They were 12-0 and averaged 40 points per game. Their *closest* game was a 49–35 victory over Air Force. Twice, they scored 63 points. Smith completed 67.5 percent of his passes for almost 3,000 yards out of Meyer's spread offense.

By the time the regular season ended with a 52–21 win over BYU, the Utes were ranked fifth and six in the two national polls, and most important ranked sixth in the BCS poll. That meant the BCS had to do something it dreaded: extend a bid to one of its five bowl games to a school *not* from one of the Power Six conferences. At the time, Utah was still part of the Mountain West conference.

In its seven-year history, the BCS had never gone out of the Power Six to fill its ten bowl spots. Utah gave it no choice.

"Of all the things we did that year, I think busting the BCS and forcing them to take us was the one that meant the most to us," Smith said. "Our attitude was, whoever we play, we're going to pound them and show them how good a non–power conference school can be."

Unfortunately, the BCS chose to send its weakest automatic qualifier, Big East champion Pittsburgh, to the Fiesta Bowl to play Utah. It was most unfortunate for Pitt, because Utah did exactly what it came to do, pounding the Panthers 35–7. Smith completed 29 of 37 passes for 328 yards and four touchdowns.

By then, everyone knew Meyer was leaving to take the job at Florida, and rumors were rife that Smith was going to pass on his senior season. He had finished fourth in the Heisman Trophy voting behind Matt Leinart, Adrian Peterson, and Jack White—one spot ahead of his high school teammate Reggie Bush, making them the first players from the same high school team to finish in the top five in the Heisman voting in the same season.

Smith's uncle, John L. Smith, had made some informal phone calls to NFL general managers and was being told that his nephew was a likely first-round draft pick. By then, he was six feet four, weighed 215 pounds, and had shown both mobility (scoring ten rushing touchdowns) and arm strength. The only question about taking the step to playing on Sundays was whether he could adapt to a pro-style offense.

After the bowl game, Smith decided there was really nothing left to accomplish in college. Meyer was gone, and so was an accomplished senior class. He had asked the NFL's official scouting service to tell him formally where it thought he might be drafted, but the word from his uncle was enough, he thought, to make a decision.

In the fourth quarter of the bowl game, he could hear the Utah fans chanting, "One more year, one more year."

That made the decision harder, but not that much harder. Three days after the bowl game, he made his announcement. He had already graduated the previous spring with a degree in economics and had done some postgraduate work, largely to be eligible to play football. Once he had decided he was headed for the NFL, there was no reason to hang around and not focus on getting ready for all the pre-draft routines players go through: the Senior Bowl; the combine; a pro day; and private workouts. So he said his good-byes and loaded up his car for the ten-hour trip back home to San Diego.

En route home, his cell phone rang. It was the NFL scouting service with their report on his draft status. They told Smith they believed he'd be drafted at some point during the second round.

He kept driving.

—

Aaron Rodgers had also decided to pass on his senior season, leaving California after a season in which he completed 67.5 percent of his regular season passes—exactly the same percentage Smith had thrown for in his twelve games at Utah.

Rodgers and Smith were considered the two top quarterback names in the draft. Rodgers was—and is—an out-of-the-box type of person. To this day, when he introduces himself on NBC's Sunday Night Football games (the starters introduce themselves rather than the announcers), he will often say, "Aaron Rodgers, Butte Junior College," rather than mentioning Cal, the school where he came to national prominence.

"Butte took a chance on me when no one in Division I recruited me," he once said. "Heck, I was only at Cal for one year longer than Butte."

Rodgers had one offer as a high school senior—to walk on at Illinois. Back then he was only five feet ten and 170 pounds. A year later, when Cal coach Jeff Tedford came to Butte to look at another player, he was surprised to learn that no one had offered or signed the six-foot-two, 205-pound quarterback who was throwing rockets.

Two years later, after Rodgers had led Cal to a 10-2 record that included a 23–17 loss to national champion USC in which Rodgers completed twenty-three straight passes at one point, there were plenty of scouts who thought Rodgers was likely to be the number one pick in the 2005 draft. The San Francisco 49ers had the first pick. Rodgers had grown up in Chico, about 165 miles north of the Bay Area. He was, for all intents and purposes, a local kid: Chico to nearby Butte, and then south to Berkeley, right across the bay.

The 49ers had a new coach that winter, Mike Nolan, the son of Dick Nolan, who had coached the team from 1968 to 1975. He had grown up a football brat, following his father from job to job, much the way a military brat moves when his parent in the military is transferred.

Nolan liked the notion that Smith had a more in-the-box personality than Rodgers. Both had strong arms and both were mobile. Both ran a 4.7 40 at the combine, not superfast for a quarterback but plenty fast enough. Smith scored a 40 on the Wonderlic, Rodgers a 35. Given that they are two of football's smartest people, those numbers are more a reflection of the fallacies of the Wonderlic than anything else.

By the time the NFL was finished putting the quarterbacks through their paces, it was clear that Smith was *not* going to be a second-round pick. The only real question was whether the 49ers would take him or take Rodgers. The other was expected to fall until later in the first round because other teams picking in the first ten were not necessarily looking for a quarterback.

The 49ers were starting from scratch. They had gone 2-14 in 2004, starting the season with Tim Rattay as their quarterback and finishing it with Ken Dorsey playing the position. Coach Dennis Erickson and general manager Terry Donahue were both fired. Nolan was hired to essentially fill both positions, a trend at the time in the NFL. The success of Bill Belichick in New England as dictator of all things encouraged other teams to follow suit.

Nolan was a defensive expert. He had been a defensive back in college at Oregon and had spent one year of his twenty-three as a coach on the offensive side of the ball. He had been the defensive coordinator for the Giants, Washington, Jets, and Ravens—the latter for three seasons after spending his one and only season on offense, coaching wide receivers in 2001.

Nolan was very smart and very confident and had lived and

breathed football his entire life. Which might explain why he laughed it off when Washington's new owner, Dan Snyder, began telling him during the 2000 season what *he* wanted to see the team's defense doing.

"He came to me one day and began explaining that he thought our defense was too vanilla," Nolan said, several years after escaping Washington. "He said he wanted the defense to have more flavor—like Ben and Jerry's ice cream."

Nolan decided he knew more about coaching defense than a guy who had made his millions through direct-mail advertising. A couple of weeks later, after a loss, he found a pint of multiflavored ice cream on his desk with a note: "THIS is what I want from my defense."

Nolan responded with a note back to the owner: "Thanks for the ice cream. My kids enjoyed it."

Then came a loss at Dallas—the ultimate disaster to Snyder. When the team's charter landed at Dulles Airport, Nolan did what many NFL coaches do on Sunday night: he went straight to the office to begin preparing for the following week. This time he found an entire crate of ice cream—melting—on his desk. There was no note. It wasn't needed.

A few years later, when Nolan told the story to a reporter, Snyder—through his spokesman—angrily denied that anything along those lines had happened. When Norv Turner, who had been Washington's head coach at the time, confirmed it, Snyder—and his spokesman—changed their story. They had now decided that it had been general manager Vinny Cerrato who sent the ice cream.

By then, Nolan, at forty-five, was a prime candidate to become a head coach. When the 49ers selected him in January 2005, it seemed to make perfect sense: thirty years after his father had last coached in San Francisco, Nolan took over.

His first and most important job was to find a quarterback.

And so, on April 23, 2005, when the NFL draft began at the Jacob Javits Convention Center on the west side of Manhattan, NFL commissioner Paul Tagliabue stepped to the microphone and announced: "With the first pick in the 2005 NFL draft, the San Francisco 49ers select . . . Alex Smith, quarterback, Utah."

Aaron Rodgers would have to wait through twenty-two more picks before the Packers took him with the twenty-fourth pick. Ryan Fitzpatrick would have to wait for 248 picks before being taken by the

Rams. The difference was Fitzpatrick wasn't surprised; Rodgers was surprised and a little bit angry.

Smith, even though he had heard his name bandied about as possibly being the number one pick, was stunned.

"It was a long way from starting my sophomore season as Utah's backup quarterback to being the number one pick in the NFL draft nineteen months later," he said. "It was a little bit like, 'Toto, we aren't in Kansas anymore.'"

He wasn't in Oz either. He was in San Francisco with an entire city—an entire league—monitoring his every step. And every misstep.

Life in the NFL would be a lot different from life in the Mountain West.

5

Alex Smith was prepared for the media blitz that he knew would come with being the first pick in the NFL draft. Talking to the media has never been a problem for him.

This, though, was different. It wasn't just the Bay Area media that wanted to talk to him; it was the national media. After all, he wasn't just the 49ers' first pick, he was the *league's* first pick.

"For the most part, it was fine," he said. "The questions weren't exactly difficult to answer and, in a lot of cases, they were questions I'd been asked multiple times.

"The hard part was knowing that all eyes were on me all the time. We'd be doing calisthenics in mini-camp and it felt as if all the cameras were on *me*. There wasn't much down time or quiet time. Some of it was fun. Heck, I hadn't thrown an interception and we hadn't lost a game. But from day one it felt as if I was the face of the franchise. That's a little bit tough when you haven't played a down yet."

The quantum change in Smith's life hit him in the face one afternoon when he went to the bank. He had opened an account locally and, at the end of the team's second rookie mini-camp, found two checks in his locker.

NFL players receive about 95 percent of their salary during the seventeen weeks of the regular season. During the off-season, they receive small checks for mini-camps (now known officially as Offseason Team Activities—OTAs) and for exhibition games.

Soon after he signed his contract in July, Smith noticed two checks in his locker. One was for $1,000, and the other was for $700. He went to the bank, filled out a deposit slip, and waited his turn in line. As he was waiting, he glanced at the checks. That was when he noticed that the $1,000 check wasn't for $1,000.

"It was for one *million* dollars," Smith said with a sheepish grin. "I had misread the zeroes. In my defense, I'd never seen a check even close to that big. It turned out it was part of my signing bonus."

Smith quickly stepped out of line and rewrote the deposit slip. "I also set up direct deposit that day," he said. "I didn't really want to get that look from the teller again.

"That was the day it really hit me that my life had undergone a radical change. It's not as if I grew up poor. But I was one of five kids, and my dad was a high school principal. I know he never found himself holding a million-dollar check. It wasn't a bad thing, but it was certainly eye-opening."

So was his rookie season. Even though Smith was the most-watched player on the 49ers' preseason roster, Mike Nolan and offensive coordinator Mike McCarthy had no intention of rushing him. Nolan had seen what playing from week one had done to Kyle Boller in Baltimore in 2003. Even though the Ravens had made the playoffs with a 10-6 record, most people—correctly—credited the defense for that success. Boller was doubted from day one and never completely recovered from the microscope he was put under.

Nolan didn't want that to happen to Smith, even though it was inevitable—whether he delayed it or not.

Tim Rattay was again the starter when the 49ers opened the season with a win against the St. Louis Rams. A week later, during a 42–3 blowout loss to the Eagles, Smith made his debut, coming in to throw one incomplete pass during the 49ers' final possession of the game. Then it was back to the bench until week four, when he again came in to mop up during a 31–14 loss to the Cardinals. This time, though, Smith completed six passes in his relief appearance.

Nolan decided it was time for the future of the franchise to become the present.

It wasn't an easy situation to step into—for anyone. The 49ers had a porous offensive line, and even though Smith was elusive, he was sacked five times by the Colts in his starting debut. He also threw four interceptions, and Indianapolis cruised to a 28–3 victory. The next week wasn't much better: Smith was again sacked five times. He threw just one interception but also lost a fumble, and Washington embarrassed San Francisco, 52–17.

Smith was in and out of the lineup the rest of the season, ultimately playing in nine games on a team that finished 4-12. He threw one touchdown pass and eleven interceptions, hardly what he or the 49ers had been hoping for when he was drafted.

"It was, to say the least, a tough year," he said, looking back. "Everything I did, good or bad—mostly bad—was dissected. We just weren't very good, and I never felt as if I was the guy, the way I wanted to be the guy. But I guess it's fair to say I wasn't the first quarterback to struggle breaking in with a bad team my rookie year."

That's certainly true. Troy Aikman had gone 1-15 as a rookie in Dallas; Peyton Manning was 3-13 his first season in Indianapolis; the Rams were 4-12 in Jared Goff's rookie season in 2016; Carson Wentz, drafted behind Goff at number two that spring, was 7-9 as the Eagles' starter.

More often than not, when a quarterback is drafted number one it is to join a bad team. Andrew Luck was drafted by a Colts team that had just gone 2-14 in 2011, but a lot of the reason for the Colts' failures that season was the loss of their star quarterback—Peyton Manning. The Colts went 11-5 in Luck's rookie season and made the playoffs. But they were the exception, not the rule.

Mike McCarthy left the 49ers following the 2005 season to become the Packers' head coach. There, he would eventually make the switch from Brett Favre to Aaron Rodgers at quarterback after Rodgers spent most of three seasons observing from the sidelines.

Smith's new offensive coordinator was Norv Turner, who had been fired at the end of 2005 as the head coach in Oakland. Nolan had worked for him in Washington and quickly snapped him up.

Smith loved working with Turner, who liked to throw the ball downfield more often than McCarthy had in the West Coast offense, which is built around shorter, more high-percentage passes. He was now the team's unquestioned starter. In fact, he took every snap during the 2006 season, and the 49ers improved to 7-9.

Smith's highlight—and the team's highlight—may have come during a Thursday Night Football national telecast against the Seattle Seahawks. Cris Collinsworth, doing the color on NBC, commented early in the game that, given a choice, he would have taken Denver rookie QB Jay Cutler over Smith if the two had been in the same draft.

He added that he also thought two other 2006 rookies—Matt Leinart and Vince Young—were clearly superior to Smith.

But after Smith scored the 49ers' last, game-clinching touchdown by running a naked bootleg, Collinsworth's tune had changed completely.

"Alex Smith is the best I've ever seen him," he said. "That drive is the best I saw. What a second half he's had."

Smith's stats improved noticeably in his second season: sixteen touchdown passes; sixteen interceptions. Hardly spectacular, but noticeably better than during his on-again, off-again rookie season.

Both he and his team went into 2007 thinking the playoffs were a realistic possibility. The once-proud team, which had won five Super Bowls between 1981 and 1994, hadn't been in the postseason for four straight seasons and hadn't had a record better than 7-9 during that stretch.

There was, yet again, a new coordinator for Smith to work with. Turner had been hired as the head coach in San Diego and Jim Hostler was the new offensive coordinator.

The season started well, the 49ers winning their first two games, including a Monday Night Football opener when Smith drove them to a late winning touchdown, using his legs for a 25-yard run and his arm for a 22-yard completion to Arnaz Battle that set up the winning score. *This* was the Smith the 49ers had drafted.

But it began to go wrong for both team and quarterback in week three. The 49ers lost to the Steelers, 31–14, bringing them back to earth. A week later, Smith was sacked in the first quarter and landed squarely on his right shoulder. The diagnosis was a separation; the way to a cure, rest. He sat and watched the 49ers lose that day and then the next two weeks. He came back with the 49ers at 2-4 and wasn't the same quarterback. He missed easy throws and often grabbed at his shoulder after making a throw. It was clear to many—notably players on opposing defenses—that he wasn't healthy.

After a 24–0 loss in Seattle, Smith admitted that his shoulder was "killing" him. Seattle linebacker Julian Peterson said it was apparent that Smith was in pain and not right.

Nolan didn't want to hear it. "That might mean something to me," he said when the comment was repeated to him, "if Julian was a doctor."

Nolan didn't want to hear Smith talking about the injury publicly. Smith has always been honest with the media. When he was asked if the shoulder was still hurting, he said it was, but that he thought he could play through it.

Smith thought he was being honest. Nolan thought he was whining—and said so. Smith went back to see Dr. James Andrews, arguably the world's most famous orthopedic surgeon. Andrews admitted he was surprised when he examined Smith to find the injury more serious than he had initially thought, and he told Smith, "This is much worse than I thought."

Once a *doctor* had confirmed the extent of the injury, Smith took Nolan on publicly. In an interview in the *San Jose Mercury News,* Smith said that Nolan had "undermined" his relationship with his teammates by questioning his toughness. Several players anonymously told the *Mercury News* that Smith had been nicknamed "the Lion" after the Cowardly Lion in *The Wizard of Oz.*

"I always liked Mike; what went on with us wasn't personal," Smith said. "It may have felt personal at times, but we were both trying to do what was best for the team. He was fighting for his job, so he was frustrated.

"I was frustrated because my shoulder wasn't supposed to hurt as much as it did, but it hurt like hell. I'm willing to play through pain—that's part of football. But I didn't think I was doing anyone any good going out there and playing horribly because every time I tried to throw the ball, my shoulder was screaming at me in pain."

On December 11th, Smith had surgery on his shoulder. But the damage to his relationship with Nolan was more difficult to repair. Nolan was going through a difficult season too: a 2-0 start with playoff hopes had dissolved during an eight-game losing streak. His father—his hero and his coaching mentor—passed away on November 7, three days after the team's sixth straight loss. Five days later came the shutout loss in Seattle, followed by Smith being shut down.

The 49ers finished 5-11, and Scot McCloughan was hired as general manager, taking away Nolan's control of player personnel decisions. Both Nolan and the quarterback he had chosen to be his franchise quarterback appeared to be on shaky ground heading into the 2008 season.

Because the offense had been awful—with or without Smith—Hostler was fired, and for the sixth straight season, the fourth since Smith had been drafted, the 49ers began the season with a new coordinator. This time it was Mike Martz, the coach credited with creating "The Greatest Show on Turf" offense that had helped the Rams win the Super Bowl in 2000 and return there two seasons later.

Martz was a believer in the spread offense, one not that different from what Smith had run under Urban Meyer at Utah. Still, Smith found himself in a battle with Shaun Hill and J. T. O'Sullivan—who had been in Detroit with Martz and knew the offense well—for the starting job during training camp.

Making life more difficult was nagging pain in his surgical shoulder. O'Sullivan was selected as the opening day starter, and the 49ers lost to the Cardinals 23–13.

Midway through the following week, the pain in Smith's shoulder was so bad he couldn't lift his arm above his head. Back he went to Dr. Andrews. This time Andrews found a broken bone in the shoulder, caused, he believed, by a wire inserted during the previous surgery that had somehow sawed through the bone.

Smith was placed on injured reserve. His season was over before it started.

On October 21, with the team 2-5, Nolan was fired and replaced by Mike Singletary, the Hall of Fame linebacker. Hill became the quarterback. McCloughan told the media there was absolutely no way the 49ers could afford to pay Smith the $9.625 million he was due to be paid in 2009, the fifth year of the record-breaking six-year, $49.5 million rookie contract he had signed in 2005.

As he rehabbed from his surgery, Smith had no idea what was coming next in his career or his life.

—

Ryan Fitzpatrick's rookie contract wasn't quite in the same neighborhood as Smith's. He was guaranteed $230,000, and with bonuses that amount jumped to about $309,000 for that first season.

Fitzpatrick was fine with it. He was also fine with wearing a baseball cap on the sidelines when the season began. He was the Rams' third-string quarterback behind Marc Bulger and Jamie Martin. In October, Bulger hurt his shoulder and was replaced by Martin, Fitzpatrick becoming the backup. Three weeks later, Bulger returned and was instantly hurt again.

The following week, with the Rams playing in Houston, Martin went down with the Texans leading 21–0 in the second quarter. Suddenly, Fitzpatrick was wearing a helmet instead of a baseball cap.

"The good news was I didn't really have time to think about it," he said years later with a laugh. "We'd lost the last two and we were in deep water when I went in. I just tried to keep the ball moving downfield."

He did so to the tune of 310 yards and three touchdowns, leading the Rams to a stunning come-from-behind 33–27 overtime victory. The Rams trailed 27–17 with under a minute to play before Fitzpatrick found Isaac Bruce for a 43-yard touchdown pass with twenty-six seconds left to make the score 27–24. The Rams then recovered an onside kick, and Fitzpatrick completed a 19-yard pass to John Smith with four seconds left. Jeff Wilkins kicked a 47-yard field goal to tie it. Then, in overtime, Fitzpatrick took the Rams 90 yards in six plays, the last one a 56-yard strike to Kevin Curtis to win the game.

It was an extraordinary debut, especially for the 250th pick in the draft who had been selected in large part because of his score—48—on the Wonderlic test.

"I had the advantage that week that the Texans had never seen me," Fitzpatrick said. "They had no idea what I did well or what I didn't do so well. NFL teams learn fast. A week later, the opponent had seen me on tape and it was a different ball game."

Indeed it was. Having played so well in Houston, Fitzpatrick was rewarded with the start a week later at home against Washington. That made him the first Harvard quarterback to ever start an NFL game.

Sadly, the results weren't the same. Washington won the game, 24–9. A week later, at Minnesota, Fitzpatrick threw five interceptions. The following week, after a poor first half against the Eagles, Martin replaced him for the second half. Fitzpatrick didn't know it at the time, but he wouldn't throw another pass for three years, until the 2008 season.

"It was the best of times, it was the worst of times," he said.

To some extent, it was a time that might try a man's soul. But Fitzpatrick had proven he could play in the NFL. The Rams hired Scott Linehan to replace Mike Martz as coach for the 2006 season, and Bulger stayed healthy all season, starting sixteen games. The team also brought in Gus Frerotte, the ex-Washington starter, as Bulger's backup, meaning that Fitzpatrick was once again the third-stringer.

Which is why, when he was traded to the Cincinnati Bengals on the eve of the 2008 season opener, he was happy to make the move. Carson Palmer was the Bengals' quarterback, and he was one of the more durable quarterbacks in the NFL. He'd needed major knee surgery in

January 2006, after getting hit as he released a pass in a playoff game against the Steelers. The thinking was that it would be difficult for Palmer to rehab in time for the start of the season, but he was behind center for the opening exhibition game.

The Bengals still needed a backup with some experience. The only other quarterback on their roster going into the season was rookie Jordan Palmer. So they traded a seventh-round draft pick to the Rams for a former seventh-round pick—Fitzpatrick. At the very least, Fitzpatrick was going to a team where he would be the backup, not a third-stringer, even though Palmer's recent history indicated Fitzpatrick probably wouldn't see the field very often.

It didn't work out that way. In the third game of the season, a loss to the New York Giants, Palmer felt a twinge in his elbow late in the game and had to come out. A week later, Fitzpatrick was the starter against Cleveland—which turned out to be the Bengals' fourth straight loss. Palmer returned to play against Dallas but felt more pain in the elbow. It turned out he had partially torn a ligament and a tendon in his elbow. He was done for the season.

Fitzpatrick started the season's last eleven games and went 4-6-1, which wasn't bad, given that the team had been 0-5 prior to that. The tie was against the Eagles. It was after that game that Philadelphia quarterback Donovan McNabb admitted he didn't know games could end in a five-quarter tie—he just assumed you kept playing until somebody scored.

McNabb was pilloried for his honesty, and some in the media brought out the old "black quarterback" stereotypes. This was several years after Rush Limbaugh, during his brief and embarrassing stint on ESPN, claimed that the media was overrating McNabb because it wanted to see a black quarterback succeed. Limbaugh was fired soon after that, only after ESPN was attacked, not only for hiring Limbaugh but for trying to sweep the McNabb comments under any rug it could find.

Still, the ugly stereotype persisted. Three years after the fifth-quarter incident, McNabb, having been traded to Washington, was benched by Coach Mike Shanahan late in a game against the Detroit Lions in favor of Rex Grossman. On his first snap, with Washington trailing 31–25, Grossman was sacked and fumbled. The ball was picked up by the Lions' Ndamukong Suh, who trotted 17 yards into the end zone.

When Shanahan was asked about his decision to change quarterbacks in his postgame press conference, he said he wasn't sure if McNabb knew the team's two-minute offense. A simple "Donovan hadn't had a great game, so I decided to give Rex a shot" would have sufficed, but Shanahan was one of those never-wrong coaches. A day later, when that explanation had failed to fly, Shanahan claimed he wasn't sure if McNabb was in shape to run back-to-back plays in the two-minute offense.

To top it all off, Shanahan—or his son Kyle, the offensive coordinator—then leaked to ESPN's Chris Mortensen the "fact" that they'd been forced to cut their playbook in half because McNabb couldn't learn the entire thing.

They'd called McNabb dumb, out of shape, and then really dumb. Talk about stereotyping. To try to prove that the Shanahans weren't putting McNabb down, the team made a huge production of announcing a contract extension for McNabb, one that could be worth $88 million. What they didn't mention was that there was a clause in the deal that said he'd receive only the $3 million signing bonus (basically hush money) if he was cut after the season. McNabb kept his mouth shut and, surprise, was cut at season's end so that the Shanahans could go with Grossman and the immortal John Beck as their quarterbacks the following season. They went 5-11.

Fitzpatrick knew the fifth-quarter rule. Like McNabb, he also failed to get his team into the end zone. No one called him dumb. He was, after all, a Harvard graduate.

And white.

———

Fitzpatrick was a restricted free agent at the end of the 2008 season and had some value as a backup who had proven he could be reasonably effective as a starter.

The Buffalo Bills offered him a three-year contract that was worth $7.5 million, a considerable step up from his rookie contract in 2005. He wasn't in Alex Smith territory, but he was making progress.

Dick Jauron—a Yale graduate—was entering his fourth season as the Bills' coach, the first coach to last that long since Marv Levy had retired at the end of the 1997 season. Trent Edwards was the starter, Fitzpatrick the backup.

Except Edwards went down with a concussion in the sixth game of the season. In came Fitzpatrick, the patron saint quarterback of comebacks for bad teams. The Bills rallied to beat the Jets, 16–13, in overtime.

By now, there were starting to be jokes told in the locker room about the "Fitzpatrick jinx." Everywhere he went as a backup—or so it seemed—the starter ended up getting hurt sooner or later, and there was Fitzpatrick leading the team. (Years later, when Fitzpatrick signed with the Tampa Bay Buccaneers prior to the 2017 season, he joked that "Jameis [Winston] has to be just a little bit nervous.")

Fitzpatrick started the next two games in 2009 for the Bills, and the team split them before Edwards returned after the bye week when the team played in Tennessee. The game didn't go well for anyone: the Bills lost, 41–17, and two days later Jauron was fired. Interim coach Perry Fewell's first act was to name Fitzpatrick the starter.

For once, Fitzpatrick got to take the opening snap because his coach thought he was the best option, not because of an injury. The Bills were 3-3 the rest of the way, and Fitzpatrick played solidly.

Chan Gailey was hired as the new coach and decided to go with Edwards to start the season. But an 0-2 start changed his mind, and Fitzpatrick became the starter in week three when the Bills played the Patriots. After a loss to the Packers, 34–7, expectations were low—to say the least. But Fitzpatrick kept the team in the game until late in the fourth quarter before the Patriots prevailed, 38–30.

The next day, the Bills released Edwards. They signed Brian Brohm—as Fitzpatrick's backup. For the first time in his career, Fitzpatrick was the unquestioned starter.

Sadly, it was for a bad team. The Bills started 0-9 but managed to go 4-3 down the stretch, with Fitzpatrick playing solidly if not spectacularly. People often forget that the number of NFL quarterbacks who play spectacularly is a lot smaller than those who are, at best, solid; at worst, awful.

That explains why Kirk Cousins, after leading Washington to a record of 24-24-1 (including one playoff loss) in three seasons as the starter, was able to command the $72 million, three-year guaranteed contract he received as a free agent in March 2018.

No one believed for a second that Cousins was anywhere close to Tom Brady, Aaron Rodgers, Drew Brees, or a healthy Andrew Luck. In the NFL, especially at the quarterback position, it isn't about who is best, it is about who is next. Most teams need to try to improve at the position, and when someone with a proven track record of goodness becomes available, teams pounce. Greatness rarely comes on the free agent market; goodness does.

Fitzpatrick was good enough in 2010 that Gailey decided to stick with him the following season. The Bills' off-season mission was to shore up the defense. That's why their first four picks in the draft were defensive players.

The 2011 season started wonderfully for Buffalo and Fitzpatrick. The Bills went to Kansas City and routed the Chiefs, 41–7, in week one, then came from way behind the next two weeks—first beating the Oakland Raiders, 38–35, and then coming from 18 points down to stun the Patriots, 34–31.

The win was the first for the Bills over New England since 2003—a streak of fifteen straight losses.

By then, Fitzpatrick had become something of a cult figure in Buffalo. He had grown a huge, bushy beard—mostly to stay warm—and it had become his trademark. "A lot of it was that I didn't much like shaving," he said. "Fortunately, my wife liked it, so I just kept it."

The Bills didn't really care about the beard one way or the other, but they liked what they were seeing on the field. And so, on October 28, during the team's bye week, they announced that they had signed Fitzpatrick to a new deal that was for six years and could be worth $59 million. There was a $10 million signing bonus, and the guaranteed money was about $18 million, ensuring Fitzpatrick a total of $28 million (NFL contracts are almost never guaranteed for their announced value).

Even for a Harvard graduate, that was pretty good money a month shy of his twenty-ninth birthday.

"It was all good right about then," Fitzpatrick said. "We liked Buffalo, the people were incredibly nice, and I got used to the cold—sort of—after a while. Best thing, though, was Chan had given me the chance to start and we were playing really well as a team."

—

The good times, however, didn't last.

Two days after the Bills announced Fitzpatrick's new contract, the team played Washington in Toronto, the game being part of the "Toronto" series that had started in 2009. Because of flagging attendance, Buffalo played one game annually in the Rogers Centre, the stadium with the retractable roof that housed the Toronto Blue Jays during baseball season. The game proved to be the last high point of the season.

The Bills won easily, 23–0, to up their record to 5-2, putting them in position, or so it appeared, to make the playoffs for the first time since 1999.

But it was downhill from there, starting with that afternoon. On a rare positive play for Washington, linebacker London Fletcher sacked Fitzpatrick, who felt pain go through him. It turned out he had broken two ribs. It didn't keep him from playing; in fact, he never even appeared on a weekly injury report. But it made playing—and throwing—difficult. He wasn't the same player the last nine games of the season, and the Bills weren't the same team.

The problems went well beyond Fitzpatrick's ribs. Star running back Fred Jackson, two starting wide receivers, and linebacker Shawne Merriman all went down for the season with various injuries. Lacking weapons, with a quarterback playing hurt and a defense missing key players, the Bills faded badly. They lost seven straight games before beating the Broncos in the penultimate week of the season. By then, it didn't matter. The victory made them 6-9. A week later the Patriots blew them out, 49–21, and the season ended with a thud.

Thinking they were close to being a playoff team, the Bills signed defensive end Mario Williams to the largest free agent contract in team history—$100 million with $50 million guaranteed.

But they began the 2012 season with back-to-back losses and never really recovered. They were 5-7 and still on the fringes of playoff contention going into December before a three-game losing streak doomed them . . . again. By the time they beat the Jets to close out the season, they were 6-10 . . . again.

Fitzpatrick had a solid year statistically, throwing twenty-four touchdown passes and sixteen interceptions. He threw for a career-high 3,400 yards. It just wasn't good enough.

Gailey, the coach who had put so much faith in him, was fired at season's end. He was replaced by Doug Marrone, and the Bills asked Fitzpatrick to take a pay cut, thinking they were going to draft a young quarterback and let Fitzpatrick keep the seat warm until he was ready to play.

Fitzpatrick didn't like the idea of taking a pay cut, especially since the team's failures had little to do with him. In March, when the new NFL season officially started, Fitzpatrick was cut. A little more than a month later, the Bills used their first-round pick on quarterback EJ Manuel.

Fitzpatrick was thirty and had been in the league for eight seasons—eight more than most people would have guessed. He'd played for four teams and had been a starter in sixty-eight games.

Now, seventeen months after signing his dream contract, he was out of work.

"Goes with the territory," he said. "When things go well, everyone loves you. When they don't, people fall out of love in a hurry."

6

Andrew Luck never had much trouble getting people to love him—especially when he was playing football.

Luck was the oldest of Oliver and Kathy Luck's four children, born almost three years after his father had retired, having played five seasons as an NFL quarterback.

Oliver Luck had starred at West Virginia and had been drafted in the second round of the 1982 draft—forty-fourth pick—by the Houston Oilers. He was the third quarterback taken that spring, behind the ill-fated Art Schlichter (fourth) and future Super Bowl winner, Jim McMahon (fifth).

Luck spent most of his pro career backing up Hall of Fame quarterbacks: two seasons with Archie Manning and three with Warren Moon. He did start for about half the 1983 season when Manning was hurt.

If nothing else, Luck and Manning had to be the first teammates to father quarterbacks who became the number one pick as quarterbacks in the NFL draft. Manning had two—Peyton in 1998 and Eli in 2004. Luck had Andrew in 2012.

When his playing career was over, Luck, who had graduated from West Virginia magna cum laude and Phi Beta Kappa, went to law school at the University of Texas. It was there that he met Kathy. Both left with law degrees and, soon after, Andrew was born in September 1989.

A year later, Luck ran for Congress in West Virginia, taking on three-term Democrat Harley O. Staggers Jr. in the general election. He lost a tight race and decided to give up politics for sports.

Within a year, he and his growing family were living overseas. Oliver took a job in Germany as general manager of the NFL-run World League of American Football's Rhein Fire. A year later, he took over the Frankfurt Galaxy and two years after that was named as the league's president. By then, the NFL, in an attempt to keep the product alive, was calling it "NFL Europe" as a marketing ploy to make sure people knew that the league was connected to the all-powerful NFL. In essence, it was football Triple-A: players who couldn't make an NFL roster went to NFL Europe to keep their careers alive and hope they would get another chance to catch on with an NFL team.

Growing up in Europe until the age of eleven, Andrew was a soccer fan first and foremost and remains one to this day. It wasn't until his family moved to Houston and his dad was hired as CEO of the Houston Sports Authority that he became involved in traditional American sports.

"I knew about football when we were living in Europe, my dad was running a football league," he said. "I knew he'd been a quarterback in the NFL, so someday being a quarterback was in my mind for sure. Back then, I sort of thought every kid's dad played in the NFL. It wasn't until I was older that I realized how unusual that was.

"But I really enjoyed soccer when I was young. That's what we played at recess in school, and, again, I just figured that's the way it was everywhere. It wasn't until we moved to Houston that I found out different. Even then, I never lost my passion for soccer. I still follow it closely."

Andrew was always one of the biggest kids in his class. Which is why when he first played Pop Warner football, he played defensive end and occasionally running back. When he got to the seventh grade, a coach named Rick Thornton decided that his height and his arm merited a chance to play quarterback. From that day forward, quarterback was his position.

He continued to play all sports through high school. He played basketball for four years and was a two-year starter. "I was a rebounder, a defender, and a fouler," he said with a laugh. "I couldn't shoot."

He also played baseball and ran track: the 300 hurdles and the 4x400 relay were his specialties. By the time he was a high school senior, he was six feet four, weighed 225 pounds, and had excellent grades and board scores. He picked Stanford over dozens of big-time schools dying to recruit him in part because of the academics, in part because of the campus, but also because the coach, Jim Harbaugh, had played in the NFL for fourteen seasons and ran a pro-style offense.

"Stanford had everything I wanted," he said. "I figured it was hard to go wrong there."

He was right. After redshirting as a freshman, he became the starter in 2009. By then, Harbaugh had recruited very good players and the Cardinals had their first winning season since 2001—a span that included two fired coaches and a 1-11 record the year before Harbaugh arrived. The 8-5 record included a bid to the Sun Bowl and a 55–21 upset of USC in Los Angeles. The Trojans weren't quite the superpower they had been a few years earlier, but they were still ranked eleventh in the national polls, and Stanford's win—three years removed from being 1-11—got national attention.

Luck didn't play in the Sun Bowl after breaking a finger on his throwing hand in the regular season finale against Notre Dame, a 45–38 win. Even so, he had emerged as a star. He was everything an NFL team was looking for in a quarterback: big, strong-armed, smart, and with experience running a pro-style offense, which would mean he wouldn't go through an adjustment period—the way, for example, Alex Smith had coming out of college—after running a spread offense.

A year later, Stanford, most notably Harbaugh and Luck, exploded into the national consciousness. The Cardinals went 12-1, the only loss coming at Oregon. Autzen Stadium in Eugene has always been one of the toughest places in the country to play because the stands are so close to the playing field. It becomes even more difficult when the Ducks are good.

The 2010 Oregon team, under Chip Kelly, wasn't just good; it was great. Oregon would go 12-0 in the regular season before losing the national championship game to Auburn, 22–19, on a field goal as time ran out. That game was the second all season in which Oregon failed to score at least 35 points.

Stanford lost at Autzen, 52–31, because their defense—like all the others Oregon faced in the Pac-10—couldn't stop Kelly's spread offense. The Cardinals went to the Orange Bowl as a consolation prize and crushed ACC champion Virginia Tech, 40–12.

Luck finished second in the Heisman Trophy voting behind Auburn's Cam Newton. The only thing that might have denied Newton the trophy that season was the NCAA investigation into whether his father had, for all intents and purposes, sold his son to the highest bidder while he was in junior college.

The last thing the NCAA wanted to do was take the star quarterback of the number-one-ranked team in the country off the field. So it came up with a unique out for Newton: it found that if the "student-athlete" (ha!) was unaware that someone *else* was breaking rules on his behalf, he would not be punished.

As a result, Newton skated, played in the national title game, and won the Heisman.

Luck was eligible for the draft after his sophomore season since he had redshirted as a freshman, and players are allowed into the draft three years after their high school class graduates. But he decided to stay at Stanford to get his degree and because the Cardinals had a chance to be a top five team again in 2011. Most of the key players from the team that had finished ranked number four after the Orange Bowl win were returning.

"We had some really, really good players," Luck said. "We had guys with NFL talent, we had a great offensive line. I was in the fortunate position that I didn't *need* the money. My family was doing just fine. So I had the option to stay in college. I loved college. So I decided to stay."

He made the decision even though Harbaugh had left to take the job as coach of the San Francisco 49ers. Luck was very comfortable with David Shaw, who had been the offensive coordinator and was promoted to take Harbaugh's place.

"Coach Shaw was definitely different than Coach Harbaugh," Luck said. "He could be fiery at times, but he was more inclusive. He wanted the seniors to kind of take charge of the team; make it their team."

Even though Luck was a junior in terms of eligibility, he was a senior academically and clearly the team's leader as the quarterback, not to mention the runner-up for the Heisman Trophy.

Luck's last college season went exactly as he had hoped . . . almost.

Again, Oregon was the Kryptonite in Stanford's national championship dreams. This time, the Ducks came to Stanford and turned it into Autzen Stadium on the second Saturday in November. The score was almost the same as it had been a year earlier, 53–30.

Because Stanford and Oregon were both in the newly formed Pac-12 North (the league had gone to divisions when it had expanded the season after Colorado and Utah joined) and each finished 7-1, Stanford didn't get to play in the conference title game, since Oregon had the head-to-head tiebreaker.

Instead, Stanford went to the Fiesta Bowl, where it played third-ranked Oklahoma State and lost, 41–38, in a shootout. Even though Luck played well—he was 27-of-31 passing for 347 yards and two touchdowns—it was a deflating end to his college career.

The first week in December, he had again finished second in the Heisman voting, this time losing out to Baylor's spectacular Robert Griffin III—Griffin receiving 405 first-place votes to Luck's 247.

Both were considered great pro prospects, although Luck was clearly number one in the minds of NFL scouts. He was considered such a lock to be the number one pick during the fall of 2011, the NFL's worst teams unofficially engaged in what was labeled the "Suck for Luck" campaign.

The Indianapolis Colts (2-14) out-sucked the St. Louis Rams (2-14) and the Minnesota Vikings (3-13) to get the number one pick. The Colts "won" the tiebreaker with the Rams based on the Rams having had a more difficult schedule.

The Colts had been in the playoffs for nine straight seasons prior to 2011. But when Peyton Manning had neck surgery and had to sit out the season, the Colts went into the tank completely, losing their first thirteen games. Two late wins made Indy fans nervous, but the team finished with a 19–13 loss in Jacksonville to wrap up the "suck" title.

To this day, one of football's more intriguing trivia questions is: "Who did Andrew Luck succeed as Colts quarterback?"

The answer is *not* Manning. It is, in fact, Dan Orlovsky, who took over midway through the season for Curtis Painter, who had been Manning's backup prior to the future Hall of Famer's injury.

Luck laughs at the question. "See, there was no pressure on me at all," he said. "No knock on Dan, but it's not as if I succeeded Peyton Manning."

Except, in reality, he did just that. The Colts released Manning on March 7, the official start of the 2012 NFL season. Manning had *been* the Colts for most of fourteen seasons, but that didn't matter in NFL-world. Sentiment leads to losing. Manning was about to be thirty-six and was coming off major surgery. The future was the twenty-two-year-old phenom from Stanford.

"I guess it happens to everyone at some point, doesn't it?" Luck said one evening in the spring of 2017. "I'm twenty-seven and I'm already starting to feel old around the rookies on the team. It goes quickly."

Luck was picked number one and Griffin was picked number two by Washington—which traded a slew of draft picks to the Rams to move up in order to take Griffin.

Both were instantly tabbed as the future—actually the present—of their franchises. The moment they got their hug from Roger Goodell, the NFL's hug-obsessed commissioner, they were the faces of their new teams.

Which is a fact of life for those who play quarterback in the NFL. Especially when they are drafted to be starters right away. That was the case with Luck and with Griffin.

Welcome! We love you! Now win . . . or else.

—

The case can be made that no quarterback in NFL history has fallen farther or faster than Robert Griffin III, after he had an astounding trip to one of the highest pedestals ever reached by a rookie quarterback.

Griffin was a hero in Washington even before he took a snap. The trade for Donovan McNabb in 2010 had turned into a disaster when he ran afoul of the Shanahans—father Mike, son Kyle. Then came the ill-fated John Beck–Rex Grossman 2011 season, which ended with Washington going 4-12.

That left the team with the number six pick in the draft. It wasn't going to be high enough to get either Luck or Griffin. There was no way the Colts were giving up the number one pick. But the Rams, who believed they had their quarterback in Sam Bradford—the number one pick in the 2010 draft—were willing to listen.

The Rams ended up acquiring Washington's top pick—the sixth in the draft; Washington's number one picks for 2013 and 2014; and a second round pick in the 2012 draft in return for the number two overall pick in that year's draft.

In NFL terms, this was a king's ransom. Most general managers would rather part with their firstborn child than give up a number one pick—much less two in back-to-back years. Washington knew that Luck was going to Indianapolis with the first pick, and the reason for the trade was to get the chance to draft Griffin.

Griffin appeared to be everything an NFL team could possibly want. In addition to his remarkable physical skills, he was the son of a military veteran, was articulate, had a great smile, and came off as completely charming in the media. The stereotypes still sometimes attached to African American quarterbacks couldn't be put on him. He had graduated from Baylor in three years with a 3.67 GPA and had started working toward a master's degree. He wasn't just smart, he was *smart*.

After taking Griffin right behind Luck, Shanahan drafted a second quarterback: Michigan State's Kirk Cousins in the fourth round. The pick was little noticed. Shanahan, having spent a miserable 2011 without an NFL-quality quarterback, wanted a viable backup for Griffin and thought Cousins could be that guy.

For one year, the Griffin trade looked like a steal for Washington. If the team had given up *five* number ones, the trade would have been the right choice because Griffin appeared to be exactly what every NFL team dreams of finding: a generational quarterback; a Brady, a Rodgers, a Brees.

Griffin wasn't good; he was great. In Washington's opener at New Orleans—arguably the league's loudest stadium—he completed 19 of 26 passes for 320 yards and two touchdowns. He also ran for 42 yards on 10 carries and led his team to a stunning 40–32 win over Brees and the Saints.

Griffin was close to perfect on and off the field. He stuck around to high-five the small group of celebrating Washington fans, then said all the right things: crediting the coaches and his teammates.

He couldn't possibly be that good every week, and the otherwise-mediocre Washington team slumped to 3-6. Then Griffin got on a roll, making remarkable plays at critical times the next seven weeks.

Washington won three straight against the NFC East—routing the Eagles, beating the Cowboys in Dallas on Thanksgiving behind another remarkable Griffin performance, and then beating the Giants, 17–16, when Griffin hit Pierre Garçon with an 8-yard-touchdown pass to cap a fourth-quarter drive.

A week later, trailing the Baltimore Ravens by eight in the fourth quarter, Griffin scrambled. He was hit by the Ravens' huge defensive tackle, Haloti Ngata, and pain shot through his right knee. It was the same knee he'd had surgery on as a Baylor sophomore.

He hobbled off the field but came back after missing just one play. After the game, Shanahan would claim that team doctor James Andrews, the renowned orthopedic surgeon, had told him it was okay to send Griffin back in, that the knee was fine. Later, Andrews would say he had no such conversation with Shanahan, that in fact, Griffin avoided him on the sideline, circled back to the coaches, and went back into the game.

"I never had a chance to look at him," Andrews said.

This was the beginning of a lengthy he-said-he-said that would consume the franchise for the next three years.

Griffin went back in for four more plays—clearly hobbled—before being relieved again by Kirk Cousins. In what would prove to be a harbinger, Cousins got Washington into the end zone, hit on the two-point conversion, and led the team to an overtime win.

Griffin's injury was diagnosed as a sprained LCL. He sat out the next week in Cleveland, and Cousins led the team to a 38–21 win. If nothing else, he had proven that Shanahan knew what he was doing when he used that fourth-round pick on him in the spring.

Griffin came back for the last two games of the regular season—a win in Philadelphia and a Sunday night victory over the Cowboys in the finale that clinched the NFC East. For Washington, a town obsessed with the Cowboys, a quarterback who swept Dallas as a rookie, including a division-clinching win as a climax to the season, was just about ready for a statue.

Not only was Washington in the playoffs, it got to play at home against Seattle in the first round.

As it turned out, that evening—January 6, 2013—was the beginning of the end for Griffin and for Mike Shanahan in Washington. Griffin was almost perfect in the first quarter, and his team jumped to a 14–0 lead.

But, scrambling to try to pick up a first down deep in Seattle territory, Griffin stumbled and fell on the sideline—and didn't get up. He came out only briefly, but when he returned he was clearly limping.

It didn't help that the turf inside Washington's home stadium is generally considered the worst in the NFL. The team has been unable to find a way to improve the quality of the field to this day, and playing an injured Griffin on *that* field was insane.

Once again, there were questions about what Andrews had said—or not said—to Shanahan about Griffin's condition. But it didn't take one of the world's great orthopedic surgeons to see that Griffin was hurting and didn't belong on a bad field against a ferocious defense.

By the fourth quarter, the Seahawks had taken a 24–14 lead—with Griffin clearly not himself, Washington failed to score after its first two drives. On a third down and long, Griffin, in shotgun, reached for a snap that was low and wide. He couldn't corral it and, as he went to try to pick it up, his knee buckled. He couldn't get up.

This time, he didn't return. As it turned out, he had torn the LCL *and* the ACL joints. He needed surgery.

The blame game began.

—

Griffin was never the same player. He insisted he would be back for the start of training camp, then complained publicly when Shanahan kept him out of the preseason lineup. Burned once, Shanahan wasn't going to rush him back.

Griffin publicly criticized Shanahan for not playing him. By then, it was clear that Shanahan and Griffin's relationship was awful and that Griffin, because he knew he had Snyder's backing, felt no obligation to pretend publicly that he and his coach were on the same page.

After he was fired, Shanahan talked publicly about a meeting he and Griffin had a month after the Seattle game in which—according to Shanahan—Griffin more or less laid down ground rules. He wanted to be a pocket passer to stay away from injuries; he didn't want to run the read-option offense that had helped make him a star as a rookie. Shanahan remembered Griffin telling him which play calls were "acceptable" and which ones were "unacceptable."

"I realized that was Dan [Snyder] talking," Shanahan said. "'Unacceptable' was one of his words. He frequently said things were 'unacceptable.'"

Without taking a preseason snap, Griffin started game one, a 33–27 loss to the Eagles. It went downhill quickly from there. Losing in Green Bay the next week was no surprise, but then the Lions came to town and walked away with a 27–20 victory to drop Washington to 0-3. It was the first time in *history* that Detroit had won in any D.C.-area stadium.

Griffin wasn't the same quarterback he'd been as a rookie. He ran less often, and when he did run some of his speed and elusiveness wasn't there in the wake of major reconstructive knee surgery. When Washington dropped to 3-10 after an embarrassing 45–10 loss to the

Kansas City Chiefs, Shanahan announced that Griffin would sit out the final three games of the season in order to prevent further injury.

Cousins started the last three games, and Washington went 1-2. Shanahan and son Kyle were both fired the day after the season ended. Snyder wanted a coach who would do what he was told—especially when it came to Griffin.

In came Jay Gruden. Remarkably, things got worse in Gruden's first season. Griffin dislocated an ankle in week two and Cousins became the starter. Four weeks later, he was benched in favor of third-stringer Colt McCoy.

Somehow, McCoy led Washington to an overtime win in Dallas and—as always happens when a new guy succeeds—became a hero in Washington. Griffin *and* Cousins became yesterday's news. Griffin's rookie year might as well have been two hundred years earlier, not two years earlier.

McCoy had star quality that Cousins lacked. He had finished second in the Heisman Trophy voting as a junior at Texas and third as a senior while leading Texas to a 12-0 record and a spot against Alabama in the national title game.

He'd been injured in that game and, apparently due to his lack of height (six feet one), hadn't been drafted until the Cleveland Browns took him in the third round. He started for a season and a half for the Browns, and was traded to the 49ers after three seasons. He threw one pass for San Francisco in 2013 and then signed with Washington for the 2014 season, presumably to back up Griffin and Cousins.

A week after the Dallas game, Griffin was healthy and—apparently at Snyder's insistence—was the starter against the Vikings. Both teams were 3-5 and hoping to sneak into playoff contention. Griffin didn't play poorly—18-of-28 for one touchdown and one interception—but Vikings rookie Teddy Bridgewater rallied his team to a 29–26 victory.

A week later, Washington went down meekly at home, losing 27–7 to Tampa Bay while the crowd spent most of the second half chanting, "We Want Colt."

Griffin had gone from *the* hero in town to someone most couldn't wait to see leave—including his coach.

When Griffin suffered a concussion in the second exhibition game of 2015, it turned out to be his last hurrah in Washington. With the uncertainty of when Griffin would return as an excuse, Gruden announced that Cousins would start the opener and would be Washington's quarterback for 2015.

"He's been our best quarterback and he deserves to start," Gruden said.

Griffin never saw the field—except from the sidelines—all season and was never once activated for a game. Cousins had a good year—not a great year, but good enough to allow Washington to win a weak NFC East with a 9-7 record.

He became the town's darling. Cousins was everything an NFL fan base can love: he was handsome, always said the right things, had a growing family, talked about his Christianity, and was healthy.

It isn't as if NFL fans won't accept an African American quarterback. They will, as long as he's great. When Griffin got married between his first and second seasons in Washington—before the fall from grace—fans sent him hundreds of wedding gifts, as if he needed them.

Those gifts provided a first small clue that perhaps Griffin wasn't quite as smart as he was articulate. Instead of tweeting a thank-you to all his adoring fans and saying he was going to make a donation to charity in honor of all of them, he tweeted photos of himself with some of the gifts.

No one minded—then.

Griffin left Washington quietly in 2016, released on March 7. Seventeen days later, the Cleveland Browns signed him. Given that no franchise in football history had ever been in more desperate need of a legitimate NFL quarterback, there really was no gamble for Cleveland in the move.

Coach Hue Jackson even made Griffin the starter for the season opener. Naturally, he hurt his shoulder in the opener and missed the next twelve weeks. He came back to start the final four weeks of the season and played well enough to lead the Browns to a 20–17 win over San Diego on Christmas Eve—their lone win of the season.

Merry Christmas.

On the first official day of the 2017 season, March 10, the Browns released Griffin.

He sat out the entire season before the Baltimore Ravens signed him to a last-chance, no-risk contract to back up Joe Flacco. Then they drafted Louisville Heisman Trophy winner Lamar Jackson—leaving Griffin in third-string limbo going into training camp in 2018.

7

"Here's the thing about playing quarterback in the NFL. There are only a handful that are good enough to make you *better*. There are quite a few who are good enough to allow you to win if you have a good team. And then there are some who play because, well, you can't line up without someone to snap the ball to, right?"

Doug Williams was relaxed, eating a light dinner—soup and salad—at one of his favorite restaurants, Eddie Merlot's, an upscale steak house about five minutes from Washington's team headquarters in Ashburn, Virginia.

Williams was talking both as a Super Bowl–winning quarterback and as an NFL player personnel director about the uncertain life of an NFL quarterback. It was November 2017, and Washington had just traveled to Seattle and stunned the Seahawks, 17–14, driving 70 yards in thirty-five seconds in the final minute for the winning touchdown.

"When they [the Seahawks] scored [to go ahead with 1:34 left], I got up to go downstairs," he said with a laugh. "I was waiting by the elevator and saw him complete the first pass. I figured I'd better wait."

"Him" was Kirk Cousins, Washington's quarterback and the only man in Washington who could compete with Donald Trump when it came to controversy.

The first pass had been a 31-yard completion to Brian Quick that had moved the ball to Seattle's 39-yard line. A moment later, Cousins threw a ball down the sideline in the direction of Josh Doctson, and Doctson used every inch of his six-foot-two-inch frame to dive and catch the ball on the 1-yard line. One play later, Robert Kelley barreled into the end zone for the winning score. Four plays, 70 yards, two big pass plays to set up an unlikely win in a place where the best teams almost never won, much less the middle-of-the-road team from Washington.

But they'd gone into Seattle with a banged-up offensive line and somehow won. Most of the screaming media in D.C. didn't pay much attention to Seattle's sixteen penalties or three missed field goals. This was a miracle, and the hero was Cousins. If there had been a mayoral election in Washington that day, Cousins would have won by acclamation. He also could have been county executive in any surrounding suburb, a congressman from Maryland or Virginia, or, if he preferred, a senator from either state.

Which, realistically, presented a potential problem for Williams.

"We're 4-4," he said. "What's our record since Kirk's been the quarterback? I think it's 21-19. We've made the playoffs once. Haven't won a playoff game. We aren't likely to win the division this year. [Philadelphia was 7-1 and had already beaten Washington twice.] Kirk has done some very good things. But when it's all said and done, he's been a .500 quarterback.

"If he wanted to sign a long-term deal, would we have to give it some serious thought? Yes. Because there are a lot of teams with quarterbacks a lot less good than Kirk. We *can* do worse. The question is, can we do better?"

Deep down, Williams knew the entire "to sign or not to sign," the NFL version of Hamlet's dilemma, was really a moot point. There was too much bad blood between Cousins and the two men who had final say in matters like this, owner Dan Snyder and his henchman, Bruce Allen. They'd had a chance to sign Cousins to a long-term contract, notably after the 2015 season, when he'd taken the team to the playoffs. But in spite of the pleadings of then–general manager Scot McCloughan, they'd made him a lowball offer and been forced to place a franchise tag on him for the 2016 season, requiring them to pay him $19.9 million.

A year later, after a similar non-mating dance, Cousins had been franchised again, this time for $23.9 million. That meant the team had paid him $43.8 million for two seasons when it probably could have signed him at the end of 2015 for about $45 million in guaranteed money for five seasons. Now the only way to guarantee that he played in Washington in 2018 would be to make him the first player ever to be franchise-tagged for three straight seasons. The cost would be $34.6 million. And then, a year after that, Cousins would be a free agent, and nothing—no amount of money, begging, pleading, or cajoling—would keep him in town for 2019.

Williams knew that. He also knew that even though the politically savvy Cousins was saying all the right things publicly about "hoping" his future was in Washington, he would be out of Dodge the first chance he got. Why stay with a team whose president (Allen) repeatedly calls you "Kurt" in public, as if to imply that you aren't all that important?

That was why Williams was looking at quarterbacks constantly on the pro level and on the college level. He'd made a point of seeing the ballyhooed college quarterbacks—Sam Darnold of USC; Josh Rosen of UCLA; Josh Allen of Wyoming; Baker Mayfield of Oklahoma; and Lamar Jackson of Louisville—in person and on tape.

He wasn't necessarily sold on any one of them as *the* guy to get, and he knew that Washington's mediocrity—as opposed to being awful—meant it was unlikely that any of them would fall far enough in the draft to reach Washington. There would be no massive trade to move up either, not after the way the Griffin trade had ultimately worked out.

He was intrigued by Alex Smith, who had one year left on his contract in Kansas City. That meant the only way to get Smith would be through a trade. There was, however, a good chance that Smith could be had for a reasonable price because the Chiefs had drafted Patrick Mahomes as his presumed heir in the previous spring's draft.

"When Andy [Reid] called to tell me they were going to take a quarterback, I wasn't shocked," Smith had said during the summer. "They hadn't made any sort of real change in the quarterback room in the four years since I'd gotten there. I understood. I knew the job was still mine for this season [2017], but after that, all bets are off. You don't take someone at quarterback in the first round with the idea that he's going to sit and watch for two years. One year, maybe. But not two."

Williams knew that just as well as Smith did. Which was why he was keeping a close eye on Smith as the season progressed. He knew Smith was a young thirty-three, still quick and agile enough to run the occasional read-option play and much better equipped than Cousins to avoid a rush and keep a play alive without forcing a pass into coverage.

There was also the advantage of knowing Smith would look at

Washington as a fresh start if a deal could be made to bring him there. Cousins wanted out; Smith would be glad to walk in and take his place.

In the back of his mind, Smith knew he was in his final year in Kansas City. He didn't *want* to think it, but after thirteen seasons as a pro, he was a realist. Which is why he wanted so much to make the most of what he expected was his last year playing for Andy Reid. He'd been part of one Super Bowl—back in 2013—when he'd watched the 49ers play the Ravens from the sideline. He very much wanted his *own* Super Bowl team. He knew this might be as good a chance as he would get.

—

Smith's journey to Kansas City had started the way a lot of player movement starts: with an injury.

After Mike Nolan's firing, the 49ers went 5-4 the rest of the 2008 season, and Mike Singletary had the interim tag removed from his title. Singletary hired Jimmy Raye, who had once competed with Doug Williams for playing time in Tampa Bay, as his offensive coordinator. That made Smith five-for-five: five seasons in the NFL, five offensive coordinators. Singletary interviewed eight coaches before hiring Raye, a sign of how uncertain he felt about what was best for the team offensively.

While Smith was rehabbing from his second shoulder surgery, general manager Scot McCloughan had told the media the 49ers intended to cut him at season's end. Smith had two seasons left on his contract and was due $24.6 million—including $9.6 million in 2009. The 49ers weren't willing to pay him that much money.

Understanding that his free agent options would be limited coming off a lost season, Smith renegotiated with the 49ers, signing a new two-year deal for $4 million annually, slightly higher than the going rate for veteran backup quarterbacks.

Shaun Hill had played well late in the season, and Singletary and Raye had him penciled in as the starter. The 49ers started 3-1, mostly on the strength of an improved defense—not surprising, since Singletary had been a Hall of Fame linebacker in Chicago and had always coached on the defensive side of the ball.

In week four, the 49ers got blown out, 45–10, in Atlanta and then, coming off their bye, trailed the Texans 21–0 in Houston when Singletary and Raye decided to see if Smith could do any better than Hill. He did—throwing three touchdown passes to Vernon Davis. The Texans won on a late field goal, but Smith had his job back. The following week, in Indianapolis, he got his first start in almost two years. The 49ers lost, 18–14, to drop to 3-4, but Smith played well enough to keep the starting job.

Things didn't go especially well for the team the rest of the season. Singletary was a Nolan disciple and friend. He had a temper but was also a self-described Christian who often made it clear to the players that he expected them to go to church or team chapel services.

"I was never comfortable with that," Smith said. "I've always thought that religion is personal and that no one should tell you what's right and wrong for *you*. I would never presume to tell anyone else what to do. Mike brought it up all the time. There was an unspoken pressure to let Mike feel as if you were listening to him on the subject of religion. It was uncomfortable."

The 49ers finished 8-8, winning their last two games after being eliminated from playoff contention. Smith had his best season statistically, and, in an upset, Raye was retained as offensive coordinator. It meant for the first time in his career that Smith would spend an off-season with a coordinator he was familiar with.

The experience didn't last long. The 49ers started 0-5, and with his support inside the team collapsing, Singletary fired Raye and promoted Mike Johnson to coordinator. Johnson opted to run a spread offense, similar to what Smith had run in college.

Things got no better—for the team or for Smith. He was now being booed regularly by 49er fans, since, after all, it is always the quarterback who is to blame when a team goes south. The 49ers did win in Johnson's debut in his new job, beating the Raiders, 17–9, with Smith throwing two touchdown passes.

A week later, in a loss at Carolina, Smith hurt his throwing shoulder and had to come out. Troy Smith started the next three games—the first two victories—before Alex Smith was reinstated as the starter after a loss in Green Bay. By then the team was in complete chaos. Singletary was fired with one game left in a 6-10 season.

His parting words going out the door were "You gotta have a quarterback."

By now, Smith was considered a top-pick blunder by almost everyone in football. He'd been in the league for six seasons, and his record as a starter was 19-51. The fact that much of that was because he had a poor team around him most of the time—most notably an awful offensive line—was irrelevant. He was the quarterback; he was the face of the franchise; and he was a loser.

He was also a free agent.

"By the end of that season my attitude was 'Get me out of here, I need a fresh start someplace,'" he said. "I honestly didn't care where it was or who it was with or how much money I was paid. I just wanted a chance to start over. It had been a tough six years."

Because he was still technically under contract to the 49ers until March, Smith was able to use the team's facilities to work out when the season was over.

Jim Harbaugh had been hired as the team's new coach after going 23-3 his last two seasons at Stanford with Andrew Luck as his quarterback. One day in January, Harbaugh walked into the weight room and said to Smith, "How about we go outside and play catch for a little while."

Smith was game. He knew Harbaugh had played quarterback in the NFL for fourteen years, and he thought it was nice of Harbaugh to offer to spend *any* time with him, since he didn't figure in the team's future.

"After a while, he asked me if I had any interest in staying in San Francisco," Smith said. "My honest answer at that point was no. But we kept talking. We'd play catch and talk. I can't remember exactly when I decided I'd like to stay, but there came a point where I thought it would be fun to play for him.

"I'd had two head coaches in the NFL. Both were defensive coaches. I'd had six coordinators. It isn't as if putting in a new offense during the off-season is rocket science or all that hard. But it is hard to build on what you've learned the previous season when you're being asked to learn something new . . . again.

"I certainly knew what kind of job Jim had done with Stanford and with Andrew [Luck]. Yes, it had been college, but he'd run a pro-style offense, which was part of the reason why the scouts were so high on Andrew even though he had decided not to come out that year."

The players and owners were in negotiations for a new contract at that point, and it wasn't going well. On March 12th, what should have officially been the first day of the 2011 season, the owners locked the players out. That meant no new contracts could be negotiated.

By then, though, Smith thought there was a good chance he'd be offered a contract, and he had decided he'd like the chance to play for Harbaugh. So, when the players decided to work out on their own, Smith was one of the leaders. He began teaching the offensive players some of the basic concepts of Harbaugh's West Coast offense. In July, when the lockout ended, he signed a one-year deal for $5 million to stay with the 49ers.

Harbaugh's arrival was like a magic elixir. The 49ers hadn't had a winning season or been to the playoffs since 2002. To start that 2011 season, they bolted to a 9-1 record, the only loss coming in overtime to the Cowboys in week two. Smith was a different quarterback: confident, under control, clearly in command of Harbaugh's offense.

The 49ers' second loss didn't come until Thanksgiving night, when they went to Baltimore to play in what was—naturally—dubbed "The Harbaugh Bowl," the Ravens' John Harbaugh matching up against Jim, his more glamorous younger brother.

Three weeks later, they clinched their first playoff spot since 2002, when Jeff Garcia had been the starting quarterback. They finished 13-3, won the NFC West, and had a first-round bye in the playoffs.

They faced the New Orleans Saints and Drew Brees in the divisional round in what turned out to be a classic quarterback shootout. Brees, who had led the Saints to a Super Bowl victory two seasons earlier, completed 40 of 63 passes for 462 yards. Smith was 24-of-42 for 299 yards. Brees threw two interceptions; Smith none.

The 49ers led 23–17 late in the fourth quarter when Brees marched his team 85 yards to a go-ahead touchdown with 4:11 left. Down 24–23, Smith responded, taking his team the length of the field, capping the drive with a 28-yard scramble for a touchdown to go ahead 29–24 with 2:18 to play. Hoping for a seven-point lead, Harbaugh went for two, but the conversion failed.

Brees wasn't close to done. It took him all of thirty-four seconds to get the lead back. He hit Jimmy Graham with a 66-yard pass and then found Darren Sproles for the two-point conversion, giving the Saints a 32–29 lead.

But he left too much time on the clock: 1:37. The 49ers needed to go 85 yards for a touchdown or, more likely, about 50 yards to get into field goal range for David Akers to tie the game and send it into overtime. Smith wasn't thinking field goal. He found tight end Vernon Davis down the sideline for 47 yards to reach the 14-yard line. Then, with the clock under fifteen seconds, he dropped back and found Davis again, running a post pattern in the end zone. The tight end reached up and made the catch with nine seconds left. The 49ers won, 36–32.

It was the first time in NFL history that a quarterback had led two lead-changing drives in the last three minutes of a game. It came almost exactly thirty years to the day after "The Catch"—Joe Montana's famous touchdown pass to Dwight Clark that beat the Dallas Cowboys in the NFC title game and led to the 49ers' first Super Bowl victory. This one was labeled "The Grab," and any doubts about Smith as the 49ers' quarterback were gone—at least at that moment.

A week later, the 49ers hosted the NFC Championship game because the New York Giants had upset top-seeded Green Bay. Ted Ginn Jr. was unable to play in the game because of a sprained ankle, and rookie Kyle Williams took his place both as a wide receiver and as the team's punt returner.

That proved disastrous.

Williams fumbled two late punts, the first in the fourth quarter to set the Giants up to take a 17–14 lead. Smith got the 49ers into position for a field goal that sent the game to overtime, tied at 17. The teams exchanged punts, but Williams fumbled Steve Weatherford's punt on his own 24-yard line. The Giants patiently ran several plays to get a little closer before Lawrence Tynes kicked a 31-yard field goal to end the game and send New York to the Super Bowl.

Afterward, Smith refused to pin the blame on Williams. "It's never one guy, win or lose," he said. "Our offense didn't do enough, and that's on me."

In other words, according to Smith, it was one guy: him.

"That's the way it is, the way it should be," Smith said, years later. "Of course it takes eleven guys to produce on offense, but if I'm going to get the bulk of the credit when we win, then I get the bulk of the blame when we lose—no matter how it happens. If you don't accept that, you better not sign up to play the position."

Having signed a one-year contract prior to 2011, Smith was a free agent again a year later. He had led the 49ers to a 14-4 record and within a couple of plays of the Super Bowl. Harbaugh wanted him back. Smith signed a three-year deal worth $24 million, his career *finally* on the right path after seven seasons in the NFL.

The following season, the 49ers did make the Super Bowl, but Smith wasn't on the field to get the credit.

In the ninth game of the year against the St. Louis Rams, with the 49ers 6-2 and cruising toward another NFC West title, Smith took a hard hit in the second quarter and suffered what was later diagnosed as a concussion. He stayed in the game long enough to throw a 14-yard touchdown pass to Michael Crabtree to give the 49ers a 14–7 lead, even though his vision was blurred.

Then he came out, not knowing his career in San Francisco had, for all intents and purposes, just ended.

Smith's backup was Colin Kaepernick, who had been drafted in the second round a year earlier out of Nevada. Kaepernick was as big as Smith, six feet four, 215 pounds, but faster and with a stronger arm. This was during the NFL's "read-option" craze.

The read-option is a version of the many option offenses that have been used in football, dating to the triple-option wishbone offense invented by Emory Bellard when he was Texas's offensive coordinator in the late 1960s.

The simplest way to explain the read-option is this: The quarterback "reads" the defensive end on the side of the field where the play is supposed to go. If he's lined up inside the offensive tackle on that side of the ball, then he runs wide to that side *or* drops to pass. If he is lined up outside the tackle, he hands off to a running back to run between the tackles *or* fakes the handoff and drops to pass or rolls out.

A quarterback with speed is essential to run the offense. Smith had the speed to run it, but Kaepernick had more speed. The downside to the read-option and the main reason it was an "in" offense for such a short period of time is that the quarterback is hit on a regular basis. (See Griffin, R III.)

With Kaepernick in the game, the 49ers ended up settling for a 24–24 tie with the Rams on the day Smith was injured. A week later, with Smith still out, the 49ers routed the Bears, 32–7. Smith was cleared to play the next week, but Harbaugh stuck with Kaepernick, saying he would decide week to week who would start at quarterback.

He decided on Kaepernick every week for the rest of the season— right through the Super Bowl. Both Harbaugh and Kaepernick would talk later about how Smith tutored Kaepernick in both practice and games every chance he got.

But it was difficult for Smith. He had done nothing wrong. In most places, when a starter gets hurt, he gets his job back when healthy. Harbaugh had made it clear right away he didn't believe that was always the case. Smith understood. Still, watching his team go to the Super Bowl, rather than playing, stung.

"Kaep played very well," he said, looking back. "I understood Jim's thinking. That didn't mean it didn't hurt. I thought I could take the team where we ultimately wanted to go if I had the chance. It'll always hurt a little that I didn't get that chance."

The 49ers ended up 7 yards short of rallying to win the Super Bowl. They trailed the Ravens, 28–6, early in the third quarter before a thirty-four-minute delay for a power outage seemed to turn the momentum around. They got to within 34–29 and had a first down on the 7 with two minutes still left. But four incomplete passes later, the Ravens got the ball back. They took an intentional safety to create more room to punt the ball in the waning seconds, and the final was 34–31.

Most of the focus in the game was on the Harbaugh brothers coaching against each other and on Ravens linebacker Ray Lewis playing the final game of his career.

Jim Harbaugh, never a good loser, complained loudly postgame about the officiating, convinced there should have been one—if not more—pass interference penalties called in the end zone on the last series. It took a while for Jim and brother John to finally speak to each other on the phone in the aftermath of the game. When someone asked John a month later how the phone call had gone, his answer was succinct: "Not well," he said.

One thing was clear in the wake of the Super Bowl: Kaepernick was now the 49ers' quarterback. Smith had two years left on his contract, which he had signed figuring he would be the team's starter for those three seasons. He was only twenty-eight and still had plenty of football left in him. But he had no desire to be a backup, and the 49ers had no desire to pay him $16 million for two years to fill that role.

On February 27, 2013, they traded him to the Kansas City Chiefs for a second-round draft pick and a conditional future pick.

It was time to start over again.

8

Joe Flacco was never supposed to start in Baltimore as a rookie in 2008—at least not at the start of the season. The plan was for him to learn Cam Cameron's offensive system and watch either Troy Smith or Kyle Boller run it until the time was right for him to take over.

Troy Smith had been the Ravens' fifth-round draft pick in 2007 after winning the Heisman Trophy at Ohio State. He had dropped that far because of his height—five feet eleven—and because he was considered a better runner than passer. And, no doubt, because he was African American. When in doubt, NFL scouts believed it was best to find another position for the "athletic" black quarterback.

Smith became Boller's backup as a rookie after Steve McNair went down for the season, and actually started the last two games of the Ravens' lost (5-11) season. That record cost Brian Billick his job and brought about the hiring of John Harbaugh—who instantly hired Cameron as the offensive coordinator.

The plan was for Smith to start the third exhibition game in August in St. Louis against the Rams. But the week of the game, he was diagnosed with Lemierre's syndrome, which is a bacterial throat infection that often afflicts young adults.

Neither Harbaugh nor Cameron was eager to start Boller in the one exhibition game where teams actually play those who will play on opening day for more than a quarter. Boller's time had come and gone. He was around for emergencies.

And so, Flacco got the start. He wasn't perfect, but for a rookie, he was very solid; clearly the best option the team had to open the season two weeks later against the Bengals.

"Maybe it wasn't ideal," Flacco said. "But I thought I was ready." He smiled. "I waited long enough when I was in college. I really didn't want to spend any more time watching."

On September 7, 2008, Flacco was introduced as the starting quarterback, just about four months after he'd been drafted. The Ravens won the game 17–10 and followed up two weeks later (after a bye week forced upon them by Hurricane Ike) by beating the Browns, 28–10. The first road game of the season produced the first loss—to the Steelers, 23–20, in a stadium and against a team that would create a lot of heartache for Flacco and the Ravens during the next ten seasons.

"Funny thing is, I've never minded playing up there," Flacco said. "It's a blue-collar crowd, I grew up in a blue-collar town. They're loud, but that's fine. It's a great football atmosphere.

"The problem isn't the locale. It's the team. They're always good."

The Ravens lost their next two, but then won four in a row to reach 6-3. By then, Flacco's nickname in Baltimore had been born: "Cool Joe."

Rarely did he show emotion. A touchdown pass didn't elicit a much different reaction than an interception. Occasionally, if you looked very closely, you might see a smile underneath his helmet. But it wasn't easy.

"It's sort of the way I was raised," he said. "For one thing, my dad always believed that you don't get in the face of your opponent celebrating. You try to remember what it's like to be on the other side of it. Plus, it's just not my way. Most of the time, there's still a lot of game left to play, whether you've just done something good or something bad. And when the game is over, there's usually another game to play.

"When you win the Super Bowl, *then* you celebrate. When you lose the last game of the season, then you're truly disappointed. Not until then."

Flacco's rookie season didn't end until the AFC Championship game. The Ravens made the playoffs as a wildcard team. After losing to the Steelers again to drop to 9-5, they had to win their last two games to make the postseason. They won in Dallas, 33–24, and then routed the Jaguars, 27–7.

Rookie quarterbacks don't make the postseason very often. They win two playoff games on the road even less often. But the Ravens went to Miami and easily handled the AFC East champion Dolphins, 27–7. That wasn't a shock. What was a shock was their 13–10 win at Tennessee a week later. The Titans had gone 13-3 and were the top seed in the AFC.

The victory meant a return to Pittsburgh—scene of the first loss of the season. The Steelers had been the second seed, with a 12-4 record. Quarterback Ben Roethlisberger had already won a Super Bowl three seasons earlier, and the Steelers were simply . . .

"Better than us," Flacco said. "We might have beaten them if we'd played an almost perfect game, but we didn't. I certainly didn't."

Flacco threw three interceptions, including a pick-six by the Steelers All-Pro safety Troy Polamalu, and the Steelers won, 23–14, in a game that wasn't that close. Two weeks later Pittsburgh beat the Arizona Cardinals in the Super Bowl, making Roethlisberger the second quarterback (Joe Montana was the first) to win the Super Bowl with different head coaches. He won the first with Bill Cowher coaching the team, the second with Mike Tomlin in charge.

The conference championship game aside, Flacco had had a remarkable rookie season. The team finished 13-6. Even in the quiet of a losing locker room, Ravens owner Steve Bisciotti, who rarely came into the locker room postgame, couldn't stop smiling as he congratulated his team and his rookie coach on their season.

"I think we got the right guys," he said, referring to Harbaugh and Flacco. "We're still a couple of steps away, but this team should be good for a long time to come."

That prediction turned out to be true. But taking those last couple of steps would not be easy.

—

By the time the 2009 season began, Joe Flacco was almost an iconic figure in Baltimore. Even though Eric DeCosta's "we got our guy" moment with Cam Cameron had been staged, it was absolutely true. It had taken the franchise twelve years to get "their guy" at quarterback, but Flacco's rookie season had made it evident that it had finally happened.

Even nine years earlier, during the 2000 season, when the Ravens became Super Bowl champions, the quarterback position was a problem. The Ravens actually went through a five-week stretch in October during which they failed to score a single touchdown. They had won the first two games: 12–0 against the Browns on four Matt Stover field goals; 15–10 against Jacksonville on five Stover field goals. They then lost to Washington, 10–3, and to the Titans, 14–6. At that point Ravens coach Brian Billick decided to bench Tony Banks in favor of Trent

Dilfer. In the team's fifth game in October, Dilfer didn't do any better, Baltimore losing to Pittsburgh, 9–6.

That meant the Ravens' offense for five October games had consisted of fourteen Stover field goals and zero touchdowns. After a 5-1 start, they were 5-4. A week later, in Nashville, the touchdown-less streak was finally broken when Dilfer hit Qadry Ismail with a first-quarter touchdown pass. Remarkably, the Ravens didn't lose again. They won the last seven games on their schedule to finish 12-4 and make the playoffs as a wildcard team, finishing a game behind Tennessee in what was then the AFC Central.

They then gave up *one* touchdown in four postseason games, beating Denver, 21–3; Tennessee, 24–10; Oakland, 16–3; and the Giants, 34–7, in the Super Bowl. New York's only touchdown came on a kickoff return. That meant the Ravens had given up 5.75 points per game in the playoffs, arguably the greatest defensive performance in history.

Dilfer may have been the first quarterback labeled a "game manager." His job was to make sure the offense didn't give up any points. The Ravens did enough on offense to win, but it was hardly spectacular. General manager Ozzie Newsome and Billick were convinced they needed to upgrade the position if they were to have a chance to win a second Super Bowl.

Dilfer wasn't re-signed. Instead, Elvis Grbac, who had been the Chiefs' starter the previous season, was signed as a free agent. Baltimore went 10-6 the following season, beating the Dolphins in a wildcard game before losing—badly—in Pittsburgh. Grbac threw three interceptions. The Ravens then asked Grbac to renegotiate his five-year, $30 million contract. When he refused, they cut him.

That led to the failed Boller experiment. In 2006, the Ravens finally found a star quarterback when they acquired Steve McNair from Tennessee. McNair was thirty-three, but he led the team to a 13-3 record in his first season before getting hurt early in 2007 and retiring soon after.

That was when DeCosta began his search for a long-term answer at quarterback. By the end of 2008, the Ravens were convinced they had finally found their man in "Cool Joe."

The Ravens made the playoffs in each of Flacco's first four seasons. They also won at least one postseason game in each of those seasons, Flacco becoming the first quarterback in history to accomplish that feat.

In 2009, they were 9-7, sneaked into the playoffs as the second wildcard team, and routed the Patriots—in Foxboro—in the opening round before losing to the top-seeded Colts and Peyton Manning the following week.

A year later, they improved to 12-4 but were again a wildcard because the Steelers won the division. They won easily in the opening round again, going to Kansas City and pounding the Chiefs, 30–7. That meant Flacco had won four road playoff games in his first three seasons.

A week later, they had to play in Pittsburgh. Flacco didn't believe that task was too daunting. The Ravens had beaten the Steelers there during the regular season, and he enjoyed the atmosphere at Heinz Field. The Ravens actually led 21–7 at halftime, but the Steelers—naturally—rallied to lead 24–21 before the Ravens tied the game at 24–24 in the fourth quarter. Then Ben Roethlisberger did what he had done to the Ravens so often in the past, driving the Steelers to the winning touchdown. Final score: Steelers 31, Ravens 24.

There was no doubt now that Flacco was becoming the face of the team as Ray Lewis began to show his age. Even though Lewis had been convicted of obstruction of justice in a double murder in Atlanta during Super Bowl week in January 2000, he was an absolute icon in Baltimore. Always the last player introduced, he would do his "war dance" after coming out of the tunnel while the entire stadium stood and cheered.

But Lewis was nearing the end, and Flacco, with his boy-next-door looks, his marriage to his high school sweetheart, and his rapidly growing family, was the perfect face for a franchise that still had actual cheerleaders, not just a dance team.

Even so, there were whispers about whether he was good enough to take the team to the next level—as in the Super Bowl. The Ravens were good. Flacco was good. But together could they be great?

"I never doubted that we could do it," Flacco said. "To me, the key is to get into the playoffs every year. If you do that, you have a legitimate chance to win the whole thing. Look at how many wildcard teams have won the Super Bowl. Baltimore's only Super Bowl before I got there was as a wildcard team in 2000. [The Colts had won Super Bowl V before their move to Indianapolis, but that was a different franchise.] I never worried about what we were seeded, we'd proven we could win on the road.

"You need some luck. You need to be healthy. You need to be playing your best football going into the playoffs. But I never doubted that we could do it."

Some in Baltimore did doubt it. Flacco was considered a good quarterback but not an elite one. He wasn't, some in the media pointed out, the best quarterback in the division—Roethlisberger was.

In 2011, the Ravens finally got over the Pittsburgh hump, beating the Steelers twice in the regular season to win the AFC North. Both teams went 12-4, but the Ravens won the division on the head-to-head tiebreaker and for the second time in their sixteen-year history had a first-round bye. The other time had been in 2006 during Steve McNair's one full season as the quarterback.

Playing at home, they beat the Houston Texans, 20–13, to advance again to the AFC Championship game. As has been the case for most of the twenty-first century, the road to the Super Bowl in the AFC ran through Foxboro.

In the week leading up to the game, Ed Reed, the Ravens' great safety, raised some eyebrows when he went on a local radio show and said that he thought Flacco looked a little rattled at times during the Texans game. That didn't exactly fit the "Cool Joe" image, nor did it fit with the Ravens' usually buttoned-up public facade. Flacco laughed it off.

"I said to him, 'Yo, bro, what are you doing to me?'" Flacco said later that week. "'I already take enough and now you're going to come out and say something like this?'"

Flacco said Reed laughed it off, told him he loved him, and the two men hugged. All was cool, according to Cool Joe.

The Ravens weren't intimidated by the Patriots' aura—especially having beaten them two seasons earlier in Foxboro in the wildcard round.

Not surprisingly, the game swung back and forth from mid-afternoon into night. Tom Brady sneaked into the end zone on fourth-and-1 early in the fourth quarter to give the Patriots a 23–20 lead. After that, neither team could score—each quarterback threw an interception—until the Ravens got the ball with 1:44 left.

Last chance.

Starting at his own 21, Flacco methodically took his team down the field, completing a number of short- to medium-range passes. He found Anquan Boldin for 29 yards to the Patriots' 23, then went right back to him for 9 yards and second-and-1 at the 14 with twenty-seven seconds left.

Flacco dropped quickly, stepped up in the pocket, and threw a strike into the right corner of the end zone to Lee Evans.

The pass was perfect, dropping into Evans's waiting arms. But as Evans gathered it in, the Patriots' Sterling Moore made a desperate slap at it. Somehow, Evans let it slip from his grasp. He had it long enough that John Harbaugh was irate that the officials didn't even look at replay to see if Evans had possession long enough to rule the play a catch.

They didn't look, and it was an incompletion. If Evans had wrapped the ball up, the Ravens would have been going to the Super Bowl.

Instead, kicker Billy Cundiff came in with fifteen seconds left to attempt a 32-yard chip-shot field goal to tie the game and send it into overtime. Cundiff had kicked for nine different teams in his NFL career but had found a home in Baltimore a year earlier, replacing the retired Matt Stover—who had been with the team since its days in Cleveland. He had converted 26 of 29 field goals and made the Pro Bowl.

Somehow, needing to make a kick he could normally hit in his sleep, Cundiff hooked it and the ball wobbled to the left of the goalpost.

Two plays after it had looked as if the Ravens had won, the Patriots were back in the Super Bowl.

The drop turned out to be the last play of Lee Evans's NFL career. The Ravens didn't re-sign him, and, after signing with the Jacksonville Jaguars, he was cut the following August and decided to retire.

Cundiff was luckier. The Ravens kept him around but drafted Justin Tucker to compete with him in training camp. Tucker won the job— and has gone on to be the best kicker in football—and Cundiff played for four more teams the next two seasons before retiring.

Flacco knew he had done everything he could have been expected to do, but that's not what he said. "We needed to get into the end zone on the last drive," he said. "We had other chances the whole game. We just weren't good enough." *He'd* been good enough, but he wasn't about to throw Evans or Cundiff or anyone else under the bus.

Flacco was now four years into his career, and the Ravens had been in the playoffs all four seasons, reaching the AFC title game twice. But no Super Bowls.

He had one year left on the five-year, $30 million contract he had signed as a rookie, and the Ravens wanted to lock him up with an extension. They offered a substantial raise—five years at an average of $14 million a year. Flacco turned it down.

People were amazed. The word around the NFL was that Flacco was rolling the dice and "betting on himself," counting on having a big year to force the Ravens to offer him a better contract; put the franchise tag on him—meaning he would be paid 125 percent of what the top-five-paid quarterbacks in the league were paid on average; or let him walk in free agency.

"I never saw it as a gamble," Flacco said, years later. "I thought I was worth more, based on what I'd done and on what other guys were getting paid. I believed I'd have a good year and, if I did, the Ravens or somebody else would end up paying me more.

"It wasn't as if I hadn't proven to myself already that I could play in the NFL. I wasn't a rookie. The only risk was if I got hurt—which I hadn't for four years. If the Ravens didn't want to pay me, I knew somebody would. To me, it just made sense. I had faith in myself and in our team."

The faith paid off—even though there were some rocky moments along the way. The 2012 season started well, the Ravens bolting to a 9-2 start. In week three, they beat the Patriots, causing some in the media to say and write that they had "gained a measure of revenge" for the loss in Foxboro in the AFC title game the previous January. Flacco didn't know whether to laugh or cry.

"You don't 'get revenge' by winning a regular season game after you lose to someone in the playoffs," he said. "We could have won the Super Bowl if we'd finished that playoff game off. We can never get that back. When we won that game in the regular season it made us 2-1. Period. Nothing more."

The season turned in the wrong direction when the Steelers came to Baltimore on the first Sunday in December. Pittsburgh was having a rare down year and would finish 8-8. Roethlisberger was hurt in week ten, and by the time the Steelers came to Baltimore, his backup, Byron Leftwich, was also out, leaving third-stringer Charlie Batch as the starter. Even so, the Steelers came from behind to win 23–20, staying alive in the NFC North race.

A week later, the Ravens went to Washington and lost again, 31–28, in overtime to Robert Griffin III's suddenly inspired team.

The next day, the Ravens did a very un-Ravens-like thing, firing offensive coordinator Cam Cameron with two games left in the regular season. The Ravens—notably owner Steve Bisciotti and general manager Ozzie Newsome—were among the least likely teams in the NFL to hit the panic button. There was irony in that a loss to Washington—one of the most likely teams in the NFL to hit the button—brought on Cameron's firing.

Jim Caldwell, who had coached the Colts to a Super Bowl in 2009 and was now the quarterbacks coach, was promoted to take Cameron's place. Cool Joe was surprised, but not shaken up. Cameron was the only coordinator he had worked with in almost five seasons but he knew that Caldwell wasn't going to try to reinvent the wheel, or the offense.

"I was certainly surprised by the timing," he said. "It wasn't as if our offense had shut down or anything. We'd had a couple tough losses, sure, but I didn't think they'd make that kind of move, especially in December. Maybe John just thought a different voice was needed in the [offense's] room. I was comfortable with Jim, he'd been my position coach all season. So it was fine."

The move didn't exactly pay off right away. The Broncos, led by a reborn and healthy Peyton Manning, came to town and beat the Ravens, 34–17, dropping them to 9-5. The Steelers' loss to the Cowboys that day clinched a playoff spot for Baltimore, but the town was in a state of near panic. What had looked like a promising season at 9-2 was starting to look like another (ho-hum) trip to the playoffs that wouldn't last very long.

A week later, the Ravens broke the streak with a 33–14 win over the Super Bowl champion Giants (they had beaten the Patriots the year before). Then the Ravens treated the finale in Cincinnati like an exhibition game, pulling most of the starters after the first quarter in a 23–17 loss.

The 10-6 record landed them a number four seed, getting to play at home against the Colts, who had gone 11-5. The Ravens got the home game because they were division champion and the Colts had finished behind the Texans in the AFC South.

Ray Lewis announced during the week leading up to the Colts game that he was retiring at season's end, and much of the pregame focus was on the fact that he was playing his last home game. That was fine with Flacco, who threw two touchdown passes and outplayed Andrew Luck in a convincing 24–9 victory. The win made Flacco the first quarterback in history to win at least one playoff game in each of his first five seasons.

That didn't matter much in Baltimore. The Ravens had to travel to Denver to face the top-seeded Broncos, who had signed Peyton Manning after he had been released the previous winter by the Colts. They had gone 13-3, and Manning, at the age of thirty-six, had looked as good as ever.

The Broncos had easily beaten the Ravens a month earlier in Baltimore, and there wasn't much reason to believe the result would be much different playing in Denver's Mile High Stadium.

The day was brutally cold, the listed temperature at game time thirteen degrees, with the windchill right around zero and the temperature dropping in the second half as the sun began to set.

The game turned into a crazy shootout. Trindon Holliday returned a first-half punt for a Denver touchdown and then returned the second-half kickoff for another touchdown. The Ravens' Corey Graham returned a Manning pass for a 41-yard pick-six in the second quarter. Flacco found Torrey Smith for a touchdown late in the first half to tie the game at 21–21. Holliday's return made it 28–21, but the Ravens answered on a Ray Rice run to tie it again. Then Manning took the Broncos 88 yards to retake the lead, 35–28, midway through the fourth quarter.

Flacco remembers telling himself repeatedly that he wasn't cold, almost as a mantra. The chance to pull the upset was still there. The Ravens' defense forced a Broncos punt late but had to spend all three time-outs in the process. The Ravens got the ball back on their own 23-yard line with 1:09 left, out of time-outs, and needing a touchdown.

In short, they needed a miracle.

Flacco's first pass was incomplete. On second down, finding no one open, he was forced to scramble and picked up 7 yards before getting out-of-bounds with fifty-three seconds left. It was third-and-3, and the Ravens were 70 yards from the goal line.

Flacco dropped again, then stepped up. For a moment it looked like he was going to run again—perhaps pick up the first down, then spike the ball to stop the clock.

"Never crossed my mind," he said. "If I run, we probably still have at least sixty yards to go and by the time we get up and spike, the clock is under thirty seconds.

"They were in cover-two [two safeties playing deep to prevent a deep pass], but it looked to me like they got confused and no one came over to take Jacoby [Jones]. I saw him behind everyone, so I stopped and threw the ball as far as I could. I knew he had the speed to get to it."

Flacco released the ball just across the 25-yard line, and Jones caught it in stride at the Denver 18, meaning he had thrown a 57-yard strike. For once, Cool Joe lost his cool—a little—spinning down the field, arms out as if he was an airplane, finding Jones to congratulate him. Then he walked to the sideline calmly.

"Still a lot to do," he remembered. "All we'd done was tie the score."

There were still forty-one seconds left and the Broncos had two time-outs to play with, but they opted to kneel and take their chances in overtime. The defenses took control: both teams had to punt three times.

Then, late in the first overtime period, Manning made a rare mental error. On second-and-6 from his own 38, he was chased out of the pocket by the Ravens' Paul Krueger. Running to his right, he tried to throw back across his body to Brandon Stokely. But because it was a difficult throw, the ball was just a little behind Stokely, and Graham—again—was in the right spot to make the interception at the Denver 47.

From there, the Ravens methodically moved the ball to the Denver 30—the key being an 11-yard run by Ray Rice as the second overtime began. Once there, Harbaugh decided the ball was close enough for Justin Tucker, who made it look easy from 47 yards, pouring the kick through 16:42 into overtime to give the Ravens a stunning 38–35 win.

To this day, the pass from Flacco to Jones is a huge part of Ravens lore—of football lore, for that matter. It has been called "The Mile-High Miracle," "The Flacco Fling," and "The Rocky Mountain Rainbow."

The Ravens, when they finally reached the warmth of the locker room and had a chance to celebrate for a few minutes, called it—in the words of the late, great basketball coach Jim Valvano—"Survive-and-Advance."

They had survived Denver. They advanced to New England for the AFC Championship game . . . again.

9

As overjoyed as the city of Baltimore was after the Mile-High Miracle, there was a great deal of trepidation in the days leading to the return to Foxboro—scene of the "The Drop" and "The Hook" a year earlier.

Painful memories.

Their quarterback had taken on and beaten Andrew Luck, the NFL's new golden boy, and then he had beaten the old golden boy—on the OGB's turf, no less.

Now, though, he and his team were facing Darth Vader—Tom Brady—and the Emperor: Bill Belichick.

It wasn't as if the Patriots were unbeatable; they were just very, very difficult to beat. The Ravens had beaten a relatively "down" New England team in the opening round of the 2009 playoffs, but the Patriots hadn't won a Super Bowl since the 2004 season and very much wanted to get back there after losing in the final minute to the Giants a year earlier.

It was the second time in five years that a 9-7 Giants team had upset the Patriots in the Super Bowl. That didn't make Darth Vader or the Emperor very happy.

And, they were playing at home, where they almost never lost in the postseason. In the Belichick-Brady era, they were 11-2 in postseason games in Foxboro—one of those losses being the 2009 game against the Ravens.

Most people expected the Patriots to win because, well, they were the Patriots. What they didn't count on was the fact that the Ravens hadn't gotten over the loss a year ago and believed they were the better team that day.

"It wasn't as if we didn't respect them and what they'd accomplished," Flacco said. "We did. But there's a difference between respecting someone and being intimidated. I think for a lot of teams going into that stadium to play that team was intimidating. We weren't intimidated.

"In my career we'd played there twice in postseason. We'd won once and lost the other game when we easily could have won. We didn't expect it to be easy, but we believed we were going to win."

Teams take their cue from their quarterback. The vocal leader of the Ravens was still Ray Lewis. He was the one who gave the rousing pregame speeches. But by now it was Cool Joe the other players looked to for their cues.

"It's a body language thing," said Dennis Pitta, Flacco's favorite third-down receiver and best friend on the team. "Joe's body language, especially when he's playing well, radiates confidence. You can see it."

You could certainly see it on that surprisingly balmy—forty-one degrees at the 6:30 p.m. kickoff—but windy New England winter evening.

The first half wasn't filled with confidence-building moments for the Ravens. Each team scored one touchdown, but the Patriots pieced together two other drives that led to field goals and a 13–7 lead at the break. Brady's record at home when leading at halftime was 67-0. Not an encouraging statistic.

But, as Han Solo once said, "Never tell me the odds."

Flacco was Han Solo in the second half. He led three touchdown drives, the first 87 yards, culminating in a touchdown pass to Anquan Boldin; the second 63 yards, Pitta getting the touchdown pass; the third 47 yards, with Boldin scoring on another pass from Flacco.

The first drive gave the Ravens a 14–13 lead. The second stretched the margin to 21–13. The third made it 28–13. Each time the Patriots tried to respond, the Ravens' defense had an answer. They stopped the Patriots on downs on the Baltimore 19 on one series; then got interceptions from Dannell Ellerbe (on a tipped ball) and from Cary Williams to end any chance of a New England comeback.

Shockingly, Brady was Darth Vader after he'd been stripped of his helmet. The Force had beaten the Dark Side.

The Super Bowl was now set up between the Harbaugh brothers, with John's Ravens facing Jim's 49ers. There was, of course, work to be done in New Orleans. But Flacco played superbly, throwing for 331 yards and three more touchdowns.

With Alex Smith watching helplessly from the San Francisco side-lines, Colin Kaepernick rallied the 49ers from a 28–6 third-quarter deficit to within 31–29 after he ran for a 15-yard touchdown midway through the fourth quarter. But a two-point conversion failed, Flacco got his team into position for one more Justin Tucker field goal, and the defense forced four consecutive incomplete passes from the 7-yard line in the waning minutes and the Ravens held on.

Flacco was voted Super Bowl MVP. In four playoff games he had thrown twelve touchdown passes and zero interceptions, one of the great postseason performances in NFL history. He had proven himself to be an elite quarterback; perhaps not Brady or Manning or Brees or Rodgers, but worthy of mention sometime soon after that.

Even if he hadn't believed it was a gamble, there was no doubt that he had bet on himself and won. One month after the Super Bowl, he and the Ravens agreed to a new contract. It was for six years and a total of $120.6 million if carried out to the finish.

NFL contracts often don't reach the finish line, which is why the dollar figure that is guaranteed is almost always the most important one. In Flacco's case it was $52 million, including a $29 million signing bonus and $51 million in the first two years. It wasn't likely that there would be any talk about changing the contract before the fourth year, when the cap hit for Flacco would be $29 million, a figure that would make it hard for the Ravens to put a competitive team together and come in under the NFL's salary cap.

Flacco wasn't worried about that. The contract made him the highest-paid player in the NFL—nice for the ego and the bio, but not that big a deal to Flacco.

"All it meant was that I was the next guy in line," he said four years later. "Don't get me wrong, I think I'd earned that opportunity. That was why I'd turned down the deal the year before. I thought I deserved better and that I would prove it to them. I did that, so I didn't feel lucky to get the contract.

"But I knew it would only last a few months and then someone else would get more. It didn't matter. I felt I got what I deserved."

Sure enough, Aaron Rodgers signed a new contract in Green Bay within a month that was worth more than Flacco's deal, and Matt Ryan signed an extension in Atlanta in July that was also worth more than

Flacco's deal. By the time Flacco got to training camp, he was "only" the third-highest-paid player in football.

He had no complaints.

———

Alex Smith wasn't making nearly as much as Flacco going into the 2013 season, but he wasn't complaining. After his breakout season in 2011, he had signed a three-year, $24 million deal with the 49ers prior to 2012.

When he arrived in Kansas City for the 2013 season, that contract was still in place. More important, Andy Reid, who had just taken over the Chiefs after fourteen seasons in Philadelphia, had traded for him with the intention of making him his starting quarterback. The Chiefs were coming off an awful 2-14 season in which neither Matt Cassel nor Brady Quinn had been able to get much done playing quarterback.

Reid wanted Smith because he was an established starter who had experience in the West Coast offense that Reid liked to run and because he was able to get him without giving up too much (a second-round pick in 2013 and a second-round pick in 2014).

Reid turned over much of the roster and completely cleared out the quarterbacks room. Chase Daniel, who had been Drew Brees's backup in New Orleans for three years, was signed as Smith's backup. Tyler Bray, an undrafted free agent from Tennessee, was the third quarterback.

From day one, it was Smith's team. After his experience in San Francisco, that was a relief.

"It wasn't as if I didn't understand what Jim [Harbaugh] did with Kaep," he said. "The guy came in and played really well. He stuck with the hot hand. It was just hard to sit there and not feel part of it while we were going to the Super Bowl, and the only thing I'd done to get benched was have a concussion.

"From day one in Kansas City, Andy made it clear I was his quarterback." He smiled. "Of course, if I'd gotten hurt, who knows what would have happened."

Reid was a second-generation branch of the Bill Walsh coaching tree, having worked for Mike Holmgren, who had worked for Walsh.

It was Walsh who, for all intents and purposes, created the "West Coast" offense—although he was working as a coordinator in Cincinnati when he first came up with it. The first offense referred to as the West Coast offense was actually Don Coryell's offense in San Diego, which was initially christened "Air Coryell." Then, some people began calling it a West Coast offense.

Air Coryell was actually completely different from Walsh's offense because it was built around deep passes—which was why Coryell's quarterback, Dan Fouts, was known as "the mad bomber."

Walsh's offense was built around short passes—horizontal passes, in the vernacular—that were meant to stretch the defense. Instead of setting up the possibility of a deep pass by establishing the run, Walsh did it with quick passes to both backs and receivers that might be caught behind the line of scrimmage, on it, or not far beyond it.

In theory, this opened up the middle for the running game and the deep pass because defensive backs were forced to move closer to the line of scrimmage to prevent the short passes from consistently picking up 8, 10, 15 yards.

Walsh brought the concept with him to San Francisco, and it worked to near perfection with Joe Montana as his quarterback. After the 49ers won their first Super Bowl in January 1982, the term "West Coast offense" was applied on occasion to the 49ers.

It was only after Bill Parcells's New York Giants had beaten the 49ers, 17–3, in a 1985 playoff game that the term began to take root. "What do you think of the West Coast offense now?" Parcells asked after the game. Parcells was an advocate of "smashmouth" offense, running the ball time after time and using the passing game—especially a vertical (downfield) passing game—only when absolutely necessary.

Through the years, there have been many different versions of the West Coast offense, including the one Mike Shanahan (who worked for George Seifert, Walsh's successor as coach in San Francisco) used in Denver that was built around utilizing the running game, not in the Parcells smashmouth way, but in a manner that used smaller linemen and "zone blocking," meant to get the backs to the outside on what were called "stretch" plays—as in stretching the defense the way the short passing game did.

The West Coast offense Reid brought to the Kansas City Chiefs was a hybrid—it incorporated the Walsh passing game and the Shanahan stretch running game. In Jamaal Charles, the Chiefs had a running back who could stretch defenses. In Smith, they had a quarterback who could make decisions on the fly and could get the ball downfield when circumstances dictated.

The new team of Reid and Smith was a smash hit from day one in Kansas City. The Chiefs, coming off the disastrous 2-14 season a year earlier, began 9-0. Charles proved to be the ideal West Coast back. He rushed for 1,287 yards and caught 70 passes for just under 700 yards—scoring nineteen touchdowns—twelve running, seven passing—in the regular season.

Smith also had an outstanding season, one that was almost identical statistically to his breakout season in San Francisco two years earlier. He threw for a career-high twenty-three touchdowns and had only seven interceptions. His numbers in 2011 had been seventeen and five. He completed 60.6 percent of his passes for 3,313 yards, compared to 61.1 and 3,144 in San Francisco.

In short, he was a Pro Bowl quarterback who felt completely at home with his new team and coach. Reid was the play-caller, and he and Smith quickly developed a comfort level with each other.

One coach communicates with the quarterback with his headset from the sideline, and, after all the different voices Smith had heard during his years in San Francisco, he soon found the sound of Reid's voice soothing as he called plays.

"I've had four head coaches," Smith said. "There's a marked difference for a quarterback—or at least for me—when the head coach is an offensive guy. With Andy, I had that. A lot of the time, I knew what he was going to call before he called it. Plus, he gave me a lot of flexibility to check [change the play] if I saw something at the line."

The Chiefs had the misfortune that season to play in the same division as the Denver Broncos, who were still smarting over their loss to the Ravens in the previous season's playoffs. They traveled to Denver to put their 9-0 mark up against the Broncos' 8-1 record. The Broncos won, 27–17.

A week later, both teams lost. The Broncos went to New England, led the Patriots 24–0, and ended up losing, 34–31, in overtime. The Chiefs lost to San Diego, 41–38, when Philip Rivers threw a touchdown pass in the waning seconds after Smith had thrown three touchdown passes and given his team the lead, 38–34, late—just not late enough.

Denver and Kansas City rematched a week later in Kansas City, and again it was a quarterback shootout, Peyton Manning versus Smith. The Broncos took a 35–21 lead in the fourth quarter, but Smith twice took his team the length of the field . . . almost. The first drive resulted in a touchdown that cut the margin to 35–28. The second stalled at the 13-yard line in the final minute.

The win pretty much wrapped up the AFC West title for the Broncos. They were 10-2, the Chiefs 9-3, and the Broncos had the tiebreaker because they had swept the season series.

The Broncos finished 13-3, the Chiefs 11-5, meaning the Chiefs had to travel to Indianapolis to face the Colts, the AFC South champions, in the first game of wildcard weekend. The Chiefs lost Jamaal Charles on the first drive of the game when he was knocked silly during a run. The teams traded early touchdowns, and then the Chiefs took control of the game, outscoring the Colts 31–3 from midway in the first quarter until early in the third. When Smith threw a 10-yard touchdown pass to Knile Davis with 13:44 left in the third quarter after Husain Abdullah had intercepted Andrew Luck at the Colts' 18, it appeared that the Chiefs were on their way to New England for a divisional playoff game against the Patriots.

But it didn't turn out that way. All of a sudden, the Colts' offense came to life. They scored touchdowns on five of their next six possessions—Luck picking the defense apart.

They closed the gap to 41–38 when running back Donald Brown was hit on the 2-yard line by the Chiefs' Eric Berry and fumbled. The ball rolled free until Luck picked it up on the 5 and, before anyone really knew he had the ball, raced into the end zone.

"Looking back, after it was over, that was the play that really won the game for them," Smith said. "We take over there, still up ten, and run some clock, it's not a lock that we win, but there's a good chance that we do. When we got the ball back up three, we *did* kill about five minutes before we kicked a field goal. But a six-point lead with five minutes left is a lot different than a thirteen-point lead."

To be exact, they took 5:02 off the clock before Ryan Succop's kick made it 44–38. It took Luck exactly 1:15 to take his team 80 yards, the touchdown coming on a 64-yard pass to T. Y. Hilton. Adam Vinatieri's kick made it 45–44.

There was still 4:21 left on the clock; plenty of time for the Chiefs to get into field goal range. Smith quickly completed two passes to

Dwayne Bowe, moving the ball into Colts territory at the 43, about 8 yards from Succop's field goal range.

The drive bogged down there. On the first play following the two-minute warning, facing fourth-and-11 from the 43, Smith found Bowe down the right sideline and the receiver made a spectacular catch inside the 10. But he couldn't keep both feet inbounds, and the pass was ruled—correctly—incomplete. The Chiefs were out of time-outs, and the Colts ran out the clock.

It was the second-biggest playoff comeback in NFL history, topped only by the Bills coming back from a 35–3 deficit against the Houston Oilers in January 1993. The Colts had scored 35 points in a little more than twenty-four minutes.

The offensive numbers for both teams were mind-boggling. Smith was 30-of-46 for 444 yards and three touchdowns and had rushed for 51 more. Luck was 29-of-45 for 447 yards. He had thrown four touchdown passes and survived three interceptions. In all, the teams combined for 1,069 yards—a playoff record.

The only numbers that mattered when it was over, though, were 45 and 44—the final score.

For Luck, it was another brick in the legacy wall he was rapidly building in Indianapolis. The Colts had gone from 2-14 in the "Suck for Luck" season to 11-5 in his rookie year before losing on the road in the first round of the playoffs. They'd gone 11-5 again in his second season but had won the division, played at home, and come from 28 points down in the second half to win.

A week later, they traveled to Foxboro and were soundly beaten by the Patriots, 43–22. Even so, they had made progress, and it appeared inevitable that he would get the Colts back to the Super Bowl and follow in the footsteps of Manning.

Smith would have loved the chance to face the Patriots. He had played well, his only mistake coming when he had been sacked from behind in the third quarter and fumbled. Overall, even though the season had ended in disappointment, the Chiefs had made a remarkable turnaround.

"The goal when you play in the NFL is simple," he said. "You want to win the Super Bowl. There's no doubt that winning a Super Bowl changes your legacy. All you have to do is look at history. Why are [Tom] Brady and [Joe] Montana looked at as the greatest quarterbacks of all time? Because they've won the most Super Bowls." (For the record, Terry Bradshaw won four, but he is often overlooked in the pantheon of great quarterbacks.)

"I know people will look at me different if I win a Super Bowl," Smith continued. "I get that. And if you're a competitor at the highest level of a sport, your goal is to win the biggest game."

He smiled. "I've gotten there once, but didn't get the chance to win it. If we'd won, I'd have felt good, but it wouldn't have been fulfilling, since I wouldn't have felt like I contributed. I want to be on the field when the confetti comes down someday."

As training camp began in 2014, Smith was entering the final season of the contract he had signed in San Francisco and was due to make $7.5 million. Like Flacco two years earlier, Smith wasn't going to sign unless he got the money he felt he deserved—which was a lot more than what he was making. In the two and a half seasons he had played since Harbaugh's arrival in San Francisco, he had emerged as one of the league's better quarterbacks.

The 49ers in 2011 and in 2012 before his injury had gone 20-6-1—including two playoff games in 2011 in which Smith had played very well. The Chiefs had gone 11-6, making his combined record 31-12-1, and he had again played well in the playoff game even though his team had lost.

Smith was willing to see how the 2014 season played out and take his chances as a free agent if need be. The Chiefs, who had seen first-hand what life was like without a quality quarterback, didn't want to take the risk.

They offered Smith a four-year extension beginning in 2015 that would be worth a little more than $17 million a year on average. That wasn't as much as Aaron Rodgers, Drew Brees, or Joe Flacco were making, but they had all won Super Bowls.

It was considerably more than what a team would pay a "game manager." Even though there were still those who looked at Smith as that kind of quarterback, clearly Reid—the final decision-maker—and the Chiefs saw him as a good deal better than that. The new contract would make Smith the tenth-highest-paid quarterback in the league. That was fine with him.

The Chiefs regressed a little bit in 2014, going 9-7 and missing the playoffs. A year later, they started 1-5, and there was talk in Kansas

City that the bloom was off the Reid-Smith rose. When Charles tore his ACL, it looked like it was going to be a lost year.

But the team righted itself, stunning the Steelers, 23–13, to start a ten-game winning streak. They won in Denver in week nine and finished 11-5. That wasn't enough to catch the Broncos (12-4) for the AFC West title, but it did get them the number one wildcard. They went to Houston and blasted the Texans, 30–0, for their first postseason win since 1993, when they had reached the AFC Championship game before losing to the Buffalo Bills. Since that time, they had lost an NFL-record eight straight playoff games—the most recent being the gut-wrenching loss to the Colts two years earlier.

The eleven-game win streak and the joyride ended a week later in—surprise—New England, where the Chiefs gave the heavily favored Patriots a scare before losing 27–20.

Smith felt as if the Chiefs were close, that they were a play or player or two away from getting to play in February. That spring, they added a major potential weapon in the draft in Tyreek Hill, a fleet wide receiver who had finished his college career at West Alabama after being tossed from Oklahoma State in the wake of a domestic violence incident. He had eventually pleaded guilty to punching and choking his pregnant girlfriend.

Remarkably, he served no jail time, getting three years' probation and being allowed to play football the following fall at West Alabama.

He wasn't invited to the NFL combine but did a pro day for scouts and ran a blazing 4.25 40. If not for his checkered (to put it mildly) off-field past, he almost certainly would have been a high draft pick. Instead, the consensus was that he wouldn't be drafted. The Chiefs took him in the fifth round and received a good deal of criticism for doing so.

Hill began the 2016 season as a kick returner but was soon part of the receiver rotation. With his deep-play ability added to tight end Travis Kelce, who had become an excellent possession receiver, Smith had a variety of weapons at his disposal. He also had a new running back: Spencer Ware, who emerged as the starter when Jamaal Charles was still slowed by the ACL injury he'd suffered in 2015.

Ware had been a sixth-round pick of the Seattle Seahawks coming out of LSU in 2013 and had spent one year with the team (their Super Bowl–winning team) before being cut prior to the 2014 season. The

Chiefs had signed him, put him on the practice squad to start the 2015 season, and activated him midway through the season after Charles was hurt. He had played well enough that the Chiefs looked at him as insurance if Charles couldn't come all the way back.

He couldn't. Charles ended up rushing the ball a total of twelve times in 2016. Ware became the starter and rushed for 921 yards. He also caught 33 passes for 447 yards. He wasn't Charles, but he was pretty good.

The Chiefs finally broke through in 2016, winning the AFC West. Peyton Manning had retired after the Broncos had won the Super Bowl, and the Oakland Raiders, rejuvenated by the emergence of quarterback Derek Carr as a star, became the Chiefs' competition for the division title.

The Raiders were 10-2 and the Chiefs 9-3 when the Raiders came to Arrowhead Stadium for a rare Thursday night game that was worth watching. Smith outdueled Carr and the Chiefs won, 21–13. That left the two teams tied for the lead, but since the Chiefs had beaten the Raiders in Oakland in October, they had the tiebreaker because of their sweep of the season series.

A week later, the Chiefs lost to Tennessee and the Raiders again had control of the division. But that same day, Carr broke his leg in Oakland's win over the San Diego Chargers. The Raiders managed to beat the Colts a week later but lost their finale in Denver, 24–6. When the Chiefs won in San Diego that day, everything flipped.

The Raiders went from the number two seed in the AFC playoffs to the number five seed as a wildcard. The Chiefs, looking at another wildcard and a trip to Houston for the first round, instead became the number two seed and, for the first time in the Smith-Reid era, had a first-round bye.

"That was a big deal," Smith said. Then he smiled. "Or should have been a big deal. Historically the bye doesn't guarantee you'll win your first game, but it certainly improves your odds."

In 2016, two teams with the first-round bye won and two lost. In the NFC, the Atlanta Falcons, the number two seed, easily beat the Seattle Seahawks. But the Green Bay Packers, the number four seed, rallied late behind Aaron Rodgers to stun top-seeded Dallas.

In the AFC, top-seeded New England won easily against the Houston Texans. But the Pittsburgh Steelers, the number three seed who had an identical 12-4 regular season record as the Chiefs, came to Arrowhead and upset them, 18–16.

The good news for the Chiefs' defense was that they kept the Steelers out of the end zone all night. The bad news was that they couldn't stop the Steelers from moving into field goal range on a regular basis.

As it turned out, Chris Boswell kicked a postseason-record six field goals—four in the first half, one in the third quarter, and one in the fourth. The Chiefs, who had scored on their opening drive, finally scored again on a 48-yard Cairo Santos field goal with ten seconds left in the third quarter to make it 15–10. Ben Roethlisberger again drove his team into field goal range, and Boswell's final kick of the day made it 18–10 with 9:49 left.

The Chiefs then put together one of the oddest 75-yard drives ever seen, needing fourteen plays and two penalties to cut the margin to 18–16. With only 2:43 left, they went for two and failed—after succeeding at first on a play called back by a hold on All-Pro tackle Eric Fisher.

The Steelers took over on their own 5 after the kickoff, picked up one first down, and ran out the clock. Game over. Season over.

"You work like hell during the regular season to get the chance to play postseason," Smith said. "You can't take making the postseason for granted because it's never easy. But once you get there, you understand that there's no guarantee you're getting back the next year or *ever*. So when you lose, there's this feeling of emptiness—especially when you've put yourself in a position where you've got a home game to reach the conference title game.

"I've been through it before. I've played in the conference championship game, and the feeling knowing you're playing to go to the Super Bowl is unbelievable. To come up short—*just* short—is unbelievably deflating."

There were, of course, the questions about whether Smith was a "Super Bowl quarterback"—whatever that means. Was Trent Dilfer a Super Bowl quarterback? Was Mark Rypien? For that matter, was Nick Foles a Super Bowl quarterback in 2018? Apparently, yes. On the other hand, was Dan Marino *not* a Super Bowl quarterback? He went to one—and lost. Was Sonny Jurgensen not a Super Bowl quarterback?

Smith wasn't worried so much about what other people were saying. He wanted to be a Super Bowl quarterback, regardless of how the term was defined. And he knew the clock was ticking.

10

As disappointing as the end of Alex Smith's 2016 season was, it was an absolute joy compared to the way Ryan Fitzpatrick felt after his last game of the season.

And his final game was a victory.

"About as hollow a win as you could possibly have," he said with a smile.

Fitzpatrick's nomadic career had taken him from St. Louis to Cincinnati, Buffalo, Tennessee, Houston, and then to New York to play for the Jets.

Fitzpatrick had officially become flat-out rich—as opposed to very well paid—when he had signed his six-year contract in Buffalo in the fall of 2011 (with $28 million guaranteed and a total potential of $59 million). He had been named the NFL's offensive player of the month that September after the Bills got off to a 3-0 start, but by mid-season Fitzpatrick had broken two ribs (during a 23–0 win over Washington in the "Toronto" series), and the Bills finished out the year at 6-10.

Still, Fitzpatrick was clearly established as Buffalo's starting quarterback, and he was financially secure—not insignificant because he and his wife, Liza Barber, had started a family in 2007 and it was growing rapidly. Fitzpatrick had met Liza at Harvard. He was captain of the football team in 2004, and she was captain of the women's soccer team. He had proposed during his rookie season—in a McDonald's—and they had been married a year later. Brady was born in 2007; Tate in 2009; Lucy in 2011. Every other year Ryan and Liza had a baby—the trend continuing right through 2017, when Jane became their sixth child, following Maizy in 2013 and Zoey in 2015.

"I think that's a wrap," Fitzpatrick said after Jane's birth. "Liza feels as if she's been pregnant nonstop for ten years."

Healthy again, Fitzpatrick had a solid year with the Bills in 2012, but the team did not, again finishing 6-10. That led to Chan Gailey being fired after three seasons. In came a new coaching staff, led by Doug Marrone.

Marrone's first important move was to decide he needed a new quarterback. He told Fitzpatrick he was going to make him the backup to whomever he brought in and asked him to take a pay cut. Fitzpatrick wasn't terribly interested in not having a chance to start or being paid less. Marrone told him it was either that or being released—Fitzpatrick opted for being released. The Bills went on to draft EJ Manuel with the sixteenth pick in the first round. Manuel tore his knee up in October of his rookie year (proving that the Fitzpatrick Curse traveled), lost his job to Kyle Orton a year later, and is now a backup in Oakland.

Six days after being released, Fitzpatrick signed with Tennessee, presumably to back up Jake Locker, another first-round draft pick. While in college at Washington, ESPN's Adam Schefter, the king of the anonymous quote, had quoted an anonymous NFL general manager as anonymously telling his colleague Chris Mortensen that Locker was "a bigger, faster, taller version of Steve Young."

Young is in the Pro Football Hall of Fame. Locker played four desultory seasons in the NFL before retiring. Granted anonymity, general managers will say almost anything—which helps explain why so many of them and their scouts lined up during the 2017 season to explain—anonymously, of course—why Colin Kaepernick had suddenly forgotten how to play football after he stopped standing for the national anthem.

It took four weeks in Tennessee for the Fitzpatrick Curse to kick in. Locker was carted off the field in the season's fourth game with a hip injury, and in came Fitzpatrick. Locker returned three weeks later, lasted another two weeks, and then went down with a Lisfranc injury to his foot, ending his season. Fitzpatrick ended up playing in eleven games, starting nine of them.

Maybe thinking that releasing Fitzpatrick would lead to a miraculous return to health for Locker, the Titans released Fitzpatrick in March 2014, replacing him with Charlie Whitehurst, whose nickname around the league was "Clipboard Jesus" because he sported a Jesus Christ–style haircut and beard and played with six different teams— almost always as a backup, thus meaning he carried the quarterback's proverbial clipboard on the sideline.

Those clipboards, for the record, have become obsolete. Because every play call is now charted by computer and backup quarterbacks wear headsets that allow them to hear all communications between the quarterback on the field and the coaches, no one carries a clipboard play chart anymore.

Exactly one year after being signed by the Titans, Fitzpatrick was signed by the Houston Texans. Coach Bill O'Brien needed a quarterback, and his notion was to let Fitzpatrick and Ryan Mallett compete for the job. That was fine with Fitzpatrick, who won the job, then lost it to Mallett in November with the team 4-5. Mallett lasted two games before he tore a pectoral muscle and went down for the season.

A week later, Fitzpatrick threw *six* touchdown passes in a 45–21 win over the Colts but, in a twist, was injured with two games left in the season when he broke his leg on a scramble during a loss to the Colts that eliminated the Texans from playoff contention.

Even though the Texans had gone 9-7 with the three-headed quarterback of Fitzpatrick, Mallett, and Tom Savage, O'Brien decided to go quarterback-hunting again. His search produced Brian Hoyer, Brandon Weeden, and B. J. Daniels—none a Pro Bowl candidate. Even so, the team went 9-7 again, thanks to its superb defense.

This time, Fitzpatrick wasn't released. He had signed a two-year contract, so the Texans traded him to the New York Jets in return for a conditional late-round pick. Fitzpatrick was proof that late-round picks could become productive NFL players.

The Jets had a new coaching staff, led by Todd Bowles, who had hired Chan Gailey as his offensive coordinator. Geno Smith was the starting quarterback, but Gailey wanted someone who was comfortable with his system to back him up, and since Fitzpatrick had played for him in Buffalo for three seasons, he made perfect sense.

"I was always comfortable with Chan, not just his system but on a personal level too," Fitzpatrick said. "So when I went there, even though it meant moving the family *again*, I was happy to be there."

The trade to the Jets meant that Fitzpatrick had to relocate the family for the third straight spring: Buffalo to Nashville in 2013; Nashville to Houston in 2014; and now Nashville to New Jersey in 2015.

"By then we'd gotten pretty good at it," Fitzpatrick said. "The good thing was that the kids were pretty young, so changing schools wasn't all that hard for them. And Liza had become an absolute pro at it by then. I told her she should start a business as a 'how to move your family' consultant."

Liza might have been able to do that if she hadn't been pregnant at the time with Zoey.

No one in New York was exactly sold on Smith as the man who would lead the Jets to glory. He had been drafted out of West Virginia as a second-round pick by then–Jets coach Rex Ryan. Smith had been seen by many as a lock first-round pick, so much so that the NFL invited him to New York to be in the greenroom and get the Roger Goodell hug when he walked onstage.

Goodell was long gone by the time the Jets took Smith with the thirty-ninth pick. Smith had a shaky rookie season and then was benched for a while the next season in favor of an over-the-hill Michael Vick. The 2015 season was viewed by many as his last chance to prove he could be an effective NFL starter. Since Ryan was gone—having been fired and then hired in Buffalo—the belief was that he would be on a fairly short leash with the new coaching staff.

It turned out there was no need for a leash. On August 11th, two days before the Jets' first exhibition game, Smith got into a locker room fight with backup linebacker IK Enemkpali, apparently over Smith's failure to pay off a bet.

When it was over, Smith had a broken jaw that would require surgery and Fitzpatrick was the starting quarterback. The curse lived.

"That one was weird," Fitzpatrick said, laughing. "Players get hurt, that's part of football. It's why it's always important for teams to have a good backup at quarterback. But you certainly don't expect to lose your starting quarterback because of a locker room fight."

The Jets were 2-0 when doctors cleared Smith to play. By then, rookie coach Todd Bowles and Gailey saw no reason to give him his job back. The Jets were 4-1 when Fitzpatrick tore ligaments in his left thumb against the Raiders. Smith had to come in for him, and the Jets lost, 30–24. Fitzpatrick had surgery on Monday and played the following week.

Even so, the team was 5-5 when Fitzpatrick made the one hundredth start of his career in early November against the Dolphins. They won, 38–20. Then they beat the Giants in overtime a week later and stretched the streak to four with wins over the Titans and Cowboys.

That brought the Patriots, who had already clinched the AFC East (again), to MetLife Stadium, the hulking monstrosity that had opened in 2010 so the Jets and Giants could cash in on more corporate sales.

The game swung back and forth, the Patriots tying it at 20–20 with under two minutes to play. Overtime.

The NFL's overtime rules had been changed in 2012 because the feeling was that the coin toss was decisive on too many occasions. A team would win the toss, receive, drive into field goal range, and win the game without the other team ever touching the ball.

The change made things more complicated: Under the new rule, if the receiving team scored a touchdown, the game was over. But if it settled for a field goal, the other team then got the ball back with the chance to match—meaning the game continued—or score a touchdown to win.

Patriots coach Bill Belichick is not just one of *the* great coaches in the history of the game, he is a true iconoclast. Most coaches will punt on fourth-and-1 except when desperate. Belichick will not only go on fourth-and-1, he'll go on fourth-and-almost-anything, and he will sometimes do it in his own territory, which is considered by most in football to be the first definitive sign of insanity.

Belichick—clearly—feels no need to feed the media sound bites. In fact, his press conferences have become famous for his toneless one-, two-, and three-word answers. Belichick may be the only man in history who could describe the history of the world in one sentence.

On this balmy (sixty degrees at kickoff) December afternoon, with the light rapidly fading, Belichick did it again. NFL coaches *always* take the ball to start overtime if they win the coin toss, knowing that a touchdown will win the game. This would seem to be especially true of Belichick and the Patriots, since their quarterback was someone named Tom Brady.

And yet when Patriots captain Matthew Slater called heads and the coin came up heads, he said, "We'll kick."

Most people thought Slater had somehow made a mistake. He hadn't. He was doing what he had been told by Belichick to do.

"I asked him like three or four times," Slater said later. "He was looking at me like I was concussed or something, because he kept saying, 'We'll kick.'"

In fact, Belichick wanted to kick in a specific direction so the Patriots would have the wind at their backs, but the rules don't allow a team to pick what direction they're going in, unless that's their first choice, as in "We'll take the north end of the field." The other team then decided whether to receive or kick off. Presumably, the Jets would have received from the south end.

Either way, the Jets ended up with the ball first because Belichick, rather than just putting the ball in Brady's hands, decided his defense would stop the Jets and give Brady the ball back in good field position.

For once, he was wrong.

Fitzpatrick coolly led the Jets straight down the field: five plays, 80 yards, culminating in a 6-yard toss in the corner of the end zone to Eric Decker for a 26–20 victory. It was Fitzpatrick's third touchdown pass of the day.

The win sent the New York fans into fits of euphoria (this was the Patriots Fitzpatrick beat, after all). It was the fifth win in a row for the Jets, and they were now 10-5, the first time since 2010 they'd had double-digit victories during a regular season. More important, it meant that they would clinch a playoff berth with a win in Buffalo the following week.

The matchup was the kind the NFL craves for TV ratings. Rex Ryan, who had twice taken the Jets to conference championship games, had been fired at the end of the 2014 season and hired in Buffalo. Now he had a chance to keep his old team out of the postseason.

The scenario was simple: If the Jets won, they were in. If they lost and the Steelers won in Cleveland against the hapless Browns, the Steelers would get in because both teams would be 10-6 and Pittsburgh had a better record against common AFC opponents. The teams hadn't played each other during the season.

As it turned out, Rex got his revenge. The Jets, clearly tight, fell behind 13–0 in the first half, but rallied to within 19–17 when Fitzpatrick hit Decker from 21 yards out with 1:10 left in the third quarter.

The defense forced a punt. Needing only a field goal to take the lead, the Jets drove to the Bills' 14 with just under eleven minutes to play. Fitzpatrick wanted a touchdown and a five-point lead. He looked to Decker yet again, this time deep in the end zone. The pass was intercepted.

The Bills then got a field goal to make the margin 22–17. Still plenty of time left. The Jets moved to their own 45 with a third-and-9 at the two-minute warning. Ryan came with a blitz. Fitzpatrick saw Brandon Marshall open down the middle but was hit as he released the ball. The pass was underthrown and intercepted again.

The Jets got one last desperate chance, taking over on their own 18 with forty-four seconds to go and no time-outs left. Fitzpatrick scrambled for 9 yards but, blitzed again, trying to find Decker deep, was intercepted for a third time in the last quarter.

Game over. Season over.

"As disappointing as any loss I've ever been through," Fitzpatrick said. "We worked so hard to get into that position, and then we just couldn't get it done in that fourth quarter. There were a lot of reasons for what happened, but ultimately, I blame myself. I got the credit the week before when we went down the field to beat the Patriots, I had to take the blame for not getting it done against the Bills.

"Most years, 10-6 gets you into the playoffs. That year, it didn't. We knew what was at stake going in, and we didn't do what we had to do. I didn't do what I had to do. That hurt."

As it turned out, the Jets were the only team in either conference with a winning record that failed to make the playoffs that year.

Even after the loss in Buffalo, there was no doubt that Fitzpatrick had just completed the best season of his career and appeared to be locked in as the Jets' starter for 2016.

Steve Serby, the longtime columnist for the *New York Post,* wrote a column about how far Fitzpatrick had come from one Christmas to the next: from sleeping on the couch in the family's home in Houston because he couldn't make it upstairs on his broken leg, to celebrating the recent arrival of child number five and the best season of his career at home in New Jersey with his Jets future secure.

Except it wasn't quite that simple. While Bowles knew he wanted Fitzpatrick over Smith as his starter, the organization wasn't sure if it wanted to commit to Fitzpatrick without at least taking a look at another quarterback. They drafted Christian Hackenberg out of Penn State in the second round—the same round where they'd selected Smith three years earlier—with the notion that maybe he would be the answer at quarterback, if not right away, then in the future.

Fitzpatrick was a free agent. He had little interest in going to another team when he had clearly established his value with the Jets.

Teams weren't exactly lining up to sign him either: he was thirty-three, which meant no one wanted to make any kind of long-term investment in him, and his play in 2015 had priced him out of the backup quarterback market.

So Fitzpatrick and the Jets went back and forth, the drama playing out in the New York tabloids. Depending on whose side you took, either the Jets were being chintzy with someone who had taken them to the brink of the playoffs or Fitzpatrick was asking too much for a player who'd had a good season but had failed with the playoffs on the line in the season's final week.

"The funny thing is, I was asking for a one-year contract worth twelve million in guaranteed money," Fitzpatrick said. "No long-term commitment, I knew how old I was, but money that you'd pay a starting quarterback with eleven years of experience in the league."

The negotiations dragged on. It wasn't until July 28—after training camp was under way—that the two sides finally agreed. The deal was for one year and $12 million guaranteed.

"Could have been done in March," Fitzpatrick said, shaking his head. "Just wasn't."

The delay in the contract and some of the public anger it engendered—some directed at the team, some at the quarterback—proved to be a harbinger.

The Jets lost their opener, 23–22, to Cincinnati, but bounced back to beat the Bills, 37–31, in a Thursday night game. Fitzpatrick was superb, throwing for 374 yards, and was selected as the AFC offensive player of the week.

It went downhill from there. A week later, in an embarrassing 24–3 loss to the Chiefs, the Jets turned the ball over *eight* times, six of them on Fitzpatrick turnovers. Three weeks later, en route to a 28–3 loss to Arizona, Bowles benched Fitzpatrick, bringing back the seemingly forgotten Geno Smith. He then named Smith to start the next week in Baltimore.

That, however, didn't last long. Smith went down in the second quarter with what turned out to be a torn ACL—ending his season. The Fitzpatrick Curse was apparently alive and well. Fitzpatrick came on to lead the Jets to a surprising 24–16 victory, and the job was his again. The Jets made it two in a row the next week against the pathetic

(1-15 for the season) Browns, but things began to fall apart again soon after that. A loss to the Dolphins was followed by a 9–6 loss to the merely awful (4-12) Rams. During that game, Fitzpatrick took a hard hit and had to come out in favor of Bryce Petty, who had been a fourth-round pick a year earlier.

Petty got the start a week later against the Patriots, but—naturally—he went down before halftime and back came Fitzpatrick. The revolving door continued to swing a week later when Fitzpatrick started against the Colts, but he was benched in favor of Petty at halftime.

At that point, the Jets' next quarterback move might have involved Joe Namath or Mike Taliaferro. (Taliaferro, as all Jets historians know, was the team's quarterback before Namath.)

Instead, Bowles announced that, with the team 3-9 and going nowhere, Petty would start the season's final four games. Might as well get a look at the young guy, was the thinking. Fitzpatrick was thirty-four, and everyone knew what he could and couldn't do.

"That was a rough, rough time," Fitzpatrick remembered. "We'd started the season feeling like we had a real chance to be good. We were 10-6 the year before, we knew we could compete with the best teams. I was comfortable as the starter and was being paid starter money because of what I'd done the year before.

"Then, starting with the Kansas City game, it began to fall apart and we went downhill fast. I was benched; unbenched because Geno got hurt; got hurt myself; came back; got benched again. By the time we got to December, I think everyone just wanted the season to be over, me maybe most of all."

Naturally, Petty got hurt—twice—first against Miami and then again at New England, a 41–3 embarrassment that summed up just how far the Jets had fallen in a year, going from an exhilarating overtime victory that had put them on the brink of the playoffs to a one-sided rout that left them 4-11 with one game to play.

The finale, as it had been a year earlier, was against the Bills—this time, though, in MetLife Stadium. The announced crowd was 78,160, about half of them apparently disguised as empty seats. On a relatively warm, mid-forties New Year's afternoon, Fitzpatrick threw two touchdown passes and the Jets easily beat Buffalo, 30–10. The two-TD, no-interceptions game meant that Fitzpatrick's final numbers for the season were seventeen touchdown passes and twenty-two interceptions.

He knew he had played his final game for the Jets, and he wondered if he had played his final game—period. Hardly a sentimentalist, Fitzpatrick brought his family down onto the field afterward to take some photos and found himself lingering for one last look around before he left for the locker room.

"The thought absolutely occurred to me that this might be the last time I saw a football field as a player," he said. "I knew the Jets weren't going to bring me back, and I didn't know if anyone was going to have much interest in a thirty-four-year-old who was coming off a terrible season.

"Beyond that, I wasn't certain if I wanted to play again even if an offer did come up. You're always beat up at the end of a season—any season—physically and mentally. I just wasn't sure I wanted to go through it again. I'd played twelve years, which is a lot longer than I'd ever thought I'd play when I got out of college.

"I'd thrown for more than twenty-five thousand yards in the NFL, and I had never dreamed I'd get the chance to do that. So if this was the end, I was prepared for it.

"But I also knew from my past experience that once my body healed from the pounding and I had some time away from the daily grind of the game, I might feel differently if an opportunity came along. I didn't have to make any decisions at that point, so I just sat back and figured I would see what—if anything—came up."

One of the things few people understand about playing quarterback is the beating you take playing the position. Because of rules designed to protect quarterbacks from getting injured, quarterbacks are viewed as pampered and protected—which, relatively speaking, they are.

They wear red jerseys in practice, which mean "Do not touch." If a rushing lineman or blitzing linebacker hits a quarterback more than a split second after he releases a pass, he's penalized. Sometimes it can be less than a split second. In the sexist culture of the locker room, players often joke that quarterbacks should wear dresses and that the rules are designed nowadays to turn tackle football into touch football.

There's no doubt that linemen and running backs take a play-to-play pounding that is almost indescribable. If you stand on the sidelines during a game and watch a routine play—a handoff to a running back, who picks up 4 yards before he's brought down—you wouldn't expect anyone to get up from the collisions that take place.

And yet, 99 percent of the time, everyone gets up and jogs back to the huddle. Most injuries aren't caused by the collisions, they're caused by flukes: someone rolling over someone's leg; a noncontact injury that tears an ACL; a twist in the wrong direction at the wrong time.

Only now, in the last ten years, have NFL trainers and doctors become more aware of the fact that a player doesn't have to be stretched out on the ground screaming in pain to be hurt.

"Almost every play hurts in some way," Joe Flacco said. "I'm a big guy [six-six, 230 pounds], but when I get hit by a lineman or a linebacker who is running full speed at me, it hurts. You lie there for a split second kind of taking inventory of your body, and if nothing is causing screaming pain, you get back and go back to the huddle. You play the game, you accept the fact that you're going to feel pain out there. You're going to be hurting when the game's over.

"A lot of times after a routine game I'll have trouble doing very much on Monday, still be sore on Tuesday, and *maybe* by Wednesday I'll start to feel normal—or what passes for normal during the season—again. That's why the Thursday night games are so tough. Just when you might be starting to feel okay again, you're back out there and it starts all over again."

Most football players will tell you that being hurt and being injured aren't the same.

"You're hurt in some way all the time," Fitzpatrick said. "Everybody is to one degree or another—especially by December, because you really don't have time to heal from week to week. I've played with broken ribs and all sorts of aches and pains. It's not being brave or anything, it's part of the job. Unless your body absolutely says, 'No, I can't do this,' you go back out there."

Alex Smith, who has been remarkably healthy for most of his thirteen seasons in the NFL, describes it best: "When I come in after a game, I can see all the bruises and the welts from the various hits. You might still be feeling the pain from a particular hit that shook you up, but unless you can't walk or can't lift an arm, you just take a shower, be thankful you're in working order, and go home. Then, when the season's over, you have a chance to heal."

Fitzpatrick needed some time to heal in all ways possible after the Jets' finale against the Bills.

"It was nice to go out with a win," he said. "But it was small consolation for the season we'd had—that I'd had."

He smiled. "It was also a year too late. We needed to beat them the year before. If we had, who knows . . ."

PART TWO

11

Andrew Luck sat at a corner table in a quiet restaurant called Vida, far off the beaten path from Indianapolis's downtown. The restaurant had been open for only fourteen months, but it had become a place Luck went to frequently.

"I can ride my bike over here easily on side streets, and when I get here, the place isn't swarming with football fans," he said with a smile. "If I go someplace downtown, it's pretty much impossible to have a quiet dinner. Here"—he swept a hand around the room—"no one is all that interested in me. Plus, the food's very good."

It isn't easy to find a quiet place to eat when you are the starting quarterback in an NFL town. It's even tougher when you arrived as the Next Great Thing and your image is on a giant billboard on the stadium where your team plays.

No wonder Luck would like a place on a quiet street where he would be interrupted only occasionally during dinner.

This was early June, with the 2017 football season approaching. Luck was four and a half months removed from shoulder surgery that he hoped would finally allow him to play football at 100 percent and to live his life pain free. It had been a while since he had been able to do either.

Luck's first three seasons in the NFL had gone about as well as anyone realistically could have hoped. The Colts had gone 11-5 each year and had improved their playoff performance annually. In 2012, they had lost on the road in the first round to the Baltimore Ravens—who went on to win the Super Bowl. In 2013, Luck had led the second-greatest comeback in playoff history in a 45–44 wildcard-round win over the Kansas City Chiefs, before losing a week later to the New England Patriots. In 2014, the Colts had beaten the Cincinnati

Bengals and the Denver Broncos—led by Indianapolis icon Peyton Manning—to reach the AFC title game.

Their 45–7 loss to the Patriots had been overshadowed by "Deflategate," the controversy that engulfed the NFL for the next twenty months over the question of whether Tom Brady had ordered that footballs be deflated in order to grip them more easily.

In the spring of 2015, prior to the start of Luck's fourth season, the Colts had picked up his fifth-year option for $16.55 million. That was on top of the four-year, $22 million deal he had signed coming out of Stanford as the number one pick in the 2012 draft.

Luck still hadn't been to a Super Bowl, but that seemed to be just a matter of time. Beyond that, life was pretty good.

Things began to change during Luck's fourth season. The Colts started slowly, losing to the Buffalo Bills and New York Jets. They had come back in week three to beat the Tennessee Titans. But Luck had felt a twinge in his shoulder during that game. He had stayed in the game and thrown two fourth-quarter touchdown passes as his team rallied past the Titans for a much-needed win.

But when the doctors took a look at the source of the shoulder pain, they found a strain in his AC joint—AC is short for acromioclavicular— which is why people just call it the AC. The recovery time for that sort of injury is two to twelve weeks, depending on the severity of the tear and the athlete's ability to tolerate pain.

Luck missed two games and then came back in week six against the Patriots, not exactly an easy return-engagement game. He played reasonably well the next four weeks, most notably in a 27–24 win over the Broncos, who came into Indianapolis unbeaten on November 8.

Throughout those four games, Luck knew something was wrong. "I was missing throws I should have made," he said. "It wasn't as if I couldn't play—I could. But it wasn't easy. I was good enough to play, but not as good as I knew I should be."

During the Broncos game, Luck took a hard hit and lacerated a kidney and tore an abdominal muscle. He couldn't play through those injuries *and* a sore shoulder, so he went back to the bench. As it turned out, his season was over. The kidney and abdominal issues healed, but his shoulder continued to feel worse.

At season's end, he met with the team doctors, and together they decided that a rehab program should heal the shoulder in time for the 2016 season. Luck didn't want to have surgery unless he had no choice. "Surgery is a long, painful recovery," he said. "It should be a last resort. We didn't think we were there."

Although missing nine games after having started fifty-seven straight games—forty-eight regular season games from 2012 to 2014; six playoff games; and the first three games of 2015—was frustrating, the general assumption was that 2015 had been a blip and that Luck, who would turn twenty-seven in September 2016, would be just fine.

In fact, the Colts' confidence was such that on June 29, just prior to the start of training camp, they signed Luck to a six-year contract worth $140 million—$87 million of it guaranteed. The deal made Luck the highest-paid player in the NFL—a title he carried until Derek Carr topped it (in terms of dollars per season) a year later when he signed with Oakland for $125 million for five years—$25 million per season versus $23 million per season.

Interestingly, when Luck signed, some observers believed he was, at least in terms of career arc, *under* paid. Luck had come into the league in the second season of a rookie salary cap. As a result, his first contract was worth far less than that of Sam Bradford, who in 2010 had been the last number one pick before the 2011 CBA (collective bargaining agreement) created the rookie cap. Bradford's deal was worth $50 million in guaranteed money—more than twice what Luck got.

Luck didn't care about any of that. He understood the money he was getting was mind-boggling and far more than he needed, especially with a lifestyle that included a lot of time riding his bicycle around town.

As it turned out, Luck had his best season—statistically—in 2016. He threw for 4,240 yards in fifteen games with a 63.5 percent completion percentage—the highest of his career—thirty-one touchdowns, and thirteen interceptions. As always, he was a surprisingly effective runner for someone six-four, 240 pounds. He rushed for 341 yards—an average of 5.7 yards a carry. Luck had surprised a lot of scouts when he ran a 4.67 40-yard dash at the combine in 2012. Ben Roethlisberger, another big quarterback who could make things happen with his legs, had run a 4.75 in 2004; Peyton Manning had run a 4.8 in 1998.

Luck missed one game, a November loss to the Steelers, after suffering a concussion the previous week against the Titans, a game the Colts won. He came back the following week and, for the season, took every meaningful snap at quarterback in the fifteen games he started.

In all, it was a nice comeback season, sullied somewhat by the Colts finishing 8-8 and missing the playoffs for a second straight season. The problem wasn't the offense; it was the defense. Indianapolis finished seventh in the league in points scored; thirtieth in points allowed—ahead of only the 4-12 Houston Texans and the 1-15 Cleveland Browns.

As solid as Luck's numbers were, there was a problem—a big one. His shoulder still hurt, and it was getting progressively worse.

"It had gotten to the point where doing simple things had become difficult," he said. "Shaking hands hurt. Opening a door hurt. Picking up my coffee cup in the morning hurt. We had done all the right rehab stuff the previous off-season.

"I felt okay for a while during the rehab, but when the season started it went the other way. I'd feel sharp pain at times. Other times, I felt like I had a dead arm. I could get by, but I didn't feel right. I knew I didn't want to go through another season feeling the way I felt on and off the field. It wasn't just affecting my football, it was affecting my life. I knew I couldn't just go on dealing with the pain. That wasn't good enough."

And so, on January 14, Luck had surgery on the shoulder. Realistically, he knew he would have been happy to be ready for the start of the season, though he held out some hope that he'd be ready for training camp. The spring OTAs were out of the question, but that didn't matter. Veterans need OTAs like a marathon runner needs to walk to work.

Which was why, as he pulled into Vida for dinner, Luck was in a good mood.

"I'm looking forward to getting onto the field pain free," he said. "It's been a while since that was the case. It's funny how quickly time goes by when you play football for a living.

"It doesn't feel like it was that long ago that I was drafted and I was the rookie everyone was looking at in training camp. In the real world, it wasn't that long ago—five years. But in football, it doesn't take very long to start feeling old. Part of it is the beating your body takes. We all go through that, with or without injuries.

"But a bigger part of it is how quickly things change. If you look at our training camp roster, there are *four* guys who were here when I first got here in 2012: [Adam] Vinatieri; [Anthony] Castonzo, and T.Y. [Hilton]. That's it. There are a lot of kids coming to the team now who don't remember the world before the internet. I'm old enough to remember a time when there was no internet. A lot of them don't—at all. It's scary.

"Truth is, there are times when I look around and I feel like an old fart."

One can only imagine how Tom Brady—twelve years older than Luck—or Drew Brees—ten years older—or Ben Roethlisberger—seven years older—must feel. Like Luck, Brees is probably thoughtful enough to think about how quickly time passes for a football player. Roethlisberger has talked for two years about knowing retirement is near. Brady is from another planet and clearly plans on playing forever.

It was Brees whom Luck talked to the most after the surgery. He had always admired Brees for never being stymied by his lack of size or by serious injuries. Brees had dropped to the second round of the draft in 2001 because teams were unsure about his height (five-eleven) and his arm strength. In the NFL, he'd become a star in San Diego but then injured his shoulder in 2005, leading to surgery for a torn labrum and torn rotator cuff.

The Chargers had then offered him a contract with very little guaranteed money, and he eventually signed with New Orleans, where he led the Saints to a Super Bowl victory, helped the city recover from the horrors of Hurricane Katrina, and consistently put up numbers that will make him a lock Hall of Famer whenever he retires.

"He's been through a lot and proven over and over again that he can do things when people doubt him," Luck said. "Plus, he's very smart and very mature. He's living proof that you can come back from serious injuries and be better than you were before. Talking to him was a big help for me in a lot of ways."

Of course, all the talking in the world wasn't going to heal his shoulder. Luck's plan as he sat and talked on a warm June night was to be on the field when training camp began in mid-July. But there was just a hint of doubt as he spoke.

"I want to be on the field throwing the ball, getting ready as soon as possible," he said. "But if it doesn't go exactly according to plan, that's okay. One thing Drew and some others have told me is you have to be patient. You can't push your body to do things it isn't ready to do. I understand that."

He smiled. "The date that matters the most is September tenth."

That was the day the Colts were scheduled to open the season in Los Angeles against the Rams. Luck was planning to be in the lineup that afternoon.

—

Joe Flacco's target date was also September 10.

He had been healthy throughout 2016 and had one of his best seasons statistically—throwing for more than 4,000 yards for the first time in his career.

He had also signed a contract extension the previous March that again made him the highest-paid player in the NFL. The contract meant he should be with the Ravens through the 2021 season, which made it at least possible that Flacco would finish his career in Baltimore.

The extension was worth $66 million, $40 million of it guaranteed. Since his pay was now stretched out over six years instead of the three left on the deal he had signed in 2013, Flacco would count far less against the Ravens' cap. A good deal, it seemed, for both sides.

The Ravens started 3-0 but couldn't continue to play at that level. Their defense, once the pride and joy of the franchise, struggled. They lost four straight games after the 3-0 start, fought back to 8-6, but then lost in Pittsburgh and Cincinnati the last two weeks to finish 8-8 and out of the playoffs for a second straight season. It was the first time since 2004–2005 that they had missed the postseason two years in a row.

That meant Flacco's gaudy numbers felt pretty hollow. "The point of your season is to get to the playoffs," he said. "Your personal numbers, good or bad, don't really matter. I got paid the money I got paid because we were consistent winners my first seven seasons. We got to the playoffs and we performed well in the playoffs. Going two years in a row without making it didn't feel good at all."

The Ravens signed veteran wide receiver Jeremy Maclin to a two-year contract during the off-season and added Danny Woodhead, a running back who specialized in being a third-down receiver. Dennis Pitta, after three lost seasons, had been healthy throughout 2016 and had been Flacco's go-to possession receiver, with 86 catches for 720 yards and two touchdowns.

There was hope that Breshad Perriman, who had been the team's first-round draft pick in 2015, might finally live up to his potential in 2017. The scouting and coaching staffs had been enamored of his 4.29 40 speed coming out of college, but all the speed in the world didn't really matter if you couldn't catch the football.

Flacco was comfortable with his receiving corps and thought the running back situation—which had never really settled down after the team had been forced to release Ray Rice in the wake of his domestic abuse case—would be better. His concern was the offensive line.

"If we can put together a group that can play together the entire season and get better, I think we can be pretty good," he said on an early June afternoon during the team's second round of OTAs. "An offensive line needs time to play together, to get used to one another. It's not as easy as it looks. If we can put the same five guys on the field most weeks, they'll get better throughout the season."

Things had not gotten off to a good start early in OTAs. During a routine Friday practice, Dennis Pitta had stretched for a Flacco pass and—untouched—had gone down. He tried briefly to get up but went back down almost instantly.

Watching, Flacco knew right away that something was seriously wrong. "As a player, you learn to read body language," he said. "Especially when it comes to guys you know well. He was grabbing at his hip, and that was where he'd had his problems in the past.

"When he finally got up and they helped him off, the look in his eyes told me he knew it was bad."

As it turned out, it was very bad—career-ending bad. Pitta had dislocated his hip again. That meant he wouldn't play that season, and whether he could return in the future would be very much in doubt. Five days after the injury, the Ravens released Pitta, meaning they would save about $2.5 million in salary cap money.

Football is not a business for sentimentalists. Because Pitta had a preexisting hip injury, a clause in his contract said that if he couldn't play because of a hip injury, the Ravens would owe him nothing. Normally when a player is released because of an injury, a financial settlement is reached. In Pitta's case there was no settlement.

Pitta's injury was tough for Flacco to take on a number of levels. Pitta was his closest friend on the team. During OTAs, he and Pitta often played golf together after the day's work was done. Flacco and his wife, Dana, had four kids; Pitta and his wife, Mataya, had three. The families often spent time together during the season, and when Flacco and Pitta were "bachelors," during OTAs, they often had dinner together.

Beyond that, Pitta was Flacco's "crutch" receiver. When the Ravens needed 5, 6, 7 yards on third down, Pitta was often the target. When Flacco couldn't find anyone deep on a play, his underneath receiver was often Pitta.

Pitta had good hands and had no trouble running over the middle to make a tough catch. A presence like his could not be underestimated. Now, in the blink of an innocent play in OTAs, he was gone. When the season began, Pitta was with the team—in the radio booth, doing color for the first four games of the season.

"On the one hand, it was very difficult," Flacco said. "You see any teammate go down and realize right away that the injury is serious, it's tough to take. Doesn't matter how many times you've seen it—which we all have—it's still tough to take. When it's your best friend on the team and a guy you rely on heavily, that makes it even tougher. It was a setback for the team and it was bad for me, personally and professionally."

The start of training camp was hardly encouraging either. Two days before the team's first practice, Flacco felt a pain in his lower back during a routine lifting session in the team's weight room. Not wanting to take any chances, he went instantly to see the team's trainers and doctors. They said he had strained a muscle and recommended rest. How much rest he would need was the key question. At that moment, standing up was a challenge—much of the pain being in his butt.

Initially, the thought was that Flacco might miss a week—maybe two—but would be ready, if necessary, for the exhibition opener against Washington.

That didn't turn out to be the case. Flacco saw no need to rush back to play in any of the four exhibition games.

Exhibition football exists for one reason: to give the league and the TV networks the chance to add a few more dollars to their coffers. In 2011, when the owners locked the players out during collective bargaining negotiations, it wasn't a coincidence that a settlement was reached just before the start of the exhibition season.

The players don't make that much during exhibitions. Most of their salaries are paid during the seventeen-week regular season. The tickets that season-ticket holders must buy and others will buy (because they can't afford a season-ticket package) are full-priced. So are concessions and parking. Since only a handful of exhibition games are part of the network TV packages, teams sell local TV rights.

The owners will argue, of course, that the games are needed to get players sharp for the regular season and to figure out who will make the fifty-three-man roster and the eight-player practice squad.

That is marginally true—at best. Nowadays, most teams schedule scrimmages with other teams that serve the same purpose as exhibition games, except they don't involve time-outs for TV or halftime. There's more coaching, because the scrimmage can be stopped at any time for coaches on both sides to make a point.

For years, players have campaigned to have the exhibition season cut in half, pointing out that during exhibition games serious injuries always occur that affect the regular season. More and more in recent years, coaches have limited exhibition playing time for regulars. Many play in only one game—the third—going perhaps a half. The fourth game is played almost entirely by players who will be cut the next day. None object to being used as fodder, because they know it may be their last chance to play football and they're hoping another team may see something in them and sign them after they're cut.

Going into his tenth season, Flacco didn't need very many snaps to be ready for the regular season. "In an ideal world, I might be ready to play a half or a quarter in the third game," he said. "But I really don't think it's that important. I can get the reps I need in practice if I don't actually get into a game. The key thing is that I'm a hundred percent healthy when we play for real."

Flacco's injury, and the uncertainty about his return time, thrust the Ravens into the middle of the brewing Colin Kaepernick controversy. Kaepernick had been in the national spotlight since the previous August, when he stopped standing for the national anthem. Initially he had sat on the bench during the anthem, and then, after a meeting with a former Green Beret named Nate Boyer—who had played in the NFL—he decided to kneel.

Boyer had explained to Kaepernick that it was a tradition to kneel in front of the graves of fallen comrades, and since Kaepernick's protest was to bring attention to racial inequality and the deaths of African

Americans at the hands of white police officers, that would be a way to protest and honor the dead.

In an interview with HBO's Bryant Gumbel, Boyer said that Kaepernick had been very receptive to his ideas and had asked him to kneel with him. Boyer had told him he couldn't do that, but would stand next to him, hand on heart during the anthem while Kaepernick knelt. When Boyer did that, he was pilloried—he said—by some of his former Green Beret comrades. Boyer said he believed it was more important to have a dialogue than to polarize the situation any further.

Kaepernick began the 2016 season on the bench behind Blaine Gabbert in San Francisco, eventually taking over as the starter on a very bad team. He played solidly, especially the second half of the season, when he threw fourteen touchdown passes and three interceptions.

When the 49ers cleaned house in the front office and the coaching staff after a 2-14 season, Kaepernick's fate in San Francisco was sealed. John Lynch, the new general manager, let him know in February that the 49ers were going to release him rather than pay him the $14.5 million he would have been due if he had been on the roster at the start of the season.

The NFL is a quarterback-starved league. Perhaps half the teams have competent starters, and very few have backups who can step in and win games for them. The two notable exceptions were the Minnesota Vikings, who reached the NFC Championship game after Case Keenum was forced to replace Sam Bradford two games into the season, and the Philadelphia Eagles, who won the Super Bowl with Nick Foles replacing Carson Wentz, who was on his way to being the league's MVP before he tore up his knee in December.

Keenum and Foles had both been starters in the past, not great ones, but starters nonetheless.

There was also Jimmy Garoppolo, the starter-in-waiting in New England, who had stepped in and played very well in Tom Brady's stead when Brady had missed the first four games of the 2016 season because of his Deflategate suspension.

Garoppolo's play had either cemented his status as Brady's successor—if Brady ever retired—or made him a more valued trading chip for the Patriots. In October, with Brady having one of his best years at age forty, Bill Belichick traded Garoppolo to the 49ers for a second-round draft pick.

By season's end, Garoppolo's presence in San Francisco had completely changed the 49ers' profile within the league—from incompetent to contenders—going into 2018.

Keenum had been undrafted coming out of the University of Houston, in part because of his size, six-one (maybe), but also because he had torn an ACL in his knee in 2009. He drifted from the Houston Texans to the St. Louis Rams, back to the Texans, and then to the Rams again prior to the 2015 season.

The Rams had traded that off-season for Foles in a swap of quarterbacks with the Philadelphia Eagles. Foles had gone to the Pro Bowl in 2013, but as the fortunes of Coach Chip Kelly faded in Philadelphia, so did his.

Keenum outplayed Foles in training camp and became the starter. Foles had been signed to a two-year, $24 million contract when he came to St. Louis. When the Rams decided to take Jared Goff as their quarterback of the future with the number one pick in the 2016 draft, Foles asked for his release. He signed with the Chiefs for a lot less money—$1.75 million for one year—and backed up Alex Smith for a year. Then he signed with the Eagles to back up Wentz prior to 2017.

Keenum stayed with the Rams when they moved back to Los Angeles and was the starter at the beginning of the 2016 season. The Rams started 3-1 and then collapsed, winning just one more game the rest of the season. Coach Jeff Fisher finally decided he had to play Goff after the team *won*, 9–6, against the New York Jets. Fisher was fired with the team 4-9, and Keenum again became a free agent at season's end.

He then signed with the Vikings for a base salary of $2 million to be Bradford's backup. When Bradford went down with a knee injury in the season opener, Keenum had to step in for him. He never stepped out.

The Vikings were 2-2 when the Green Bay Packers came to town with a record of 4-1. Already there was talk that Aaron Rodgers was on his way to a second MVP award.

But Rodgers was hurt in the second quarter that day, going down with what turned out to be a broken collarbone. By the time he returned in week fifteen, the Packers had gone from a Super Bowl favorite to a team trying to hang on for dear life—unsuccessfully as it turned out—at sneaking into the playoffs.

The Packers went 3-5 after Rodgers got hurt and were 7-6 when he returned. Clearly not 100 percent and still rusty, Rodgers threw three interceptions, and the Packers lost to the Carolina Panthers. Their chance for the playoffs gone, the Packers opted not to play Rodgers in the season's final two games and lost both.

As Keenum stood on the sidelines watching Rodgers come off in obvious pain, his emotions weren't mixed in the least. He was upset.

"I've been through a serious injury, so I know how awful it feels, especially when you come off and you're almost certain the injury is serious," he said. "Aaron Rodgers is good for the NFL. He's a true star. You want to compete against him and you want to try to beat him.

"My heart just went out to the guy. You don't want to see anyone hurt, but we all know injuries, sometimes serious ones, are part of football. Quarterbacks take a beating—even when they aren't injured. You know when someone like Aaron goes down, it changes the entire season for a team."

Which is exactly what happened to the Packers. Keenum and the Vikings beat the Packers that day, and when the extent of Rodgers's injury was learned, millions of hearts within Packer Nation fell.

There are only a handful of quarterbacks in the NFL who are that vital to a team's hopes: Tom Brady, Drew Brees, Cam Newton, Russell Wilson, Andrew Luck—and Ben Roethlisberger. There are also a handful of quarterbacks not on that level whose loss to injury would ruin a team's season: Flacco, Philip Rivers, Dak Prescott, Eli Manning, and, as of last season, Carson Wentz and Jared Goff.

A team might be able to survive without them for a game or two, but not long term. As remarkable as Foles's performance was in the 2018 playoffs, it isn't likely that the Eagles would have been the Eagles if Wentz had gone down when Rodgers did. Then again, Foles might be the exception that proves the rule—someone who had been a Pro Bowler in the past.

When Luck was unable to play for the entire 2017 season, the Colts had to give up a second-round pick to the Patriots to acquire Jacoby Brissett just to have a respectable quarterback, and they completely tanked, going 4-12. There are plenty of other examples: even though Kirk Cousins played admirably once he was given the job in Washington following Robert Griffin III's injuries, the entire arc of the franchise changed. The team went from having a potential Hall of Famer at quarterback to a solid quarterback the owner and team president never really wanted as their starter.

Keenum, bolstered by a superb defense, had a remarkable season in 2017. The Vikings won ten of their last eleven regular season games and were the number two seed in the NFC (behind Philadelphia) in the playoffs.

Even though Keenum played very well in Bradford's stead, there were still those in Minneapolis who hoped Bradford would come back after the team's bye week to take his job back. He didn't. By the time he was ready to play in the postseason, Keenum had played so well there was no thought at all of benching him.

Keenum and Foles were exceptions. More often than not, when a team loses a starter, the effects are catastrophic. When Flacco clearly wasn't ready to play in the exhibition opener, the Ravens began looking for another quarterback. They didn't want Ryan Mallett, Flacco's backup, to play too much because they needed him healthy if Flacco wasn't ready to play in the opener in Cincinnati. The only other quarterback on the roster was Dustin Vaughan, who had never taken a snap in a regular season game.

That's where Kaepernick came in—potentially.

The fact that he had not been signed since opting out in March had become a polarizing topic. The quality of some of the backups being signed was well below Kaepernick's career résumé—including the 2016 season.

When Flacco's injury was announced, there were questions right away about the possibility of signing Kaepernick. Coach John Harbaugh had nothing but good things to say about him as a quarterback and as a person. Kaepernick came to Baltimore to meet with team officials.

But when the dust cleared, the Ravens signed someone named David Olson, whose most recent team had been the Kansas City Phantoms of the Champions Indoor Football league—a second-tier—Arena Football League.

Olson's career in Baltimore lasted four days. He was cut on July 31, and the Ravens signed Josh Woodruff, who had also never taken an NFL snap and had most recently been released by the Bills in May.

The Ravens' given reason for not signing Kaepernick was that they hadn't felt he was still passionate about playing football when they'd met with him. There had been a report that owner Steve Bisciotti didn't want to sign him because he was afraid of fan backlash. General manager Ozzie Newsome issued a non-denial/denial of that story, saying—in a statement—that Bisciotti had never told him he couldn't sign Kaepernick.

A month later, just prior to the start of the season, Ray Lewis, the Ravens' iconic former linebacker, went on the NFL Network and said he had pushed the team to sign Kaepernick but the battle had been lost when Kaepernick's girlfriend, Nessa Diab, posted a tweet that was perceived as "racist."

The tweet showed a photo of Lewis with his arm wrapped around Bisciotti and a second photo from a movie called *Django Unchained,* which showed an almost identical photo of Samuel L. Jackson—playing a slave—with his arm around a dying Leonardo DiCaprio—his owner.

Clearly, Diab was making a point about the relationships between NFL players and owners. Whether it was racist was open to interpretation, but it apparently gave the Ravens another reason not to sign Kaepernick, even though he was clearly a better and more experienced quarterback than David Olson or Josh Woodruff—or, for that matter, Ryan Mallett.

Flacco, working to be ready for the season, was bemused by the whole thing.

"If I hadn't been able to start the season, I would think he'd be someone who would be pretty good insurance behind Ryan," he said. "I don't think anyone in the locker room would have had a problem with him being signed. For the most part, guys just want to know if you can help the team."

Several Ravens, most notably Terrell Suggs, the leader of the defense, had emphatically made that point. But the Ravens didn't sign Kaepernick. Neither did anyone else.

Clearly, in spite of the excuse-making going on, each of the thirty-two owners had decided they weren't going to sign Kaepernick. As the season went on, the excuse-making grew louder, with anonymous front-office executives insisting that Kaepernick wasn't that good a player anymore or that he wasn't "worth the trouble"—as in booing fans.

No doubt if Kaepernick had been signed and played well, the boos would have quieted quickly.

Fortunately for the Ravens, Flacco was cleared to play the opener. All was well in Baltimore.

12

There were no health issues for Alex Smith during the 2017 preseason. But his life did change in April.

The Chiefs had again had an excellent regular season in 2016, going 11-5 and winning the AFC West, edging the Oakland Raiders on the last day of the season thanks to having beaten them twice, giving them the tiebreaker when the two teams finished with identical records.

That meant the Chiefs were the number two seed in the AFC— behind the Patriots—and got to play their first playoff game at home under Andy Reid. Unfortunately, the opponent was the Steelers, a team they always seemed to struggle with. This time was no different. The Steelers defense shut down the Chiefs' offense for most of the day, and when the Chiefs finally scored late in the game to cut the margin to 18–16, the Steelers stopped the two-point conversion attempt and hung on to win.

Smith had been in Kansas City for four seasons. The Chiefs had reached the playoffs on three of those occasions but had not made it to a conference championship game. Smith was about to turn thirty-three and had two years left on his contract.

"There's a window for players," he said. "Just like there's a window for teams. I felt as if I was playing as well as I had ever played, but I also know football's a business and that coaches and general managers have to try to be one step ahead when it comes to personnel. If they're not, they become former coaches and general managers pretty quickly."

Which is why Smith wasn't terribly surprised when he got a text from Andy Reid two days prior to the draft letting him know that the Chiefs were planning to use a high draft pick on a quarterback. Who it would be and exactly when it would come, he didn't say. The point of the text was to let Smith know the Chiefs were beginning to think about Life After Alex.

"The quarterback room hadn't really changed much in terms of me being the leader for four years," Smith said. "They hadn't drafted anyone before the fifth round, and they had brought Nick [Foles] in specifically to be my backup. In the NFL, four years is a long time not to make any change in the QB room. It's so important to the team that you can't afford to get caught short."

During Smith's four seasons playing for Reid, there had never been any doubt that the other quarterbacks in the room were his backups, there to play only if he got hurt. Reid's text didn't change that. Clearly, Smith was going to be the starter in 2017. But there were no guarantees beyond that.

"What it did was make me aware that the window was starting to close," he said. "It didn't represent any sort of change of life for me at that moment. If they *hadn't* drafted someone, my future would have still depended on whether I played well or not. If I played well, I'd have a job. If I didn't play well, I wouldn't have a job. The only difference really was an understanding that if I played well, I'd still have a job, but there was no guarantee that it would be in Kansas City."

Reid wasn't completely sure the Chiefs would get the chance to draft Patrick Mahomes, the quarterback they liked, but he felt Smith deserved a heads-up.

"I knew we liked the kid, and I knew there was a chance we were going to be able to get him," Reid said. "I told Alex, 'You just keep being you. Don't look over your shoulder, because there's no need to do that.' I wasn't really worried about whether he could do that or not because he's got NFL scar tissue. I knew, if we did it, that he'd handle it well."

As it turned out, the Chiefs decided to go all-in on drafting a quarterback they believed would be Smith's successor. They had the twenty-seventh pick in the first round but ended up trading with the Buffalo Bills to move to the tenth spot. To do that, they had to give up their first pick, their third pick, *and* their number one pick in the 2018 draft.

That was a heavy price to pay to move up seventeen spots, but they had decided to push all their chips in on Mahomes, who had left Texas Tech after his junior season. Mahomes was actually a little shorter than Smith: six-two to six-four, and a little slower: 4.80 in the 40 at the combine, compared to Smith's 4.67. He had a rifle for an arm and, perhaps most important, was eleven years younger than Smith.

"I'm realistic," Smith said after the season had started. "You don't spend that much to get someone with the intention of sitting them on the bench for two years. But for the moment, I'm worried only about this season. If I play well, the future will take care of itself one way or the other."

Colin Kaepernick had talked about how supportive Smith had been after he had taken over for him as the starter in San Francisco. This was different, but Smith was very comfortable being in a mentoring role for someone he knew had been anointed as his successor.

"I've heard about quarterbacks, Tom Brady among them, who don't want to share stuff with younger players," he said. "I'm just not built that way. There's absolutely no reason for me not to help Patrick out in any way I can. When I was young, there were older guys who went out of their way to try to teach me. There's no reason why I can't do that too.

"There are certain things you can tell someone player to player that's different from coach to player. When I first got to San Francisco, I had to go from spread and shotgun to taking snaps under center. The coaches were always on me about my footwork. I was always counting steps, three steps, five steps, seven. It got to the point where, at times, I wasn't even looking at the defense or at my receivers. Footwork, footwork, footwork.

"I think it's okay to work on those fundamentals in practice. But when you get in a game, that has to all go out the window. You can't think about that. The most important thing is your eyes. You have to *see* the game: know who needs to be blocked; know where the defense is; see your receivers—read the defenders. That's all with your eyes. That's the kind of thing I tried to work with Patrick on."

No one was more aware of Smith's mentoring of Mahomes than Reid. "What he did for him you can't pay back with money," he said. "He helped him with things in ways that a coach simply can't do. There was complete trust from pupil to mentor. Knowing Alex, I wouldn't have expected anything different."

It helped that Smith and Mahomes hit it off from the beginning. All three quarterbacks—Tyler Bray was in his fourth season as the

Chiefs' number three quarterback—got along well. Smith and his wife, Elizabeth, often had Mahomes and his girlfriend and Bray and his wife over to their house for dinner during the week.

"It was a very comfortable dynamic in the room," Smith said. "You can never underestimate how important that is because the three quarterbacks and the quarterback coach [in this case, offensive coordinator Matt Nagy] spend a *lot* of time together. If you aren't comfortable with one another, that can be a problem."

As is often the case with the too-long preseason, the Chiefs took a couple of key hits. Playing in Seattle in week three, the game in which the starters get the most playing time, starting running back Spencer Ware caught a short pass from Smith and zigzagged his way inside the 10-yard line before suddenly going down.

Just like Flacco with Pitta, Smith knew right away the injury was serious. "When it's noncontact, when someone like Spence just goes down like that, you know it's bad," he said. "My first thought was how unfair it was for him. Jamaal [Charles] was gone and the stage was all his. He'd played well the year before, and we all thought he was ready to be a star. Then this happens."

Andy Reid felt the same way: "Any injury like that is tough to deal with, no matter how often you've seen it happen," he said. "But this was gut-wrenching. It wasn't that I didn't have confidence in our kid [rookie Kareem Hunt] but that Spencer deserved better than that."

The NFL chews up running backs and spits them out. Charles had been one of the league's dominant running backs—he'd had five 1,000-plus-yard seasons—prior to a torn ACL in 2015 and had needed a second surgery in 2016 after playing in just three games. Ware, who had been released by the Seahawks once and waived by the Chiefs before being re-signed, stepped in and rushed for 921 yards on 214 carries and had caught 33 passes for another 447 yards.

Even though Ware was carted off the field, the initial reports were that he had just sprained the knee. Smith suspected that further tests wouldn't be quite as encouraging. He was right.

Two days later, after the team had flown home from Seattle, Ware underwent an MRI that showed multiple torn ligaments in the knee. He was done for the season. All of a sudden, Kareem Hunt, who had played in the Mid-American Conference the previous fall at the University of Toledo, was the starting running back.

Next man up. Life in the NFL.

The Chiefs were less than two weeks away from opening the NFL season in Foxboro against the Patriots, the Super Bowl champions. Smith had been thinking about that game since the NFL had unveiled its schedule—with all the bells and whistles you can possibly imagine—on April 20.

"You always start thinking about the first opponent when you see the schedule," he said. "But this was different. We were playing the very first game of the season. The entire league would be watching. We'd be playing a team that almost never loses at home, and we'd be walking into the stadium in the middle of their celebration of winning the Super Bowl. We all knew what the atmosphere would be like.

"It was the kind of challenge you have to crave if you're a competitor—no matter how difficult you think it may be."

Now the Chiefs would be going into that crucible on Thursday night, September 7, with a rookie drafted in the third round at running back.

"I think we all had a lot of confidence in Kareem," Smith said. "He'd shown us that he had plenty of talent in preseason. Of course, preseason is one thing, playing in Foxboro against the Patriots is another."

The game began almost exactly as most of America expected it to begin. The Patriots, as they always seem to do, took the opening kickoff and drove right down the field, 73 yards in nine plays, and scored on a 2-yard run by rookie running back Mike Gillislee less than three minutes into the game, taking their usual 7–0 lead.

On came the Chiefs' offense. On first down at the 25, Smith handed to Hunt, who bolted through a hole to pick up 7 quick yards. There was just one problem: he fumbled when hit, and the Patriots' Devin McCourty scooped up the fumble at the Chiefs' 32.

Quickly, Brady got the Patriots to the Chiefs' 20 and found Rob Gronkowski in the end zone for a diving touchdown catch. The season was less than five minutes old and the Chiefs, playing in arguably the toughest place in the NFL to win on the road, were down 14–0.

"I was thinking, 'Holy shit, we're down 14–0 and we've run one play on offense,'" Smith said. "One minute we're coming out of the tunnel pumped and ready and knowing we've got a really good plan, and the next minute we're down 14–0."

Only they weren't. The touchdown pass was reviewed. This was the first test of the NFL's new rule by which all replay decisions came out of New York, rather than ultimately being made by the referee. The play was overruled—correctly—as an incomplete pass. The score reverted to 7–0.

Two plays later, on fourth-and-inches from the 10, Belichick, as always, went for it. And the Chiefs' defense rose up and stuffed Gillislee for a half-yard loss.

Just like that, the Chiefs had life.

Smith promptly drove his team 90 yards in twelve plays, culminating with a 7-yard pass to Demetrius Harris. That tied the game at 7–7 and allowed the Chiefs to take a deep breath. Reid, offensive coordinator Matt Nagy, and Smith had believed coming into the game that they could move the ball on the Patriots' defense. Now they had tangible evidence that they were right.

"Right there the tone of the entire night changed," Smith said. "It went from people thinking blowout to shootout."

It became a shootout. The Patriots led 17–7 late in the second quarter when the Chiefs took over on their own 10 with 2:47 left. Mixing short passes with runs and using his time-outs deftly, Smith took the Chiefs down the field on their second 90-yard drive of the night, this time climaxed by a 3-yard pass to Hunt with thirteen seconds to go that made the halftime score 17–14.

"That drive was so key," Smith said. "We'd fumbled on our first offensive play, had terrible field position the whole half, and got out of there down three with the ball coming to us to start the second half. Plus, we hadn't used a lot of the stuff we thought would work against them. It was a very up locker room."

It probably helped that the Chiefs were unaware that the Patriots had led at halftime eighty-one times in regular season games played in Gillette Stadium since it opened in 2002, and had won all eighty-one.

Except at the Super Bowl, with its endless overhyped show, halftime in the NFL is quick. It lasts a total of thirteen minutes, which doesn't leave a lot of time for adjustments or rah-rah speeches.

"By halftime, you're usually too tired to give a rah-rah speech even if you wanted to," Smith said.

Most halftime routines are the same: Coach talks briefly to the team, then offensive coaches and defensive coaches go to separate rooms to discuss adjustments or changes—either in play-calling or personnel.

The medical staff updates the head coach on injuries. Then each unit meets briefly before the coach has a few final words before returning to the field.

Reid, Nagy, and defensive coordinator Bob Sutton didn't think any major changes were needed. They wanted to run the ball a little more often, since Hunt had run well and with confidence after his fumble. They were hoping to get more pressure on Brady, because not doing so was always suicidal.

On the second play of the second series of the second half, Smith looked deep and found the fleet Tyreek Hill behind the defense. He hit him in stride, and 75 yards later the Chiefs had the lead, 21–17. The Patriots answered with a touchdown and a field goal and led 27–21 after three quarters. It looked like 82-0 with the halftime lead was inevitable. The Chiefs had played well and hung in, but, as usual in Foxboro, it wasn't going to be enough.

And then the fourth quarter happened. The defense finally got some pressure on Brady. And the offense kept him off the field most of the quarter. The Patriots had two series and went three-and-out on both of them. Meanwhile, the Chiefs kept pounding at a tiring Patriots defense. Hunt was slashing and breaking tackles all over the field. He would finish the night with 239 yards in total offense—the most *ever* by a rookie running back in his first game since the AFL and NFL had merged in 1970.

The running game opened up the passing game for Smith. The Chiefs took the lead, 28–27, on the second play of the quarter on a 78-yard Smith-to-Hunt pass. Then, with 5:14 to go, Hunt scored again on a 4-yard run to make it 35–27. The Patriots, needing a touchdown and two-point conversion to tie, meekly went three-and-out. It took all of two plays—a 58-yard Hunt run and a 21-yard touchdown run by backup Charcandrick West—to up the lead to a stunning 42–27.

Game over. The Chiefs had outscored the Patriots 21–0 in the fourth quarter to win by that 42–27 margin. The result stunned the sellout crowd, the Patriots, and the entire league. One of the most oft-asked question in preseason had been, can the Patriots go 19-0?

Answer: no, emphatically.

"It was amazing to contrast the end of the game from the beginning of the game," Smith said, smiling at the memory. "We came out there and the place was still going crazy from their trophy ceremony and all the speeches. Then they go right down the field and score and we fumble. Loud beyond belief. Then, in the fourth quarter, I watched as people went up the aisles to get to the parking lot in complete silence. The place was like a tomb—except on our sideline. It was amazing."

Smith had outplayed Brady, throwing for four touchdowns and 368 yards. No quarterback had *ever* thrown for four touchdowns without an interception against Belichick's defense. In seventeen seasons under Belichick, the Patriots had *never* given up 42 points.

It was quite a start to what the Chiefs all believed might be a special season.

There was one down note. Late in the fourth quarter, Eric Berry, the Chiefs' All-Pro safety, went down with what turned out to be a ruptured Achilles tendon—meaning his season was over after one game. Berry was more than just an excellent safety; he was the leader of the Chiefs' defense, someone who had survived cancer to come back and be an All-Pro for the third time in his career in 2016.

"Very hard to take seeing Eric go off on a cart," Smith said. "It sounds like a broken record sometimes when you talk about how hard it is to see your teammates get hurt, but it is. That was especially true with Eric because of all he's been through and because he's so important to us emotionally. It took a little edge off the night."

The good news was that the Chiefs had pulled off something almost no one had expected. They had a head start on the rest of the league with a 1-0 record. And they had ten days off to prepare for their home opener against the Philadelphia Eagles.

Most people didn't know at that point just how good the Eagles were. Smith had a pretty good idea, but he would have an even better idea once the game was over.

13

It had taken Ryan Fitzpatrick a while to recover from his lost 2016 season in New Jersey. Even after twelve years in the NFL, even though he understood blame for losing always started with the quarterback, the 180-degree change in fortune was stunning to him.

"Intellectually, I understood it," he said. "In this case, it wasn't just being the quarterback, it was also about being in New York. Everything there is exaggerated. When you play well, you're not just a hero, you're a superhero. When you don't play well, you aren't just a goat, you're whatever is beyond being a goat.

"It wore me down. By the end of any season, if you've been playing, you aren't just worn-out physically, you're worn-out emotionally. You have to put so much into every game. This time was different. This time I wasn't sure if I wanted to play again—even if I had an opportunity to play."

After a few weeks at home with his family, with the physical and emotional pounding of the season behind him, he began to relax a little.

"Actually, I got to a place where my approach was 'Let's see what happens,'" he said. "As in, 'Let's see if anyone comes looking for me with some kind of an offer.'"

He knew, realistically, he was again part of the backup market. There would be no $12 million deals on the table. That was okay, though, because money wasn't the question. He'd already made millions more than he'd ever dreamed of making coming out of Harvard. Chances were good, he knew, that he was the highest-paid member of Harvard's class of 2005—and that was probably saying something. (Facebook founder Mark Zuckerberg would have been class of '06 had he graduated.)

The question, then, was twofold: Did he want to go play again, and, just as important, was he ready to subject his family to yet another move?

"We liked it in New Jersey," he said. "We lived about ten minutes from the facility and the kids liked their schools. But by then, Liza had become such a pro at moving that neither one of us saw that as a big issue."

A short time later, the Tampa Bay Buccaneers came looking for someone to back up Jameis Winston. Mike Glennon, who had been the Bucs' third-round draft pick in 2013, had left Tampa Bay to sign a stunning three-year, $45 million deal with the Chicago Bears. The Bucs were looking for a veteran who could counsel the sometimes immature Winston and also be ready to step in and keep the team competitive if Winston got hurt.

The offer was one year, $3 million. This was in May, two months after the free agent window had opened. With Glennon gone, the only other quarterback on the Bucs' roster behind Winston was Ryan Griffin, who had been the team's third-string quarterback for two years and had never taken a snap in an NFL game. When the team didn't find anyone in the middle rounds of the draft to their liking at quarterback, they began looking for an unsigned free agent who wasn't going to be controversial (Colin Kaepernick), had plenty of game experience, and wasn't going to be too expensive.

Fitzpatrick checked all the boxes.

"By May, I felt like I wanted to play," he said. "If no one made an offer, I was at peace with it. I'd played twelve years, I'd had a lot more success than I'd ever dreamed. I still remember when I went past twenty-five thousand yards passing in my career, my dad calling me and saying, 'I can't believe you've passed for more than twenty-five thousand yards.' I wasn't that far behind my boyhood hero Jake Plummer [29,253] at that point. The number was kind of mind-boggling to me.

"But when the Bucs came along, I saw it as an opportunity. Liza encouraged me too. She's an athlete, and she reminded me I'd be an ex-NFL player for a long time, why not continue to be one for as long as possible. So I jumped back in with no doubts."

Once again, Liza handled the move. Some things went back to Arizona or into storage. The rest of it went to a new house in Tampa. The kids had to be registered for school and signed up for sports.

Ryan was free to focus on learning another offensive system and on adjusting—again—to being a backup.

He liked Winston right away and could see his potential up close after a few snaps in practice. The Bucs had gone 9-7 in 2016, only the twelfth winning season in the forty-one years of the franchise's existence, and their first since 2010, and they went into 2017 with high hopes. Many of those hopes were built around Winston, who had won the Heisman Trophy in 2013 and had been the number one pick in the NFL draft in 2015.

His life had not been without controversy. There had been a sexual assault allegation; a shoplifting incident; a profane sexist meme shouted from the top of a table in the Florida State student union; and very little genuine regret from Winston in the wake of any of the incidents. He was, in many ways, typical of the coddled athlete who is told by those around him that he is never wrong.

Fitzpatrick viewed Winston with a clean slate: Winston was friendly, outgoing, and bright. He was willing to listen when Fitzpatrick brought some of his "old man" wisdom to the table.

"Jameis still has some learning to do, like a lot of young quarterbacks," Fitzpatrick said early in the season. "People tend to forget he's only twenty-three and he's been in the public eye for a long time.

"He's a *talker*. He is never brief on any subject. One of the things he's getting better at is listening. He doesn't have anything against it, he just has to be reminded every now and then to do it."

One thing about the Bucs' training camp was different from any other camp Fitzpatrick had been in: the presence of *Hard Knocks*.

The HBO series had started in 2001 and was a joint venture between the network and the NFL. Each summer, it chronicled one team's training camp—from the arrival of the rookies through the final cuts. It ran for four consecutive weeks once the first exhibition games began.

HBO had complete access to everything and everyone in the camp, although the NFL—through NFL Films—had the ability to censor anything that might be embarrassing for a team, a player, or the league. There would be no discussion of Colin Kaepernick—for example—on *Hard Knocks*.

The star of the 2017 version of *Hard Knocks,* from beginning to end, was Winston. The series has become formulaic in recent years: the producers pick a couple of star players to focus on and a couple of players on the bubble to make the team. They also focus on the coach and the general manager.

When the series began, the scenes in which a coach and/or GM told a player he was cut were dramatic. Now they feel staged. Every player has done a great job, worked hard, is a great guy, and will no doubt get another chance. Every player is grateful for the chance he's been given, and everyone hugs when it's all over. It has become a reality show—in other words, very little of it is real.

Since Fitzpatrick lockered next to Winston, he was often on camera while Winston talked—whether to the camera or to teammates.

Fitzpatrick had his moments in the spotlight. He had started a preseason tradition years earlier requiring the starting quarterback for each exhibition game to come up with a poem that all the quarterbacks—usually four during preseason—would recite before taking the field. Although HBO never credited him with the idea, it did show the recitation of the poem each week.

He had brief on-camera moments throughout the series. But the producers were a lot more interested in Winston's burgeoning stardom than with the story of a seventh-round draft pick from Harvard playing for his seventh team. Fitzpatrick was fine with that.

"I had no problem with them being around," he said. "I think we all kind of enjoyed it. But Jameis was the star—as he should be—and I wasn't one of those guys whose career hung in the balance. I was going to be the backup quarterback unless Jameis got hurt or I got hurt. There wasn't that much of a story line there."

Training camp passed without incident. *Hard Knocks,* which at times in the past had made news, made none. The Bucs were scheduled to open the season in Miami. But that didn't happen. With the massive Hurricane Irma headed for south Florida, the NFL made the sensible decision to postpone the game. Both teams had their byes in week eleven, so the game was rescheduled for then. That meant the two teams would have to play sixteen straight weeks beginning in week two of the season, but there really wasn't any choice.

And so, the Bucs opened their season at home against the Chicago Bears.

Chicago, which would finish the season 5-11 and fire Coach John Fox, proved to be the perfect opening game opponent. Glennon, whose $45 million contract had become even more baffling when the Bears used the number two pick in the draft to take Mitchell Trubisky, was still the starter. He threw two interceptions and fumbled once. In all, the Bears had four turnovers, and the Bucs led 29–0 before Chicago scored a late consolation touchdown to make the final 29–7.

Winston was 18-of-30 for 201 yards, all he needed since the Bucs scored most of their points on short-field drives after turnovers. Their first touchdown of the season came on a one-play, 13-yard drive, Winston finding wide receiver Mike Evans for the score. Fitzpatrick came in to mop up on the final two series of the game, throwing one incomplete pass and then ending the game with two kneel-downs.

"It certainly wasn't the same feeling you have when you're the starter or even when you come into a game suddenly after an injury," he said. "But it was nice to be part of a win and to get back on the field in a real game, even if the game was decided.

"In a perfect world every game would be like that. But I knew that wouldn't be the case. It's always a long season in the NFL."

Neither Fitzpatrick nor Winston nor the rest of the Bucs had any idea just how long this one would be.

—

Joe Flacco hadn't taken a single snap during the exhibition season. He knew he would be a little bit rusty going into the Ravens' opener in Cincinnati, but he wasn't that concerned about it. He'd felt good in practice the week prior to the game and was looking forward to getting back on the field.

"I've been in the league long enough now that playing in exhibition games isn't that big a deal one way or the other," he said. "If I'd been completely healthy, I might have two or three quarters—four max. I really didn't look at it as a big deal."

It turned out not to be a big deal at all, thanks to the performance of the Bengals' Andy Dalton—and the Ravens' defense. Dalton threw four interceptions and the Bengals had five turnovers in all.

Flacco threw only twelve passes, completing nine of them. One was a 49-yard second-quarter touchdown pass to Jeremy Maclin, who had been picked up in June after the Chiefs had released him for salary cap reasons. That pass climaxed the only sustained touchdown drive of the game. The Ravens got another touchdown later in the quarter after Lardarius Webb returned one of the Dalton interceptions to the

Cincinnati 2-yard line. It was 17–0 at halftime, and the Ravens cruised to a 20–0 victory.

A week later, the Ravens opened at home against the hapless Browns. For a lot of the game, Cleveland didn't look hapless, keeping the game competitive for much of the afternoon.

The Browns, who would become the second team in NFL history (2008 Lions) to go 0-16, split time during the game between quarterbacks DeShone Kizer, a rookie from Notre Dame, and Kevin Hogan, a second-year player from Stanford who had been cut by the Chiefs.

Neither was exactly a Pro Bowl candidate. And yet, at times, each moved the ball against the Ravens' defense. Their undoing, not surprisingly, was turnovers—five in all, meaning the Ravens had turned their opponents over ten times in two games.

The Ravens led throughout, scoring the first two touchdowns of the game, but the margin was only 21–10 after three quarters. Flacco was solid, completing 25 of 34 passes. He threw two touchdown passes and an interception; the latter coming when he threw the ball up for grabs on a third-and-long and defensive back Jason McCourty intercepted it at the Cleveland 9-yard line. It was the equivalent of a good punt—no real damage done.

The Ravens were never in serious danger of losing. A Justin Tucker field goal early in the fourth quarter extended the margin to 24–10, but the Ravens couldn't get the Cleveland offense off the field in the final minutes, allowing a twelve-play, 57-yard drive they finally stopped on downs in the final minute.

"It wasn't pretty," Flacco said afterward. "But it really doesn't matter how you win as long as you win."

That's what he told the media in his postgame press conference. Flacco, like any experienced quarterback, knows what to say and what not to say. He took responsibility for the interception, saying he shouldn't have just thrown the ball, hoping one of his guys would grab it. He didn't bring up the fact that he had very little time to throw and very little to lose by attempting the pass. If a receiver drops a ball, you shrug and say maybe you could have led him a little more. If the O-line isn't giving you enough time to throw, it's still on you to get the ball out quick enough.

Flacco knew that there was some fool's gold in the first two wins. Neither the Bengals nor the Browns were very good—the Browns, in fact, were awful. The Ravens' defense wasn't going to continue to average five turnovers a game. The running game was still suspect, and, perhaps most important, the team's best offensive lineman, right guard Marshal Yanda, had gone down in the second quarter when Cleveland defensive lineman Danny Shelton rolled up on his right ankle.

When Yanda didn't get up, the trainers and doctors came out to check on him. Standing nearby, Flacco knew right away it was serious—just as he had known in June that the injury to Pitta was serious.

"It was the look on his face," Flacco said. "He was in a lot of pain. Marshal is about as tough as it gets. He played most of last season [2016] with one arm after he hurt his shoulder and was still one of the best linemen in the league."

Flacco wasn't exaggerating. One website had selected Yanda as *the* best lineman in the league, and he had made the Pro Bowl for the sixth straight time. The Ravens were already thin on the offensive line. Center John Urschel had stunned the team by suddenly retiring on the first day of training camp in late July.

Urschel wasn't exactly your typical football player. He was only twenty-six and had been spending his off-seasons working toward a PhD in math at MIT. He had missed three weeks in preseason with a concussion a year earlier and had later said that the concussion had affected his ability to make sense of some of the math problems he was working on.

He retired two days after a new study had been published showing that CTE—chronic traumatic encephalopathy—had shown up in 99 percent of the brains that had been donated by ex–football players after their death.

Urschel never publicly discussed whether the new CTE study affected his decision, saying only that he was looking forward to pursuing his studies at MIT on a full-time basis. But inside the locker room, the sense was that he had been shaken—like many players were—by the latest study.

The NFL had done everything it possibly could to downplay the effects of concussions and playing football on the minds and bodies of its players. It had dismissed the initial discovery of CTE by Dr. Bennet Omalu and had acknowledged it only after the evidence had become overwhelming and after CTE had shown up in the brains of a number of well-known former players, notably Hall of Fame linebacker Junior Seau and Pro Bowl safety Dave Duerson.

Both committed suicide by shooting themselves in the chest while leaving behind notes for their families asking that their brains be studied for CTE. Both were found to have suffered from the disease.

When Seau was inducted into the Hall of Fame in 2015, the Hall, which is technically run by an independent group but is almost solely funded by the NFL, refused to allow his daughter Sydney to give his induction speech, even though Seau had specifically said prior to his death that if he was voted into the Hall, he wanted her to speak in his place.

Under tremendous public pressure, including from a number of Hall of Famers, the Hall finally agreed to a five-minute onstage "interview" with Sydney, during which there was no mention of Seau's death or CTE.

The Hall's blowhard director, David Baker, defended the decision by saying that induction into the Hall was about a player's career, not his life. Except that most Hall of Fame speeches practically drown in discussions of what a great *man* the player was, not just his playing career.

Two weeks after Urschel retired, starting left guard Alex Lewis also went down for the season, requiring surgery on his left shoulder. Yanda's injury meant the Ravens were down three starters, including their best up-front player.

Tony Bergstrom, who had been acquired from Arizona just prior to the start of the season to provide depth, suddenly was the starting right guard.

"You have to deal with injuries, it's simple as that," Flacco said. "Every team has players get hurt. But some guys are harder to replace than others. Marshal was going to be very hard to replace, especially on a young line that was trying to jell."

Winning tends to overshadow problems. The Ravens were 2-0 and, for some, the preseason doubts had quickly become a thing of the past. Game three would be in London against a Jacksonville team that had gone 3-13 the previous season. There was good reason to believe the Ravens would be 3-0 when the Steelers came to town the following week for the first of their two meetings.

The Jaguars had opened with an easy win in Houston, against a

Texans team that for some reason was quarterbacked by Tom Savage, even though the team had drafted Deshaun Watson with the twelfth pick in the draft to be the team's quarterback of the future.

Once upon a time it was a given in the NFL that rookie quarterbacks would spend the season holding a clipboard and learning their craft by watching. As recently as 2003, there were still teams doing that: Carson Palmer, taken with the first pick by the Bengals in the 2003 draft, never took a snap that season. Instead, the immortal Jon Kitna was the quarterback.

But that had become the exception. Both Troy Aikman and Peyton Manning had been thrown into the fire right away as rookies on bad teams—the 1-15 Dallas Cowboys in 1989 and the 3-13 Indianapolis Colts in 1998. Flacco had also started game one but probably would not have done so if Troy Smith hadn't gotten sick during the preseason. Andrew Luck and Alex Smith, each the number one pick in the draft, had started from the beginning, although Smith had been in and out as a starter in 2005.

The Bears had started Mike Glennon over Mitchell Trubisky at the start of the 2017 season, if only to justify the $45 million they had spent on him. By game four, Trubisky was the starter. Bill O'Brien had done the same with Watson, going with Savage, a proven mediocrity, over Watson to start the season.

O'Brien cited Savage's experience as the reason for going with him to start the season (Savage had started two games in 2016). It's no secret that NFL coaches—Bill Belichick being the most notable exception—almost always choose the conservative route because any out-of-the-box thinking that fails is going to cause media and fan outrage. That's why they almost always punt on fourth-and-less-than-a-yard, even though the odds are in their favor if they go for it. Fail once, and all sorts of criticism will come down on their head. Belichick, with five Super Bowl rings, is immune to criticism. Most coaches see it as Kryptonite.

It took exactly one half and a 19–0 deficit for O'Brien to realize that Savage could have fifty years of experience and he still wasn't going to be a very good NFL quarterback. Watson replaced him at halftime, but it was too late and the Jaguars won, 29–7.

These weren't the Jaguars of the recent past. They had become a solid team, especially on defense, as the Ravens would find out a short time later in London.

—

The Ravens flew to London on Thursday prior to the game. They practiced Friday, and then everyone tried to catch up on sleep and get acclimated to the five-hour time difference on Friday night.

They awoke Saturday to find that the NFL-world they had been living in before they went to bed had changed considerably.

On Friday night, President Donald Trump had spoken at a rally for Luther Strange, who had been appointed to the Senate seat vacated by Jeff Sessions when Trump made him attorney general.

Strange was running in a special election primary the following Tuesday, and Trump was speaking on his behalf. Knowing his audience—decidedly right-wing—Trump decided to attack NFL players who had not been standing for the national anthem.

"Wouldn't you love to see one of these NFL owners, when somebody disrespects our flag, to say, 'Get that son of a bitch off the field right now—he's fired. He's fired!'" Trump said. "You know, some owner is going to do that. He's going to say, 'That guy disrespects our flag, he's fired.' And that owner, they don't know it, but they'll be the most popular person in this country."

Trump, who once owned a team in the United States Football League (a league that failed miserably in an attempt to challenge the NFL—both on the field and in court), then attacked the entire league.

"The NFL ratings are down massively. Now, the number one reason happens to be they don't like watching what's happening; because you know today, if you hit too hard—fifteen yards! Throw him out of the game! They're ruining the game! That's what they want to do—they want to hit. They want to hit! It's hurting the game.

"But do you know what's hurting the game more than that? When people like yourselves turn on the television and you see these people taking the knee when they're playing our great national anthem. The only thing you could do better is, if you see it, even if it's one player, leave the stadium.

"I guarantee things will stop. Just pick up and leave. Pick up and leave. Not the same game anymore anyway."

Trump's rant instantly did what he does best—divided the country. Clearly he saw the players in much the same way the Romans saw the gladiators once upon a time: whether they lived or died (of CTE rather than the sword) didn't matter as long as he and his fellow Romans were entertained. How dare they protest in any way about racial injustice. They should just shut their mouths and go out and blast one another into next weekend.

NFL commissioner Roger Goodell, who was in London for the Ravens-Jaguars game, labeled the president's comments "divisive." Many players took to Twitter to attack Trump. The irony was that the anthem protests that Colin Kaepernick had started a year earlier had slowed to a trickle once the season started.

As soon as Trump's comments went viral, it was apparent that many players were going to feel compelled to respond. In London, there was no formal discussion among the Ravens players, but it did come up in the locker room.

"The general consensus was that we didn't need a consensus," Flacco said. "I think everyone wanted to make sure that no one felt pressured to do one thing or another. If guys wanted to kneel, that was fine. If guys didn't want to kneel, that was fine too. There was no arguing, no one saying, 'This way is right.' There was just an understanding that each of us had to do what we felt was right for us."

Like most teams that Sunday, the Ravens fell into two groups: one group, which included Coach John Harbaugh, locked arms in a show of unity while the anthem was played. Flacco was in that group. The other group knelt together, arms locked. There were ten Ravens who knelt, as did Ray Lewis, the retired Hall of Fame linebacker, who knelt with the players in uniform.

On the other sideline, Jaguars owner Shad Khan, who had given money to Trump, locked arms with his players who were standing. A dozen Jaguars knelt.

All the players on both sidelines then stood for the playing of "God Save the Queen," the British national anthem.

Because the game was the first one played that Sunday—kicking off at 9:30 a.m. Eastern time—and because it was played in a foreign country, it received a great deal of attention.

Some right-wing pundits were outraged that players would kneel for "The Star-Spangled Banner" and then stand for "God Save the Queen."

"It's embarrassing that they show respect for another country's anthem but not for their own," screeched one Fox News anchor.

Another yelped that it was "disgusting" that players making "hundreds of millions of dollars" would stage such a protest. "I'd like to know," she demanded, "what are they protesting, what exactly are they protesting?"

Apparently working for Fox News doesn't require knowing anything about the news.

The Ravens-Jaguars game was just the beginning of a day filled with protests. Three teams: the Tennessee Titans and Seattle Seahawks, who were playing each other in Nashville, and the Pittsburgh Steelers, who were playing in Chicago, stayed in the locker room during the playing of the anthem, violating normal NFL protocol.

Thirty-two members of the Denver Broncos and twenty members of the Cleveland Browns knelt. Many owners followed Khan's example and locked arms with standing players during the anthem—including Washington's Dan Snyder, another major Trump contributor and supporter.

Seven of Snyder's players chose to kneel and, on the opposite sideline, more than half of the Oakland Raiders knelt or sat.

Ravens owner Steve Bisciotti, also a Republican, issued a statement that said: "We recognize our players' influence and support them 100 percent. All voices need to be heard. That's democracy in its highest form."

In Los Angeles, Alex Smith was truly torn by what was going on. Prior to Trump's rant, only one Chiefs player, cornerback Marcus Peters, had knelt during the anthem. Most of the players who had protested in the past had been African American. Most of those who had knelt throughout the day were also African American, with a handful of exceptions. In spite of Trump's claims that "This is not a racial issue," it was clearly a racial issue.

Kaepernick had started his protest in response to what he believed was white police brutality directed at African Americans. Smith understood this and felt for his African American teammates.

"They were in a no-win situation," he said. "If they knelt for the anthem, they would be viewed by many people as betraying their country in some way. But if they didn't kneel, didn't protest in some way, they would be viewed by many in their race as betraying them. It was a terribly unfair position for them to be put in."

Chiefs coach Andy Reid had taken the same approach as the Ravens'

John Harbaugh. What the players did was up to them. They wouldn't be judged, regardless of what they did during the anthem.

The players knew that was true of Reid, but weren't so sure how true it would be when it came to the team's chairman, Clark Hunt, who had inherited the team from his father, Lamar Hunt. Clark Hunt had been one of the more outspoken owners on the subject of anthem protests in the past. Now, though, his public stance softened: "We believe in honoring the American flag and supporting all of those whose sacrifices protect the many freedoms we have in this country, including the right to have differences of opinion," he said in a statement that day.

The last eight words were different from what Hunt had said in the past, when he had made it clear he expected his players to stand for the anthem after Peters had stopped doing so.

Smith wasn't going to kneel for the anthem, but he and Patrick Mahomes stood behind the bench rather than just off the field, the traditional place where players lined up during the anthem.

By the time the day was over, more than two hundred players had knelt or sat during the anthem—and that didn't include the players on the three teams who stayed in the locker room. The week prior to Trump's comments, a total of six players had failed to stand for the anthem.

Alejandro Villanueva, the Steelers' starting left tackle who had been an Army Ranger and served three tours in Afghanistan, accidentally became a hero of the right when he stood just outside the tunnel during the playing of the anthem.

Villanueva said later he had planned to join his teammates in the locker room because it had been decided they would *all* do the same thing, but got caught short of the tunnel when the anthem began. "Out of respect for other veterans and those who have been wounded overseas, I had to stop," he said. "I feel like I threw my teammates under the bus."

His teammates didn't see it that way and understood what had happened. Asked to comment on Trump's comments, Villanueva said he had no comment one way or the other.

Many of his fellow players made their feelings crystal clear with their actions.

—

Joe Flacco was relieved once the anthems had been played in London because once the game started, the political turmoil would fade to black—at least for a few hours.

Unfortunately, the game brought very little relief. The Jaguars were in complete control right from the start. The Ravens' initial first down of the day came with 4:18 to play before halftime. By then, their first five possessions had produced four three-and-outs and a Flacco interception—caused by Jeremy Maclin being separated from the ball, and his senses, as he went over the middle, with Jacksonville's A. J. Bouye ending up with the football.

The Jaguars, who were publicly doing a Hamlet routine about whether Blake Bortles, who had been the number three pick in the draft in 2014, was good enough to be their quarterback long term, scored on five of their first six possessions: field goal, touchdown, field goal, touchdown, field goal.

It was 23–0 at halftime.

"There's really not much for anyone to say in a situation like that," Flacco said. "I'm the offensive captain, but if I get up and give a rah-rah speech, it isn't going to do much good. As poorly as we'd played, believe it or not, we weren't thinking the game was over. Our attitude was—had to be—if they can score twenty-three in a half, we can too. We'd scored that many, more in fact, in the past, so why not go out and do it again? You can't hang your head at that point. If you do, things are only going to get worse."

They certainly didn't get any better. Flacco *was* surprised when offensive coordinator Marty Mornhinweg, who had taken over in October of the previous season when Marc Trestman had been fired, told the players that they would be running their regular offense in the second half.

"I thought, given the score, that we might go two-minute right away," Flacco said. "We needed to speed up the game, and given that we'd done nothing on offense the first half, I didn't think we had anything to lose by going two-minute."

In the end, it didn't really matter. The Ravens could have come out in the old Texas wishbone and it probably wouldn't have changed anything. The second half went much like the first, and Jacksonville heaped on more points. The final shellacking of 44–7 was every bit as humiliating as it appeared to be.

The good news was that the Ravens' archrival, the Steelers, were coming to Baltimore the following Sunday.

"Seriously, that *is* good news," Flacco said two days after the game, tucked into a corner of the Ravens' team dining room. "If the Steelers coming to town can't get our minds moving forward and off of what happened Sunday, nothing can."

14

Doug Williams had been named Washington's senior vice president for player personnel in June. Depending on your point of view, that position could mean three things. He was either the team's general manager—but without the title—or the chief scout, or a figurehead given the position because owner Dan Snyder and team president Bruce Allen were desperate to do *something* that would create goodwill among their fans and the local media.

There was no one better to do that than Williams. He was, after all, a Super Bowl hero—the MVP of Super Bowl XXII, the second of Joe Gibbs's three championships in Washington. He was respected in football and in the D.C. area, both as a person and as someone who knew the game. And, unlike former general manager Scot McCloughan, he wasn't likely to clash publicly with Snyder or Allen. It just wasn't his way.

So, in a very real sense, Williams's new position was all-of-the-above: he had the kind of scouting and personnel background that would make his voice a respected one in Washington's war room; he knew the team's scouts well, having been on the staff for three years; and he could be a respected public face for a franchise whose owner and president were about as popular and respected as deposed Los Angeles Clippers owner Donald Sterling (who had been run out of the NBA).

Williams hadn't had final say in the Washington draft room two months earlier, in April 2017, but he'd played a major role in what had been considered a very solid draft—especially after the chaotic ending to McCloughan's run in Washington, which had been filled with animosity, rumors, and all sorts of lying by the team and by McCloughan.

It was clear by the end of the 2016 season that McCloughan was at odds with Snyder and Allen. At the Senior Bowl, where one might expect the man in charge of personnel to be the spokesman for the team, McCloughan was barred from speaking to the media by Allen.

Several weeks later, he no-showed at the scouting combine—arguably the most important pre-draft week of the year—and he and the team put out statements that he was absent because his grandmother had died. It turned out she had died almost a month earlier.

Two weeks later, the team fired him and then began floating rumors that his drinking issues had resurfaced during the season. By then, few people in D.C. would have believed Snyder or Allen if they had said the earth was round.

Soon after that, Allen, knowing the team needed some positive publicity—*any* positive publicity—approached Williams about the idea of becoming director of player personnel—McCloughan's old job without the general manager's title. Williams was fine with that.

"The point was I wanted the job," he said. "I wanted to prove I could do the job and earn the title at some point. If I didn't do well, it didn't really matter what my title was, I'd be gone. If I did do well, the other stuff would come soon enough."

Just as he never blanched at being referred to as a "black quarterback" because, as he likes to say, "I was a black quarterback. The important question was whether I was a *good* quarterback, regardless of color," Williams didn't mind taking on the responsibility without the title that should have come with it.

In that sense, he was much like Ozzie Newsome. When the Cleveland Browns moved to Baltimore in 1996, owner Art Modell made Newsome the player personnel director. In the first draft in which he had final say, Newsome drafted Jonathan Ogden with the number four pick and Ray Lewis at number twenty-six. Both are now in the Hall of Fame. And yet, it wasn't until midway through the 2002 season—after winning a Super Bowl—that Newsome was finally given the title of general manager. It was another four years before the Houston Texans made Rick Smith the second African American GM in the NFL, and a year later that Jerry Reese was named as GM of the Giants.

Going into the 2017 season, there were six African Americans who held the general manager title: Newsome, Smith, Reese (who was fired prior to the end of the season), Reggie McKenzie in Oakland, Sashi Brown in Cleveland, and Chris Grier in Miami. Williams was the seventh. He didn't have the GM title, but he was the highest-ranking personnel man in the organization outside of Allen (who spent much of his time organizing alumni events and making sure Snyder's many needs were tended to at all times).

Which is why Williams had a nervous stomach on September 10 as he walked into FedExField the morning of the home opener. He knew the new season would not be easy, but he also knew it would be an important one for the team and for him.

The biggest question—no surprise—was the quarterback position. But there were many other challenges heading into Washington's season, like the Snyder-Allen decision to let receivers Pierre Garçon and DeSean Jackson walk in free agency—Garçon to San Francisco and Jackson to Tampa Bay. The two had helped make Kirk Cousins a 4,000-yards-plus quarterback the previous two seasons. Jackson was the deep threat; Garçon the clutch possession receiver. Both were gone.

Another issue was Washington's defense, which had been porous in 2016. The solution was to fire coordinator Joe Barry and promote outside linebackers coach Greg Manusky, who, if you believed the Washington media, was the next Bill Belichick when it came to defense. Remarkably, Manusky had been a coordinator for three other teams and somehow those teams hadn't won the Super Bowl. There was also a new offensive coordinator, Matt Cavanaugh, who had been promoted from within after Sean McVay had left to become coach of the L.A. Rams.

Surprisingly, Jay Gruden was back for a fourth season as head coach. The joke around Washington was that Snyder had thought he was hiring Jon Gruden, only to be stunned to find his new coach was the complete opposite of his brother: plainspoken, low-key, and perfectly happy if he never saw another TV camera again.

But Gruden was a good coach. The players liked him and so did the media, because, unlike his predecessor Mike Shanahan, who would prevaricate if asked the time of day, he answered questions directly and honestly.

Gruden was the eighth coach to work under Snyder since he'd purchased the team in 1999, so four years in charge amounted to a dynasty. But like everyone who worked for Snyder—other than the seemingly untouchable Allen—his job could be in jeopardy at any moment.

And yet, the most important person in this whole equation was Cousins. It wasn't just that he was the quarterback, it was that he had become a polarizing figure by *succeeding*.

When he was drafted out of Michigan State in the fourth round in 2012, Cousins was supposed to be the guy who occasionally stepped in for Robert Griffin III. His rookie season played out perfectly: Griffin was brilliant in leading the team to the playoffs in that first year, and when he had to miss a game late in the season, Cousins was good enough to start and win in Cleveland during the team's seven-game winning streak.

Good job, Kirk, now put your headset back on.

Griffin's injury in that year's playoffs changed everything—though not right away. The following season, Griffin came back to play week one—too soon, as it turned out—and he and the team struggled throughout the season, which was his and Cousins's second year in the league. With three weeks left and the team 3-10, and Shanahan feuding with Snyder and clearly on his way out, Shanahan benched Griffin for the remainder of the season. Cousins started the last three games—all losses. Gruden was hired to replace the fired Shanahans (father Mike and son Kyle, who was his offensive coordinator). The thinking around the league was that Gruden, who had never been a head coach before, would do what Snyder wanted and play Griffin without any questions or doubts.

He did that for two games. In week two, Washington's only win in its first six games, Griffin dislocated an ankle and had to be carted off the field. That began a fourteen-week quarterback merry-go-round. Cousins started for a while and then was benched in favor of Colt McCoy—who actually led the team to a shocking Monday night win in Dallas. Griffin came back to start in week nine, and the team lost three in a row, dropping to 3-8.

Gruden decided to go back to McCoy—Cousins was by now a forgotten third-stringer—and McCoy promptly injured his neck against the Indianapolis Colts and was out for the season. Back came Griffin. The team finished 4-12.

There's an old saying in football that if you have two starting quarterbacks, you don't have a real starter. Washington went into training camp the following summer with *three* quarterbacks who had been starters the previous season and various people campaigning for each of the three.

Gruden wanted Cousins to start. He believed his skills were best suited to his offensive system, which was West Coast with an emphasis on running the football and quick-decision, three-step drops in the passing game.

Snyder wanted Griffin to start. After all, he had given up a boatload of draft picks to get him in 2012 and Griffin was a *star*, even if he hadn't played like one in 2013 and 2014. Naturally, the owner had the final say.

It all changed in week two of the exhibition season against the Detroit Lions. Griffin fumbled the ball, fell on it, and took a blow to the head. He left the game with a concussion and Cousins came in. That turned out to be Griffin's Wally Pipp moment; he never played another down for Washington.

After a week of utter confusion about the seriousness of Griffin's injury—the team first announced he had been cleared to play, then said he had been ruled out of that week's game against the Ravens—Cousins started in Baltimore in the third exhibition game, the only one in which the starters play any serious minutes.

Cousins played well, and with Griffin's health still questionable, Gruden announced that Cousins would start the opener in two weeks against the Dolphins. His stance on the quarterback position was made clear by the way he worded the announcement: "I think Kirk has earned the right to be our starting quarterback for this season," he said.

That comment was clearly directed not at the media, but at the owner.

Finally the no-doubt starter, Cousins flourished—most of the time. Washington went from 4-12 to 9-7 and won a very weak NFC East, clinching their playoff spot by winning their last four games—including a 34–23 victory over Dallas at home in the Sunday night finale to the NFL regular season.

Even though they lost to Green Bay at home the following week in the wildcard game, their improvement made Cousins a local hero. Griffin became the forgotten man. He had never been activated for a single game all season. McCoy had served as Cousins's backup.

Cousins ended up passing for more than 4,000 yards. And because he was almost blindingly polite, local fans and media loved him. He rarely said anything interesting, but no one really cared, especially with the team winning again after two miserable seasons.

Cousins was now clearly Washington's quarterback. Griffin was released as soon as the 2016 league season officially began in March. But there was a wrinkle: Cousins was without a contract. McCloughan urged Snyder and Allen to sign him to a long-term deal, one that probably would have cost the team about $45 million in guaranteed money to lock up Cousins for five years.

Snyder had finally been forced to give up on Griffin, but he still wasn't convinced that Cousins was *the* guy, and so he didn't pull the trigger on the long-term contract. Negotiations commenced and went nowhere, and finally Washington was forced to place a franchise tag on Cousins, meaning he would be paid $19.8 million for 2016. If he had not been "franchised," Cousins could have left Washington, and the team couldn't afford to let that happen.

The Cousins non-signing began a two-year soap opera in Washington. He had not been the Chosen One, but Cousins had become the Man anyway. He played well—if not brilliantly—said all the right things, and frequently gave all the glory to God.

Hallelujah.

—

Sitting in his box, watching the opener on that September day in 2017, Doug Williams was pretty convinced he was watching a franchise quarterback, the person who would lead his team to a lot of wins for the next dozen years.

The problem was, he was playing for the other team.

Carson Wentz had been the number two pick in the 2016 NFL draft coming out of North Dakota State, where he hadn't started until his redshirt junior year. He had then led the Bison to their fourth and fifth consecutive national titles at the FCS level. He was the physical prototype for a modern NFL quarterback: six feet five, 240 pounds, with a strong arm and speed: he'd run a 4.77 40 at the combine. He'd also scored a 40 on the Wonderlic test; not Ryan Fitzpatrick–like, but impressive nevertheless.

Wentz and Jared Goff had emerged as the hot quarterbacks in the 2016 draft. With all the money NFL teams spend on scouting, it is remarkable how often teams miss on quarterbacks. In 1998, scouts had been split on whether Peyton Manning or Ryan Leaf should be the number one pick. Fortunately for the Colts, they took Manning. Unfortunately for the Chargers, picking number two, they took Leaf.

The list of highly drafted washout quarterbacks is a long one. What do the names Tim Couch, JaMarcus Russell, and David Carr have in common? Each was the number one pick in the draft, and each did almost nothing worth remembering in the NFL. How about Matt Leinart, Akili Smith, Vince Young, and Heath Shuler? Each was picked number three in the draft. And did little in the NFL.

That doesn't even count other first-round draft picks since 2000 like Blaine Gabbert, Jake Locker, Kyle Boller, Johnny Manziel, JP Losman, Daunte Culpepper, Cade McNown, Brady Quinn, Christian Ponder, and, yes, Tim Tebow—the twenty-fifth pick to Denver in the 2010 draft.

In 2016, the next five quarterbacks picked after Goff and Wentz were Paxton Lynch (also a first-rounder), Christian Hackenberg, Jacoby Brissett, Cody Kessler, and Connor Cook. It wasn't until after all of them had been picked that the Cowboys took Dak Prescott with the 135th pick (fourth round), and they took Prescott only after failing to move up in order to take either Lynch or Cook.

That's how inexact the science can be; figuring out who will succeed in the NFL at quarterback and who won't.

The Rams, who were moving from St. Louis to Los Angeles, decided to go with Goff, who had spent three years at Cal-Berkeley and came off more glamorous than the kid from North Dakota. The Eagles, who had traded with the Browns to move up to the number two pick, happily took Wentz.

Initially, the plan had been to let Wentz back up Sam Bradford during his rookie year, perhaps even "redshirt" for the entire season. Then, just prior to the start of the season, Teddy Bridgewater, the Vikings' starting quarterback, went down with a gruesome leg injury, and Minnesota was desperate for a quarterback with starting experience. The Vikings were willing to give up a number one draft pick in the 2017 draft and a number four the following year to get Bradford.

Since the long-term plan was for Wentz to be the starter anyway, the Eagles made the deal and Wentz went from redshirt to starter in the blink of an eye. He'd had his "rookie" moments in 2017 but had also shown why the Eagles had been so happy to get him. There was little doubt that he was a star in the making.

Early in the opener, Williams saw very clearly why that was true. On the Eagles' first drive of the game, they faced third-and-12 from their own 42-yard line. Wentz retreated under heavy pressure. He dodged one tackler, then slipped another. Finally, just before he could be brought down, he found wide receiver Nelson Agholor running free down the sideline. The extra time Wentz had bought allowed Agholor to get open, and he raced into the end zone for an early 7–0 lead.

Williams sat back in his seat. He knew what he had just seen: a quarterback who was truly a difference-maker.

"Three kinds of quarterbacks in this league," he would say later. "First, there are the guys who you hope don't lose the game for you. There are *a lot* of those. Then there are guys who can win for you some of the time, but not all of the time. I call them 8-8 quarterbacks. And then, there's the smallest group, the guys who will win games for you that maybe you shouldn't win: [Tom] Brady; [Aaron] Rodgers; Cam [Newton]; [Russell] Wilson; [Drew] Brees, [Andrew] Luck, when he's healthy.

"Wentz is going to be one of those guys."

The only reason Williams put it in the future tense early in the 2017 season was that he'd also seen Wentz throw a pick-six to Ryan Kerrigan that same day and make some mistakes born of inexperience. But there was no doubting the talent and the potential.

The Eagles beat Washington 30–17 that day. Cousins, the most discussed man in town, was 30-of-40 passing but threw a terrible interception in the fourth quarter, overthrowing an open receiver in the end zone with the Eagles up 19–17 and the ball on the Philadelphia 14-yard line. Then, with Washington still alive with 1:38 left, trailing 22–17, Cousins got hit as he tried to throw from his own 29-yard line, and the officials ruled it a fumble.

It was a close call that left much of the rah-rah Washington media grumbling as if it was a *lock* that the offense would have marched the remaining 72 yards if an incomplete pass had been called.

"I thought my arm was going forward," Cousins said. "I know it was very close. But that's not where we lost the game. There were some plays before that which really hurt us."

And so, the Washington quarterback debate was off and running for another season.

—

Andrew Luck wasn't in the Colts' lineup that same day for their opener against the Rams. The Colts' starting quarterback was Scott Tolzien, and the results were disastrous. The Rams led 27–3 at halftime and cruised to a 46–9 win, getting year two of the L.A. Rams 2.0 off to a rousing start.

When it had become apparent that Luck wasn't going to be ready to start the season and there was no timetable for his return, the Colts had traded Phillip Dorsett, a former number one draft pick to New England, to acquire Jacoby Brissett.

Brissett was the Patriots' third-string quarterback behind Tom Brady and Jimmy Garoppolo and was considered expendable by Bill Belichick. He had played in two games the previous season when Garoppolo had gotten hurt while Brady was serving his four-game Deflategate suspension. He had played well enough to become a legitimate trading chip.

Brissett had arrived in Indianapolis a week before the Rams game and Colts coach Chuck Pagano, whose hot seat had turned red-hot in Luck's absence, decided to start Tolzien in the opener, if only because Tolzien had spent the entire 2016 season in Indianapolis and had actually started the one game Luck had missed. If Brissett had been with the team for eight days rather than seven, Pagano might have started him.

As it was, Tolzien lasted three quarters—throwing two pick-six interceptions—and went to the bench for good at the start of the fourth quarter.

Luck watched from the sidelines, feeling helpless and "weird"—his word.

"When you're hurt and you're around your team, whether in the locker room, in practice, or on the sideline during a game, it feels weird," he said. "You're there, but you're not really there. You can't do anything to help the team win. It's just a terrible feeling, no getting around it. I wanted to be there at the games to support the guys any way I could. But the honest truth was there was nothing I could do. I hated it—I mean, I hated it."

A week later, with Brissett now the starter, the Colts played much better before losing to the Arizona Cardinals 16–13 in overtime. They managed to beat the even more hapless Browns, 31–28, a week later.

That was the weekend that Donald Trump decided to profanely insult the players who hadn't been standing for the national anthem. There was no time to really discuss Trump's comments as a team, so nothing was organized for that Sunday. More than twenty Browns knelt during the anthem, and about ten Colts did the same.

That week, with a trip to Seattle looming, about twenty players met with general manager Chris Ballard, several front-office members, and Coach Chuck Pagano. Even though Luck wasn't playing, he was a team captain, so he took part in the meeting.

"My heart really went out to some of the African American guys in the room," Luck said. "They were getting emails and texts and tweets from people saying, 'How can you not side with us [other African Americans] on this?' They were clearly torn by the whole thing. Listening to them talk was heartbreaking in a lot of ways."

The decision was made that the players would lock arms as a team. No one was told they could *not* kneel for the anthem. They also agreed to wear T-shirts in pregame that said, "We will" on the front and "Stand for equality, justice, unity, respect, dialogue, choice, opportunity" on the back.

"The point was it wasn't *anti*-anything," Luck said. "It was just a statement that we all believe in those ideals for everybody."

The game played out in another embarrassing loss. The Colts were blown out 46–18, dropping their record to 1-3, and everyone in Indy began preparing for what looked like a very long season.

And then, on October 4—three days after the loss in Seattle—hope appeared. It came in the form of Luck walking onto the practice field, taking some snaps, and actually making a few throws to receivers.

Luck spoke to the media that day for the first time since the start of the season. He talked about how rusty he felt, that he even had to *think* about how to take a snap, but he also talked about how good it felt to be in a uniform—even a practice jersey—and to be on a football field with his teammates. It had been, he said, a long nine-plus months since the surgery.

"I knew when I had the surgery it would be a long process," he said. "I knew it would take patience. It's all been positive, I've been going in the right direction the entire time. I feel like I'm near the finish line."

He was asked the multimillion-dollar question: Would he play this season?

"Yeah, oh yes," he answered.

It turned out that day was the highlight of the season for Luck and the Colts. The plan was to bring him along slowly, allowing him to practice only in a limited way every other day—one on, one off. No sense pushing the shoulder when it appeared to be close to healthy.

For almost two weeks, Luck followed the schedule, trying to throw a little bit harder each day. Colts general manager Chris Ballard regularly reported to the media that it was all going well, that the "zip" was coming back to Luck's throws.

Then, on October 19—fifteen days after The Return—the mood and the message changed. Ballard announced that Luck was going to be shut down again for a while. There was "some soreness" in the shoulder, and he had been given a cortisone shot to try to "calm things down in there."

In truth, Luck had felt pain in the shoulder almost from the day he first set foot back on the practice field.

"I went back to practice because that had been the plan," he said. "I was *supposed* to be feeling good enough to practice, so I told myself I was—when I wasn't."

Luck had been commuting weekly to Birmingham, to see one of James Andrews's partners. If you ever read Andrews's name in print, you would think his actual name was "renowned orthopedic surgeon Dr. James Andrews."

Luck *wanted* to believe he was making progress, that he was close, that he would return during the season.

But he was none of those things. "I just felt like I *had* to play, I couldn't miss the entire season," he said. "But the fact was I wasn't there and I wasn't really close. When I felt the pain, it wasn't as bad as it had been before the surgery or right after, but it was there. I was in denial, though. I kept thinking it would somehow go away miraculously. That wasn't going to happen.

"When I finally had to stop, I don't know which pain was worse: the pain in my shoulder or the emotional pain realizing I just couldn't do it."

When Luck stopped throwing, Ballard insisted it wasn't a major setback; it was just the Colts being cautious and making certain they didn't push Luck too hard, too fast.

Ten days later, Ballard reported that Luck was going to see doctors again, perhaps different doctors than the ones he had been seeing up until that point. Was there any thought, he was asked, to simply shutting him down for the season?

"Not at this time," he answered—ominous words for a team that had just dropped to 2-6—the two wins being over teams (the Browns and 49ers) that at that moment were winless.

Four days later, "not at this time" became now. The Colts put Luck on injured reserve, officially ending his season. Since he was clearly nowhere close to being ready to practice again, much less play, and the team was going nowhere fast—except a high pick in the 2018 draft—there was no sense in even thinking about pushing him to come back to perhaps play a game or two at the end of a lost season.

By then, Luck had left the country to go to a clinic in Holland that was run by a personal trainer he had worked with in the past and whom he felt comfortable with. Nicole, his fiancée whom he had dated since the two were Stanford freshmen, went with him.

Naturally, given all the happy talk of the previous month, there were those who wondered if the injury was more serious than anyone had been letting on. There was speculation from some—including former teammate D'Qwell Jackson—that Luck's career might be over.

Ballard was asked the question: "Could this be career-ending?"

"I've not heard that from one doctor," Ballard said. "Career-ending would be putting him on the field before he's ready to play, that's where you would be concerned," perhaps the most accurate thing he had said all year.

Luck didn't speak after shutting down or before leaving the country.

"I've always understood that part of my job is to talk to the media and to try to be honest with them," he said. "But I felt awkward during that entire period. There were some questions I couldn't answer and some questions I didn't want to answer. I've never felt uncomfortable talking to the media. Right then, though, I did."

Luck knew he didn't have answers to a lot of the questions they would ask. Like "What's happened since October fourth when you were close to the finish line?" And "What are you going to do next?" Or "Do you have any idea at all where the finish line is at this moment?"

Luck knew the answer to all those questions was essentially the same: "I have no idea. All I know is my shoulder still hurts."

Rather than repeat the same nonanswer over and over, Luck put out a statement through the team: "I wish I was better and 100 percent this season but that's not the case. I know I'll be better from this. I know I'll be a better quarterback, teammate, person and player from this and I'm excited for the future."

It was the best possible spin that could be put on a depressing situation. With that, Luck went looking for answers. The finish line was nowhere in sight.

15

One of the most surprising facts about week two of the 2017 NFL season was that the game between the Philadelphia Eagles and Kansas City Chiefs had become one of the must-see games of the weekend.

Both teams had been expected by most to come into the matchup 0-1. The Chiefs had been a playoff team the previous January, but opening up against the Patriots in Foxboro had looked to most people like a lock loss. Add in the fact that many so-called experts were wondering if New England might go 19-0, and there weren't a lot of folks expecting the Chiefs' 42–27 victory that included a 21–0 fourth-quarter margin.

"I guess it's tough to go 19-0 from 0-1," Alex Smith had joked.

The Eagles' opener wasn't nearly as daunting, facing a Washington team that had gone 8-7-1 the previous season and didn't appear likely to be a whole lot better a year later. Then again, the Eagles had been 7-9 that same season, had been swept by Washington, and had won one—that's one—road game from September to January.

The 7-9 had come after a surprising 3-0 start that included a stunning 34–3 rout of the Pittsburgh Steelers in week three. After that game there had been suggestions that both rookie coach Doug Pederson and rookie quarterback Carson Wentz begin polishing their Hall of Fame speeches. Canton was 401 miles—and just a matter of years—from where the two were residing in Philadelphia at that moment.

Reality hit soon after that. The Eagles went 4-9 the rest of the season. Pederson's play-calling was questioned, and Wentz finally made some rookie mistakes. Some in Philadelphia wondered aloud if Pederson was too much like his mentor, Andy Reid, under whom Pederson had both played and coached. Reid was semi-revered in Philadelphia for making the Eagles a consistent winner until his final season, but he was questioned because the team had gotten to the Super Bowl (in

2005) but had never won it in fourteen seasons under Reid—and in the fifty-one years since the game had been invented.

The Eagles' last title of any kind had come in 1960. Their quarterback was Norm Van Brocklin. Dwight D. Eisenhower was president, and no one in the United States had heard of the Beatles yet.

Now, though, the Eagles had a chance to be good. Very good. At least that was the way Alex Smith saw it.

"You didn't have to watch their defense on tape for very long to know it was going to be a long, grinding day," he said. "They were fast, aggressive, and mean. I was very glad we had a couple of extra days to get ready after playing on Thursday night."

They also were playing at home.

Arrowhead Stadium opened in 1972 and was part of a two-stadium complex: a football stadium adjacent to a baseball stadium. This was during the time when multipurpose stadiums were the rage and most NFL teams played in stadiums that also housed baseball teams.

Because Arrowhead was built strictly for football, it had better sightlines than a multipurpose stadium and became a model for future NFL football stadiums. By 2017 only two NFL teams were still playing in multipurpose stadiums: the Oakland Raiders, who were in the process of fleeing to a new $2 billion, football-only stadium in Las Vegas no later than 2020, and the Miami Dolphins, whose Hard Rock Stadium had been built for both football and baseball and now houses only football since the Miami Marlins moved downtown in 2012.

Arrowhead is always loud. Everyone dresses in Chiefs red, and the stadium currently holds the Guinness World Record for noise in a stadium: officially measured at 142.2 decibels in a 2014 game against the Patriots.

Of course, home field will carry a team only so far. "It probably affects the home team more than the visiting team, and then only at certain times," Smith said. "As a visitor, it may mean you have to use silent signals to call audibles because it's too loud to hear, but you get used to that. The home team can, on occasion, draw some adrenaline from the crowd amping up, but even that only lasts for a few plays.

"Best team usually wins."

The Chiefs would prove to be the best team against the Eagles, but regardless of the noise level, it was a sixty-minute donnybrook.

"Definitely one of those games where you check yourself when you're taking off your uniform to make sure everything is in the right place," Smith said. "I was sore everywhere coming off the field that day."

The game was a defensive struggle until midway in the third quarter, the Chiefs leading 6–3 with neither team having threatened the end zone. Then it changed very quickly.

"Sometimes, for whatever reason, it takes falling behind to get your offense into gear," Smith said. "Maybe you come out on the next series with an extra sense of urgency. When you're in the lead, even if you aren't moving the ball well, maybe you don't quite feel that."

Wentz and the Eagles got the Chiefs' attention with a seven-play, 81-yard drive. Wentz went 5-of-5, culminating the march with an 18-yard pass to Alshon Jeffery to put the Eagles up, 10–6, with 4:08 left in the third quarter. Given that new sense of urgency, the Chiefs quickly responded with a drive of their own—83 yards, five plays, with Kareem Hunt, the suddenly budding star, going 53 yards for the touchdown.

The first play of the drive was a 12-yard run by Smith, whose legs were often something of a secret weapon for the Chiefs.

"People still don't know just how good a runner he is," Andy Reid said. "I remember early on, he took off on a broken play during a fourth-quarter drive and I turned to [then–offensive coordinator] Brad [Childress] to tell him I wanted to get into hurry-up after the play and he said to me, 'You might want to wait until he's finished.' I looked up and Alex was still going . . . and going. People miss that a lot."

Smith had run a 4.67 40 at the combine in 2005, so it wasn't as if people didn't know that he had speed. But he was also quick and shifty and could occasionally break a tackle or make a tackler miss. That was why Reid, as the play-caller, wasn't shy about calling running plays for him when the defense was clearly geared to stop someone else.

The Hunt touchdown made it 13–10 with 1:20 left in the third. The Eagles responded with a tying field goal early in the fourth before the game turned on a Wentz mistake.

Philadelphia had forced a Chiefs punt after tying the game, and had a second-and-12 on its own 33. Wentz dropped, trying to set up a screen. Once again, he came under a heavy rush—he was sacked six times in the game—and, trying to avoid the rush, he tossed a sidearm pass in the direction of running back Darren Sproles, who was surrounded by red shirts.

The ball was tipped and ended up in the hands of defensive tackle

Chris Jones, who actually lost 3 yards trying to run, meaning the Chiefs took over at the Eagles' 31. Three plays later, facing third-and-4, it was Smith facing onrushing linemen, notably defensive end Vinny Curry, who appeared to have him trapped.

But Smith managed to dodge him and, again using his speed, picked up 5 yards for a critical first down. If Curry had sacked him, the Chiefs—at best—would have had a long field goal attempt. Instead, two plays later, Smith found Travis Kelce for a go-ahead touchdown, making it 20–13 with 6:25 left.

That proved to be the decisive moment in the game. The Chiefs' defense forced a three-and-out and, facing a now-tired Eagles defense, the Chiefs upped the margin to 27–13 with 2:14 left on another run by Hunt, this one from 2 yards out. The Eagles managed to score with eight seconds left against Kansas City's prevent defense, but the Chiefs recovered the ensuing onside kick and it was over, 27–20.

Smith's 5-yard first-down scramble on the lead-taking drive was one of those plays that often go unnoticed. If he hadn't escaped Curry, Chiefs field goal kicker Harrison Butker would have faced a field goal in the 50-yard range—not exactly automatic. Instead, the Chiefs ended up with a game-turning touchdown a couple of plays later.

The game had been tough physically on both quarterbacks. Wentz had not only been sacked six times, he'd been knocked down a total of ten. Like Smith, he'd been able to escape several other near disasters, scrambling four times for 55 yards. The only scramble that hadn't worked out had been the intercepted screen pass. He had finished 25-of-46 for 333 yards, forced to throw all day because the Chiefs completely stifled the Eagles' running game. Smith was 21-of-28 for 251 yards, the biggest difference being that he hadn't turned the ball over.

"I'm not sure people realized at the time what a good win that was," Smith said. "But we knew we'd beaten a very good football team. In its own way, that game was as much of a confidence builder as the Patriots game had been. We caught the Patriots a little off guard. That wasn't the case with the Eagles."

As it turned out, the Chiefs had opened the season by beating the two teams that would play in the Super Bowl. Of course, they couldn't possibly know that at the time, especially since, at that moment, they had every reason to believe that *they* would be the AFC team traveling to Minneapolis the following February.

—

While the Chiefs continued to win after their impressive victories the first two weeks of the season—they would start 5-0 and be the last team to lose a game—the Ravens had come down to earth very quickly and emphatically after their 2-0 start.

Joe Flacco had hoped the loss in London would be a wake-up call, a reminder that the team wasn't nearly as good as the two relatively easy victories over bad teams might indicate. Just as importantly, he didn't think the loss to the Jaguars was an indication of how bad the Ravens were. If it had been, there wouldn't have been much point in even showing up to play the Steelers the following week.

Flacco has never been one to dwell on outcomes—wins or losses—during his career. He sees no point in it, other than perhaps learning from mistakes, regardless of the final result.

Which is why he sat in a corner of the Ravens' dining room two days after the London debacle and calmly talked about what had gone on.

The Jaguars played a game annually in London (because of flagging home attendance), so perhaps their experience with the five-hour time change had given them an advantage.

"If we lost in overtime or on the last play you *might* say that was a factor, but not at 44–7," Flacco said with a smile. "I felt fine. I think we all felt fine. We just played bad."

What about the national anthem controversy? Had that somehow been a distraction?

"Same for them as for us. They were ready to play. We weren't. Happens to everyone—even the very best teams in the league. You see a score and you say, 'How's that possible?' What was it, four, five years ago that the Patriots got crushed in Kansas City early and Belichick was actually asked if he would consider changing quarterbacks? They ended up winning the Super Bowl."

In fact, the Patriots had dropped to 2-2 early in the 2014 season after a 41–14 Monday night loss in Kansas City, and Bill Belichick *had* been asked if he would give any thought to benching Tom Brady. He had simply shaken his head in disgust in response. His answer to every question the rest of that week was "We're on to Cincinnati."

Brady had one of the worst games of his career that night, completing 14 of 23 passes for a mere 159 yards while being intercepted twice. Alex Smith had looked like the lock future Hall of Famer, going 20-of-26 for 248 yards and three touchdowns. Rookie Jimmy Garoppolo had come in with the Patriots down 41–7 and driven the team to a late consolation touchdown. Apparently someone in the media thought that might mean something.

It didn't.

The Patriots went on to play Cincinnati (at home), beat the Bengals 43–17, and did go on to win the Super Bowl.

Flacco would never be as taciturn as Belichick. But his approach was about the same: on to Pittsburgh.

That's why Flacco didn't mind the idea of playing the Steelers next. He knew there would be no chance of coming out flat playing their archrivals at home. Coach John Harbaugh wouldn't need to give any fire-and-brimstone speeches in the wake of the embarrassing loss. Both teams were 2-1 and both had lost the previous Sunday—the Steelers having been stunned in overtime in Chicago by the winless Bears.

Harbaugh had a temper. There were times when he would jump on his team for what he thought was lack of effort or carelessness or failure to pay attention to detail. All that had been evident in London. But Harbaugh had been calm in the aftermath.

"I think he understood there wasn't much point," Flacco said. "It isn't as if we needed him to point out that we were awful. Plus, with the Steelers coming in, he really doesn't have to say anything to get us excited about playing. If we aren't ready to go Sunday, *then* something's wrong."

Unfortunately, the week wasn't going to just be about the Steelers. It was going to be—again—about Donald Trump. The vitriol was still going back and forth across the country: Trump, naturally, doubled down on his comments, demanding in a Saturday tweet that all players stand for the national anthem.

The players wanted to be seen as united, but many, insulted by Trump or not, weren't comfortable with the idea of kneeling or sitting for the anthem. Most teams decided to compromise. They would show that they were together and aware of the issue without disrespecting the flag.

The Ravens came up with a plan that they thought would at least keep the peace for another week. Prior to the anthem, PA announcer Bruce Cunningham read a statement written by Ravens PR vice president Kevin Byrne: "Before the singing of the national anthem, please join Ravens players and coaches and the entire Ravens organization to pray that we as a nation embrace kindness, unity, equality, and justice for all Americans."

That seemed reasonable enough, and some fans applauded. But as Cunningham finished, the Ravens players took several steps forward, joined hands, and took a knee.

—

The minute the players knelt, the booing began. Loud booing. It didn't let up until the anthem singers from the United States Air Force Heritage of America Band were introduced and began to sing.

They were there because earlier in the week, Joey Odoms, an African American singer who had deployed to Afghanistan while serving in the Maryland National Guard, had resigned as the team's anthem singer. He had won a contest in 2014 to sing the anthem at their home games but, in the wake of the protests the previous week, didn't feel he could continue.

"The tone/actions of a large number of NFL fans in the midst of our country's cultural crisis have convinced me that I do not belong there," he said in an Instagram post.

Privately, Odoms told team officials he was afraid he might be attacked in Baltimore by white people.

It was in that semi-hostile, semi-confused atmosphere that the game finally began. The sounds coming from the stands sounded more like hushed murmurs than the screaming that was expected under normal conditions.

"It was impossible not to notice," Flacco said. "It's not an excuse at all for the way we played, but you couldn't help but notice it. On the road, you get used to getting booed. Not at home."

Maybe the booing shook the Ravens. Or maybe they were just a team with a banged-up offensive line that wasn't quite ready for a game like this in week four of the season.

Whether they were ready to go or not, the Ravens' performance in the game was a disaster for most of sixty minutes.

The Steelers' first drive lasted more than ten minutes and produced a field goal for a 3–0 lead. A poor kickoff return pinned the Ravens on their own 10-yard line. Flacco's greatest strength as a quarterback may be his ability to throw deep—"go vertical," in today's football vernacular—and he decided to air the ball out, throwing a perfect pass down the left sideline to Mike Wallace, who was open by a step.

The ball dropped perfectly into Wallace's hands. Wallace is known for his sure-handedness. Throw it near him and he will catch it. Not this time. He dropped the ball.

Things went downhill quickly from there. Two possessions later, Alex Collins, the Ravens' gifted second-year running back, fumbled on his own 31-yard line, leading to a short Steelers touchdown drive that made it 13–0. On the ensuing possession, Flacco completed three straight passes: to Jeremy Maclin for 3 yards; to Benjamin Watson for 5; and then on third-and-2 to Watson again—for a loss of 3 yards. The Ravens were forced to punt, and Roethlisberger did his Roethlisberger thing, as he had seemingly done to the Ravens on hundreds of occasions, running a perfect two-minute drill that led to an 11-yard touchdown pass to JuJu Smith-Schuster with thirty-eight seconds left. Even though the Steelers went for two and failed, the score was 19–0 at halftime, and boos—again—filled the stadium.

The Ravens briefly made a game of it in the third quarter, getting a field goal after an Eric Weddle interception deep in Steelers territory and a touchdown after a 50-yard run by Collins set up a 16-yard Flacco-to-Wallace touchdown pass. The score was 19–9—the Ravens also went for two and failed—there was still 6:02 left in the third quarter, and just like that the boos were gone and the stadium was rocking.

It didn't last. Flacco was under constant pressure when he tried to pass, and other than the one long run by Collins, there was no running game to speak of at all.

Flacco threw two fourth-quarter interceptions—which, naturally, reignited the booing. The Steelers scored a clinching touchdown on a 1-yard run by Le'Veon Bell with 2:26 to go to make it 26–9, and the booing stopped in large part because most fans began stampeding for the exits. Bell finished with 144 yards on 35 carries. Flacco was 26-of-49 on the day with one touchdown pass, two interceptions, and a number of flat-out drops.

Alex Smith and Andy Reid. "We could read each other's minds most of the time." *Courtesy of the Kansas City Chiefs*

Alex Smith on the move—one of his most underrated skills.
Courtesy of the Kansas City Chiefs

Alex Smith, offensive coordinator Matt Nagy, and Patrick Mahomes look over a computer printout on the bench. Nagy's now in Chicago as the head coach and Smith is in Washington. *Courtesy of the Kansas City Chiefs*

Often a quarterback's most important attribute: his eyes. *Courtesy of the Kansas City Chiefs*

Joe Flacco with John Harbaugh, the only head coach he's ever played for in the NFL. *Courtesy of Shawn Hubbard, Baltimore Ravens*

Even the less-mobile quarterbacks have to be able to throw on the move to survive. *Courtesy of Phil Hoffmann, Baltimore Ravens*

Joe Flacco with any quarterback's ultimate prize: not the big contract . . . the Super Bowl trophy. *Courtesy of Shawn Hubbard, Baltimore Ravens*

The best of times, the worst of times—Ryan Fitzpatrick's two years with the Jets. *Courtesy of the New York Jets*

Fitzpatrick on his best day as a Jet: the OT win over the Patriots. *Courtesy of the New York Jets*

Ryan Fitzpatrick felt completely at home—in his seventh NFL home—as a backup, stand-in, and mentor for Jameis Winston. *Courtesy of the Tampa Bay Buccaneers*

Doug Williams in his glory—Super Bowl—days in Washington. *Courtesy of Washington NFL Football Team*

One of the reasons Dan Snyder and Bruce Allen promoted Doug Williams is because the media likes and respects him. *Courtesy of Washington NFL Football Team*

Doug Williams (third from left) and his staff watch their
team in practice. *Courtesy of Washington NFL Football Team*

Andrew Luck pointing out protections to his
offensive line. *Courtesy of the Indianapolis Colts*

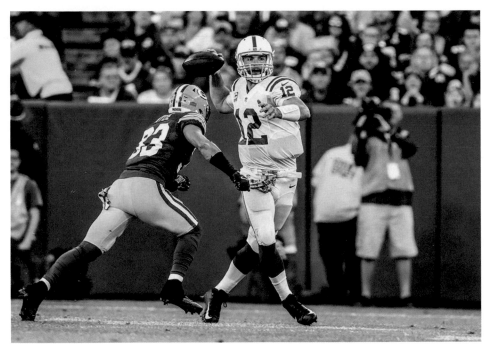

Andrew Luck is surprisingly nimble for a man his size. Here, he scrambles extending a play. *Courtesy of the Indianapolis Colts*

Andrew Luck's arm was one of the best in the NFL pre–shoulder surgery. Can he come all the way back? *Courtesy of the Indianapolis Colts*

Eli Manning started 210 straight
games for the Giants and led
them to two Super Bowl wins . . .
Courtesy of Evan Pinkus, New York Giants

But that didn't protect him from being benched by a desperate coach
about to lose his job . . . *Courtesy of Evan Pinkus, New York Giants*

No one really noticed or cared about the drops. Flacco was the guy making more than $20 million a year; he was the guy who could be seen and heard all over town selling product. With Ray Lewis gone, he *was* the face of the franchise. He certainly wasn't going to point out the dropped balls.

"That certainly doesn't do any good," he said, forcing a smile. "I know the guys are doing the best they can. I know the frailties we have as a team, and, God knows, I'm not perfect by any means.

"Plus, if I ever started whining publicly that way, my dad would kick my butt. The way I was raised, you don't gloat when you win and you don't sulk when you lose. So when you lose, you suck it up and take responsibility. It comes with the job."

Flacco was working with a rebuilt offensive line, but the bigger problem may have been a flawed receiving corps. Ozzie Newsome had signed Jeremy Maclin, a solid possession receiver, during the off-season. Maclin had been available because he'd been hurt while playing in Kansas City most of the 2016 season, and the Chiefs released him in a salary cap move. He had trouble staying on the field again in 2017, and when he did play he was inconsistent.

Wallace was the big-play threat, a guy who had had more than 1,000 yards receiving in two different seasons in Pittsburgh. He was thirty-one, perhaps a half-step slower; still solid but not what he had once been.

Then there was Breshad Perriman. The Ravens had been dazzled by his speed—he twice ran 4.29 in the 40 on his pro day—when he came out of Central Florida in 2015 and had drafted him in the first round.

The Ravens had let Torrey Smith, who had been their best deep threat for four years, leave as a free agent. They had decided signing him would be too expensive given their salary cap limitations, and because they believed they could replace him for a lot less than the $40 million, five-year contract he was given by the San Francisco 49ers.

Perriman was supposed to be that guy. There was just one problem: he wasn't especially good at catching the football. He could get where he needed to go very fast, but it didn't do much good when the ball ended up on the ground.

Perriman was hurt in 2015, then caught 33 passes in 2016. In 2017, when he was on the active roster, he caught a grand total of 10 passes for 77 yards. He was the rarest of the rare: a Ravens first-round bust.

Throw in the fact that Dennis Pitta—Flacco's most reliable possession receiver—was in the radio booth, and moving the ball through the air was a challenge. On the other hand, moving the ball on the ground was often nonexistent.

By the end, as the Ravens tried to drive for a meaningless final-minute touchdown—they were stopped on downs inside the 10—Gerry Sandusky, their longtime radio voice, looked around at the largely empty stadium and said, "The only people left right now are friends, family, and people on the payroll."

Most of them undoubtedly would have left if they could.

The Ravens were 2-2. The city where they had been so beloved only four years earlier was restless. To say the least.

16

The NFL season was now four weeks old, and, in what would prove to be a harbinger for what was to come, there had already been a number of genuine surprises.

In the AFC, the Buffalo Bills sat atop the Eastern division, a place seemingly reserved in perpetuity for the New England Patriots. The "Can they go 19-0?" Pats were 2-2. The "Can they go 0-16?" New York Jets were also 2-2. If he had been in the right mood, Bill Belichick would no doubt point out that four-week records only rarely proved significant.

The Kansas City Chiefs were 4-0, and the various pundits were already talking about Alex Smith as an MVP candidate. The Los Angeles Chargers had started 0-4 and weren't even selling out their temporary home, a 27,000-seat soccer stadium. The joke around the league was that if the Chargers tried to go back to San Diego, the city might not take them.

In the NFC, the Philadelphia Eagles, after their close loss in Kansas City, had bounced back to win their next two games: beating the New York Giants at home and the Chargers on the road to lead the East at 3-1. Both games were close, but in the NFL the margin of victory matters only to gamblers.

The Dallas Cowboys, who had won thirteen games a year earlier, were off to a 2-2 start and the New York Giants, an eleven-win playoff team in 2016, were off to an 0-4 start in what would become a lost season in the New Jersey Meadowlands.

The Green Bay Packers, one of the favorites to represent the NFC in the Super Bowl, were 3-1 in the North, and the Detroit Lions were also 3-1, with the Vikings at 2-2.

Minnesota was an intriguing team. It had an excellent defense but was forced to rely on Case Keenum, a career backup, at quarterback, after Sam Bradford was injured (again) in the opener. The Vikings had believed they had found their quarterback in 2014, when they traded into the bottom of the first round so they could draft Teddy Bridgewater out of Louisville. He had played solidly as a rookie and, a year later, had led the Vikings to a division title while making the Pro Bowl. But the gruesome noncontact leg injury he had suffered in an August preseason practice just prior to the start of the 2016 season had forced the Vikings to trade for the oft-injured Bradford. Keenum had been signed by the Vikings during the off-season to a one-year, $2 million contract—pretty much the minimum for an NFL quarterback with any starting experience at all.

When Bradford went down late in the opener against the New Orleans Saints, Keenum was suddenly the starter. The Vikings had opened with a win over the Saints but then lost, 26–9, in Pittsburgh the next week, the offense failing to produce a touchdown. Everyone wondered how soon Bradford might be back.

The Rams, Keenum's team a year earlier, had started 3-1 under new coach Sean McVay, and with Jared Goff now the clear-cut starter. No one was getting too carried away, though, since the team had started 3-1 a year earlier before plunging to 4-12. That had led to Keenum being benched after nine games in favor of Goff and Jeff Fisher being fired before the end of the season.

There were also surprises in store in San Francisco. Their new coach, Kyle Shanahan—the son of Mike Shanahan—was something of an enfant terrible. At twenty-eight, he had been the NFL's youngest coordinator when the Houston Texans gave him the job in 2008. He'd then followed his father in 2010 to Washington, where he had been in the middle of two messy situations: the Donovan McNabb fiasco, when both Shanahans didn't want McNabb as their quarterback but were overruled by owner Dan Snyder, and then the entire Robert Griffin III debacle.

While in Washington, the younger Shanahan developed a reputation for being arrogant and condescending, apparently believing *he* had been the one to win two Super Bowls in Denver, not his father. On the other hand, his father seemed to believe he was Vince Lombardi. It led to an ugly ending for the Shanahans in D.C.

There was no doubt, though, that Kyle was talented, and he quickly landed a job as offensive coordinator in Cleveland, before Dan Quinn hired him to run the offense in Atlanta in 2016. He was given a good deal of the credit for Matt Ryan's MVP season—and the Falcons' run to the Super Bowl. He was also given a good deal of the blame for the Falcons blowing a 28–3 Super Bowl lead and losing in overtime to the Patriots because he kept putting the ball in the air when killing clock almost certainly would have won the game for Atlanta.

A day after that loss he was named head coach in San Francisco—he had just turned thirty-seven—and, along with new general manager John Lynch, who had been plucked from a Fox TV booth—began tearing down the 49ers in order to rebuild them. The quarterback position would see major upheaval.

The two quarterbacks who had led the team to a 2-14 record were soon gone: Colin Kaepernick opted out of his contract when Lynch and Shanahan told him they were going to cut him rather than pay him the $14.5 million he would have been owed for the coming season. Blaine Gabbert wasn't re-signed. Kaepernick's departure had at least as much to do with politics as football; Gabbert's was just a football decision.

The 49ers signed journeyman Brian Hoyer to be their starter. Most saw him as a placeholder until the team could go after Kirk Cousins, whom Shanahan had worked with in Washington, when Cousins would very likely become a free agent early in 2018.

With Hoyer and rookie C. J. Beathard as their quarterbacks, the 49ers started 0-9. That was the biggest difference between Los Angeles and San Francisco: the Rams (in Goff) had a rising young star playing quarterback; the 49ers did not . . . yet.

Most had thought the NFC South might be the deepest division in football before the season began, and the first four weeks provided no reason to believe differently. The division was one of the most stable at quarterback (Cam Newton, Matt Ryan, Drew Brees, and Jameis Winston). The Carolina Panthers, with Cam Newton healthy after a banged-up 2016, were 3-1. So were the Falcons, having recovered from their stunning Super Bowl loss. The Saints were 2-2, and the Tampa Bay Buccaneers, having already had their bye week because of Hurricane Irma, were 2-1.

The Bucs had beaten the Bears easily in their opener before losing in Minnesota and winning at home against the hapless Giants, 25–23. Their fourth game, at home against the Patriots, was a hard-fought battle and Winston played well, but ultimately—no surprise—the Patriots came out on top, hanging on to win, 19–14.

As it turned out, the game was a turning point for both teams. The Patriots started an eight-game winning streak that night, and the Bucs would start a five-game losing streak. It wouldn't end until mid-November.

By then, their starting quarterback was Ryan Fitzpatrick.

The jinx lived.

—

A week after the loss to the Patriots, the Bucs were in Arizona, inside University of Phoenix Stadium, which is twenty-seven miles up I-10 from Sun Devil Stadium, where Fitzpatrick had watched his hero, Jake "The Snake" Plummer, play for Arizona State.

"It was definitely a homecoming for me," Fitzpatrick said. "I had a lot of family and a lot of friends at the game. Of course, I never dreamed it would turn out the way it did."

Fitzpatrick had thrown one pass going into the game—in the opening win against the Bears. He wasn't getting very many snaps in practice either because once the season starts, the starting quarterback usually takes about 90 percent of the snaps during the three full days a team practices most weeks.

In Winston's case, it was closer to 100 percent. "He's a reps hog," Fitzpatrick said, laughing. "It's understandable. The guy loves to play, and he has a real thirst for getting better. You can't possibly knock that."

Late in the first quarter, Winston was taken down on a scramble by linebacker Chandler Jones and landed hard on his right shoulder. He stayed in the game, but two series later, he threw three incomplete passes and was clearly in pain. On the next series, Coach Dirk Koetter put Fitzpatrick into the game.

The move made sense for two reasons: first, Winston was clearly hurt even if he insisted he was fine, and second, with the Bucs down 21–0 already, there was no sense taking a chance he would hurt himself more by taking another hard hit.

The lead grew to 31–0 as a rusty Fitzpatrick tried to get into game shape in a matter of minutes, having last played serious time in a real NFL game on New Year's Day—more than nine months earlier—in the Meadowlands.

Then the muscle memory began to kick in. Trailing 31–6 entering the fourth quarter, Fitzpatrick got the Bucs on a roll. He drove the team 63 yards in six plays, culminating in a 10-yard pass to Cameron Brate to make it 31–12 after the Bucs' second two-point attempt of the day failed. The defense chipped in, with Lavonte David picking up a fumble and running 21 yards into the end zone. This time, the two-point conversion worked and it was 31–20.

A few minutes later, after a Cardinals punt had pinned the Bucs on their own 1-yard line, Fitzpatrick made his only mistake of the day. Trying to create some room to work with, he threw a quick out to Evans. But defensive back Tramon Williams was sitting on Evans's shoulder, and he gambled. He intercepted the ball on the 8 and was tackled on the 1.

On the next play, Adrian Peterson, making his Cardinals debut, scored his third touchdown of the day. Peterson had been traded earlier in the week from New Orleans to Arizona and, at least for one day, brought back memories of his Hall of Fame Minnesota heyday by rushing for 134 yards on 26 carries.

Trailing 38–20 with 7:34 left, the Bucs looked finished. But they weren't. Fitzpatrick quickly drove them down the field, and Doug Martin scored from the 1 to make it 38–26, another two-point conversion failing. Then Fitzpatrick again took his team the length of the field, hooking up with Evans for 37 yards, and, remarkably, the margin was 38–33 with 2:02 to play.

The Bucs had used up all their time-outs, knowing they needed multiple scores and trying to save as much time as possible. As a result, they had to attempt an onside kick. Unfortunately for the Bucs, the ball was fielded by Larry Fitzgerald, whose hands were just about as good as anyone who had ever played in the league. Fitzgerald fell on the ball and, with Tampa Bay out of time-outs, the game was abruptly over.

Fitzpatrick was disappointed he hadn't gotten one last chance to pull off a miracle victory. He was unhappy with himself for the interception. But he knew he had played well: 22-of-32 for 290 yards and three touchdowns, coming in cold after Winston had gotten hurt, and after a nine-month hiatus.

"That was the day when I really knew I'd done the right thing coming back for another year," he said. "I had signed because the opportunity was there and I honestly wasn't sure what I'd do next when I stopped playing football.

"To be able to go back to where football began for me, to get into the game when I hadn't really expected it, and play well, was very emotional for me. It wasn't perfect and the ending was kind of flat, but I felt I had proved to myself that I still belonged in the NFL. That was a very good feeling."

The next day, sitting in the quarterbacks meeting talking about the game, breaking down what had gone right and had gone wrong, Fitzpatrick was surprised when he heard a catch in his voice as he talked about some of the plays he'd been able to make.

"Next thing I knew I had tears in my eyes," he said. "It caught me off guard. That's not me, I don't get emotional like that. In fact, I kind of looked down and said, 'What is this stuff coming out of my eyes?' I realized that being a football player has meant a lot to me, and being able to kind of put the nightmare that was 2016 behind me not by walking away from it but by playing well again was a big deal."

The question, then, was Winston's status for the following week in Buffalo. His injury had been diagnosed as a mild sprain of the AC joint. It hurt, but Winston and the team doctors believed he could play through it and that he was no more at risk for a serious injury than he would be playing completely healthy.

Fitzpatrick got plenty of reps in practice that week, and all sorts of stories flew around the internet and the various weekly football shows that "the Fitzpatrick jinx lives!"

By Sunday, Winston was ready to play and he played well, completing 32 of 44 passes for 384 yards. If his shoulder bothered him, it didn't show in his throwing. A late turnover, however, doomed the Bucs: Stephen Hauschka making a 30-yard field goal with fourteen seconds to go for a 30–27 Bills victory.

The Bucs had now lost three straight to drop to 2-4, the total margin in those three weeks being 13 points.

Winston was the starter again the following week at home against the Carolina Panthers, but this time the Bucs mustered little offense in a 17–3 loss. And a week later in New Orleans, they cratered.

It began with a bizarre pregame pep talk from Winston. Standing in the middle of his offensive teammates on the field before warm-ups, he implored them to "eat a W," forming his fingers as best he could into a W and then sticking them in his mouth—repeatedly. He was met by confused looks from everyone.

Clearly not fired up, the offense sputtered again, and Dirk Koetter decided to pull Winston at halftime with his team trailing, 16–3. Winston had taken another hit on his shoulder while being sacked in the second quarter, but insisted there was no more pain than he'd had since the initial injury.

Fitzpatrick started the second half but couldn't find the magic that had been there in Arizona, in part because he never really had a chance. The Saints scored twice quickly in the third quarter—once after taking the kickoff, then again after an O. J. Howard fumble. That made it 30–3.

On the next series, Fitzpatrick tried to find DeSean Jackson running down the left sideline, but rookie cornerback Marcus Lattimore had him well covered and Fitzpatrick threw the ball over both their heads.

Suddenly, as Lattimore started to return to his huddle after a brief celebration of his coverage, Winston came off the bench behind him, poking his fingers not into his own mouth but into Lattimore's helmet, shoving him in the process. Lattimore turned on Winston and shoved him back. From out of nowhere came Mike Evans, piling into Lattimore.

A brief melee ensued, and it ended with Evans only called for unnecessary roughness. A day later, after looking at the replay, the NFL handed down a one-game suspension.

The rest of the game was pretty much playing out the string. The Bucs scored late to make the final 30–10.

Things didn't get any better the next day. An MRI on Winston's shoulder revealed "a bunch of medical terms I can't pronounce," Koetter said. The bottom line: the doctors wanted Winston to rest for at least two weeks. At the very least, that would give him time to calm down and work on his pregame speeches.

Koetter readily admitted that he was furious with both Winston and Evans for the incident on Sunday. "You just can't do that," he said of both players' behavior.

Then he was asked for the mood of the team, now 2-6 with its star quarterback out for at least two games and its best wide receiver out for one.

"Frustrated, upset, disappointed," Koetter answered. "Pretty much what you'd expect from a team that started with high expectations and is 2-6."

The starter the following Sunday would be Ryan Fitzpatrick. The opponent would be the New York Jets.

Naturally . . .

The twists and turns kept coming.

—

After the Philadelphia Eagles had gone into Washington and opened the season with a somewhat surprising victory, the naysayers in D.C. had a field day.

This has become a fall tradition in the nation's capital in the last twenty years, in part because even the most loyal fans of the team can't stand owner Dan Snyder.

Snyder is the poster boy for rich guys who think that having a lot of money—regardless of how it's acquired—makes you somehow better than other people. According to one former employee who worked in Snyder's house, she was handed a list of rules after being hired that included an admonition to never look "Mr. Snyder" in the eye when speaking to him and to leave any room he walked into unless "Mr. Snyder" needed her to fulfill a task.

That wasn't what bothered most fans. Losing bothered them. And Washington, which had won three Super Bowls under the ownership of Jack Kent Cooke and the stewardship of general manager Bobby Beathard and Coach Joe Gibbs, didn't win very often.

Early on, Snyder tried to sign every big-name free agent he could find, if only so he could stand up and hold a team jersey with their name on it at the press conference announcing their new deal. He signed a washed-up Bruce Smith and a washed-up Deion Sanders.

After a rare successful season in 1999 with Brad Johnson at quarterback, Snyder signed Jeff George, famous for two things: a cannon arm and being a cancer in every locker room he ever walked into. Johnson went on to lead the Tampa Bay Buccaneers to a Super Bowl victory after the 2002 season.

Washington was George's fifth team. He played in six games in 2000 before being cut two games into the 2001 season by Coach Marty

Schottenheimer. He signed three different times with NFL teams over the next five years but never again appeared in an NFL game.

Late in 2009, Snyder hired Bruce Allen—the son of George Allen—to be team president and, more than anything, to take the brickbats being hurled at Snyder.

Allen became the public face of the franchise's decision-making, and many people forgot that it was Snyder who was really calling the shots. Snyder and Allen had reached a new low early in 2017 when, after firing Scot McCloughan as general manager, they leaked allegations to *The Washington Post* that McCloughan, a recovering alcoholic, had started drinking again months earlier and that was what had led to his firing.

Whether the rumors were true or not, the actions of the two men in the wake of the firing were about as despicable as anything they'd ever done, and the anger at the duo was as loud as it had ever been.

It didn't get better as the Kirk Cousins contract situation began to heat up—as Allen repeatedly referred to Kirk Cousins as "Kurt" when discussing the team's failed negotiations with the quarterback. Once again, the team had to put the franchise tag on him—this time for $23.9 million for 2017.

Cousins became the first quarterback ever franchised two years in a row. The tag meant that Washington would pay him $43.7 million for 2016 and 2017 as opposed to the $45 million guaranteed that would have locked him up for five years if Snyder and Allen had followed McCloughan's recommendation.

Donald Trump's presidency was only mildly controversial compared to the screaming and yelling going on in the media and on sports talk radio about Cousins.

Most fans supported the player. His numbers for two years had been outstanding: he'd completed 68.3 percent of his passes, and the team had gone from 4-12 in 2014 to 9-7 in 2015—and a division title—and 8-7-1 in 2016.

Both team and player maintained that there was still hope that a long-term deal could be agreed on after the 2017 season. There was no truth to that. For all his boy-next-door sweetness in public, Cousins felt dissed by Snyder and Allen—a feeling that only grew stronger during the strange "Kurt" period. The team knew he wasn't coming back.

—

There were Cousins critics who pointed out that he had a tendency to throw interceptions at critical moments and had failed miserably in the season finale in 2016 against a Giants team that had already clinched a playoff spot. That loss had kept Washington from making the playoffs in back-to-back seasons for the first time since 1992, when they had made the postseason for a third straight time in the final season of Gibbs's first tenure as coach.

The opening day loss made the critics' voices louder. The interception on a poorly thrown pass into the end zone early in the fourth quarter brought back memories of other key failures.

Then the team turned around and won against the Rams in Los Angeles—which, in retrospect, might have been their best win of the season—and followed that up with a stunning 27–10 victory at home in a Sunday night game against the Oakland Raiders.

The Raiders were going through their own ups and downs. They had finished 12-4 in 2016, their first winning record since 2002. But their season had been derailed in the penultimate game of the regular season when their quarterback, Derek Carr, broke his leg with the team leading the Colts, 33–14.

The injury to Carr and what happened to the Raiders in the aftermath—a complete meltdown the rest of 2016—were emblematic of what often happens when a star quarterback, or for that matter a good quarterback, goes down. The second Carr hit the ground and began grabbing at his leg, the Raiders' season was over.

He was healthy again to start 2017 and had signed a five-year, $125 million contract extension in June, making him (for the moment) the highest-paid player in the NFL. That was why the Raiders were being mentioned as a serious Super Bowl contender. They had opened the season with easy victories over the Titans and the Jets.

The game in Washington—Maryland actually—was the last of a long NFL Sunday that had begun in London with the Titans-Ravens game and had continued through an afternoon of protests, linked arms, kneeling, and teams staying in the locker room.

Snyder and Doug Williams were both on the field for the anthem, although neither one knelt before it was played. About a half-dozen

Washington players, most notable among them starting tight end Jordan Reed, knelt during the anthem.

Just prior to kickoff, the team put out a non-statement statement, calling football "the great unifier" in the U.S. and paying tribute to those who served in the military. Unlike other statements that had been signed by owners, this one was unsigned. That was hardly a surprise, since Snyder, according to the Federal Election Commission, had given $1 million to Donald Trump's inaugural fund.

He was one of seven NFL owners listed as giving at least that much to Trump—among them Cowboys owner Jerry Jones, who did briefly take a knee with his players the next night in Arizona prior to the playing of the anthem.

Raiders owner Mark Davis, who was (and is) in the process of abandoning Oakland to move his team to Las Vegas, did not come down on the field for the Sunday night kickoff. He did, however, say in an ESPN interview that, under the circumstances, he didn't feel he could ask or order his players not to protest in some way.

Most of them sat, arms linked, on their bench during the playing of the anthem. Then they went out and got clocked by the home team.

Cousins may have had his best game ever that night. He completed 25 of 30 passes for 365 yards and three touchdowns. The game was never really in serious doubt, and the final was 27–10.

As it turned out, that loss was the beginning of the end for the Raiders. A week later, their downward spiral continued when Carr was hurt again—this time a back injury—in a loss in Denver, and the season never got back on track again after that.

Meanwhile, as people all over town scrambled for seats on the 2-1 "Sign Kirk now!" bandwagon, Washington headed to Kansas City for a Monday night game with the undefeated Chiefs.

There would be more scrambling—much more—on and off the bandwagon before the season was over.

17

Alex Smith was surprised to see how easily Washington had handled Oakland in the Sunday night game at the end of week three. The Chiefs had traveled to Los Angeles that day and beaten the winless Chargers, 24–10, to raise their record to 3-0.

There were only two undefeated teams left in the league after just three weeks: the Chiefs and the Falcons. Smith had thought it very possible the Raiders would also be unbeaten.

"They just got outplayed the entire night," Smith said after watching Washington's dominant win. "Kirk [Cousins] was terrific and their defense did a great job on [Derek] Carr. I figured we would have our hands full on Monday night."

Washington would be coming to Arrowhead the following Monday for the Chiefs' second home game of the season.

As Smith had feared, Cousins and his offense picked up right where they had left off the previous Sunday, taking the opening kickoff and driving 75 yards to open the scoring with a touchdown. A few minutes later, it was 10–0 and Smith and his offense were struggling.

The Chiefs slowly began to get their offense moving in the second quarter. Finally, with halftime approaching, they put together their first sustained drive of the night, driving 73 yards and ending with a Smith-to-Kelce 17-yard touchdown pass that closed the margin to 10–7. It should have been tied at halftime, but Harrison Butker missed a field goal attempt for the Chiefs from 46 yards in the final seconds and Washington retained the lead.

But Smith was rolling now. Coming out of halftime, the Chiefs put together a ten-play, 79-yard drive, with Smith scoring from the 1 to take their first lead of the night, 14–10. Washington's offense, which had been dormant since the first quarter, got that surge of urgency that so often comes from falling behind and answered right away, Cousins hitting Ryan Grant for the touchdown that made it 17–14.

Then it became a battle of field goals, both defenses bending without breaking. When Washington's Dustin Hopkins hit from 40 yards to tie the game 20–20 with forty-seven seconds left, it looked like overtime was inevitable.

But in the hands of an experienced NFL quarterback, forty-seven seconds can be forever. Starting at his own 25, Smith threw a quick out for 4 yards to Charcandrick West, who stepped out-of-bounds with forty-two seconds left. Then Smith made a play with both his arm and his legs. He dropped back, knowing he needed to pick up a chunk of yardage, and, finding no one open, scrambled to his right to avoid the rush. As he approached the line of scrimmage, he made a leaping throw down the sideline to Albert Wilson, who had come open as Smith kept the play alive. Wilson picked up 37 yards before being brought down.

Smith used one of his two time-outs to stop the clock with thirty-three seconds still to go. The ball was on the Washington 34, which was within Butker's range—although the miss from 46 in the first half gave Smith some pause.

"Harrison's a really good kicker," Smith said. "He's got plenty of leg to make a field goal from that distance. But we had some time and a time-out, so why not try to give him some breathing room?"

He did that, this time finding Chris Conley, again over the middle. The pickup was 10 to the 24. Smith used the last time-out with twenty-seven seconds left. At that point, he felt comfortable that the kick would be well within Butker's range. There was no need to put the ball in the air and take any risk, so he simply handed it to Hunt, who ran to the middle of the field to make the kick straightaway. Smith spiked the ball with eight seconds left.

Butker came in and calmly drilled the kick from 43 yards for a 23–20 lead with only four seconds remaining.

Washington had one last desperation chance. Butker kicked off into the end zone, and there was time for one final snap. Cousins threw a quick out pass to Jamison Crowder, who tried to throw it back to him to set up a trick play. The ball ended up on the ground, and Justin Houston finally picked it up and ran into the end zone, creating a deceiving final score of 29–20.

Of course, gambling being as huge as it is in the NFL, many—most—were aware of how the last-second touchdown affected betting outcomes. The spread on the game had been 7 points—Chiefs favored. The over-under was 48.5. That meant those who had bet Washington with the points went from winners to losers and those who had bet the under also went from a win to a loss on a meaningless final play.

Prior to the Supreme Court ruling allowing gambling on sports in all fifty states, the NFL strictly forbade its TV "partners" from talking about betting lines on air. Given that much of the NFL's appeal is because of people betting hundreds of millions of dollars on the league each year—a number that will skyrocket in light of the Supreme Court ruling—it is laughable the way the league liked to wring its hands as if it disapproved of betting.

While claiming on the one hand that betting on football is a bad thing, the league clamped down on teams that failed to submit honest injury reports each week—or in-game—knowing full well that hiding injuries affects betting lines.

Teams are often required to submit practice tape to the league if a player not listed as injured doesn't play, or if someone listed as "doubtful," or "out," miraculously makes it to the field on Sunday. This is done in part because opponents will complain when such things happen, but also because the NFL knows if those who take bets can't rely on honest injury reports, they might have to give money back to bettors—which won't make them happy. After Houston's touchdown, ESPN's Sean McDonough settled for "this might be meaningful to some."

The win was certainly meaningful to the Chiefs, who, with the victory, were the NFL's last remaining unbeaten team (the Falcons had lost on Sunday at home to the Bills).

Smith was already getting early mention for MVP—understandably, given his play. The Chiefs had become a media darling team, not just because they were unbeaten but because they were entertaining and had a locker room full of good talkers, notably Smith, tight end Travis Kelce, and Justin Houston.

"Ask Kels what day of the week it is and he'll give you twenty good minutes," Smith liked to say of his voluble—and talented—tight end.

Like most starting quarterbacks—Joe Flacco being a notable exception—Smith was always the last player to speak to the media postgame. He would talk briefly at his locker with the Chiefs' superb public relations man Ted Crews, just to make sure there wasn't something Crews didn't know about: a possible injury, a play that had bothered Smith, something he didn't want to talk about.

"Never happens," Crews said of the last possibility. "Alex is an absolute pro."

While the other players went through their media paces in front of their lockers, Smith would get out of his uniform, shower, and dress, usually wearing a sharp suit, often black, occasionally pinstriped with a white shirt and a matching tie and pocket square. Waiting for the quarterback in the interview room can be like waiting for Godot for the media, especially if they are deadline-pressed.

Like Flacco—and most others—Smith knows it doesn't do any good to throw anyone under the bus. He can be self-critical and might express occasional frustration with an officiating call, but that's as far as it usually goes.

By the time he's finished, the locker room is almost always empty and, on the road, the bus is waiting. He will grab a snack put out by the staff outside the locker room and jump on the bus. At home he meets his family for the short drive home. His mood is dictated by the outcome. That usually doesn't change until the next day, when it's time to move on to the next opponent.

"I sleep like a baby six nights a week," he said. "Sunday night [any game night] is different. I don't sleep much at all, win or lose. Some of it is just the adrenaline of the day. It's hard to slow it down, it's still there.

"When I get home, once the [three] kids are down, Elizabeth and I will usually stay up for a while talking the day through. Mostly she listens, although there are times when she gets frustrated by things too. I know it's often harder to watch than play, so I get it. We sort of try to talk until we're too tired to talk.

"Then I go to bed and lie there and replay every play that could have gone better. Obviously, I do it a lot more after a loss than a win, because I know there's almost always something I could have done to change the outcome. Either way, it's part of the process for me to let go of the game and be ready Monday to walk into the quarterback room with that game behind me and the next one in front of me."

For the first five weeks of the season, Smith slept about as well as he possibly could on game nights—the Chiefs went to Houston in week five and won 42–34 in an old-fashioned Texas shootout, with both Smith and Deshaun Watson shining.

Smith was 29-of-37 and threw three touchdown passes; Watson was 16-of-31 for 261 yards and *five* touchdowns. That game proved to be the beginning of the end for the Texans: J. J. Watt broke his leg and was done for the season. The Texans remained competitive thanks to their offense until Watson tore his ACL in practice in early November.

The Chiefs were 5-0 after the win over the Texans and flying high. They hadn't lost since the painful playoff defeat in January to the Steelers at Arrowhead.

Next on the schedule? The Steelers, at Arrowhead.

—

The direction of the NFL's 2017 season began to take shape for real in week five. The winless Chargers went to the Meadowlands and beat the winless Giants. The game began a turnaround for the team formerly from San Diego that would lead them—shockingly—into contention in the AFC West in December. The loss kept the Giants spiraling in a direction that would lead to some of the low moments in franchise history.

The Eagles easily beat the Arizona Cardinals to be 4-1. In a game that would prove to be a harbinger, the Jaguars walked into Pittsburgh and routed the Steelers, 30–9. The loss left Ben Roethlisberger questioning his ability to be effective in his fourteenth NFL season and began to make people believe that the Jaguars might be for real.

The Ravens had to travel to the West Coast, meaning they would travel a little more than 12,000 miles in just over two weeks, playing in London and then, after a week at home, in Oakland.

Even so, they bounced back from their embarrassing loss to the Steelers with a 30–17 victory in Oakland. It certainly didn't hurt that Derek Carr had to sit out the game and the Raiders were quarterbacked by EJ Manuel. He was a considerable upgrade from Carr's replacements the previous January, but still several levels below Carr.

The first offensive play of the game for the Ravens was the same deep pass down the sideline from Joe Flacco to Mike Wallace that Wallace had dropped against the Steelers. This time the ball floated perfectly into Wallace's hands, and he caught it in stride for a 52-

yard gain to the Oakland 23. Four plays later, running back Vince Mayle scored from the 2-yard line, and the Ravens had scored as many touchdowns in 2:15 in Oakland as they had scored in sixty minutes a week earlier in Baltimore.

On the Raiders' opening series, tight end Jared Cook caught a short pass from Manuel and fumbled. Baltimore's Jimmy Smith picked the ball up at the Raiders' 47 and raced into the end zone, making it 14–0. The Ravens never really looked back. When the Raiders managed to creep within 24–17 late in the third quarter, Flacco took the offense on two long, clock-killing drives that led to Justin Tucker field goals. The final was 30–17, and with the Steelers' loss, the Ravens were again tied for first place in the AFC North at 3-2.

Suddenly, all was well in Mudville.

The game of the day, though, as everyone expected, was in Dallas. The Packers had destroyed the Cowboys' dream season the previous January with an Aaron Rodgers miracle in the NFC divisional playoff round.

The Cowboys had gone 13-3 after rookie Dak Prescott, a fourth-round pick out of Mississippi State, had taken over at quarterback when Tony Romo again went down, this time with a back injury, during preseason.

The Cowboys had gotten lucky. With the 135th pick in the 2016 draft and their second pick of the fourth round, they took Prescott.

Prescott was a perfect example of how flawed NFL scouting can be—especially at the quarterback position.

He wasn't that tall—six feet two—and his arm wasn't a cannon. He was labeled "an athlete" by scouts, which is often code for: he's black. All that added up to Prescott being just the eighth quarterback chosen in the draft.

The Cowboys had released Brandon Weedon when Romo returned, and they let Matt Cassel leave to sign with Tennessee. That left Prescott to compete with Matt Moore to be Romo's backup. When Prescott played superbly in exhibition games, the general thinking was that he might be ready to replace Romo in a year or two.

It didn't take that long. Romo got hurt at the end of preseason, and Prescott became the starter. The Cowboys lost their opener at home to the Giants, 20–19. They then won eleven in a row.

They entered the playoffs with a 13-3 record and the number one seed in the NFC. The Packers had beaten the Giants easily in the wildcard round and came to Dallas to play a team that hadn't been to the Super Bowl since the 1995 season.

The game was a back-and-forth duel between an old master— Rodgers had turned thirty-three in December—and a young one— Prescott was twenty-three.

It came down to a battle of two-minute offenses and two of the best field goal kickers in the game. Rodgers drove the Packers to the Cowboys' 38, but the drive stalled and Mason Crosby came in to nail a 56-yard field goal with 1:33 to go.

That was plenty of time for the rookie Prescott. His drive bogged down on the Green Bay 33, and Dan Bailey tied the game again with a 51-yarder.

Remarkably, the Cowboys had left too much time—thirty-five seconds—on the clock for Rodgers. After a sack and an incompletion left the Packers with third-and-20 at their own 32, overtime appeared to be a certainty. It would have been, with almost any quarterback on the field other than Rodgers.

Rodgers took the snap with twelve seconds left. Pressured, he rolled left and made a throw that perhaps no one else in the game—including Tom Brady, who couldn't possibly escape the rush the way Rodgers did—could make. He put the ball right on the outstretched hands of Jared Cook (the same Jared Cook who would hand the Ravens a touchdown in Oakland on that October afternoon in week five of the 2017 season), who somehow got both feet down before falling out-of-bounds.

The play had to be reviewed for several minutes before officials in New York confirmed Cook had made the catch at the Dallas 32, a gain of 36 yards. With three seconds left, Crosby came on and was perfect—again—this time from 50 yards. Game over. Season over for the Cowboys. Shocked fans exited the stadium headed to another long off-season.

Now, nine months later, the Packers returned to Dallas. Rodgers was playing at an MVP level and the Packers were 3-1. The Cowboys were a surprising 2-2—having been routed in Denver in week two and then losing at home the week before to the resurgent Rams. With the Eagles already 4-1, the game was surprisingly important to Dallas.

The game was different from the playoff game—but the result was the same. Prescott gave the Cowboys a late 31–28 lead with an 11-yard scramble that came at the end of a remarkable seventeen-play, 79-yard drive that took 8:43 off the clock.

That, however, was not enough, because Rodgers still had 1:13 and a time-out left to work with. For Rodgers, that's almost like working out of an easy chair.

The Packers quickly drove into Crosby's range for a tying field goal. Rodgers was having none of it. On third-and-8, he again made a play very few quarterbacks could make, scrambling left, pulling the ball down, and racing to the Cowboys' 12 before stepping out-of-bounds.

First down. Still twenty-one seconds on the clock. Rodgers threw incomplete to Davante Adams. Sixteen seconds left. Rodgers went back to Adams, throwing a perfect pass on a straight fly route to the corner that Adams leaped for and caught with eleven seconds left.

As Yogi Berra might say, it was déjà vu all over again. The Packers won 35–31, and most Cowboy fans went home cursing the name Aaron Rodgers. Dallas was 2-3 and, as it turned out, would never challenge the Eagles in the NFC East. Green Bay was 4-1, seemingly poised to run away with the NFC North.

But the NFL is often like the weather in San Francisco: if you don't like it now, be patient, things will almost certainly change in the near future.

—

There were a surprising number of empty seats at kickoff in Baltimore on October 15, even after the Ravens win the previous week in Oakland. It was something Joe Flacco and his teammates couldn't help but notice. The Ravens were hosting the Bears on a warm and humid day approaching seventy degrees.

"We'd just won in Oakland and, even though we played lousy against the Steelers, we were tied for first place," he said. "It [the empty seats] was something I think we all couldn't help but notice as the season went along because we weren't used to it."

For the most part, Baltimore loved its football team. The Ravens had arrived in Baltimore in 1996 after the city had been without an NFL team for twelve years—the Colts stolen from the city by owner Robert Irsay, who packed up and left town for Indianapolis in the middle of the night in the spring of 1984.

There were some people who didn't feel right about Baltimore getting a team stolen from another city—Cleveland—but that passed quickly, especially after the NFL awarded an expansion franchise to Cleveland soon after the Browns had become the Ravens.

The Ravens played in Memorial Stadium, the former home of the Colts—and the Orioles—for two seasons while the new stadium the city had committed to building for them was completed. Then, in their third season in the new place—which has had various corporate names on it since opening in 1998—they won the Super Bowl. They had been a solid, competitive franchise for most of the twenty-first century and had won a second Super Bowl in February 2013. Tickets to what was now M&T Bank Stadium became very tough to find.

There are two statues outside the stadium: one of Johnny Unitas, the great Colts quarterback, and one of Ray Lewis, the iconic linebacker generally considered the greatest Raven of them all.

Flacco is, without question, the Ravens' greatest quarterback. Unlike many franchises that move, the Ravens were forced to leave all Browns records and history behind. When the Indianapolis Colts talk about their greatest players and history, both Johnny Unitas and Peyton Manning are part of it, as is the Baltimore Colts' Super Bowl V victory over the Cowboys. But Jim Brown and Otto Graham aren't mentioned in the Ravens' record books. Their legacies remain in Cleveland with the expansion (1999) Browns.

The Ravens' victory in Oakland had been a relief, not just because it stopped the two-game losing streak (three straight losses in the NFL is roughly the equivalent of a thirty-game losing streak in baseball), but because the offense showed some life. Flacco threw the ball well, the receivers caught the ball well, and the running game was effective.

Still, Flacco knew there was no reason to get comfortable. The Bears were not a good team, but that didn't mean there wasn't reason to worry—even playing at home.

The Bears were 1-3 when Coach John Fox decided he had seen enough of quarterback Mike Glennon, the $45 million off-season acquisition. Mitchell Trubisky, the much-ballyhooed number two pick in the draft, had gotten the start in Minnesota on the previous Monday night in week five and had played reasonably well, driving the Bears to a late tying touchdown.

The Vikings started Sam Bradford that night, thinking his knee had healed enough for him to play. He could play—just not effectively. He looked like a statue in the pocket and could barely move at all. That led to a sack for a safety late in the first half, which meant the halftime score was 3–2.

Given the score, Vikings coach Mike Zimmer went to the bullpen to start the second half, bringing Case Keenum in for Bradford. Keenum got the offense going, leading two touchdown drives. The Bears tied the game at 17 early in the fourth quarter, but the game turned on Trubisky's one truly bad mistake of the night—a pass he intended for tight end Zach Miller that was intercepted by safety Harrison Smith at the Bears' 26 with 2:32 left.

Keenum kept the ball on the ground and ran the clock down to twelve seconds before Kai Forbath came in and kicked the winning field goal from 26 yards.

That meant the Bears came into Baltimore still planning to keep the game plan fairly simple, with Trubisky getting his second start.

"The thing you need to do in a game like that, especially at home, is not give the other guys hope," Flacco said. "Let them know you're the better team right away."

The Ravens did exactly the opposite. The offense sputtered the entire first quarter—picking up one first down in three series. The Bears weren't much better, and the score was 0–0 after one.

It got worse in the second quarter. The Bears managed a drive that led to a field goal—the key play being a 12-yard *run* by Trubisky—and took a 3–0 lead. The Ravens quickly moved the ball to the Chicago 26. On third and 6, Flacco completed a short pass to tight end Maxx Williams, one of several players trying to fill the large shoes vacated by Dennis Pitta. Williams made the catch and appeared to have a first down when he was hit by linebacker Christian Jones and fumbled. Danny Trevathan fell on it at the Bears' 20, and the boos started again.

They got louder a few minutes later when Flacco, trying to throw deep to Breshad Perriman, was intercepted. Perriman was open at the Bears' 35, but the ball hit him in the worst possible spot—his hands. He bobbled it, then was hit hard by Kyle Fuller as the ball bounced into the air and into the hands of diving safety Ryan Callahan.

For a split second, no one but Callahan realized he had scooped the ball up before it hit the ground. He scrambled to his feet untouched and took the ball back to the Ravens' 20.

Most game stories described Perriman as bobbling the ball because of Fuller's hit. But replays showed that Perriman was bobbling the ball even before being hit. Even so, the interception was charged to Flacco, and the boos rained down. As always, the quarterback takes the best and the worst.

The Bears scored two plays later on a trick play, Trubisky flipping the ball to running back Tarik Cohen, who ran right, pulled up, and found Zach Miller open in the end zone. That made the score 10–0 with 3:36 to go.

Flacco was able to get the Ravens into position for a 27-yard Justin Tucker field goal to make it 10–3 at the half, but the Ravens had already committed the cardinal sin of giving a bad team hope.

Things didn't get any better at the start of the third quarter. The Ravens went three-and-out on their first series, and the Bears proceeded to drive 67 yards to extend the lead to a stunning 17–3.

And yet, just when fans were thinking about heading for the exits—come late, leave early—the game turned on one play. The Bears did what bad teams do: with one mistake, they let a team back into the game when it was down. It happened on the kickoff after the Bears' touchdown, when Bobby Rainey returned the kick 96 yards for a touchdown, appearing to be down at one point but continuing on because no one on the Bears ever touched him. Suddenly, it was 17–10 and people went back to their seats.

It looked like the Ravens had tied the game early in the fourth quarter when, with the ball on the Bears' 10, Flacco scrambled and found Mike Wallace in the end zone for a touchdown.

But this was a Murphy's Law day for the Ravens. Flacco, hardly known for his ability to scramble, had crossed the line of scrimmage just before throwing the pass to Wallace. Instead of a tying touchdown, the Ravens had to settle for another Tucker field goal, making it 17–13.

Murphy showed up again a few minutes later. With the Ravens driving, Flacco rolled right on third-and-4 from the Bears' 33 and found Chris Moore down the right sideline. But Moore was hit as he tried to catch the ball and—naturally—it bounced off his hands into the air and was intercepted 10 yards farther downfield by third-year cornerback Adrian Amos—who had never had an NFL interception.

Amos weaved his way 90 yards for a touchdown to make it 24–13, and it seemed the Ravens had been put out of their misery.

But remember that thing about bad teams?

Tucker kicked another field goal with 3:01 left to make it 24–16. Then, with the Bears trying to run out the clock on the ground, Jordan Howard, who was having a career day, was stopped for a 2-yard loss on third-and-1 at the Chicago 26, forcing a punt with 1:55 left after the Ravens spent their last time-out.

The Ravens still had a chance, but they would have to go the length of the field with no time-outs to score a touchdown—which the offense hadn't done all day—and then make a two-point conversion to tie.

Long odds. Or so it seemed.

Then, Michael Campanaro, who returned punts largely because he had good hands and was unlikely to fumble, fielded the punt at his own 23. Somehow, he got outside the Bears defenders and went untouched 77 yards down the sideline to score.

Much of the crowd was gone by then, having departed after the Amos interception. Those who were left went nuts as Flacco and the offense came on to go for two. Flacco found Nick Boyle, another Pitta wannabe, for the two-point score and, remarkably, the game was tied.

Even Cool Joe shook his fist at that development.

"The game looked lost after the interception," he said later. "Then, all of a sudden, we've got a real chance to win—to really steal a win. They gave us a chance. At that moment, I thought we were going to get it done."

Any thought of the Bears trying to get into field goal range with 1:37 left went away when Trubisky fumbled a shotgun snap and had to retreat to the 19 to recover.

Overtime.

The NFL had shortened overtime at the start of the season from fifteen minutes to ten minutes, largely to reduce wear and tear on teams forced to play an extra quarter—at least a little bit.

The Ravens had all the momentum. And when the Bears were forced to punt and punter Pat O'Donnell semi-shanked the punt so it went out-of-bounds on the Ravens' 40, all Flacco and his offense had to do was move the ball 20 yards—maximum—to be within Tucker's range.

But they couldn't do it, going three-and-out when Flacco's third-and-2 pass to Moore was knocked down. Punter Sam Koch pinned the Bears at their 7. If the Ravens could get the Bears off the field in a three-and-out, they might get the ball back *already* in field goal range.

The Bears had run the ball well all day, and, pinned deep, it seemed unlikely they'd try anything fancy. They didn't. On first down, Howard—who would finish the day with 164 yards—ran left and appeared surrounded. One tackler missed, then two, then three. He kept spinning free. By the time he was done, he'd pulled free and gone 53 yards to the Ravens' 40.

Just like that, the stadium deflated again—as did the Ravens' sideline. With room to work, the Bears allowed Trubisky to throw. On a third-and-11, still not quite in field goal range for kicker Connor Barth, Trubisky found Kendall Wright open down the seam for 18 yards to the Ravens' 23.

That, finally, was the dagger. The Bears ran three up-the-middle running plays (why they waited for three plays, no one quite knew) and brought Barth in for a 40-yard attempt with 2:11 to go. The kick was down the middle, and—mercifully for those watching—the game was over: Bears 27, Ravens 24.

John Harbaugh went into the interview room before Flacco, even though Flacco very much wanted to do his thing and get the heck out of the building.

Harbaugh didn't really have much to say. Asked about the Bears' 254 yards rushing, he shrugged and said, "I can't answer that [what the problem was]. I just saw them running for a lot of yards."

He insisted his players had "played their hearts out," which is straight out of the coach's handbook for not calling your team out in public. NFL teams are asked to show up sixteen times a year. Anyone who doesn't play his heart out shouldn't be playing.

Flacco was asked if losing this way to a bad team was especially tough to take.

"When it looks like you're out of a game and then you have a chance to win . . ." He paused. He could see the headlines: "Flacco calls loss devastating" or, "Flacco says Ravens never should have lost . . ." He regrouped, shrugged, and said, "Every loss stings. They all sting."

This was more than a stinger. Very few teams in the NFL have any margin for error, because the season is so short. A bad loss can knock you out of home-field advantage, out of a bye, or, worst of all, out of the playoffs.

The Ravens were now 3-3 rather than a rosier 4-2, and this loss wouldn't go away anytime soon.

"To be successful, unless you're the Patriots, you probably have to win two games in a season you don't deserve to win," Flacco said later. "That was one of those games. We had too many turnovers and didn't move the ball nearly enough." He paused and shook his head. "We [the offense] didn't score a touchdown. That's on me."

Both interceptions he had thrown had been good throws that went off his receiver's hands and into the hands of Bears defenders. Didn't matter. It's always on the quarterback in the NFL.

18

On the same afternoon that the Ravens were losing a game that their quarterback claimed was on him, the Green Bay Packers were losing something far more important: their quarterback.

The Packers arrived in Minneapolis to play the Vikings in two-year-old U.S. Bank Stadium, on a roll. They were 4-1 coming off their stunning win in Dallas. The Vikings were 3-2, and their quarterback was again Case Keenum since Bradford was out again with his recurring knee problems.

U.S. Bank Stadium would be the site of the Super Bowl in February. Many believed this would be a good chance for the Packers to get a feel for the place.

On the Packers' second possession, they faced a second-and-9 at their own 39. Out of the shotgun, Rodgers dropped, looked left, and found no one open. He rolled right, found some space, and spotted Martellus Bennett wide open 10 yards downfield. His pass hit Bennett in the hands—and he dropped it.

That wasn't the important part of the play. As Rodgers scrambled, outside linebacker Anthony Barr had a clear path to him and ran straight at him. Barr hit Rodgers a split second after he released the ball. There was no penalty and, later, when the league looked at the hit, Barr wasn't fined. It was one of those bang-bang football plays in which it would have been virtually impossible for Barr to pull up.

He hit Rodgers on his left side, but as Rodgers went down, he tried to cushion his fall with his right hand. The minute he hit the ground and rolled over, clearly in pain, it was apparent he was hurt.

Or, more accurately, injured. Quarterbacks are hurt every time they take a hit. Most of the time they get up, shake it off, and walk back to the huddle.

Not this time.

Rodgers rolled onto his back and lay there as the Packers' medical staff rushed out to see if he was okay.

As he watched from the far sideline, Case Keenum's football and quarterback instincts told him that he wasn't okay.

"You could see by the way he was holding his arm as he came off that it didn't look good," he said. "It was very upsetting. We all know it's a violent game and people get hurt. All of us get hurt at some point. But as a quarterback, I could almost literally feel his pain. And as someone who loves football, I knew—I know—that the game, the sport is a lot better when Aaron Rodgers is playing. He makes it better."

As Keenum described, Rodgers was holding his right arm at his side as he came off. He was taken off on a cart, and the report came back pretty quickly after an in-stadium X-ray: his collarbone was broken. At best, he might return for the final few weeks of the season.

At that moment, the axis of the NFL changed. The Packers went from being a Super Bowl favorite to just another team. Brett Hundley, who had been drafted in the fifth round coming out of UCLA in 2015, came into the game to replace Rodgers. Hundley hadn't played a down in 2015 and, in 2016, had thrown ten passes, completing two of them.

Under the absolute best of circumstances, trying to replace Aaron Rodgers would be almost impossible for anybody. These weren't close to the best of circumstances. Hundley came into a 0–0 game on the road against one of the league's best defenses.

What happened was predictable: on Hundley's first full series (he simply handed off on third-and-9 after the Bennett drop and the Packers punted), he was intercepted by safety Xavier Rhodes at the Packers' 27-yard line. Two plays later, Keenum found running back Jerick McKinnon and he raced into the end zone for a 7–0 lead.

The Packers did manage to tie the game 7–7 after Clay Matthews returned a McKinnon fumble 63 yards to the Minnesota 18. Hundley threw a 14-yard pass to Davante Adams, who had caught the winning touchdown pass from Rodgers a week earlier, to tie the score.

That, though, was Green Bay's last real hurrah. The Packers scored three points the rest of the afternoon, while Keenum patiently directed a long drive to make it 14–7, and then the Vikings happily settled for three Forbath field goals in the second half.

The Packers' second-half possessions went like this: punt, interception, punt, stopped on downs, interception. They never came close to scoring. With Rodgers playing, there was no way that would happen.

The reality, though, was that Rodgers wouldn't be playing for a long time. By the time Barr (who had hit Rodgers) turned on his phone after the game, he had more than 3,000 tweets—"most of them not very nice," he said later—from people telling him what they thought of his hit. He was called a "Minnesota terrorist," among other things that shouldn't be repeated. The vitriol continued to pour in long after the game was over.

"I'm truly sorry it happened," Barr said later that week. "I don't want to see anybody get hurt and certainly not Aaron Rodgers, he's one of the best players in the game. It wasn't a dirty hit. Clearly I didn't mean to hurt him."

Rarely do players mean to hurt another player. Sometimes they commit dirty plays because they get overamped in the heat of the game or because they think it's the best way to make a play. That's one reason why targeting has become a major penalty, although the NFL still hasn't gotten around to making ejection mandatory when a player is whistled for targeting.

The Packers' season was ruined after the injury. Hundley simply didn't have the experience to step in and play well enough for the team to compete—much less be a Super Bowl contender.

The Vikings' victory that week made them 4-2 and, for the moment, left them tied with the Packers at the top of the division. There were still plenty of questions about how good the Vikings were. The defense was excellent, but the question was, could a team actually compete at the top levels of the league with Case Keenum as the starting quarterback?

Unlike Hundley, Keenum *did* have experience. He had been in the NFL for six years and had played in Houston; St. Louis; Houston again; St. Louis a second time; and Los Angeles—when the Rams moved there from St. Louis after the 2015 season.

His was an intriguing story. He had spent six seasons at the University of Houston, redshirting as a freshman, then tearing his ACL in the third game of his redshirt senior season. The NCAA had granted him a sixth season of eligibility (he was a graduate student by then), and he'd had a remarkable season. The Cougars finished 13-1. They had gone into the Conference USA title game 12-0, with dreams of perhaps getting a New Year's Day bowl bid. But they were upset by Southern Mississippi and ended up in the less-than-glamorous Ticket City Bowl game in Dallas.

Their opponent was Penn State, which had fallen off its pedestal two months earlier in the wake of the Jerry Sandusky scandal that had led to the firing of legendary coach Joe Paterno. The Nittany Lions had been 8-1 when the Sandusky scandal became public. They had beaten Illinois on October 29 for Paterno's 409th win, which allowed him to break Eddie Robinson's all-time record for victories.

No one knew that day that the game would not only be Paterno's last win, but the last time he coached a football game. A week later, with Penn State off, Sandusky was arrested and charged with multiple counts of child rape. Four days after that, Paterno was fired.

In the midst of the scandal, the Nittany Lions lost to Nebraska, then beat a bad (6-6) Ohio State team before being crushed in the regular season finale by Wisconsin. By the time they got to Dallas, most of the players just wanted the season to be over.

Keenum and the Cougars took full advantage, winning 30–14 with Keenum throwing for 532 yards. He finished the season with an astonishing 5,246 yards passing. In other words, he *averaged* more than 400 yards a game.

And yet, when the NFL draft came, Keenum sat and watched seven rounds go by without hearing his name called. He was a classic example of a player overlooked because of his size. At the combine, he had measured six feet and a half inch. His arm strength was considered average. Speed (4.8 in the 40), slightly above average.

But as is always pointed out when quarterbacks who should (according to the scouts) succeed don't, and quarterbacks who shouldn't succeed do, you can't measure heart.

Drew Brees and Russell Wilson, both of whom have won Super Bowls, are shorter than Keenum. Aaron Rodgers, also a Super Bowl winner, is about an inch taller.

But scouts are conditioned to fall back on things like hand size and arm strength. Prior to the 2018 draft, when various quarterbacks were being bandied about as a potential number one pick, scouts kept bringing up the fact that Wyoming quarterback Josh Allen had huge hands, which was one big reason he might go number one.

Big hands might help, and so might arm strength, but they are rarely the reason why a quarterback succeeds. Tom Brady dropped to the sixth round because he was much too slow (5.28 40) to survive in an NFL pocket. His arm strength was solid but not great.

If you ask those who have coached him, they will tell you what was missed by the scouts were two things: ability to communicate to your teammates exactly what you want done, and decision-making—both at the line of scrimmage and in the pocket, Brady may be the best decision-maker of all time. If he audibles, it is almost always to the right play. He's almost never intercepted because he knows when to take a sack. More often than not, when Brady does throw an interception it's because he's hit as he's throwing or because the ball is tipped or deflected in some way.

In 2016, he threw twenty-eight touchdown passes and was intercepted twice. In 2017, he wasn't quite as good, throwing thirty-two touchdown passes while being intercepted seven times. In thirty-seven postseason games, facing good teams with good defenses in almost every game, Brady has thrown seventy-one touchdown passes and thirty-one interceptions. The Patriots are 27-10 in those games, including eight trips to the Super Bowl and five Super Bowl titles.

Communication and decision-making. Hand size and arm strength don't accomplish either one of those things.

Keenum ended up in Houston as a practice squad player in 2012. The next year, injuries pushed him into a starting role, but the team went 0-8 in the games he started. He was waived at the end of training camp the following year so that the Texans could bring in Ryan Mallett, and Keenum was signed by the Rams, cut by the Rams, and re-signed by the Texans.

Late in the season, after Ryan Fitzpatrick broke his leg, Keenum got two starts, and the Texans won both games. Then he was traded back to the Rams for a seventh-round draft pick.

He began 2015 as the Rams' backup to Nick Foles. When Foles played poorly, he was benched and Keenum became the starter.

Playing against the Ravens, Keenum was clearly knocked silly in the second quarter. He was examined by the team's doctors and returned to the game. If he went through the NFL-mandated concussion protocol, he did it in record time. The NFL "investigated," but of course nothing came of it.

The Rams moved back to L.A. in 2016 and were that year's *Hard*

Knocks team. Naturally, much of the focus was on the quarterbacks: Keenum, named the starter by Coach Jeff Fisher before camp started, and Jared Goff, the number one pick in the draft. Keenum and his wife, Kimberly, became stars of the four shows because they were outgoing and smart and because the notion of someone who had been an undrafted free agent coming out of college and had bounced around competing with the number one pick in the draft was intriguing.

Keenum started the first nine games. The Rams were 3-1 before the roof caved in on them. Keenum's low point came in a game in London against the Giants in which he threw four interceptions. Fisher decided to bench him after a *win*—a 9–6 slogfest against the Jets—deciding it was time to see what Goff could do.

The answer was not very much. The Rams didn't win again and, after a 42–14 loss to the Falcons dropped their record to 4–9, Fisher was fired. The interim coach was John Fassel, son of former Giants coach Jim Fassel, who had once taken New York to the Super Bowl.

The switch to Fassel changed little. The Rams, with Goff starting, lost out, ending the season by being routed 44–6 by the Cardinals at home before an announced crowd of 66,125 that looked a lot closer to 125 by the time the clock mercifully hit all zeroes.

Knowing that the Rams' new coaching staff wasn't going to bring him back, Keenum signed a one-year deal with the Vikings in March worth $2 million. He was supposed to be an insurance policy for Sam Bradford and for Teddy Bridgewater, whose return from his shattered leg remained a huge question mark. Keenum, at least, had starting experience if something went wrong.

And then it did. Bridgewater clearly wasn't close to coming back when the season began, and Bradford went down in game one. He came back for game four and looked so bad that Coach Mike Zimmer quickly went back to Keenum.

He never went back to Bradford again. Such is life in the NFL.

—

One week after Aaron Rodgers had been injured, the Ravens limped into U.S. Bank Stadium. The limp was more figurative than literal. The loss to the Bears hadn't been crippling, but it had been damaging.

The game wasn't exactly must-see TV or must-watch football.

Once upon a time, the Vikings had played their home games in

Metropolitan Stadium, which had been built primarily for baseball. In fact, the configuration of the stadium was so odd that the two teams shared the same sideline.

During the years of Fran Tarkenton and the Purple People Eaters, the Vikings were almost unbeatable at home in late-season games because no one—with the possible exception of the Packers—knew what it was like to play in such cold conditions on a regular basis.

In 1982, the Metrodome opened and both the Twins and Vikings left Metropolitan Stadium—the Mall of America is now on the old stadium site—to move indoors. The Vikings lost their cold-weather edge. In 2014 and 2015, while waiting for U.S. Bank Stadium to be built, the Vikings played in the University of Minnesota's outdoor stadium. In 2016, they moved back indoors. The new stadium sits in the same place that the Metrodome sat, but it is gleaming and bright as opposed to the Metrodome, which often felt like a giant cave.

Playing the Vikings in Minneapolis is always a unique experience. Throughout the game, something called a Gjallarhorn—which sounds like a Viking ship approaching in the fog—is almost a constant both before and after key plays. Many of the fans, men and women, show up in "Helga" hats, which, if you envision what Vikings' headwear looked like, you have the correct visual. The band is called "The Skol" band, and the Vikings' "Skol" song is played repeatedly after scores.

"Loud," Joe Flacco said. "That's all I can say about it. It was loud—all day."

The noise wasn't the Ravens' biggest problem. The Vikings' defense was. The Ravens scored one touchdown in the game, and it came on the last play of the day and only made the final score—24–16—appear closer than the game had been.

On the game's first series, Flacco dropped to pass on third-and-5 and was sacked before he even had a chance to look downfield.

Things didn't start too auspiciously for Keenum either. After Marcus Sherels had returned Sam Koch's punt 48 yards to the Ravens' 36, Keenum decided to take a deep shot right away.

"I just felt the momentum of the game," he said later. "After the punt return, I thought we could get them down early and go from there."

It didn't work out that way. Keenum's pass down the right sideline bounced off the hands of receiver Laquon Treadwell and went into the hands of Baltimore's Brandon Carr—who dashed from the 2-yard line to the 36. From there, the Ravens were able to get into field goal range for Justin Tucker and a 3–0 lead.

Most of the game was a duel between the field goal kickers—Tucker and Kai Forbath. The Vikings' kicker ended the half by making a 60-yarder to give his team a 9–6 lead—neither team having come close to a touchdown.

Forbath made it 12–6 before the Vikings finally proved that there was an end zone in the new building when Latavius Murray scored on a 29-yard run with 7:58 left in the third quarter. Ironically, Forbath, who had made the 60-yarder look easy, missed the extra point. Still, the 18–6 lead looked insurmountable, and it was. Tucker made another field goal, but Forbath made two more, and Flacco's 13-yard touchdown pass to Chris Moore on the game's last play did little to make anyone in the Ravens' locker room feel better.

The Ravens were now 3-4, and the offense had produced one touchdown—a meaningless one—in two weeks.

"I believe we have the talent in the room to play well," Harbaugh insisted.

Flacco didn't disagree. "I can't afford to disagree," he said later. "For one thing, I really do have faith that we can play better. If it turns out I'm wrong, well, then it's a long season."

The Vikings were 5-2 after the win. Keenum was in no rush to speak to the media when the game was over. He was the starter now. It was his team. There was still talk that Zimmer would have a decision to make when Bradford came back, but it was apparent the team's confidence in Keenum was growing every week.

After he had met with the media, Keenum stood in the empty locker room and talked patiently for a few minutes to a reporter.

"I've always had confidence in myself, no matter where I've played," he said. "I feel very good about where I am in my life right now. I believe I'm right where God wants me to be."

At that moment, he was also right where the Vikings wanted him to be: patiently guiding a team that was gaining confidence with each passing week.

—

While the Vikings were on an upward trend, the Kansas City Chiefs were going in the other direction. No one was more surprised than their quarterback.

The Steelers had returned to Arrowhead for week six of the season, bringing with them the ghosts of the previous January.

"For whatever reason, they've just got our number," Smith said. "You look at tape and say, 'Is there one thing they're doing to us?' The answer's no. They're a good team, but we've played some of our best games against good teams. Their defense stopped us for most of the playoff game in January and their defense did it to us again in October."

Kareem Hunt came into the game as the leading rusher in the NFL. Against the Steelers that week, he carried nine times for 21 yards. On the other side of the ball, Le'Veon Bell carried thirty-two times for 179 yards. That explained a lot.

After an early safety had given the Steelers a 2–0 lead, the Chiefs got a Butker field goal to lead 3–2. That came midway in the first quarter. They didn't score again until midway in the fourth. They had one sustained drive, which began late in the third quarter and carried over into the fourth. With the Steelers leading 12–3, the Chiefs drove the ball from their own 20 to a first down at the Steelers' 12. But on fourth-and-2 from the 4, Andy Reid decided his team needed a touchdown, not a field goal. Smith tried a quick pass over the middle to backup tight end Demetrius Harris, but it was batted down.

The Chiefs finally scored on a 57-yard Smith pass to De'Anthony Thomas to make it 12–10 midway through the fourth, but Roethlisberger answered right away, finding Antonio Brown for 51 yards and a 19–10 lead. The Chiefs cut the margin to 19–13 with 2:17 left.

They forced a three-and-out and had a real chance to win the game when they got the ball back with 1:42 still remaining. But Smith was sacked on a third-and-10 from the Steelers' 40, and his fourth-and-18 deep throw to Thomas was knocked down.

"They did it to us again," Smith said. "Frustrating. Still, just one loss. The key was that we had to have a quick bounce-back mentally and physically, because we had to play again on the road on Thursday. There was no time to mope."

Thursday night football games exist for the sole purpose of making more money for the owners. In 2017 CBS and NBC paid a combined

$100 million for Thursday night rights. In 2018 that number jumped to a staggering $550 million from Fox.

That's why it doesn't matter how many doctors, trainers, coaches, or players come forward to talk about how difficult it is for teams to turn around and play two games in four days—the Thursday night games aren't going away.

"There are weeks where it might be Wednesday before you feel like you can walk pain free, much less play football," Smith said. "Some guys who would be ready to play Sunday, can't make it by Thursday. It means you get very little prep—of course that's the same for both teams. Still, it's rough."

It's rougher for the road team of course, because it has to travel on Wednesday. The issue isn't so much unfairness—everyone plays one Thursday game a year—as the potential danger for players trying to play when they're hurt and really shouldn't be playing.

Doesn't matter. Money talks, and NFL owners, who make more money than any other owners in sports, laugh their way to the bank while their players hobble back onto the field.

The Chiefs had to go to Oakland for their Thursday night game. Derek Carr was healthy again, and the Raiders desperately needed a win, their losing streak having grown to four games.

That desperation was apparent when they rolled out a flea-flicker play in the first quarter. Teams usually save trick plays for moments when all else has failed. The Chiefs were up 3–0 midway in the first quarter when Carr found Amari Cooper for a 38-yard touchdown flea-flicker pass. As it turned out, that play was a launching pad for Cooper, who had been the fourth player chosen in the 2015 draft and had caught passes for more than 1,000 yards his first two seasons. He had picked up only 120 yards in the first five games of the season—and would finish the year with just 680 yards total. But for one night, Cooper was a star again, catching 11 passes for 210 yards.

Both quarterbacks were outstanding all night. Carr would finish with 417 yards on 29-of-52, and Smith would throw for 342 yards on 25-of-36. Each threw three touchdown passes and no interceptions. Smith not throwing any interceptions wasn't a surprise since he hadn't thrown one all season, and the Raiders' defense hadn't picked anyone off in its first six games.

The Raiders led 14–10, but the Chiefs then took a 20–14 lead. The

Chiefs were up 30–24 when the Raiders had one last chance to rally in the fourth quarter, taking over with 2:25 left.

They sputtered initially, pushed back to a second-and-20 at the 20 after a holding call, with the clock down to 1:27. But Carr hit Cooper down the seam to the Chiefs' 39, and suddenly the Raiders had life.

Most of the time, quarterbacks sit on the team bench, usually close to midfield, when the defense is on the field. They do this for any number of reasons: when it's hot or cold, there is always a fan or a heater nearby; it gives them a chance to sit and look at computer printouts of the defense's formations or potential offensive plays. Most of the time, though, it's just to get off their feet so they can stay as fresh physically as possible during the course of a game.

Now Smith had given up his seat and moved to the sideline, where all the Chiefs were getting as close to the playing field as the rules allowed so they could see what was going on.

What they saw in the game's final minute was baffling, frustrating, and astounding. With twenty-three seconds left, Carr appeared to hit Jared Cook with a 29-yard touchdown pass. Smith and the offense began preparing for what would be a desperate drive to try to get into field goal range with little time on the clock but two time-outs available.

But when the officials in New York looked at the play, they ruled that Cook had come down just outside the goal line, and they put the ball on the 1-foot line. On the next play, Carr found Michael Crabtree for what would be the deciding touchdown.

Except, it wasn't. Crabtree was called for pushing off, and the offensive pass interference call moved the ball to just outside the 10-yard line. Three seconds remained. Last play of the game.

Except, it wasn't. Carr tried to find Cook in the end zone, but Ron Parker knocked the ball loose. Game over. Except there was (another) yellow flag on the field. This time the call was defensive holding. The ball was moved to the 5-yard line and, with ":00" on the clock, the Raiders were given an untimed play since the game can't end on a defensive penalty.

Carr threw into the corner for Cordarrelle Patterson, who came down with the ball, clearly out-of-bounds. Game over . . . again.

Game *not* over . . . again. Defensive holding, again, the call going against Eric Murray.

On the sidelines, Smith didn't know whether to laugh or cry. No one could remember ever seeing *two* untimed plays with a game on the line because of defensive penalties.

"All night, these same guys [the officials] didn't call defensive holding at all," he said. "You could make a case for that on almost every play involving Kels [Travis Kelce] because he's so hard for guys to stay with when he gets into open space. It's not like Tyreek [Hill] where it's a matter of pure speed. Kels is shifty, hard to follow, so guys often just grab at him."

The teams lined up for the third last play of the game. By then, Smith sensed doom. "You almost felt like they were just going to keep throwing flags until the Raiders scored," he said, laughing. "Not saying that was the case, but it *felt* that way."

On the third untimed play, this one from the 2-yard line, Carr rolled left and found Crabtree (again) and he made the catch cleanly. No flags. The game wasn't over because the score was 30–30, but Raiders kicker Giorgio Tavecchio (who had been shaky at times) made the extra point and the Raiders celebrated.

At 3-4, their season was still alive. The Chiefs were 5-2, still in control of the division but wondering exactly what had hit them in the previous five days.

Carr had been the Raiders' second-round draft pick in 2014—the thirty-sixth player chosen in that draft. He'd been the fourth quarterback chosen that year, going behind Blake Bortles, Johnny Manziel (yes, him), and Teddy Bridgewater. The next quarterback chosen had been Jimmy Garoppolo.

One of the biggest reasons Carr had dropped according to the scouts and the draft-geek experts: he didn't have big hands. Apparently, they were big enough. The Chiefs could certainly attest to that.

That draft was not atypical. Clearly Bridgewater, Carr, and Garrapolo should have been the first quarterbacks drafted, and they went with the last pick of the first round and in the second and third round, respectively. For all the time and money poured into scouting, quarterback remains the most elusive position for scouts to get right.

It's called "Ryan Leaf syndrome." But there are plenty of other names whom the syndrome could be named after.

It could also be called "Johnny Unitas syndrome." In 1955, Unitas was drafted in the ninth round of the NFL draft by the Steelers. They cut him in training camp, and he spent that season playing semipro ball for the Bloomfield Rams.

A year later, the Baltimore Colts gave him a tryout. The rest is Hall of Fame history.

19

Washington's loss to Kansas City in week four had, in many ways, been typical of Kirk Cousins's stewardship as Washington's quarterback. The team had gone into one of the toughest environments in the NFL and played even-up with the league's only remaining undefeated team until the final seconds.

At times, they looked like a very good football team. In the end, they were just good enough to lose.

The flip side came two weeks later. Washington's bye had come in the fifth week of the season, which is normally the first bye week. That had changed because Miami and Tampa Bay had been forced to take their byes in week one because of Hurricane Irma.

The byes are spread out from week five to week eleven, and most teams would rather have theirs late, when they're banged up and need the rest more. Washington, Atlanta, New Orleans, and Denver had the week-five byes.

A week later, at home, Washington played against the only remaining winless team in the league, the San Francisco 49ers—in a game that ended up being about as close as the game in Kansas City against a very strong Chiefs team. On occasion, Washington had dropped these games—notably to a banged-up, playing-for-nothing Carolina team a year earlier and in the season finale when, with the playoffs at stake, they had lost at home to a Giants team using a lot of backups because their playoff spot was locked in.

This time, though, they survived, beating the 49ers 26–24.

With a record of 3-2, they went to Philadelphia the following Sunday to play the now-red-hot Eagles, who had won four in a row since their second-week loss in Kansas City. That meant if Washington was going to have any chance to compete for the NFC East title, they had to slow the Eagles down.

The game was close for a half. Washington took an early 10–3 lead on a Cousins–to–Chris Thompson 7-yard pass. But Carson Wentz, who was becoming a bigger star with each Eagles win, threw two touchdown passes before halftime, one a 64-yard bomb to Mack Hollins, the other a 4-yarder to Zach Ertz just before halftime that capped a ten-play, 86-yard drive.

Wentz started the third quarter with another drive and another touchdown pass—this one to Corey Clement—to make it 24–10. Washington briefly closed to 24–17, but Ertz caught Wentz's fourth TD pass of the day and Philly cruised from there, winning 34–24—the last Washington touchdown a meaningless one late when it was down 34–17.

The Eagles were flying and becoming the talk of the league. Washington was back in a familiar spot: .500. The next week would be critical because the Cowboys, also 3-3, would be coming to Washington for what would be a crusade game for Dan Snyder's team, a must-win game for Jerry Jones's team.

In Washington, dating back to the days when George Allen was the coach, any week when the Cowboys were the opponent was "Dallas Week." Christmas may have been a bigger deal in Washington, but not by much.

It was sort of like playing the Army-Navy game twice a season, except for one thing: the Cowboys didn't look at it that way. Tom Landry and Roger Staubach had made the Cowboys "America's Team" in the 1970s, and they had been marketed as such for years.

The Cowboys' archrivals were whoever was the most dangerous team in the NFC East in a given year. It had been Washington for a while under George Allen; then for a lengthy run under Joe Gibbs. But the Giants had been the archrivals when Bill Parcells was the coach and then when Tom Coughlin won two Super Bowls in the early 2000s. The Eagles had their moments under Dick Vermeil too. There was no such thing as "Washington Week" in Dallas. In any given year it could just as easily be "New York Week," or "Philadelphia Week." The average Cowboys fan probably hated the Patriots far more than he hated Washington.

But in week eight, with the season teetering on a cliff and Dallas coming to town, there was plenty of tension around D.C. that had nothing to do with the latest Donald Trump tweet.

This was seen by many fans and local media types as another "Kirk test." Cousins had been very good at times in the first six games, not so good in others. That mirrored his career. Going into the Dallas game, Washington was 20-18-1 since Gruden had made Cousins his quarterback. That included one playoff game, the loss to the Packers in the 2015 postseason.

Most of those fans didn't know that in reality, there were no more "Kirk tests." There really wasn't any more "Kirk" discussion in the team's offices. Team insiders knew Cousins was leaving at the end of the season. Doug Williams was already scouting quarterbacks—college and NFL—to find someone to take his place for the 2018 season.

"We can say all we want about wanting him back, and he can say all he wants about coming back," Doug Williams said. "Bottom line is we have to be scouting other quarterbacks right now."

Underneath the choirboy looks and words, Cousins was a lot more savvy than people thought. The most honest thing he had said about his situation and the way he felt about management had come at the end of a Sunday night game the previous November.

Washington had routed the Green Bay Packers, 42–24, a rare bravura performance in prime time for an organization famous for Sunday night/Monday night pratfalls.

Cousins had outplayed Aaron Rodgers, throwing three touchdown passes and no interceptions. As he came off the field after the final whistle, Cousins walked smack into general manager Scot McCloughan.

Forgetting for a moment that there were cameras and microphones around him, Cousins shouted in McCloughan's ear: "How do you like me now!" Then he repeated it with equal fervor: "How do you like me now!"

"I'm very proud of you," McCloughan answered. "Good stuff, man."

The irony, of course, was that it had been McCloughan who had pushed Dan Snyder and Bruce Allen to get Cousins signed long term after the 2015 season. At that moment, when Cousins saw McCloughan, all he saw was management—management that had dissed him.

Later he claimed there was nothing to his words, that he'd just been excited. Then he added, "I wish there hadn't been cameras and microphones around."

Of course he wished that, because those five seconds defined the way Cousins really felt, not the carefully restrained public face he had shown. Which was why Williams and those inside the team building in Ashburn, Virginia, really weren't taking a side on the Kirk debate—or as Allen might put it, the "Kurt debate."

The only way for Washington to keep Cousins for 2018 would be to pay him $34 million for one season—and *then* lose him a year later. "That's not going to happen," Williams said. "There might be two or three quarterbacks worth that kind of money, but . . ."

His voice trailed off. He was about to say, "Kirk isn't one of them." Which he wasn't.

Regardless of what anyone called him, there was one thing the quarterback was going to call himself at season's end: gone.

—

As it had been so often in the past, "Dallas Week" was again a letdown in Washington. The score was 13–7, with Washington in the lead, when Cousins was sacked late in the second quarter on a third-and-6 at the Dallas 14. Nick Rose came on for a 36-yard field goal that would have made the margin two scores just before halftime.

The kick was deflected at the line by defensive end Tyrone Crawford, and it bounced around until Orlando Scandrick picked it up at the Dallas 10 and returned it all the way to the Washington 4. Two plays later, with the stadium still murmuring in shock, Ezekiel Elliott scored from 2 yards out. What could have been a 16–7 Washington lead became a 14–13 Dallas lead at the break.

The Cowboys led 23–13 after three quarters and appeared to have the game under control until Washington finally scored with 4:39 left in the fourth quarter to make it 26–19—Rose, not having a good day, missed the extra point. He was kicking in place of an injured Dustin Hopkins and was waived a few weeks later when Hopkins returned. Such is the life of an NFL placekicker.

Both teams were using replacement kickers that day. Mike Nugent was in his thirteenth season in the league, and the Cowboys were his sixth team—although most of his career had been spent in Cincinnati. He'd been cut by the Bengals after almost seven seasons there the previous December; signed during training camp by the Giants; cut at the end of camp; and then signed by the Cowboys when Dan Bailey had been injured.

Nugent made four field goals against Washington and was 7-of-9 in four games before Bailey returned and Nugent was cut again. In December, when Bears kicker Cairo Santos was hurt, they signed Nugent—meaning he'd been on four rosters in less than twelve months.

Washington got one last chance to tie the game against Dallas. The Cowboys were able to run eight plays and force Washington to use all three time-outs before punting with fifty-four seconds left. Cousins needed to take his team 88 yards to score—a daunting task for anyone; even Aaron Rodgers.

Cousins didn't come close. On the second play, Cowboys defensive tackle David Irving got penetration and tipped Cousins's short pass over the middle intended for Chris Thompson. The ball wobbled into the hands of Cowboys free safety Byron Jones at the 21 and he returned it to the end zone for the clinching score.

The Eagles had won easily that day against the 49ers to raise their record to 7-1, meaning Philadelphia was three and a half games in front of 3-4 Washington—with the head-to-head tiebreaker. That pretty much ended any hope of a division title, even in Washington, where *The Washington Post* once headlined an A-1 story "Playoff Hopes Live," after a December victory had raised the team's record to 5-7—meaning they were still mathematically alive for a wildcard. A week later the hopes were no longer alive.

The Cowboys were 4-3 and in better shape than Washington. But with Ezekiel Elliott's six-game suspension for alleged domestic abuse still looming, Jerry Jones's team didn't look to be in very good shape either.

The four division leaders in the NFC were the Eagles, the Vikings, the Falcons, and the Rams. Only the Falcons were not a surprise. The Eagles and Rams were doing it with second-year quarterbacks who had been the top two picks in the draft. The Vikings were being led by an undrafted retread, signed with the intent of being an emergency quarterback.

Playing quarterback in the NFL is the most important position in professional sports, and there is no one way to stardom. That was never more apparent than in 2017.

—

It can be argued that no city in the country has a worse reputation as a sports town than Philadelphia. It can also be argued that the reputation is about 99 percent unfair.

The tired generalization is that Philadelphia is "the city that booed Santa Claus."

That isn't an urban legend—it happened—fifty years ago. The date was December 15, 1968, and the Eagles were finishing a miserable season by playing the Minnesota Vikings at Franklin Field, the ancient stadium on the Penn campus that was their home at the time.

The Eagles were 2-11, having lost eleven straight to start the season, and then, with the number one pick in the NFL draft in their sights, they managed to win two games. That ultimately dropped them from number one to number three in the draft's pecking order. The Buffalo Bills, drafting first, took a running back from USC named O. J. Simpson. The Eagles ended up with another running back—Leroy Keyes. The Eagles couldn't even figure out how to lose right in those days.

The day of the finale was miserable. It had snowed the night before and was still snowing at kickoff. The Eagles had planned a Christmas-themed halftime show, complete with their cheerleaders (the Eaglettes) dressed in elf costumes and Santa Claus being pulled around the field in a sleigh with eight life-size reindeer leading the way. Except by halftime, the field had been turned into a sea of mud and ice and there was no way to get the sleigh to plow through it. There was another problem: the guy hired to play Santa Claus was a no-show. To this day, no one is certain what happened.

In the movie *Miracle on 34th Street,* when Santa turns up drunk on the morning of the Thanksgiving Day Parade, Kris Kringle—the *real* Santa Claus—shows up to save the day. At Franklin Field, with a remarkable 54,000 people in attendance (this was before the NFL started basing attendance numbers on tickets sold as opposed to fans actually in the stadium), an Eagles marketing person spotted Frank Olivo sitting in the stands wearing a Santa costume, complete with fake beard.

Olivo was hired on the spot to play Santa, handed a bag of toys (or something), and told to parade around the field (on foot) waving to the crowd while the band played "Here Comes Santa Claus."

Olivo was nineteen and game to try, but the fans were already angry, not surprising given the cold and miserable conditions they were dealing with while watching their equally miserable team play. The booing began almost right away, and then someone in the upper deck threw a snowball. That started the onslaught.

Olivo, a lifelong Eagles fan, took it well. "I understood why they felt that way," he said, years later.

Thirty-five years later, the 76ers staged a promotion in which they tried to break the record for most Santas in a building—who knew there *was* such a record—and Olivo was invited to take part and was introduced as the Santa who had been booed all those years ago.

"At first there were cheers," Olivo was quoted as saying. "Then they realized they weren't supposed to be cheering and they booed. It was fine, actually. At least no one threw anything at me."

When Olivo died in 2015, it was a major news story in Philadelphia. After all, he is very much a part of the city's lore.

There have been other incidents through the years, but what the fans and media from other cities miss—intentionally—is that Philadelphia is one of the best sports towns in the country. To begin with, all four major sports teams play in south Philadelphia within walking distance of one another. Citizens Bank Park is one of baseball's best venues, and it is directly across the street from Lincoln Financial Field, where the Eagles play. "The Linc," as it is called in Philadelphia, is across the street from the Wells Fargo Center, home to the 76ers and Flyers. There is parking for all three venues all around, and a subway stop that takes fans right to the doorstep of all three on Broad Street.

What's more, Philadelphia is also the best college basketball city in the country. It has six Division I teams—Drexel is the only one of the schools that isn't part of the "Big Five." The Big Five schools—Villanova, St. Joseph's, Temple, La Salle, and Penn—all play one another every season. That's been the case almost every year since 1954.

Once, all Big Five games were played in the historic Palestra, *the* best arena in college basketball, which opened in 1927. Politics and money-hungry presidents have changed that, but the Palestra is still Penn's home, and on occasion the other schools host games there.

Philadelphia fans aren't just passionate (which leads to sporadic ugly incidents), they are loyal. They show up to watch their teams play whether the team is winning or losing. By contrast, Washington fans (who love to put Philadelphia down) are famed front-runners. The only Washington team that consistently sells out is the Capitals—even before they won the Stanley Cup in the spring of 2018.

The Nationals, who have been a contender now for seven straight seasons, sell out for the playoffs and the occasional important regular season game, but that's it. The Wizards almost never sell out during the NBA regular season, and football fans unfailingly show up . . . if the team is winning. Late in a losing season, most of the fans in the stadium—which is in an awful location and might be the least fan-friendly stadium in the NFL—are fans of the visitors.

On the morning of November 5, 2017, in Philadelphia, the parking lots around the Linc were almost full by 10 a.m.—three full hours before the Eagles kicked off against the Denver Broncos.

It was a warm, humid, overcast day with occasional drizzle, but that didn't dampen anyone's spirits. The Eagles were 7-1, they had finally found a star quarterback, and all was right with the world.

Ultimately, 69,596 people would make their way into the stadium, and, in this day of ticket resales to out-of-town fans, if there were any Bronco fans among them, they were invisible.

It took the Eagles and Wentz a little while to crank up, but when they did, it was a sight to behold.

The Broncos were a mess. They had gotten off to a surprising 3-1 start but began to slide after losing to the winless Giants coming off their bye week. They came to Philadelphia on a four-game losing streak, and rookie coach Vance Joseph had decided to bench Trevor Siemian in favor of Brock Osweiler.

Once upon a time, Osweiler had been Peyton Manning's anointed successor as Denver's quarterback. He'd been taken in the second round of the 2012 draft, at least in part because, at six feet seven, scouts were in love with his height. The scouts seemed to forget that the last too-tall quarterback to be coveted had been JaMarcus Russell, who came out of LSU at six-six with a cannon arm. The Raiders had taken him with the first pick in the 2007 draft, and he'd been a bust. To be fair, none of the eleven quarterbacks selected that year became a star— Brady Quinn was the only other QB taken in the first round—but only the Raiders had used the draft's top pick to take a lousy quarterback.

Osweiler actually replaced Manning during the 2015 season when Manning threw four interceptions against the Chiefs. He remained the starter until halftime of the season finale against the Chargers. The Broncos had a lot at stake in the game: a win would give them the AFC West title and the number one seed in the AFC playoffs. A loss would mean a tie for first in the division with the Chiefs and a number five seed as a wildcard team, since the Chiefs held the tiebreaker.

Denver led 7–6 at the break, but Osweiler had thrown two interceptions. Even though CBS analyst Phil Simms said there was no way Coach Gary Kubiak would change quarterbacks at halftime, Kubiak did, bringing Manning back.

Manning did nothing spectacular: 5-of-9 for 69 yards, but he didn't turn the ball over. The Broncos won 27–10 and, helped by home-field advantage and a bruising defense, went on to win the Super Bowl.

Manning retired, presumably leaving the job to Osweiler. But Osweiler was offered a four-year deal by the Houston Texans worth $72 million, $37 million of it guaranteed. He took it and was benched before the end of the season, then traded to the always-desperate-for-a-quarterback Cleveland Browns during the off-season.

As awful as the Browns' quarterback situation was, Osweiler didn't make it out of training camp in Cleveland. Shortly after he was cut, he was re-signed by the Broncos, who needed a backup for Trevor Siemian because of an injury to Paxton Lynch—who had been a first-round pick coming out of Memphis in 2016, but had lost the job to Siemian in back-to-back training camps.

Osweiler was a bargain for the Broncos, who had to pay him only the NFL's veteran's minimum of $775,000 because the Browns were on the hook for the rest of the $16 million in guaranteed money they had taken on when they made the trade for Osweiler.

There were times when it must have felt to Cleveland fans as if a combination of Vince Lombardi, Don Shula, and Bill Belichick wouldn't have been able to do anything right coaching their team.

Siemian had played well in the first four games but had plummeted after that. Desperate, Joseph decided to turn to Osweiler in Philadelphia.

The game wasn't exactly the Christians vs. the Lions, but it wasn't that far away. After the Broncos had taken a 3–0 lead by driving to the Eagles' 34 to set up a Brandon McManus 52-yard field goal, Wentz went to work.

Philadelphia's first three series produced a touchdown on a 34-yard

Wentz–to–Alshon Jeffery pass; a Jake Elliott field goal; and another touchdown, this one on a 15-yard Wentz–to–Corey Clement pass. That touchdown was set up by Patrick Robinson intercepting Osweiler and returning the ball to the Denver 15.

It was 17–3 after one. The Broncos managed two more field goals in the second quarter, but it didn't matter much because the Eagles scored twice more. It was 31–9 at the break, and no one got booed during halftime. By the end of three quarters, it was 44–9. Coach Doug Pederson, who had once been an Eagles quarterback under Andy Reid, cleared the bench in the fourth quarter and the final was 51–23. It really wasn't that close.

They were dancing in the streets—or in the parking lots—afterward. The once-proud Denver defense had been humiliated. The offensive balance was perfect: Wentz threw for 199 yards and four touchdowns, and the Eagles rushed for 197 yards. The Eagles were 8-1, and the rest of the NFC East was fading fast in the rearview mirror. The question now was whether they could keep winning enough to secure home field throughout the playoffs.

Wentz's day ended early in the fourth quarter with the Eagles leading 44–16. Nick Foles, who had been signed during the off-season to provide a veteran backup for Wentz, came in and produced two touchdowns—one for the Broncos on a sack/fumble and one for the Eagles on a Clements run.

The Broncos' defense hadn't given up more than 29 points all season. The Eagles scored 31—in the first half.

Like most home locker rooms in the newer NFL stadiums (the Linc opened in 2003), the Eagles' dressing area is massive. In theory, space is needed for forty-five players, since only forty-five of the fifty-three players on the active roster actually dress for a game. If the Eagles wanted to dress ninety players for an exhibition game, there was ample space.

The green walls are adorned with all the usual football coaching clichés: Trust . . . Community . . . Precision . . . Progressive collaboration and integrity . . . Respect . . . Leadership . . . Passion . . . Unity.

One can't help but wonder if any of the players ever actually look at the words, much less give them much thought. The word that means the most to a football player at any level is *kill*. That may sound over-the-top, but if you listen to players talk in a locker room pregame, it is apparent that they think of their sport as kill or be killed.

"Nothing personal," Ray Lewis used to say to his Raven defensive teammates while urging them to make sure the other team's offensive players felt pain. "It's just football."

He was right. Inflicting pain or feeling pain *is* football.

As with most starting quarterbacks, Wentz had plenty of room in a corner of the Eagles' locker room. To his left, backup quarterbacks Foles and Nate Sudfeld had lockers. To his right was the locker of Darren Sproles, who was out for the season.

Zach Ertz, Wentz's most reliable receiver, hadn't played against the Broncos. He had been the team's leading receiver, with forty-three catches through the first eight games, but a sore hamstring had sidelined him that day.

Ertz lockers near Wentz and watches him closely. "His maturity level, on and off the field, is just off the charts," he said. "He's a very serious guy. He takes preparation very seriously and working away from the field the same way. Doesn't matter how well he's playing, he just wants to get better. He's never content. The great ones are never content."

Out of uniform, Wentz doesn't look as big as six feet five, 237 pounds. Maybe it's the boyish face and the reddish beard that make him look like a guy who would be typecast as a boy next door from North Dakota. A devout Christian, he has two tattoos: one is a cross on his back; the other is on his wrist and says "AO1" (Audience of One), which he quotes when he occasionally delivers sermons, and is also the name of his foundation. He will frequently wear caps and shirts to press conferences with quotes from scripture on them and dots his Twitter feed with them.

But Wentz isn't Ray Lewis. He doesn't imply that God is responsible for Eagles victories, and he understands that many people would rather not be lectured on religion at all. He believes he should use his platform to spread the Word, but he tries to do it in a quiet way so as not to come off as either self-righteous or insistent that everyone see the world his way.

He has also adopted the starting quarterback's MO of waiting almost until the locker room is empty before he walks across the hallway to the interview room to speak to the media. After the Denver games, he said all the right things—credited his teammates for his success, talked about not getting too giddy—even with an 8-1 start.

The only time his eyes lit up during his post-Broncos press conference was when someone asked him about his plans for the upcoming bye week.

"Can't wait to get home and do a little hunting," he said with a grin.

You can take the boy out of North Dakota and make him a hero in South Philly, but you can't take the North Dakota out of the boy.

20

On the Monday after the Tampa Bay Buccaneers' embarrassing 30–10 loss in New Orleans, Dirk Koetter's announcement that Jameis Winston would be "rested" for two to three weeks did not shock anyone— especially Ryan Fitzpatrick.

As a quarterback, he could always tell when another quarterback was hurting. Watching from the sideline during the first half in New Orleans, it was clear that Winston was trying to play through pain, which is why he wasn't surprised when Koetter told him he'd be starting the second half.

There had been talk prior to the New Orleans game about sitting Winston down until his shoulder was fully healed, but Koetter had decided to give him one more shot. It hadn't worked out.

And so, once again, the Fitzpatrick jinx made news, especially since he was going to be stepping back into the limelight the following week against the New York Jets—the team that had practically made the Fitzpatrick jinx (not to mention jinxes of all kinds) a part of the football vernacular.

It had been there, prior to the 2015 season, when starting quarterback Geno Smith had gotten his jaw broken in a locker room fight with a teammate.

There was a fair amount of tension in the Bucs' facility that week. If you are an unproven coach in the NFL, you are almost always on a short tether. Koetter's hiring at the end of the 2015 season had been somewhat controversial. The Bucs had hired Lovie Smith in the wake of the disastrous Greg Schiano tenure, and Smith had gone from 2-14 in his first season to 6-10 in his second. He was a coach with a résumé that included a trip to the Super Bowl in 2007 with the Bears. The most impressive part of that run was that he had done it with Rex Grossman as his quarterback.

The Bucs fired Smith the day after the season ended, claiming that Koetter was a better coach to develop a young quarterback (Winston) and that they were afraid someone else would hire him as head coach if they didn't.

Koetter had never been an NFL head coach. The fact that Smith was African American and had been given such short shrift also came up in the media after he was let go.

Koetter had quieted the critics by going 9-7 in 2016 while Winston, in his second season, made clear progress. Now, with the Bucs 2-6 and Winston not just hurt but continuing to act strangely at times, there were whispers that Koetter could be gone after the season.

The man faced with trying to right the ship? Fitzpatrick.

Fitzpatrick also knew that facing the Jets would mean the media would relive his two years in New York—the good, the bad, the ugly. He just wanted to get to Sunday and hope for a win—the Bucs' losing streak had reached five in a row. The good news was that the game was in Raymond James Stadium in Tampa, not MetLife Stadium in New Jersey. The boo birds would have been out in force if Fitzpatrick had jogged onto the field wearing a visiting uniform.

Most analysts had predicted prior to the season that the Jets would easily be the worst team in football and would likely have the top pick in the 2018 draft, giving them another chance to draft a franchise quarterback. Their last decent quarterback had been Mark Sanchez, who in spite of becoming a national laughingstock after his infamous "butt fumble" on Thanksgiving night in 2012, had taken the Jets to back-to-back conference championship games in 2009 and 2010.

The butt fumble—which has its own Wikipedia page—doomed him in New York, and he was released after the 2013 season. Geno Smith had been drafted the following spring as his successor. That hadn't worked out, although Fitzpatrick had played extremely well in his place in 2015.

When Fitzpatrick exited early in 2017, the Jets had signed Josh McCown, who had been cut by the Browns. McCown was one of the few quarterbacks in the NFL who was not only older than Fitzpatrick (thirty-eight) but had been with more teams—ten. He and his younger brother Luke, who was also older than Fitzpatrick (thirty-six), had played for seventeen teams combined—some of them crossovers.

Both brothers were among the twenty-nine men who had started for the Browns since their rebirth in 1999. The Jets had drafted Christian Hackenberg out of Penn State in 2016 with the hope that he might be the answer, but he had only been the answer to the question "Who did Josh McCown outplay in the summer of 2017 to become the Jets' starting quarterback?"

The Jets started the season 0-2, adding fuel to the speculation that they could potentially go winless. But the team responded by winning three in a row—one against the Browns in what many had seen as a battle for the number one pick—to be a startling 3-2. At that moment they were tied with the Patriots, the team some had thought might go 19-0. As the old saying goes, this is why they play the games.

Not surprisingly, the Jets then came back to earth, losing their next three games. But they were all close: a 24–17 loss in New England, a 31–28 loss in Miami, and a 25–20 loss to the Falcons. They had broken the string with a Thursday night win over the Bills and came to Tampa as one of the league's more pleasant surprises: 4-5 and still nominally in playoff contention, especially if they could get a win against the struggling Bucs and the man who had been their quarterback the previous two seasons.

It didn't happen. The first half was a 3–3 slog, the Jets tying the game at the buzzer. Although the Bucs drove the ball 77 yards in seventeen plays to set up Patrick Murray's 29-yard field goal in the first half, they had little luck on offense other than that.

In the third quarter, Fitzpatrick was able to get his team into field goal range twice more to make it 9–3. Then, early in the fourth, after yet another New York punt, the Bucs took over on their own 19 and put the game away. The drive lasted fifteen plays and took 7:25 off the clock. It culminated with a 6-yard Fitzpatrick touchdown pass to Charles Sims with 6:05 left in the game. The pass was the fourth third-down conversion for the Bucs on the drive.

That made it 15–3 and pretty much wrapped things up. The Jets finally got into the end zone with twenty-eight seconds to go on a 38-yard McCown–to–Robby Anderson pass, but the Bucs recovered the onside kick and Fitzpatrick had the pleasure of kneeling at midfield while the clock ran out.

The loss all but wiped out the Jets' postseason chances, dropping them to 4-6. At 3-6, the Bucs were just happy to win again. It had been six weeks since they had beaten the Giants to be 2-1, thinking then that they had a chance to improve on their 9-7 record of 2016.

To an outsider, a 15–10 win at home over a team that was struggling at 4-5 hardly seemed like a big deal. But one cliché coaches use often is true in the NFL: every win is a big deal.

"You don't ever throw them back, that's for sure," Fitzpatrick said.

A win that makes a team 3-6 hardly makes it a lock for the playoffs or, for that matter, a long shot. It keeps you mathematically alive and not much else. But the mood in a winning locker room—any winning locker room—is almost always euphoric. A losing locker room, whether the game had meaning in the standings or not, is funereal.

For Fitzpatrick, the Jets' win was more than worthy of celebration. He had proven he could start in the NFL and lead his team to a win. He hadn't been spectacular—17-of-34 for 187 yards, a touchdown, and an interception. But he'd been good enough.

Koetter allowed players' sons in the postgame locker room after wins. To Fitzpatrick, that was the best part of a win. He would walk to the front row of seats, and Liza would hand down their two oldest kids—Brady, who was ten, and Tate, who was eight. Six-year-old Lucy could not understand why she couldn't go into the locker room with her brothers.

"As it is, the boys have heard some words I'm not quite sure I want them to hear yet," Fitzpatrick joked.

Knowing how disappointed Lucy was, he brought home the game ball, which he had hung on to after the final play, and presented it to her. The next morning, Ryan and Liza found her curled up with the football—which she had autographed.

"I think she had seen me autograph footballs so many times she just thought that was what you did with them," Fitzpatrick said, laughing.

In all, it was a fun Sunday and a fun week. The bitter memories of the previous season in New York were finally behind Fitzpatrick. He wished the team had a better record, and he hadn't wished for Winston to get hurt. But in all, he felt pretty good about being where he was: in Tampa, starting for an NFL team at thirty-five, almost thirteen years after being taken with the 250th pick in the draft.

—

On that same Sunday, Fitzpatrick's good friend Alex Smith, the number one pick in that same 2005 draft, wasn't nearly as sanguine. After the Thursday night loss in Oakland—"one of the strangest games I've ever seen, much less been a part of," he said, referencing the double do-overs that ended the game—the Chiefs had come back to beat the Broncos before losing in Dallas.

That left them 6-3 going into their bye week. Teams like to go into their bye weeks off a win, if only because it makes the week off that much more enjoyable.

"I certainly sleep better," Smith said. "Normally, I lose my sleep on Sunday, and then Monday you have to move on to preparing for your next game. The bye week, there's nothing to start getting ready for on Monday. So if you lose, it tends to linger."

The good news was that Andy Reid–coached teams almost always played well coming off the bye. In eighteen years as a head coach, Reid was 16-2 post-bye, the only losses coming in his final season in Philadelphia (en route to a 4-12 record), and his first season in Kansas City (2013), when they had lost to the Broncos.

The other piece of good news for the Chiefs was their post-bye opponent would be the New York Giants, a team that was hardly the 2013 Broncos (Denver had finished 13-3 and been the number one seed in the AFC going into the playoffs).

The Giants of 2017 were an awful 1-8 and came into the game at MetLife Stadium fresh off a humiliating 31–21 loss to the winless 49ers a week earlier. This was *before* Jimmy Garoppolo had taken over as San Francisco's quarterback. The 49ers had made the trade to get him from the Patriots ten days earlier, but Coach Kyle Shanahan didn't think he'd had enough time to learn the offense. C. J. Beathard, the rookie from Iowa, started the game and led the 49ers to the win.

At that point, it was only a matter of time before the Giants' second-year coach Ben McAdoo was fired. General manager Jerry Reese, who had been in charge for two Super Bowl wins, was under the gun too.

The Giants, it seemed, were exactly what the Chiefs needed to get their season turned around in the right direction.

The Meadowlands has never been an easy place for a visiting team to play—whether facing the usually mediocre (or worse) Jets or the usually good (or better) Giants. One thing that hasn't changed since MetLife Stadium replaced Giants Stadium in 2010 is the winds that swirl through the place constantly, especially in the second half of the season.

On the eleventh Sunday of the NFL season—each team had already had its bye and was playing its tenth game—the winds were even worse than usual: twenty-three miles per hour at game time with gusts well over thirty. It was an odd mid-November day, the temperature fifty degrees but humid, overcast, with a gray sky dark enough that the lights were on for a one o'clock kickoff.

Even though the announced paid attendance would be 76,363, the stadium appeared half-empty at kickoff, many fans apparently deciding a few extra minutes of tailgating would be more enjoyable than watching the Giants—whose only win had been in Denver—play for three long hours. By the time the second quarter began, the lower deck was almost full, but there were still plenty of empty seats in the upper deck. Quite a few ticket holders had stayed home.

Maybe it was the winds, or the weather, or perhaps it was just the Chiefs playing down to the Giants' level, but the game was torture to watch for everyone.

Both teams had spasms of offensive efficiency—the Chiefs ended up with 363 yards, the Giants 317—but neither could sustain much once in the other team's territory. The offensive star of the day was Giants running back Orleans Darkwa, not so much because he rushed for 74 yards on 20 carries, but because he scored the game's only touchdown, early in the second quarter.

That score was set up by a completely blown play by the Chiefs. Smith came into the game having thrown one interception all year—in Dallas, after eight games without throwing one. His second interception came against the Giants. The Chiefs had driven from their own 4-yard line and had a first down at their own 34. Then, on second down, they called a semi-trick play that would backfire.

Smith, in the shotgun, took the snap and flicked a quick shovel pass to Travis Kelce, who had cut to the middle of the field, the hope being that there would be a hole there.

There wasn't. The Giants had gotten penetration, and when Smith shoveled the pass to Kelce, it was deflected and landed in the hands of defensive tackle Damon Harrison, who lunged forward with it to the Chiefs' 26.

The Giants were able to get into the end zone from there, although it wasn't easy. Eli Manning, whose scrambles in his fourteen-year NFL career could probably be counted on one hand, took off on a third-and-8 when no one was open and picked up the first down at the 16. Then, on a third-and-7, Manning threw incomplete to Tavarres King. But Marcus Peters was called for pass interference, moving the ball to the one. From there Darkwa scored for a 6–0 lead, which stayed 6–0 when Giants kicker Aldrick Rosas pushed the extra-point attempt wide right.

It seemed like the Chiefs were getting their offense in gear after that, driving 61 yards to the Giants' 13—hanging on to the ball for more than nine minutes—but the drive stalled and the Chiefs settled for a 31-yard Harrison Butker field goal to make it 6–3.

The second half was memorable more for penalties, turnovers, and missed opportunities than anything else. Smith was intercepted twice more—both times by Giants cornerback Janoris Jenkins—but only one of them counted. Kelce threw an interception on an option pass and, just to be fair, Manning also threw an interception. It was an anemic second half, and the game ended with the Chiefs kicking a tying field goal with five seconds left on the clock. The score was 9–9.

There was probably no one in the building who wanted to see overtime—although it did provide for one moment of comic relief. When the captains came to midfield for the coin toss, referee Brad Allen actually *congratulated* them for their play. Apparently, he had averted his eyes for much of the afternoon.

The Chiefs won the toss but were forced to punt after a holding penalty wiped out a 9-yard Kareem Hunt run and created second-and-12 instead of third-and-1.

Since the Chiefs had already possessed the ball, the Giants needed only a field goal to win the game. Manning mixed Darkwa runs with short passes to reach the Kansas City 36—probably just outside Rosas's range, especially in the swirling winds. He then surprised the Chiefs' defense: instead of trying to pick up the first down with a short pass, he went deep down the left sideline to Roger Lewis, who hauled the ball in at the 2-yard line in spite of a desperation push by the Chiefs' Phillip Gaines.

After that, it was pretty much over. Manning dropped back to the 5 and knelt to put the ball in the center of the field. Rosas came in and, with 1:57 left in the overtime, made the 23-yarder to mercifully end the game, the Giants winning 12–9.

Smith stood in front of his locker in the almost-silent Chiefs locker room, taking longer than usual to get dressed. He leaned against a locker and shook his head.

"Say anything you want, we just didn't do our job on offense today," he finally said. "You can't ask much more of the defense—they gave up nine points in sixty minutes. We have to be better than that."

He stood up, starting to put his sports coat on to walk into his press conference. "The good news is, as bad as we were, there's time to get back on track. We've still got six games left, and we're still in first place. That's the cushion our start has given us."

He smiled wanly. "But we all have to understand that the cushion is just about used up."

—

Actually, the Chiefs still had some cushion left, thanks to the fact that the AFC West was turning out to be one of the weaker divisions in football. Even with Derek Carr back, the Raiders continued to struggle and were 4-6—two games behind the Chiefs. Surprisingly, the Los Angeles Chargers were also 4-6 after starting 0-4.

Coach Andy Reid wasn't thinking about the Raiders and Chargers the week after the Giants loss as much as he was thinking about how a team that had looked so good racing to a 5-0 start could now have lost four of five.

"It was a little bit baffling," he said. "We had some injuries, sure, but everyone in the NFL has injuries—especially as you get deep into the season. Our quarterback was healthy, his main weapons were healthy. We had to look at ourselves, not anybody else."

Smith was just as baffled. "We know it's there," he said. "We've seen it, we've done it. There's no doubt people figure things out watching tape. Defenses have a handle on Kareem [Hunt] now, and that's made it tougher to run. They know they have to stop Kels [Travis Kelce] because he's so key to what we do. But it isn't as if we don't have talent anymore—we do. Defenses adjust to us, we now have to adjust to defenses."

Easier said than done. Even playing at home wasn't a salve. The

Buffalo Bills, who were starting to draw attention with one of the best defenses in the league, came to Arrowhead the Sunday after Thanksgiving and won, 16–10.

The Bills led the entire game, but the Chiefs had one last chance to steal a win late. The Bills got the ball with 2:49 to go, needing one first down to put the game away. But the Chiefs defense forced a three-and-out, using all three time-outs to keep the clock from melting to nothing.

The Chiefs got the ball back with 2:28 left and one chance to stop the clock—the two-minute warning.

Starting from his own 14, Smith patiently took his team to a first down at the Bills' 38 with 1:33 still on the clock. Plenty of time. But two plays later, from the 36, Smith looked for Tyreek Hill over the middle to pick up a first down. Bills rookie cornerback Tre'Davious White stepped in front of Hill and made the interception that clinched the game.

After throwing zero interceptions in eight games, Smith had thrown four in three games. The Chargers won again that day to be 5-6, meaning they now trailed the Chiefs (6-5) by one game. The Chiefs would be returning to the Meadowlands to play the Jets on the first Sunday in December. The cushion was continuing to deflate.

—

The loss in Tampa Bay had pretty much ended any long-shot playoff hopes for the Jets. After their bye week, they'd hosted the Carolina Panthers and had—again—lost a competitive game, this one 35–27. They were 4-7 when the Chiefs showed up, and the two hot questions were who would be coaching them next season and, perhaps more important, who would be their quarterback?

Josh McCown had played solidly as the successor to Ryan Fitzpatrick, and the Jets had been respectable—far better than the 0-16 projected for them by many of the experts during preseason.

The only difference between the weather the Chiefs had encountered against the Giants and what awaited them in the same stadium two weeks later was the wind. There was none—or virtually none, remarkable for early December in the Jersey swamps.

The Jets and Giants not only have separate (massive) locker rooms in the stadium they share, they have separate visiting locker rooms.

The one the Chiefs had used while playing the Giants was smaller than most Texas high school locker rooms. It looked as if the new stadium had somehow been built while leaving the old visiting locker room of its predecessor, Giants Stadium, intact.

Against the Jets, the Chiefs were in a larger—though equally shoddy compared to the home locker rooms—space, and entered the field through the tunnel opposite the one where they had entered to play the Giants.

A good omen, perhaps.

Andy Reid had decided to make one major lineup change for the game. He benched himself, giving the play-calling duties to offensive coordinator Matt Nagy.

This didn't represent a major change for Smith. He and Nagy spent hours and hours together every week in the quarterback room, on the practice field, and on the sidelines during games. They had the kind of relationship where they could scream at each other and no feelings got hurt.

"In the heat of a game, on the sidelines and in the locker room, a lot of things get said," Smith said. "You better be able to take it because there's a lot of adrenaline flowing and very few guys tone themselves down. Nags and I can stand there and dog-cuss one another about play-calling, about my execution, about anything, and we *mean* it. Monday, it's forgotten. It has to be.

Nagy calling plays made things a bit simpler logistically: instead of Reid telling Nagy the play and Nagy relaying it into Smith through the microphone in his helmet, Nagy sent the play in directly.

"It helped," Smith said. "It gave me an extra five seconds or so to check off at the line. Couple times we had big plays on checks [audibles] that I got off with one second on the clock."

The Nagy play-calling era could not have started better. It took the Chiefs a little more than four minutes to build a 14–0 lead. Smith, as planned, came out flinging. The thinking was that the offense had been too passive, too much dink-and-dunk and try to get Kareem Hunt going, in recent weeks.

In the opening five weeks, when the Chiefs were unbeatable, Hunt had rushed for at least 100 yards four times and had 81 yards in his only sub-100-yard game. He averaged just under 122 yards a game and was also an excellent third-down receiver. In the next six weeks, Hunt's *best* game was 87 yards against the Raiders, not coincidentally the Chiefs' best offensive performance during that stretch. He averaged 50 yards per game in those six games, bottoming in the Buffalo game when he carried eleven times for 17 yards. The Chiefs' leading rusher in that game was their quarterback: Smith picked up 35 yards on seven carries.

And so, Smith came out firing. The Chiefs quickly went 75 yards in five plays—four passes, one rush (for zero yards) by Hunt—and Smith's second completion of the drive to Travis Kelce from 22 yards out made it 7–0 with 12:22 left in the first quarter.

The Jets quickly went three-and-out, and Tyreek Hill returned Lachlan Edwards's punt 40 yards to the New York 36. Smith promptly hit Kelce again for another touchdown to make it 14–0, with many of the alleged 77,562 listed as the paid attendance still in the parking lots.

It looked as if the Chiefs had found a cure for what had been ailing them. Except this was the week that the defense let down. The Chiefs had given up 25 points total in regulation the previous two weeks and had lost twice. When the offense finally found its rhythm again, the defense suddenly sagged.

By the end of the first quarter, the Jets had tied the game at 14–14, thanks to two lengthy drives. The Chiefs' offense slowed in the second quarter, and at the end of the half McCown hit running back Matt Forte for a touchdown with twenty-three seconds left—culminating in yet another long drive. The Jets led at halftime, 21–17.

"Not the way we had it planned," Smith said, forcing a smile. "When we went up 14–0, I thought, 'Okay, we're back.' But it wasn't that simple. You might have thought they wouldn't fight back, but it was still very early. There was no need for them to panic—and they didn't."

It was tough for the Chiefs' offense to get going for most of the third quarter because the Jets had the ball. They took the second-half kickoff and McCown moved the ball efficiently, executing an astonishing series that took 9:31 off the clock—in eighteen plays—before the Jets settled for a field goal that made it 24–17.

When Smith finally got his hands on the ball, he didn't keep it for long: on the Chiefs' first offensive play of the third quarter, he launched a bomb to Tyreek Hill that fell right into his arms as he outraced the defense for a 79-yard touchdown to tie the game at 24–24.

Jets: eighteen plays, 72 yards, 9:31—three points. Chiefs: one play, 79 yards, sixteen seconds—seven points. What's the old fable about the tortoise and the hare?

Sure enough, the tortoise responded with another Chandler Catanzaro field goal that made it 27–24. The Chiefs went three-and-out, and the Jets slowly moved into position for another field goal—eleven plays, 58 yards—making it 30–24. At that point, with 11:28 left in the game, the tortoise had run thirty-four plays in the second half, the hare had run four.

The Chiefs kept the ball only five plays on their next possession—the last one being a 40-yard Smith-to-Hill pass (Hill had six catches for 185 yards on the day)—for Smith's fourth touchdown pass of the day. Most important, it put the Chiefs back in front, 31–30.

The problem, though, was that the defense barely had time to catch its breath before finding itself back on the field. Again, the Jets began moving the ball. This time, though, McCown went for a Smith-like strike, finding Jermaine Kearse for a 51-yard gain to the Chiefs' 5.

That's when things got weird. The Jets actually snapped the ball ten times starting with their first-and-goal at the 5. Officials called three penalties, the most critical after the Chiefs had forced a Catanzaro field goal attempt. Chiefs defensive tackle Bennie Logan was called for hitting a defenseless player during the kick—a strange call, to put it mildly—on a field goal attempt.

The Jets got a new set of downs, first-and-goal at the 1. Remarkably, the Chiefs held *again*. This time, on third down from the 4, the Chiefs' Steven Nelson was called for holding and the Jets got *another* first down.

Twice, the Chiefs kept the ball out of the end zone. Finally, on third down, McCown quarterback-sneaked and (at last) scored to make it 36–31.

Just to make sure the entire game became Keystone Kops, Nelson was *again* called for holding on the Jets' two-point conversion. At that point, Marcus Peters, the Chiefs' All-Pro cornerback, lost his mind, picking up the flag lying in the end zone and hurling it into the stands. He was, of course, whistled for unsportsmanlike conduct. The Jets then scored on the second conversion attempt, making it 38–31.

"The whole thing was insane," Smith said later. "They hadn't called defensive holding the entire game and, just like that, every play was defensive holding. We're all on the sidelines going, 'What the hell is going on here?' It was unreal."

The Chiefs still had 2:15 left to try for a tying touchdown. Smith completed yet another long pass to Hill, this one for 40 yards to the Jets' 23. There was still plenty of time left—1:19—but no time-outs.

Smith completed a short pass to Kelce for 4 yards to the 19. But then he threw incomplete to Hunt; incomplete to Demarcus Robinson; and finally, on fourth down, incomplete to Kelce—who looked open for a split second inside the 10. It looked as if Kelce had been bumped as he was about to come open, but there was no flag.

Game over.

Smith almost never yells at officials. There is often an ongoing dialogue between quarterbacks and referees. Sometimes it's just chatter— how's the family; can you believe how cold it is; long time, no see. Other times the referee might warn a quarterback to tell his left tackle he's very close to a holding call. Other times the quarterback might ask, "What was that call about?" Or "I got clocked, where's the flag?"

As with anything else, quarterbacks get along with some officials better than others. Referee Brad Allen was one of Smith's favorites— both on a personal and a professional level.

Not at that moment. He turned and screamed at Allen, "Where's the flag?" and a few other things not repeatable if children are in the room.

"I was furious," Smith said. "There's probably no one in the league who gets held more than Kels. They'd called our guys for breathing on theirs again and again five minutes earlier. Now they saw *nothing?*"

The final was 38–31. If Smith and the Chiefs never saw a "Welcome to New Jersey" sign again, that would be just fine.

They had lost six of seven and were 6-6. The cushion was gone. They were tied for the AFC West lead with the Chargers. Twelve weeks into the season, they were, essentially, back on square one.

"The good news," Smith said, knotting his tie before going to meet the media, "is everything we wanted from this season is still in play. We just have to figure out how to get pointed in the right direction again."

He smiled. "And we need to do it soon. Very soon."

21

On the same day (November 2) that Andrew Luck's 2017 season officially ended—when the Indianapolis Colts put him on season-ending injured reserve—the league lost another star quarterback.

This time, it was Deshaun Watson, the Houston Texans' brilliant rookie, who tore an ACL in practice that day—ending his season and, for all intents and purposes, the Texans' season.

For some reason, Coach Tom O'Brien had decided to start Tom Savage in the season opener against Jacksonville, and the result was a 27–9 loss. A week later, O'Brien came to his senses and turned the reins over to Watson, who soon made the quarterback-starved teams that had passed on him in the draft look silly. The Texans were 3-3 with Watson as the starter before he was injured.

That meant the game that Sunday in Houston between the Texans and Colts would be a battle of backup quarterbacks, something that happens all too frequently in the NFL: Savage, restored to the starting role when Watson went down, and Jacoby Brissett, who had done a respectable job since taking over the Colts' offense in week two.

The Colts won 20–14 to raise their record to 3-6. They would not win again until the final week of the season, even though they were competitive most weeks. They beat the Texans again in their finale, 22–13. By then, T. J. Yates, who had been signed after the Watson injury, was Houston's starting quarterback.

The New Year's Eve win in Lucas Oil Stadium was bittersweet—to say the least. The announced attendance was 60,577, although the crowd was probably closer to 50,000—not a bad number given the Colts' record.

Even though it wasn't Chuck Pagano's fault that his starting quarterback had missed the entire season, someone had to take the fall for the team's 4-12 record. General manager Chris Ballard had been hired only a year earlier, and unfortunately NFL owners don't fire themselves— even when they deserve firing (see Snyder, Dan; Jones, Jerry et al.).

That left Pagano, who had arrived at the same time as Luck (in 2012), only to miss much of his quarterback's rookie year when Pagano was diagnosed with leukemia. He came back for the final game of the regular season after missing eleven weeks.

Luck remembered that stretch vividly. He had often gone to the hospital to visit Pagano. "Coby Fleener and I went over pretty regularly. We would stop at Jimmy John's, pick up sandwiches, and then go sit with Chuck. The way he handled the whole thing was amazing. Never complained, even though you knew the chemo was no fun."

With his cancer in remission, Pagano led the Colts to the playoffs the next two seasons, and to the AFC championship game at the conclusion of the 2014 season. The Colts lost that game—the infamous Deflategate game—45–7, and it was mostly downhill after that. Luck first hurt his shoulder three games into the 2015 season, and the team that had won eleven games three seasons in a row began to slide.

—

After going on injured reserve, Luck spent two months in the town of Laren, Holland—a town of about 11,000 that was about a thirty-minute drive from downtown Amsterdam. Having spent much of his boyhood in Europe, Luck was comfortable being there. It also got him away from all the questions and the glare of a white-hot spotlight he couldn't avoid.

He and Nicole settled in to a small Airbnb apartment, and Andrew went to work. "I took two days off from the rehab work in two months," he said. "I wanted to do the work, and I knew I needed to do it. We took a day trip to Antwerp, and I took one rest day. That was it. Honestly, though, I wouldn't have gotten through it if not for Nicole."

If anything, Nicole Pechanec had been through more in her athletic career than Luck. She was born in Newark, New Jersey, to Czechoslovakian parents and was homeschooled beginning in third grade so she could focus time on her gymnastics career. At fifteen, she moved to Czechoslovakia to train with the Czech national team and represented that country in the World Games and the European Championships.

She came back to the United States to go to Stanford, which is where she and Luck met as freshmen. She got a degree in architectural design—the same degree Luck holds—from Stanford and then, in the spring of 2017, got a business degree from Indiana—commuting the fifty miles down SR-37 each day to Bloomington. Going up and down SR-37 between Indianapolis and Bloomington is a difficult drive, especially in winter when the weather's bad, and even more so because it is one of *the* speed-trap havens in America.

"It isn't just that she was willing to do anything she could to help me," Luck said. "It's that she's tough. She knows what training is like, what it's like to feel pain, and what it's like to have to work really hard. There's no way I get through those two months without her."

After arriving in Holland, Luck got worse before he got better—physically, but even more so, emotionally.

"First few weeks weren't good," he said. "I was in pain and I was wondering when I was going to start to feel better. I don't remember exactly when I bottomed, but I did. But then, slowly, I started to get better. By the time we came home in late December, I knew I still had a ways to go, but now I *knew*—really knew—that I was getting better. I stopped trying to talk myself into feeling better and just listened to my body. Once I started doing that, I was headed in the right direction."

He didn't even bring his phone with him so as not to be in a position where he might be tempted to return phone calls from media members he knew who were bound to try to reach him. "We communicated with people through Nicole's phone," he said. "That was it."

He and Nicole spent Christmas in their Laren apartment, eating a traditional Czech Christmas dinner of codfish stew and potato salad. Nicole cooked. "I was the sous chef," Luck said, laughing.

Two days later, they flew home to be at the Colts' finale against the Houston Texans.

By then the Colts were 3-12 and it was a foregone conclusion that Pagano was going to be fired. Luck wanted to be there.

"I mean I didn't know a hundred percent," he said. "No one had told me—I'd been completely out of the loop anyway. I came into the league with Chuck as my coach. We did some great things as a team under Chuck. Made the playoffs three straight years, a conference championship game. I know now just how hard it is to do that."

The Colts beat the Texans, 22–13—meaning two of their four wins were against Houston—and team owner Jim Irsay presented the game ball to Pagano in the locker room.

A few minutes later, he fired him.

"I'm pretty sure he'd told Chuck beforehand," Luck said. "I was just glad to be there to see him go out with a win."

He was also glad to be back in the United States and ready to face the media and his future. He was no longer trying to convince himself he was getting better.

"I *was* better," he said. "Not ready to play better, but this time actually on the way to getting there. That was a long way from where I'd been in October."

—

After the Ravens' loss to the Vikings in late October dropped Baltimore to 3-4, there was something approaching panic in Baltimore. There was talk that if the Ravens missed the playoffs for a third straight season, Coach John Harbaugh's job might be on the line. There was serious grumbling about Joe Flacco's play, and even the sainted Ozzie Newsome was being questioned. What had he been thinking with some of his draft picks? Notably the 2015 number one pick wasted on the ironhanded wide receiver Breshad Perriman.

The Miami Dolphins came to Baltimore for a Thursday night game and proved to be an almost perfect salve for what was ailing the Ravens.

The Dolphins were one of the NFL's surprise teams. They had lost quarterback Ryan Tannehill for the season during preseason and had coaxed Jay Cutler, the mercurial ex-Broncos and ex-Bears quarterback, out of retirement to take his place. Cutler had played reasonably well, and the Dolphins had beaten Tennessee and then won at Atlanta in mid-October before playing the New York Jets in the fabulously named Hard Rock Stadium.

In the third quarter, Cutler was hammered (by the Jets' Janoris Jenkins) as he threw a deep ball to wide receiver Kenny Stills. Cutler had to be helped off, his ribs cracked.

Matt Moore came in and led a fourth-quarter rally, the Dolphins coming from 28–14 down to win 31–28, raising their record to a surprising 4-2.

There's an old saying in football that when a team is struggling, the most popular man in town is the backup quarterback. The Dolphins were actually playing better than most people had expected, but Moore was still the most popular man in town: fans had chanted "We want Moore" during the team's home opener.

When Moore led the Dolphins back against the Jets, the local media took up the cry, saying the Dolphins were clearly better off with Moore playing quarterback. Many said that the Dolphins were fortunate that they were playing in Baltimore on Thursday because the short week made it less likely Cutler would be able to play.

The media and fans got their wish. Moore started against the Ravens. He threw two touchdown passes—both to the Ravens. The final was 40–0. It was as if someone forgot to tell the Dolphins the game was on Thursday.

Flacco threw a 34-yard touchdown pass to Jeremy Maclin in the first quarter, then Justin Tucker kicked a 55-yard field goal (ho-hum for him) in the second quarter to make it 10–0.

The Ravens began driving again late in the quarter. On a third-and-10 from the Dolphins' 20, Flacco did something he rarely does—he took off on a scramble. As tacklers closed in on him, he went toward the ground into a quarterback slide. The rules say once a quarterback slides, he isn't supposed to be hit. He's already conceding yardage because the ball is marked where he slides, not where his feet end up.

As Flacco went down, Dolphins linebacker Kiko Alonso flew at him and appeared to make no attempt to avoid a direct hit to Flacco's head. His shoulder slammed into Flacco, knocking his helmet off. Flacco rolled onto his right side briefly, and his left hand came up in a "check, please" signal.

Watching the game on TV, Alex Smith, who had taken plenty of hits like that himself, saw the "check, please" signal and shook his head. "He was not of this world at that moment," he said. "I know what that feels like. The only good news is, he won't remember much of anything."

While Flacco rolled onto his back out cold, Ravens center Ryan Jensen flew at Alonso and knocked *his* helmet off. Alonso ended up right in front of the Ravens bench and found himself in a shouting match with a furious John Harbaugh.

The medical staff came out, got Flacco to his feet, and helped him walk to the locker room.

"I have absolutely no memory of walking to the locker room," Flacco said. "I remember feeling the hit and maybe for a split second thinking, 'Oh boy, this isn't good.' I felt some serious pain in my neck from the helmet coming off. After that, the next few minutes are blank."

Upstairs, in the Flacco family box, Dana Flacco had been chatting with her friend Ashley Heap—wife of the Ravens' former tight end Todd Heap. The Flaccos and Heaps were close friends. The Heaps had been through an unspeakable tragedy in April when Todd, unaware that their three-year-old daughter Holly was playing in the driveway, pulled his SUV forward and hit her. The little girl died soon after arriving at the hospital.

The Flaccos had flown to Mesa, Arizona, to spend time with the Heaps after the accident. The family had four other children and was still grieving when the Heaps came to Baltimore for a visit.

"I was sort of half watching, talking to Ashley," Dana said. "I saw Joe get hit and, at the time, didn't think that much about it. Joe gets hit all the time and he always gets up. I think of him as sort of unbreakable.

"Then I turned and watched the replay on the TV and I thought, 'Uh-oh.' When they took him off the field, I figured I better get downstairs and see how he's doing."

Flacco came back to planet earth sitting on the training table in the locker room. The doctors were giving him phase one of the NFL's current concussion protocol. The questions were simple: What's today? (Might have been confusing since it was Thursday.) Who are you playing? What's the score? By then, Ryan Mallett had come in, and the Ravens had gone the last 5 yards to make it 20–0. Alonso had been given a personal foul penalty but hadn't been ejected—which infuriated the crowd. At that moment Flacco was *their* Joe again.

Flacco did well enough with the test that the doctors didn't give him phase two at that moment. In phase two, the player is given a number of facts and then, ten minutes later, is asked to recite them back. There wasn't much point in giving Flacco phase two there and then. He had been out cold. He had a concussion. No way was he going to play again that night. He would have to be reexamined and pass the protocol before he could practice or think about playing the next week in Tennessee.

"I remember I could answer every question, but I struggled with 'Who did we play last week?'" he said. "At first I couldn't remember. Then it came back to me that we'd been in Minnesota."

Dana Flacco had arrived outside the Ravens' locker room just as the players were filing in for halftime.

"Obviously I couldn't go in right then," she said. "But Harry Swayne [a former offensive tackle, now the Ravens' director of player engagement] came out to tell me Joe was okay, that he was conscious and talking and answering questions. That was a relief."

Dana waited until halftime was over, then went inside to see her husband. She could tell that he wasn't quite himself, but there didn't appear to be any serious damage. By the end of the third quarter, the doctors allowed her to drive him home.

"I'm not sure if I knew the final score," he said. "I was able to follow on my phone. I knew we were in control and won pretty easily."

They won 40–0, the three second-half touchdowns coming on a recovered fumble in the end zone and two pick-sixes.

The Ravens were 4-4 and had ten days off. The fans and media who had been questioning Flacco's play were suddenly very quiet. They knew the Ravens weren't going anywhere with Mallett as their starting quarterback.

Flacco has often played hurt—as almost every player in the NFL does at some point. But this wasn't as simple. He couldn't just say, "Coach, I'm good to go." The doctors had to clear him.

They did—on Wednesday. The one remaining issue for Flacco was getting his helmet on and off, because he'd needed two stitches in his right ear where the helmet had been ripped off his head.

Alonso was fined $9,115 for the hit but not suspended—which surprised many, if not most. His defense was that the play was bang-bang and he couldn't avoid the contact. The replays showed that he might not have been able to avoid contact, but he had clearly lowered his shoulder into Flacco's helmet. One person not upset about the lack of a suspension was Flacco.

"It's football," he said. "People like to see us do battle. That's part of the game. Things happen."

What mattered most was that the Ravens had their oft-maligned starter back. They lost a tight game in Tennessee but then took advantage of a schedule that turned out to be a lot softer than it had looked at the start of the season.

A trip to Lambeau Field in November to face the Packers and Aaron Rodgers looks daunting in April when the NFL releases its schedule.

A trip to Lambeau Field in November to face the Packers and Brett Hundley isn't nearly as daunting.

The list of NFL teams that can withstand the loss of a starting quarterback is a short one. When the quarterback is the caliber of Rodgers—or Andrew Luck or even Deshaun Watson based on just six games—the drop-off is massive. It isn't as if Hundley, in his second season, was terrible. He was okay, maybe even fine. But the trip from Aaron Rodgers to fine is a long one, especially given Rodgers's capacity for winning games in the last two minutes.

There was no chance for Hundley to win the game against the Ravens in the last two minutes. On the game's opening drive, the Packers drove to the Ravens' 5-yard line. From there, Hundley tried to find Randall Cobb in the end zone. But Jimmy Smith dove in front of Cobb and intercepted the pass.

That pretty much summed up the day for Hundley and the Packers. The quarterback threw three interceptions, and Green Bay turned the ball over five times—the third five-turnover game of the season for the Ravens' defense.

Baltimore's offense hardly lit things up. It was only 6–0 at halftime, even though the Packers had turned the ball over three times. The Ravens took the opening kickoff of the second half and quickly drove 59 yards in just four plays, Flacco hitting Mike Wallace from 21 yards out for the touchdown that made it 13–0. Given the state of the Packers' offense, that was an insurmountable lead. The Ravens got a final late touchdown after Marlon Humphrey intercepted Hundley at the Packers' 18 and returned it to the 3. Alex Collins scored on the next play, and the final was 23–0—the Ravens' second shutout in three weeks against a backup quarterback.

Although the Ravens' offense had sputtered in the first half, it was plenty good enough for an easy win. Flacco was 22-of-28 for 183 yards and the touchdown pass to Wallace.

Flacco knew that Rodgers's absence made the afternoon entirely different than if he had been on the field.

"There's always a part of you that wants to go out and compete against the best," he said. "The thing you say before a game like that is, 'It's not me against Aaron Rodgers, I don't play defense.' But you know who is on the other sideline.

"On the other hand, the goal is to win games. Nothing's been especially easy for us this season. Every team gets good breaks and bad, that's part of football. We lost Dennis [Pitta], and that certainly hurt us. We lost Marshal [Yanda], that hurt. Those are two of our best players. There's a reason why people like to say the healthiest team wins. You can't whine about injuries, you have to move forward and win with whoever is out there with you. No one really cares if you have injuries.

"Was it good luck for us that Aaron couldn't play? Sure. But it was out of our control. You go out and play with your best against their best—whoever it happens to be.

"The best thing is we now control our own fate. The one and only goal is to get to the playoffs. Once you're there, anything can happen—we've proved that in the past. It doesn't matter how you get there, just that you do."

Remarkably, the Ravens, at 5-5, were sitting in the second wildcard spot in the AFC based on tiebreakers. There were still six games left, but the schedule—if it could be believed—seemed to favor them.

"That's the thing," Flacco said. "People like to look at the schedule and say, 'Win, loss, win,' and it's meaningless. You never know where teams are going to be when you play—your team and the other team.

"I'm sure when people looked at our schedule before the season they saw the Bears at home—that's a win. Then they saw the Packers on the road—that's a loss. How'd that work out?"

It worked out that the loss to the Bears was mitigated by the win over the Packers.

A week later, the Ravens faced their third backup quarterback in four weeks in a Monday night game in Baltimore.

Once upon a time, playing on Monday night was considered a big deal by NFL players. It was a chance to play on network television with everyone else in the league watching. The presence of ABC and Frank Gifford, Howard Cosell, and Don Meredith was an *event* in whatever city was hosting the game.

From 1970 to 1983, MNF—as it came to be known—became an iconic part of the sports landscape. Although Meredith left for three seasons for big money from NBC and then returned, what made the broadcasts unique was Cosell. There has never been a more polarizing figure in sports broadcasting than Cosell. *TV Guide* once did a poll among viewers in which Cosell was found to be the most beloved *and* the most hated television voice in the country.

Cosell was brilliant. Because he was not an ex-jock, he was willing to be critical and to ask tough questions in interviews. He and Meredith played off each other perfectly: the ex-lawyer from New York City pairing off with the ex-quarterback country boy, born and raised in Texas, who had starred in Dallas as the Cowboys became America's Team in the 1960s.

Meredith called Cosell "Harrd" in his Southern twang, and Cosell called Meredith "Danderoo" in his nasal Brooklyn accent. It was TV magic.

But the act broke up after the 1983 season, when Cosell decided he wanted nothing to do with football anymore. For years, ABC ran one jock after another into the booth—among them O. J. Simpson, Joe Namath, and Alex Karras. None came close to Cosell and Meredith. In fact, Meredith was never the same after Cosell left.

Al Michaels became the play-by-play man in 1986 and had a decent run with Dan Dierdorf as the color commentator. It was only when ABC was able to hire John Madden to partner with Michaels in 2002 that MNF got some of its magic back.

By then, though, MNF simply wasn't that big a deal. The NFL, which can never get enough of a good (read: profitable) thing, had added a Sunday night game in 1987, which took away the uniqueness of the Monday night games.

By 2005, ABC had cut way back on sports programming—by then it was owned by Disney, as was ESPN—and decided to let go of a thirty-six-year franchise.

When the new television contract began in 2006, Monday Night Football had become a cable franchise—on ESPN—and Sunday Night Football had moved from ESPN to NBC. What's more, the NFL started televising games on Thursday night in the second half of the season.

Playing at night became not only ho-hum but a nuisance for teams, players, and fans. Teams didn't mind Sunday nights so much because it just meant a later Sunday kickoff—although all athletes would rather play earlier in the day. No one likes to sit around all day waiting to play. Monday nights meant you had a short week to prepare for the next opponent.

That had always been the case, but in the early years no one minded much because of the glam factor of playing in the game. Thursdays were considered a pox from day one, but the league didn't care because it meant more money.

The Texans-Ravens game was a perfect example of how far Monday Night Football had fallen. The most important regular season property to the NFL had become the Sunday night games. NBC had hired Michaels and Madden in 2006, and when Madden retired, Cris Collinsworth had very ably taken his place.

More important, the NFL had added "flex" games to the late-season schedule, meaning NBC could cherry-pick games based on which ones were most important. ESPN didn't have that flexibility and often got stuck with duds, especially late in the season.

The importance and fragility of NFL quarterbacks were never more apparent than in the ESPN press release promoting the Monday night schedule for 2017. After ballyhooing an opening night doubleheader, the release mentioned one or both starting quarterbacks in fourteen of their fifteen game summaries.

October 9—"Sam Bradford and the Vikings travel to Chicago to take on the Bears." Except by then, Case Keenum was the Vikings' quarterback.

November 6—"Matthew Stafford and the Lions travel to Green Bay to face the Packers and Aaron Rodgers." Unfortunately, "the Packers and Brett Hundley" didn't have quite the same ring.

A week later it was "Ryan Tannehill and the resurgent Dolphins take on Cam Newton and the Carolina Panthers in Charlotte." Tannehill was long gone. The good news—sort of—was Jay Cutler had returned to replace Matt Moore.

For the December 4 Steelers-Bengals game, both starting quarterbacks—Ben Roethlisberger and Andy Dalton—were healthy. The problem was that Dalton's Bengals were 5-6 by then.

And finally, on December 25, Christmas night was to be lit up by a matchup between Carson Wentz's Eagles and Derek Carr's Raiders . . . but it was Nick Foles's Eagles who lit up the Raiders, 19–10, as Oakland limped to a 6-10 finish.

If Watson had been healthy, the Texans and Ravens might have been worth watching for non-Texans and non-Ravens fans. Instead, after Tom Savage led the Texans on a touchdown drive to start the game, the Ravens' defense pretty much dominated the rest of the night.

Flacco and the offense were again conservative and efficient. Trailing

7–0, they scored touchdowns on back-to-back second-quarter series, the second coming on a 46-yard drive set up by a Savage interception. The second TD, on a short Alex Collins run, made it 14–7. The teams spent the second half trading field goals, and the Ravens won 23–16.

A week later, the Ravens' offense came to life against the Lions in a 44–20 rout. The Ravens led 20–0 at halftime. The Lions twice got within a touchdown, but each time Baltimore responded with a drive that widened the lead again. A late pick-six by safety Eric Weddle produced the last touchdown.

The win made the Ravens 7-5 and put them alone in second place in the wildcard standings. They weren't going to catch the Steelers, who were 10-2 and riding a seven-game winning streak. The Steelers were next up on the Ravens' schedule, and even though the game was in Pittsburgh, there was hope.

In Flacco's first nine seasons, the Ravens and Steelers had played twenty-one times. The Ravens had lost the first three in 2008, Flacco's rookie year, but had gone 10-8 since then, including 6-4 inside Heinz Field.

"I like playing there," Flacco said. "It's a great atmosphere to play football. There's never any problem getting wired for the game: the opponent and the setting do that for you. Doesn't matter where we play, the games always seem to be close."

A year earlier, on Christmas, the Ravens and Steelers had played in Pittsburgh with the AFC North title on the line. The Steelers were 9-5, the Ravens 8-6. A Steelers win would clinch the division title, but a Ravens win would put them in control with one week to go, since both teams would be 9-6 and the Ravens would own the tiebreaker with two victories over Pittsburgh.

The Ravens led 20–10 early in the fourth quarter. The Steelers rallied to lead 24–20, but then Flacco took his team the length of the field to a touchdown that gave the Ravens a 27–24 lead with 1:18 left.

"Too much time," Flacco said later. "For Ben, that's an eternity."

As great as Tom Brady is in late-game situations, Roethlisberger is every bit as good. Like Brady, he's cool under pressure, but he has one thing Brady doesn't have: the ability to extend plays. He's so big and strong, at six feet six and 235 pounds, that he's hard to bring down in the pocket, and yet he's quick enough to escape a rush and keep a play going.

It took him ten plays and 1:09 to take his team 75 yards, capping the drive with a 4-yard pass to Antonio Brown with nine seconds left. With a win, the Ravens would almost certainly have been in the playoffs for the seventh time in nine seasons in the Harbaugh-Flacco era. Instead, they were home in January for a second straight season.

The exception to Flacco's rule about always playing close games against Pittsburgh had been the 26–9 Steelers win in Baltimore in October. The team had been booed loudly during that game—first for kneeling prior to the national anthem, then for playing poorly. Both teams had improved greatly since then. Normally, playing the Ravens at home would be the most important game on the Steelers' December schedule. But with the AFC North wrapped up and the Patriots coming to town in another week in a game that would almost certainly decide home-field advantage for the playoffs, there was reason to think the Steelers might be looking ahead just a little.

It certainly didn't start out that way, the Steelers taking a quick 14–0 lead that had everyone on the Baltimore sideline wondering if this was going to be a "here we go again" game. It wasn't. Flacco got the offense going, and the Steelers' lead was 20–14 at halftime. The Ravens actually led 31–20 in the third quarter—meaning they'd outscored the Steelers, 31–7, during a two-quarter stretch.

Naturally, though, Roethlisberger rallied the Steelers, as he's done so many times in his Hall of Fame career. The game came down to Flacco's offense going three-and-out with a 38–36 lead and Roethlisberger taking his offense into range for a 43-yard Chris Boswell field goal with forty-two seconds left that provided a 39–38 final margin.

Roethlisberger made play after play throughout the fourth quarter, bringing back some nightmarish memories for the Ravens. He'd been doing this for fourteen seasons.

This loss was different from the 2016 loss, though, because it came with three games left to play. The Ravens dropped to 7-6, but if they could win out, they would still make postseason, which, as Flacco says, is the only goal when the regular season begins.

Their final three games were at Cleveland and then at home against the Colts and the Bengals. The combined record of those three teams was 8-31.

It was December in the NFL. The weather was cold and mostly miserable. There was no room left for excuses. No one believed that more passionately than Joe Flacco.

22

In the aftermath of the Chiefs' second loss in three weeks in the Meadowlands, Kansas City coach Andy Reid was asked in his postgame press conference how he felt about his quarterback's play.

"I saw some good things," Reid said. "We had some explosive plays out there. Our biggest problem today was that the defense couldn't get off the field."

Alex Smith had actually played his best game in a month against the Jets. He threw four touchdown passes and took off on a dazzling 70-yard run, which had made him his team's leading rusher for the game.

No one expects any quarterback to run for 70 yards on one play. But Reid had seen early on in Smith's tenure in Kansas City that his quarterback had both the speed and the shiftiness to turn a broken play into a big one.

That's what happened in the second quarter against the Jets. On a second-and-10 from the 14, Smith had dropped, found no one open, and took off around the right side. He had plenty of running room and admitted later his mind flashed back to when he was a kid and felt like he could outrun anyone on the field.

"We're eighty-six yards from the goal line, I'm not thinking about anything but getting a first down," he said. "Then I got near midfield and I sensed someone coming up from behind looking to strip me, so I ducked and he missed. Then I made someone else miss. For an instant I thought, 'Maybe I can score,' but then they pinned me at the sideline and got me out-of-bounds. I have to admit, I was a little bit winded."

Coincidence or not, the offense bogged down there, settling for a field goal. That didn't mean Smith didn't get a good deal of ribbing the next day back home in Kansas City about his surprising speed: surprising for thirty-three and surprising for a white guy.

"There was a lot of that in the quarterback room," he said, smiling.

"Both about my age and my skin color. If you're going to be in that room, you better be able to take it as well as dish it out."

No one was happy with the loss, but for Reid, there was some sense of relief that the offense had looked more like the offense of the first seven weeks than the offense of the previous four. He had come under a good deal of pressure in the wake of the loss to the Giants to consider benching Smith in favor of Mahomes. It wasn't surprising that the local media would bring it up—which someone had in the postgame press conference—because no one had ever seen Mahomes make a bad play and because of the old football cliché about the backup quarterback being the most popular guy in town.

But even some in the national media had publicly wondered if it wasn't time to make the switch to Mahomes, including the highly respected Mike Florio of *Pro Football Talk* and NBC.

Smith knew he hadn't been playing well. He also knew he wasn't the only one, but he wasn't about to say that publicly.

"It was frustrating," he admitted. "I was doing a weekly radio hit, and for the first half of the season the hosts introduced me as 'the highest-ranked passer in the National Football League.' Well, I had dropped all the way to number two—behind Tom Brady—and it seemed like everyone out there wanted me benched."

Smith was in his thirteenth season in the league and had been through as many ups and downs as anyone who had ever played the quarterback position. He might have been frustrated, but he knew this sort of thing came with the territory. On the other hand, his wife, Elizabeth, saw it differently: it was all unfair, not to mention wrong.

"I think it's harder to watch than it is to play when someone you care about is involved," Smith said. "After the Giants game, when it seemed as if I was getting killed by everyone, I got home and she was very fired up.

"We always sit up and talk after games once the kids are in bed—win or lose—because we're both a little too wound up to sleep. She wasn't at all happy that night."

When Reid, who lived across the street from the Smiths, heard that, he laughed. "I wondered about the smoke coming out of their house that night," he said. "I guess that was what it was."

Smith's play against the Jets quieted the mob to some degree. Reid had promised to "look at everything, starting by looking in the mirror," after the Giants game and had lived up to his promise by handing the play-calling duties to Matt Nagy. He did not, however, want to leave his players with the impression that others might not get looked at—including his quarterback.

"If I'm looking at myself, that means I'm looking at everybody," he said. "I've always believed when things go wrong, the first person you need to look at is you. I did that. Fortunately, the change in play-callers seemed to work, so I didn't feel as if I had to do anything radical."

While the performance of the offense in New Jersey against the Jets was encouraging, the bottom line was that the Chiefs had lost—again—to a bad team. Most of the national media that week focused on the fact that the Chargers, who had bounced back from their 0-4 start to tie the Chiefs and Raiders for the division lead at 6-6, were now the clear favorites to win the West.

Smith didn't see it that way. "We certainly haven't played well for a while," he said. "But we're tied for first place, and the two teams we're tied with are coming to our place the next two weeks. We still have our fate in our hands. That's about all you can ask for at this stage of the season."

Actually, if you were the Patriots, you could ask to have your division wrapped up at this stage of the season. Or, in 2017, if you were the Eagles, the same was true. The Steelers and Vikings were very close to that status. Everyone else was scuffling to fill the eight remaining playoff spots.

By now, Smith knew it was pretty much a given that Mahomes would be the Chiefs' quarterback in 2018. He had known that on the night they drafted him. He and Reid hadn't discussed it at all once the season started. There would be time for that when it was over. It seemed as if the only way Smith *might* return was if the Chiefs won the Super Bowl: it's awfully hard to trade or release a quarterback who has just held the Vince Lombardi Trophy in his hands. The Ravens had done that with Trent Dilfer in 2001, and that hadn't worked out so well.

John Elway had retired after the Broncos' Super Bowl win in 1999, and Peyton Manning had done the same after leading Denver to the title in 2016. Jeff Hostetler, who had led the Giants to the Super Bowl in 1991 after Phil Simms had been injured, was placed into open competition with Simms for the quarterback job going into the next season. That didn't work out too well either.

For the moment, Smith wasn't thinking about the Super Bowl. He only wanted to be sure his team would have the chance to compete in the tournament that led to the Super Bowl.

The Jets game, even though it had been a loss, proved to be a turning point—or, at the very least, a nadir. The Chiefs had started out 4-0 at home but had lost their last two at Arrowhead. The thought of losing three in a row there was . . . well . . . unthinkable.

They jumped on the Raiders right from the start. The defense *did* get off the field, completely bottling Derek Carr up for three quarters.

Leading 3–0 late in the first quarter, the Chiefs drove 86 yards in fourteen plays—mixing runs with Smith passes. For the first time since early October, Hunt looked like the back who had been the scourge of the league throughout September. He would finish the day with 116 yards on 35 carries—his first 100-yard day since week five of the season. He also scored the game's first touchdown on a 1-yard plunge after what had looked like a 17-yard Smith–to–Travis Kelce touchdown pass was reversed on review and the ball was placed on the 1.

The score was 16–0 at halftime and grew to 26–0 by the end of three quarters. Carr threw two interceptions, and his lone touchdown pass came with 3:22 left and made the final a much-closer-than-it-really-was 26–15.

The Chiefs had finally gotten all three units—offense, defense, special teams (Harrison Butker, who had clanked a 38-yard field goal in the Jets game, was 4-of-4)—going all at the same time. It was, to put it mildly, a relief.

"Knew it was in there somewhere," Smith said with a laugh. "We just had to dig around and find it."

They had to be sure not to misplace it, though, because the Chargers were coming to town for one of those late-season Saturday night specials in six days.

The Chargers were one of football's hottest teams. Since their terrible start, they had two losses: one in New England to the Patriots and the other in overtime in Jacksonville. They were coming off an easy 28–6 win over Washington a week earlier and brimming with confidence.

Even though the game was in Kansas City, most experts leaned to the Chargers in their pregame predictions. Las Vegas made the Chargers a one-point favorite. Even Joel Thorman, writing for the website Arrowhead Pride, picked the Chargers: 28–27. Philip Rivers, the Chargers' quarterback, who had been the number four pick in the same 2004 draft that had produced Eli Manning and Ben Roethlisberger, was playing as well as ever at the age of thirty-seven. Manning and Roethlisberger had won two Super Bowls. Rivers had never gone beyond a conference championship game, but he had been the Chargers' glue throughout most of his career.

For two and a half quarters the game swung back and forth, which was pretty much what the 75,011 in the stadium had expected. The Chiefs led 10–0 early after Smith found Tyreek Hill for a 64-yard score midway through the second quarter. The Chargers came back with two touchdown drives of their own, one late in the second quarter, one early in the third, and took a 13–10 lead. The Chiefs responded with a time-killing drive (rare for them) that ended with Hunt catching a 3-yard pass from Smith to make it 17–13 with 2:10 left in the third.

It set up what should have been a wild fourth quarter. But a funny thing happened next: the Chargers collapsed. Or the Chiefs' defense became the Monsters of the Midway. Probably something in between.

In thirteen prior games, Rivers had thrown a total of seven interceptions: four in twelve games against teams not from Kansas City and three against the Chiefs in their September game in Los Angeles.

All of a sudden, he and the Chargers became a turnover machine.

It started when Marcus Peters intercepted a Rivers pass at his own 32 and took it back 62 yards to the Chargers' 6. Peters hadn't played the previous week against the Raiders because Reid had suspended him after he'd thrown the flag into the stands late in the Jets game and then had left the field thinking he'd been ejected when he hadn't been.

Peters was a handful. He was also a major talent. The Chiefs were hurt by a false start after the interception and settled for a Butker field goal that made it 20–13. One possession later, Austin Ekeler caught a short pass from Rivers, got hit by Peters, and coughed the ball up. Ron Parker came up with it. That led to another Butker field goal and a 23–13 lead.

Then Parker intercepted Rivers trying to find Antonio Gates, his Hall of Fame-to-be tight end, down the seam at the Chiefs' 35. From there, Smith patiently took his team to the end zone. Hunt scored from the 5 to make it 30–13 with 3:57 to go. Just for good measure, Peters intercepted Rivers for a second time, meaning the Chargers' four possessions after taking the 13–10 lead had produced, in order: interception, fumble, interception, interception.

Rivers would not be intercepted in the Chargers' final two games of the season—both wins—meaning he finished with ten for the year; six against the Chiefs.

None of that mattered to the Chiefs. They had pulled themselves out of their funk and beaten their two rivals for the division title by a combined 56–28 in back-to-back weeks. They had virtually clinched the division.

A week later, they made it official with a 29–13 win in Miami. It was the first time in the franchise's fifty-eight-year history that it had won back-to-back division titles. Smith's leadership was no longer being questioned in Kansas City.

In four games, starting with the loss to the Jets, he had thrown seven touchdown passes and one interception. He had been almost flawless, and Hunt, who had rushed for 155 yards against the Chargers, appeared to be back where he had been early in the season.

Smith walked off the field in Miami with a warm feeling of satisfaction. The Chiefs had bottomed and then returned to the top when it mattered most.

But the NFL is an unpredictable place to work. Smith had no idea that he had just won a game for the last time in a Kansas City uniform.

—

Before the end of the season, seventeen NFL teams had, for one reason or another, started a quarterback other than their starter. Some were just for rest—as with Patrick Mahomes starting the Chiefs' finale in Denver in place of Smith (since Kansas City's seed in the playoffs—number four—was already locked in).

Most of the twelve teams that would make the playoffs had the benefit of healthy, consistent play from their quarterbacks for all or most of the season: Tom Brady in New England; Ben Roethlisberger in Pittsburgh; Blake Bortles in Jacksonville; Drew Brees in New Orleans; Cam Newton in Carolina; and Matt Ryan in Atlanta started all sixteen games.

Smith and Jared Goff in Los Angeles sat out their finales with their teams' playoff positions set in stone. Tyrod Taylor was benched in Buffalo for a half when his coach, Sean McDermott, had a mind-block and decided that rookie Nathan Peterman gave his team a better chance to beat the Chargers in week eleven. The experiment lasted thirty minutes—and five Peterman interceptions—leading to a 52–24 Los Angeles win. Marcus Mariota missed one game in October for Tennessee with a pulled hamstring. That meant the quarterbacks from ten of the playoff games missed zero games or one game.

Only two teams who played postseason had any real issues at the quarterback position. The Vikings had believed Sam Bradford was their answer at quarterback, but after Bradford was hurt and then returned to play poorly, Case Keenum won the job and went on to have an impressive season.

Carson Wentz appeared to be on his way to being the league's MVP before he tore the ACL and MCL in his left knee on December 10 in Los Angeles against the Rams. That had been one of the season's most anticipated late-season games: Goff vs. Wentz, the top two picks in the 2016 draft, who had both had breakout second seasons.

Goff and Wentz had spent a good deal of time together during all the events leading up to the draft and regularly texted each other. One could almost hear the ghosts of Bobby Layne and Johnny Unitas groaning at the thought of regular communication with an opponent.

The Goff-Wentz matchup lived up to expectations, both quarterbacks moving their teams up and down the field all afternoon. With the Rams leading 28–24 in the third quarter, Wentz drove the Eagles the length of the field and plunged into the end zone from the 2-yard line for a touchdown.

But his left knee got twisted between two Rams linemen on the play, and he hobbled getting up. To add penalty to injury, the Eagles' Lane Johnson was called for holding, nullifying the touchdown and pushing the ball back to the 12.

Wentz stayed in the game. On third-and-goal from the 2, he missed Alshon Jeffery in the end zone. Coach Doug Pederson—who, like his mentor, Andy Reid, wasn't afraid to go for it on fourth down—went for it. From the shotgun Wentz dropped and waited for someone to come open. And waited. Finally, just as it looked like the play was going nowhere, he threaded a pass to Jeffery, who caught it just above his shoe tops.

The Eagles led, 31–28. It was Wentz's last play of the season.

When the doctors looked at him on the sidelines, they could tell right away that something was wrong inside his knee. He went to the locker room, where an X-ray made it apparent the injury was serious. It turned out he had torn both the ACL and the MCL.

In came Nick Foles, signed more or less off the scrap heap in the off-season. He had actually considered retiring to go to seminary until the Eagles offered him the chance to back up Wentz.

While the entire city of Philadelphia was going into a state of complete depression, Foles led the Eagles on two drives that set up field goals after the Rams had taken the lead back at 35–31. The Eagles won the game 43–35, clinching the division title. It should have been a day of celebration. Instead, most Eagles fans—most people in the city—were saying, "Again, again? When do we catch a break?"

Which is what happens when your football team last won a championship in 1960 when Norm Van Brocklin—who *really* would have disapproved of texting with an opponent—was the quarterback.

—

There were other late-season jaw-droppers when it came to star quarterbacks, particularly in the largest NFL market, one with a QB who was a two-time Super Bowl champion and MVP. Eli Manning sat out a game, and the events that led to it were stunning.

The Giants were a disaster from day one of the 2017 season. There were injuries—notably to Manning's two best targets, Odell Beckham Jr. and Brandon Marshall—but that didn't explain why they started the season 0-5 and dropped to 2-9 on Thanksgiving night in a loss in Washington.

It was pretty apparent at that point that general manager Jerry Reese, who had played a major role in two Super Bowl wins, and Ben McAdoo, the coach Reese had hired after Tom Coughlin had been forced out following the 2015 season, were both sitting on very hot seats.

That may have explained McAdoo's announcement on November 28 that his team's starting quarterback the following Sunday in Oakland would be Geno Smith—the same Geno Smith who had lost his job with the Jets to Ryan Fitzpatrick because he got slugged in the locker room by a teammate, IK Enemkpali.

Manning had started 210 consecutive regular season games for the Giants, dating to November 21, 2004. That was the second-longest streak in history. Brett Favre had started 297 consecutive games and was the all-time leader. Third on the list was Peyton Manning, who had made 208 straight starts for the Colts.

In all, Eli Manning had started 222 games in a row—playoffs included—including his two MVP Super Bowl wins over the Patriots. He might not have been a Hall of Fame lock the way Peyton is, but he was going to receive serious consideration when the time came. Earlier in the season, he'd become the seventh quarterback in history to go past 50,000 yards in career passing.

McAdoo clearly didn't care about any of that. He'd gone 11-5 in his first season, and the Giants had made the playoffs as a wildcard team. But the team's complete collapse put him in serious jeopardy because, even in that first season, no one had seen him as the second coming of Bill Belichick. Or, for that matter, Tom Coughlin.

So, desperate to try to find some way to save his job, McAdoo made a desperate move: benching a quarterback who was beloved—2017 record aside—by Giants fans, not to mention his teammates, current and former.

McAdoo might have gotten a more positive response in New York if he had announced his undying allegiance to the Boston Red Sox. Or if he'd said that Lawrence Taylor was overrated. Or Phil Simms.

Manning made it worse for McAdoo by handling the whole thing with calm and class. He turned down McAdoo's offer to start the game and then come out in order to keep the streak alive, saying, "If they want to play the other guys, then play the other guys. Starting that way would only taint the streak."

He was clearly emotional that Tuesday afternoon talking to reporters, but was still calm and professional.

The day after the announcement, Giants owner John Mara said the decision could have been "handled a little differently." Then he expressed surprise at Manning's comment about not wanting to be a token starter.

Like most owners, Mara had no understanding of a locker room. How do you handle a benching differently? Why would Manning not react the way he did?

The Giants' locker room was a maelstrom by the time the team flew to Oakland to play the Raiders. No one, with the possible exception of Geno Smith, agreed with the decision.

Ex-Giants and broadcasters weighed in, including Phil Simms. And around the league, other players, especially quarterbacks, expressed shock and dismay at the benching.

"It's just baffling," Alex Smith said. "We all understand—and I know Eli understands—that when you're losing, the person who gets blamed first is the quarterback. But was there *anyone* in New York saying Eli should be benched? I don't think so. It just makes no sense, I mean no sense at all."

Geno Smith played reasonably well that Sunday, completing 21 of 34 passes for 212 yards and one touchdown. But he fumbled twice while being sacked, and the Raiders won with relative ease, 24–17, the last score of the game coming on a New York field goal in the last two minutes. The Raiders recovered the ensuing onside kick and ran out the clock.

Mara waited until the Giants flew back home before he fired McAdoo—and, just for good measure, Reese. It was a sad ending for Reese, who had followed in the footsteps of Ozzie Newsome as an African American Super Bowl–winning general manager. It may have been his failure to stop McAdoo from pulling the trigger on the Manning benching that cost him his job, although several less-than-sterling drafts probably had more to do with it.

If there had been any doubt that McAdoo was done, the Manning benching removed it. The team was 2-10, and he had clearly lost his locker room before sitting Manning down. Once that happened he had one supporter left: Geno Smith.

Steve Spagnuolo, the defensive coordinator, was named the interim coach for the remainder of the season. His first move was to announce that Manning would start the following Sunday against the Cowboys.

Upon hearing the news, Smith said he didn't understand it. "It's not like I played bad," he said of the Oakland game. "I don't know why I'm not still starting."

The answer was pretty simple: the guy taking his place was Eli Manning.

23

On November 5, Washington-east faced Washington-west, the team from D.C. traveling to the team from Seattle.

Washington-east was banged up, especially on the offensive line and coming off a second loss to the Dallas Cowboys, this one at home. The defeat dropped the team to 3-4 and, having to travel to face the 5-2 Seahawks in one of the NFL's toughest venues, the season looked close to over.

Doug Williams understood that. And so, when Russell Wilson found Doug Baldwin for a 30-yard touchdown pass with 1:34 left in the game, he packed his briefcase, left his seat in the press box at CenturyLink Field, and headed for the elevator.

He had seen this show before. His team had led the Seahawks, 10–2, entering the fourth quarter. The defense had pitched a shutout, Seattle's only points coming when Kirk Cousins was sacked in the end zone for a safety in the first quarter.

But the lead hadn't lasted. Wilson finally got his team moving early in the fourth quarter and capped a drive by finding Luke Willson for a touchdown with 11:48 left. Coach Pete Carroll elected to go for two to try to tie the game at 10–10, but the attempt failed and Washington still led, 10–8.

The teams exchanged punts, and the Seahawks took over at their own 29 with 2:22 left, needing a field goal to take the lead. They did better than that, going 71 yards in five plays, culminating with the Wilson-to-Baldwin pass for a 14–10 lead.

That's when Williams sighed, stood up, and walked to the press box elevator to go meet his team downstairs and thank the players for a great effort against a team that was almost unbeatable at home.

Then came Cousins's two strikes for 70 yards that came while Williams was waiting for the elevator.

The first one, from the Washington 30, found wide receiver Brian Quick for 31 yards. Quick had been signed in the spring as a free agent after five years with the Rams. He would finish the year with six catches. This was his longest catch of the year and, by far, his most important.

With the ball at the 39, Cousins looked down the left sideline for Josh Doctson. A year earlier, Doctson had been Washington's number one pick in the draft, chosen out of Texas Tech by Scot McCloughan, who thought he was getting the big-play wide receiver Washington needed—especially with the team's one deep threat, DeSean Jackson, going into the walk year of his contract.

Doctson had hurt an Achilles heel in preseason in 2016 and ended up catching two passes for the entire year. Most of Washington was still waiting for him to show the potential McCloughan had seen in him.

Now, for one play, he showed it. Cousins laid the ball out so that Doctson had to dive and stretch his six-foot-two-inch frame as far as it would go and reach for the ball as it came down practically on the goal line. Somehow, he got both hands under the ball and hung on as he was being hauled down at the 1-yard line by Seattle safety Bradley McDougald.

The officials reviewed the play, but it was clearly a catch. Williams watched as running back Robert Kelley plowed into the end zone before jumping on the elevator.

Washington led 17–14, and suddenly a memorial service had a chance to become a celebration.

The game wasn't quite over.

Wilson actually drove the Seahawks as far as Washington's 38, starting at his own 25 with fifty-nine seconds left and no time-outs.

On a third-and-8 from his own 36, he found Paul Richardson over the middle for a 22-yard gain. The play must have impressed Williams and his scouts, because they signed Richardson to a five-year, $40 million free agent contract during the off-season.

With no time-outs left, Wilson rushed his team to the line. Instead of spiking the ball to stop the clock, Wilson tried to get off a real play and it backfired. He was sacked by defensive tackle Terrell McClain for an 8-yard loss, which took the Seahawks out of field goal range.

McClain got his hand on Wilson's foot as he tried to scramble free, and officials had to go to replay to be sure that Wilson was down by contact. He was. With one final play, Wilson heaved a Hail Mary into the end zone in the direction of Tanner McEvoy, and it was knocked away.

It was one of the more remarkable wins Washington had pulled off in several years. Their offensive line was missing four starters, and they were playing in a place where visitors usually go to be humiliated. The ever-effusive Washington media reacted as if the team had won the Super Bowl. Or at least a conference title.

Williams and his staff weren't quite as enthusiastic. They loved that Cousins had been able to take the team the length of the field in the last two minutes, and Doctson's catch gave them hope he might become the star they had thought they'd drafted.

But the offense had produced one touchdown in fifty-eight minutes when not facing a prevent defense, and Washington had barely won the game even though Wilson threw two interceptions; the Seahawks missed three field goals and committed twenty penalties.

Glass half-full or half-empty?

Again, the Kirk-yes or Kurt-no arguments raged in Washington.

Williams wasn't paying any attention. He was scouting the top college quarterbacks and checking on NFL starting quarterbacks who might be available in one form or another for 2018.

He knew he was going to need a new quarterback. Both Kirk and Kurt would be leaving the building for good whenever the season ended.

There was no point arguing his value. Other teams would ultimately decide that.

—

Ryan Fitzpatrick, on the other hand, was very happy right where he was. The win over the Jets in his first start in Jameis Winston's place meant a lot of him. A week later, he started again, this time in Miami against the Dolphins.

This was the game that was supposed to open the season but had to be postponed until week eleven because of Hurricane Irma. If the game had been week one, Winston would have been the starter. But a lot happens in the NFL during the course of a sixteen-week season.

By mid-November, the Bucs' high preseason hopes had been, for all intents and purposes, shot down. Winston, the star of *Hard Knocks,* was watching from the sideline. The Dolphins had lost their star quarterback, Ryan Tannehill, in preseason, brought Jay Cutler out of retirement, lost Cutler to injury, and seen Matt Moore play very well and very poorly. Cutler got the start against the Bucs. He would not, however, finish.

Once again, Fitzpatrick played the kind of game that had kept him in the league for thirteen years. The Bucs led 20–7 at halftime before the Dolphins rallied behind Matt Moore, who took over in the third quarter after Cutler—who had thrown three first-half interceptions—was diagnosed with a concussion.

The Dolphins tied the game at 20–20 after Moore completed a 61-yard pass to Kenny Stills with exactly three minutes left in the game.

Playing on the road, having struggled on offense in the second half, it looked as if the Bucs were going to let another one get away. But they didn't. Fitzpatrick's veteran cool paid off. He marched his team 58 yards in nine plays, letting the clock run down while the Dolphins used their time-outs to try to keep the game from ending on a Tampa Bay field goal.

It didn't—but there were just four seconds left when Patrick Murray, the kicker from Fordham whom the Bucs had re-signed in October (after Nick Folk had missed three field goals in the Thursday night loss to the Patriots), drilled a 35-yarder for a 23–20 lead.

The Dolphins tried to run a trick play on the ensuing kickoff—some version of the famous "Music City Miracle" of 1999—and ended up fumbling to allow a final, unneeded Bucs touchdown.

The victory made Fitzpatrick 2-0 as a starter, the Bucs 4-6 overall, meaning he had matched Winston's pre-injury victory total.

"I really never doubted that we could go down the field and score after they tied the game," he said. "It helps when you've done it before. It's like with anything—having done something makes it easier to think you can do it again. I'd been in that situation countless times. Everyone knew what we had to do. It was just a matter of doing it."

When Dirk Koetter had announced that the Bucs were going to rest Winston, the plan had been for him to sit for two or three weeks. With the team playing well and Fitzpatrick—who was 22-of-37 for 275 yards, two touchdowns, and no interceptions in Miami—making the offense hum, there was no need to rush Winston back.

At 4-6, the Bucs were technically still in the playoff picture. Realistically, especially with games at Atlanta and at Green Bay next up, they probably weren't going to make postseason. There was no reason *not* to keep playing Fitzpatrick.

The Falcons, coming off the most devastating come-from-ahead Super Bowl loss in history, had started the season 3-0. There appeared to be no hangover from their remarkable defeat to the Patriots, who had rallied from 28–3 down in the third quarter to win in overtime.

Then the Falcons went into a slide, losing four of five. But they had beaten the Cowboys and Seahawks (in Seattle) back-to-back when the Bucs came to their plush new domed stadium on the last Sunday in November.

The Falcons had no quarterback issues. Matt Ryan was in his tenth season in the league and hadn't missed a game since 2009. He had made 125 straight starts leading into the game against the Bucs, which put him fifth on the all-time list behind Brett Favre, Eli Manning, Peyton Manning, and Philip Rivers—who had 186 straight starts and would become the active leader a week later when Ben McAdoo infamously benched Eli Manning.

It looked as if the game was going to be a rout when the Falcons took a 27–6 lead, but Fitzpatrick and the Bucs rallied to within 27–20 early in the fourth quarter, twice driving the length of the field.

They even had a chance to tie when they again drove into the so-called red zone, with a second-and-2 at the Falcons' 19-yard line with more than seven minutes still to play. Fitzpatrick went for it all, trying to find DeSean Jackson in the end zone, but the pass was broken up. A quick pass to Adam Humphries picked up only a yard, setting up fourth-and-1.

With so much time left, the right move might have been to kick a field goal to keep momentum going and get into position where a touchdown might win the game. But Koetter was keenly aware of who the opposing quarterback was and knew there was a decent chance Ryan would take the Falcons down the field for a clinching score if his team was still up four. Plus, the Bucs were going to need a touchdown at some point to tie or take the lead, so why not go for it inside the 20 with only a yard needed to get the first down.

"To me, as the quarterback, it made complete sense to go for it," Fitzpatrick said. "Every team practices for moments like that late in the game. You talk in quarterback meetings about what you might do on fourth-and-one, fourth-and-ten, fourth down *from* the one. It's not like you're thinking, 'What are we going to do now?' You know exactly what you're going to do. You have options, and you choose one and hope it's right and you execute."

The Bucs didn't have a lot of confidence in their running game. They hadn't rushed the ball poorly—94 yards on 23 carries—but the passing game had gotten them back in the game and gotten them down the field on this drive. They'd rushed the ball once for 3 yards.

So Koetter called a quick slant to Cameron Brate, hoping he'd pick up at least 1 yard, maybe 2 and the first down. But the Falcons sniffed the play, and Brate was double-teamed and the pass was knocked away.

"It's a quick-decision play," Fitzpatrick said. "Short drop, get the ball there right away. It isn't as if you go through a progression. You drop and throw and hope it's the right call."

Koetter's notion that Ryan would take his team down the field proved correct. The Falcons went 82 yards in eleven plays, taking the game clock under two minutes before scoring the clinching touchdown on a 14-yard Tevin Coleman run. The final was 34–20.

Fitzpatrick was, of course, disappointed, even though he had played well again: 27-of-44 for 283 yards and, for the second straight week, no interceptions. In three starts he'd thrown one interception and had proven to the team and to himself that he was still an effective NFL quarterback.

"I really felt I was back when I came into the game in Arizona and we almost rallied to win," he said. "That was emotional for me. I think it gave me the confidence I needed when I had to step in and start. It reminded me that I was still a legitimate NFL quarterback. So did the three starts. It convinced me that I wanted to come back and play another year and that I was good enough that someone would want me, whether the Bucs or someone else.

"After the last year with the Jets, I was damaged goods on the free agent market. I was fortunate the Bucs made me an offer. After the three starts, I felt pretty confident someone would want me when the season was over."

He was hoping it would be the Bucs. He was comfortable with the team and the quarterback room. His family liked living in Tampa, and not having to move again would be nice.

"Of course in the NFL, when both sides want something to happen, it often doesn't," he said with a laugh. "We'll see."

Winston was ready to go the next week in Green Bay, and Fitzpatrick returned to the sidelines. He was happy Winston was healthy again, sad not to be playing. But at the very least, as he watched the Bucs lose in overtime, he could smile about his present—and his future.

—

Even after the disappointing loss to the Steelers in Pittsburgh, the Baltimore Ravens had a clear path to the playoffs.

They had three games left against three teams with a combined record of 8-31. At 5-8, the Cincinnati Bengals were easily the most formidable opponent in the group. The Indianapolis Colts were 3-12 and the Cleveland Browns were 0-13. The only road game left was in Cleveland.

It was somewhat remarkable that the Browns actually ranked above eight teams in home attendance, averaging an announced 63,882 per game. By the time the Ravens came to town for the Browns' home finale, the fans could hardly be blamed for being worn-out after two seasons that had produced exactly one win.

The crowd on Sunday December 17 was announced at 56,434 on a mid-thirties, cloudy afternoon, but it looked closer to half that. By the fourth quarter, only the 434 appeared to be accurate.

Even so, the Ravens didn't make it easy on themselves. They trailed 7–3 in the first quarter before a Flacco 2-yard touchdown run—the sixteenth rushing touchdown of his ten-year career—and a Flacco–to–Benjamin Watson 33-yard touchdown pass gave them a 17–7 second-quarter lead.

Watson's touchdown came with fifty-nine seconds left, and it looked like the Ravens would take a ten-point lead to the locker room at halftime. But in what would later prove to be a harbinger, the defense allowed DeShone Kizer to take his team 47 yards to the Ravens' 27-yard line and, with four seconds left, Zane Gonzalez kicked a 45-yard field goal to narrow the margin to 17–10 at the break.

The third quarter was a slog, the teams twice exchanging punts until the Browns made the kind of play that bad teams always seem to make. The Ravens had reached the Browns' 32, only to take a Flacco sack back to the 41 on third down. Rather than send Justin Tucker in to try a 59-yard field goal on a breezy day, John Harbaugh decided to play field position and sent Sam Koch in to punt.

Koch dropped the ball on the Browns' 4-yard line. Hoping, no doubt, to fool the Ravens by not trying to run the ball from the goal line's shadow, Kizer dropped into the end zone to pass and was about to be buried by blitzing linebacker Za'Darius Smith, when the ball squirted loose. Brandon Williams, the 340-pound defensive tackle, fell on it on the 1-yard line and, untouched, rolled into the end zone.

The touchdown made it 24–10, and whatever fight the Browns had left was gone. The Ravens played their offense very close to the belt the rest of the way and the final was 27–10.

One hapless team down, two to go. The Ravens were now 8-5 and had won five of six since the loss in Minneapolis in October. In an ideal Flacco-world, the offense would have been wide open, and he would have been consistently throwing the ball downfield to his wide receivers.

But that's not the way the team was built. The defense made mistakes, but it also created a lot of turnovers. Kizer had been intercepted twice in Cleveland in addition to his game-changing fumble. The offensive line had improved during the season, and so had the running game, but it was far from lights out. The tight ends who had replaced Dennis Pitta had been workmanlike, nothing more.

The wide receivers had been, to put it politely, disappointing. Mike Wallace had been Flacco's best wideout. He would end up catching 52 balls for 748 yards, well short of his best seasons. Jeremy Maclin was hurt for part of the season and ended up with 40 catches for 440 yards. Breshad Perriman had the not-so-small issue with holding on to the ball—he ended up with 10 catches on the season.

In all, it made sense for the Ravens not to take chances on offense unless they had to. Flacco understood that, and as long as the team was winning, he was content to hand off and throw short passes. But it went against his quarterbacking instincts.

"You always feel as if you can do more given the chance," he said. "I have a lot of self-confidence and belief in the offense—even if we were banged up early. We got better as the season went along, but I could see the coaches felt comfortable making sure we didn't make mistakes and let the defense make the plays we needed to win.

"That strategy made the most sense. But if you play it close to the vest, it means you're going to be in close games. There isn't very much margin for error."

The Ravens had never been a wide-open, fling-it-down-the-field team under Harbaugh. Flacco had thrown more interceptions than touchdown passes in a season only once: 2013, the year after the Super Bowl win, when he threw nineteen touchdowns and twenty-two interceptions as the Ravens went 8-8—the first time they had missed the playoffs in six seasons with Harbaugh as coach and Flacco as quarterback.

In 2017, after throwing for just four touchdown passes and eight interceptions in the first six games, Flacco threw fourteen touchdown passes and had six interceptions in the last ten. Some of that was that he grew stronger and healthier as the season wore on; some of that was that his offensive line, even minus Yanda, became more comfortable with experience; some of that was the competition. The Ravens' second-half schedule turned out to be easier than expected—only three of their last nine opponents had winning records.

The win in Cleveland was fairly typical of what the Ravens had become. The game wasn't pretty, none of the stats were spectacular, but the final result was a 27–10 victory. Which was all that was important.

The Ravens would finish with two home games. Two victories, and they would be guaranteed a spot in the playoffs.

"Which, in the end, is all that matters," Flacco said. "Once you're in, anything can happen. Sixth seeds have won the Super Bowl. The year we won, we were a fourth seed and had to win two road games. All you want is a shot at it."

Two wins at home against bad teams, and the Ravens would get their shot.

24

The Colts were up next for the Ravens, in one of those late-season Saturday games that the NFL plays when there is no college football going on.

The weather in Baltimore was strange: temperature at kickoff—just a few minutes before sundown—was sixty-three degrees, two days before Christmas. But it was a miserable, rainy day that left the stadium dark even before kickoff. Although the Ravens announced a sellout—70,590—there were plenty of empty seats. This was, no doubt, due in part to the weather.

But as with much of the NFL, it was more than that. The Ravens were sold out for the season, but the players had noticed empty seats almost every week.

"You sort of couldn't miss it," Flacco said. "You'd look around before kickoff and you'd see a lot of empty seats. It wasn't something I was used to. In my ten years, we almost always played to a full house."

Even though the NFL continued to announce only how many tickets had been sold—once, years earlier, it had also announced actual attendance—there were so many empty seats in so many stadiums that it had even acquired an internet name: the empty seat epidemic.

There were plenty of theories attached to the declining attendance around the league. It wasn't just that more people were staying home and watching on TV, because TV ratings had also been down the last two seasons. In 2016, the average number of fans watching an NFL game had dropped from 17.9 million to 16.5 million.

Much of that had been attributed to the most bitter presidential election in history, between Donald Trump and Hillary Clinton. Once the election was over, ratings had improved a little, but in 2017, with no election going on, the ratings dropped again, this time to 14.9 million viewers on average.

The Donald Trump theory, of course, was that football fans had been turned off by two things: players kneeling for the anthem and new rules designed to cut down on head injuries. Trump took the Christians vs. Lions theory that football was played to entertain viewers like him. In the same Alabama speech in which he profanely "demanded" that NFL players stand for the national anthem, Trump said this about the NFL: "Today, if you hit too hard, throw him out of the game! They're ruining the game, right? They're ruining the game. It's hurting the game."

Trump went on to say that while watching a game "for a few minutes," he had seen what he called a "beautiful tackle" that had drawn a flag.

In the 1980s, Trump had owned a team in the upstart United States Football League, which had tried to take on the NFL on the field and then, failing that, in court, where it had filed an antitrust lawsuit against the NFL. A jury found that the NFL *did* violate the law and had established a monopoly.

As a result, the jury awarded the USFL's owners $1 in damages, which trebled to $3 because it was an antitrust suit. In the game of Monopoly, that award would not be enough to pay the bill for landing on Mediterranean Avenue—with no houses on it.

Given that Trump tends to hold a grudge, it's probably fair to believe he never completely got over the sting of that outcome, the irony being that most NFL owners probably voted for him and at least seven had given him $1 million in campaign contributions.

In truth, there was no one thing that had caused attendance to drop and TV ratings to crater—a 20 percent drop in two seasons. There was a laundry list of factors that all added up to the empty seats and unwatched TV sets.

Included: TV saturation—the NFL kept pushing the envelope, adding Thursday night games and adding to the late-season Saturday schedule to go along with a Monday night schedule that was often not attractive, not to mention the hyped Sunday night games.

To most football fans, Sunday was their day to watch football. An attractive Monday night game might get their attention—but the days of the Gifford, Cosell, Meredith phenomenon were long gone. No one was tuning in exclusively to watch Sean McDonough and Jon Gruden in 2017, nor would anyone get wound up about watching Joe Tessitore and Jason Witten in 2018.

There was only one Cosell and only one Meredith.

Then there were the games themselves. Because the NFL squeezed every last billion out of its TV "partners"—CBS, Fox, NBC, and ESPN—the games were loaded down with commercial breaks. Through 2016, broadcasts followed a brutal sequence: touchdown or field goal . . . followed by a commercial break . . . kickoff . . . followed by a commercial break. There could be six minutes of commercials broken up only by a (usually not returned) kickoff. In 2017, in an attempt to get away from this pattern, the NFL decreed there would be fewer breaks—but the breaks would be longer.

Then there were the delays for replay—all of which seemed to take forever.

Plus, the NFL had so many different new rules that flags seemed to fly on every other play. Games with more than twenty-five penalties called were not uncommon. In the Ravens-Browns game in September, thirty-four penalties had been called. When the NFL was at the peak of its TV powers, games rarely lasted more than three hours. By 2017, three and a half hours was not uncommon.

Attendance was down because going to games had become so expensive. In addition to the ticket prices, fans had to pay parking fees that were pure price gouging—up to $50 in many places, almost never under $30, unless you wanted a very long walk to the stadium. Concession prices were bloated and, late in the season especially, conditions could be miserable.

Add it all up, and it wasn't that hard to understand why fewer people—even those with tickets—were making the effort to come and why fewer casual fans didn't want to sit through entire games at home.

The Ravens-Colts game was a classic example of why the empty seat epidemic existed. The weather was awful; it was, essentially, a night game; and it was two days before Christmas. That's why many people paid for tickets and didn't use them.

The game wasn't much different from the game in Cleveland a week earlier. The Ravens got out to a 10–0 lead; an early Tucker field goal followed in the second quarter by a 6-yard Flacco–to–Michael Campanaro touchdown pass.

But, as they had done in most games, the Colts hung around; and, as they had done in most games, the Ravens let a weaker opponent stay in the game.

In the second quarter, Jacoby Brissett found the ageless Frank Gore (a thirty-four-year-old running back is roughly the equivalent of a fifty-year-old quarterback) out of the backfield for a 14-yard touchdown pass to make it 10–7.

Then it became a field goal battle: Tucker kicked two for Baltimore, and Adam Vinatieri (speaking of ageless) kicked two for the Colts, the second making it 16–13 at the end of three quarters.

Vinatieri was five days short of turning forty-five. He was in his twenty-second NFL season. How long had he been around? Well, his injured teammate Andrew Luck remembered going with his father to see Vinatieri play for the Amsterdam Admirals of the World League of American Football in 1995. Luck was six at the time.

"And now I'm one of the old men on our team and Adam's still kicking," Luck said with a laugh.

As the fourth quarter began, the stadium was dark, rain-filled, and at least half-empty. After Vinatieri had closed the gap to three, the Ravens and Flacco pieced together a time-consuming fourteen-play, 75-yard drive that ended with Flacco finding tight end Maxx Williams from the 4-yard line for a touchdown. That gave the Ravens some breathing room, and they held on to win, 23–16.

"I don't think anyone's going to call that one of the great games of all time," John Harbaugh joked, standing in the hallway outside his team's locker room after the game. "But as long as we keep winning, it's all good."

Flacco felt the same way. He knew there were no style points in the NFL. The Ravens were 9-6 and one win away from the playoffs. Given how he'd felt standing in the locker room after the loss to the Vikings in October, at a time when the offense hadn't scored a meaningful touchdown in back-to-back weeks, it was a nice place to be.

—

The first sign that the last week of the season might not go as planned for the Ravens came on Monday—Christmas Day—when the NFL announced that all one o'clock games the following Sunday that had playoff implications would be moved to 4:25. The Ravens-Bengals game was one of those that got moved.

The NFL made the change for two reasons: first, so that no one scheduled to play late would have the advantage of knowing what their competition for a playoff spot or playoff seeding had done (and therefore have nothing left to play for in the later kickoff slot); second, to increase TV ratings by playing the key games in the late-afternoon window.

The Ravens, notably Harbaugh, weren't happy with the time change. "I don't think the NFL did us any favors moving us back," Harbaugh said. "But they don't care about us. So we just have to care about ourselves. We have to take care of our own business. That goes for our team, our fans, and our city. So, let's go win the football game."

Harbaugh was right about one thing: the NFL didn't care about the Ravens. It cared about what it perceived to be best for the league, not any one team.

Harbaugh was concerned that a 4:25 start on New Year's Eve would affect attendance, even with a playoff berth on the line.

A week earlier, team president Dick Cass had publicly acknowledged the empty seat epidemic in a lengthy letter to Ravens fans. After citing all the Ravens community activities through the years, Cass pinned much of the blame for the empty seats on the fact that twelve Ravens had knelt for the national anthem prior to the game in London, saying that the anthem controversy had been "an emotional and divisive issue."

He noted that in past seasons empty seats had popped up when the team wasn't performing well, but that this season "the numbers are higher and it is noticeable."

He again referenced the "one time" protest in London at that point, without mentioning that the 44–7 loss to Jacksonville that day might have been a factor too.

Clearly, Cass's concerns were long-term: he was worried that some fans might not renew season tickets for 2018. That was, no doubt, why he also pointed out the "120 million dollars in ongoing renovations to M&T Bank Stadium" and added that the first escalator to the upper deck would be open for the 2018 season.

Harbaugh's concerns were short-term. He knew that a third straight season out of the playoffs might put his job on the line, while a win against the Bengals might earn him a contract extension. The margin between success and failure in the NFL can be that thin.

As it turned out, Harbaugh was right about fans not showing up for the 4:25 start. One could hardly blame them. The unseasonable warmth of a week earlier was long gone. The game time temperature was nineteen degrees, and the gusting winds made it feel considerably colder.

Flacco, a New Jersey boy who had played in the cold most of his life, noticed it. "One of those days," he said, "where you just couldn't get warm no matter how much clothing you put on when you were on the sideline."

Then the Ravens came out as if they thought it was a 5:25 start.

Andy Dalton, the Bengals' quarterback, was in his seventh season and was a poster boy for what it's like to be a successful, but fallible, NFL quarterback.

He had been drafted out of TCU in the second round in 2011 and had become an instant starter and star in Cincinnati. Two years earlier (in 2009) the Bengals had won the NFC North, going 10-6, and Marvin Lewis had been named coach of the year. But they slipped to 4-12 a year later, and quarterback Carson Palmer demanded to be traded—which he was—to Oakland. The Bengals also decided that year they'd had enough of prima donna wide receivers Chad Johnson and Terrell Owens—both superb talents but constant headaches. They traded Johnson (aka "Ochocinco" after he renamed himself in honor of his number, eighty-five) to New England. They released Owens and, as it turned out, he never played in another NFL game.

To replace their quarterback–wide receiver combination, the Bengals drafted Georgia wide receiver A. J. Green in the first round and then took Dalton in the second round.

The duo led the Bengals to the playoffs in 2011 and became instant heroes in Cincinnati. The Bengals made postseason for five straight years, and in the summer of 2014 Dalton signed a six-year contract with a potential value of $115 million.

But the team went through one postseason disappointment after another, including an 18–16 loss to the Steelers at home after finishing the 2015 season 12-4. Dalton hadn't played in that game because he had broken a thumb four weeks earlier against the Browns. The team was 10-2 when he went down. AJ McCarron filled in competently, but not competently enough to break the team's playoff bugaboo.

The Pittsburgh loss made Marvin Lewis 0-7 in playoff games and had some people screaming for his head, even though he had made the Bengals into an almost perennial postseason team.

The screams grew louder when the Bengals went 6-9-1 in 2016.

Then the team got off to a brutal start in 2017, losing the opener 20–0 at home to the Ravens, with Dalton throwing four interceptions, then following it up with a 13–9 loss to the Texans. Two games, two losses, zero touchdowns. Offensive coordinator Ken Zampese took the fall. He was fired and replaced by quarterbacks coach Bill Lazor.

Things improved after that, but the Bengals never reached .500—coming closest at 5-6 after a win over the Browns. On December 17, ESPN's Adam Schefter reported that Lewis had decided to leave the Bengals at season's end. With his contract up, Lewis—according to Schefter—was going to pursue "other opportunities." Schefter, as he almost always does, cited "league sources" who had told him this.

And so the Bengals came into Baltimore with a 6-9 record and many expecting Lewis—who had denied the Schefter report—to be gone within twenty-four hours of the finale. At one time, the day after the NFL season ended had been called "Black Monday," because that was almost always the day coaches got fired. Now, however, impatient owners and front-office executives had started pushing "Black Monday" to "So-Long Sunday," as the Colts' Chuck Pagano and the Raiders' Jack Del Rio would learn that day.

Ben McAdoo had already been fired by the Giants, and Jim Caldwell and John Fox would exit on Black Monday. Bruce Arians of the Cardinals announced his retirement that day.

Lewis, in spite of what Schefter's "league sources" had told him, did not resign, nor was he fired.

And, unfortunately for the Ravens, his team played as if their coach's job was on the line and they wanted him to stick around for a fifteenth season.

Right from the start, Dalton looked very much like the $115 million quarterback—as opposed to the bumbler the Ravens had faced seventeen weeks earlier. Mixing short passes with Joe Mixon runs, the Bengals quickly moved 78 yards in eight plays—plus a key penalty when Green was interfered with by Brandon Carr on a pass into the end zone—to take a 7–0 lead on a Dalton–to–Tyler Kroft pass.

Once again, it was clear the Ravens weren't going to do this the easy way. Their first series was stopped by two dropped passes—one by Mike Wallace, one by running back Buck Allen. When Wallace dropped another pass on a third-and-3 late in the quarter, many of the chilled fans began to boo.

The Ravens closed the gap to 7–3 early in the second quarter after forcing a Mixon fumble at the Cincinnati 34. The offense went three-and-out, but Justin Tucker got something out of the turnover by kicking a 46-yard field goal.

With the Baltimore offense still sputtering, Dalton led another lengthy drive, this one culminating in a 5-yard touchdown pass—again to Kroft. He'd had five touchdown catches for the season coming into the game. His seventh made it 14–3 with 4:14 left in the half.

When Randy Bullock kicked a 32-yard field goal with twenty-three seconds left, the Bengals were up 17–3. Many natives were restless; others restlessly headed to the warmth of their cars.

But then the Ravens' special teams gave them life. Chris Moore fielded Bullock's short kickoff at the 7 and returned it 87 yards to the Cincinnati 6. Given a surprising last-second opportunity, Flacco found Moore for a 6-yard touchdown pass to cut the margin to 17–10 at the break.

The Ravens were still breathing. Some of the restless returned to their seats.

The Ravens maintained their momentum to start the second half, moving the ball to the Cincinnati 22, apparently on their way to tying the game.

But on second-and-5, Flacco looked over the middle for Moore, his hot receiver. The pass wasn't perfect, a little behind Moore, who reached back, got his hands on it, and then bobbled it—right into the hands of backup cornerback Darqueze Dennard. Before the Ravens could react, Dennard had broken to the sideline and had a clear path to the end zone. The only one with any kind of angle on him was Flacco, but he was cut down at the Baltimore 13 by Cincinnati defensive end Jordan Willis, and Dennard jogged into the end zone.

Suddenly—shockingly—it was 24–10.

The Ravens didn't quit—with half a year of constant work at stake, one wouldn't have expected them to.

They drove right back into Cincinnati territory but faced a fourth-and-3 at the Bengals' 17. Realizing a field goal wouldn't accomplish much, Harbaugh decided to go for it. For a moment, it looked as if the decision had backfired when Alex Collins was hit behind the line of scrimmage. Somehow, he squirmed free, got to the outside, and scored, cutting the margin to 24–17.

The momentum swung back to the Ravens, and those who had stayed were making as much noise as possible.

Another Tucker field goal made it 24–20. The Cincinnati offense, which had carved the Ravens apart in the first half, suddenly couldn't do anything. It hadn't gotten onto the field the first nine minutes of the third quarter because the Ravens had gotten the ball right back after the Bengals' pick-six, and Dalton and company had picked up only one first down before punting. Now, after the Tucker field goal, it quickly went three-and-out.

Flacco sensed that his team now had the chance to—finally—take control of the game.

"The key had been scoring the touchdown right away after the pick-six," he said. "At least that's the way it felt to me. A lot of times when teams get up on the road and then something goes wrong, they start to think about games they've lost before. I felt we were very close to putting them in that position if we could just score."

They did. Michael Campanaro, the little wide receiver, set it up with an 18-yard punt return to the 40, which became an even better return when the Bengals' Brian Hill was called for a late hit. Starting from the Bengals' 45, Flacco quickly got his team into the end zone, finding Wallace for the final 6 yards with 8:52 left. For the first time on the long day's journey into night, the Ravens led, 27–24.

When Wallace caught the pass that gave his team the lead, Flacco did something he almost never does: he threw his arms into the air in triumph and ran to join his teammates in celebration. Cool Joe didn't get that pumped very often, but with postseason now very much in sight, he let go—if only for a moment.

The Bengals' offense now seemed officially dead. On third-and-6, Dalton was sacked at his own 20 on a blitz by Matthew Judon, and the Bengals punted again. The Ravens took over with 6:33 left and the chance, perhaps, to run out the clock.

They got a first down on a 19-yard Allen run to their own 46. The clock was at 4:20. But on third-and-7, trying to throw a pass that would keep the clock running but perhaps pick up the first down, Flacco looked for Danny Woodhead, the third-down running back who had been hurt for much of the season. But the pass was broken up, and the clock stopped with 2:51 to go.

That conservative play call was exactly what Flacco had been talking about. If the Ravens had taken a shot downfield—perhaps a seam pass over the middle—the game could have been over, because a first down, arguably, would have made it impossible for the Bengals to win. They had already used up two time-outs and, at best, might have gotten the ball back with about a minute to go, deep in their own territory with no time-outs left.

Instead, they got the ball back deep in their own territory—the 10-yard line—with 2:43 left and a time-out and the two-minute warning—which is nothing more than an excuse for another TV time-out—still left.

They were at their own 33 when the two-minute warning struck and TV went to commercial.

Five or six commercials later, on second-and-10, still at the 33, Dalton threw incomplete to Brandon LaFell. But Brandon Carr was called for pass interference, giving the Bengals 10 yards and a first down at the 43. Two plays later, Dalton looked for Green—who had been held to two catches for 17 yards all day—and Eric Weddle, the Pro Bowl safety, stepped in front of Green and intercepted the pass.

On the Baltimore sidelines, they were in full celebration. Flacco sat on the heated bench in his usual spot near midfield, not thinking about how cold he was. All he was thinking about was the playoffs. The Ravens had come a long way to get there.

But they weren't there yet. There was another yellow piece of cloth on the field. Cornerback Marlon Humphrey had been called for defensive holding before Dalton had released the ball, clearly taking Green down.

Instead of it being the Ravens' ball—game over—it was the Bengals' ball at the Ravens' 47, first down. A second later it was back in Bengals territory, at the 48, after Green was called for an illegal shift.

Dalton threw two incomplete passes, then hit Kroft for 3 yards, making it fourth-and-12 at the Baltimore 49. There were fifty-three seconds left. The Bengals used their final time-out. They probably needed to go at least 15 yards, perhaps 20, to get into Bullock's field goal range.

At that moment, though, they needed 12 yards or the game would *finally* be over. It had started almost three and a half hours earlier. The Buffalo Bills, who had beaten the Dolphins to keep their slim playoff hopes alive, were already in their locker room, hoping for a Bengals miracle that would end their seventeen-year playoff drought—the longest in all four major sports.

The Ravens' defense had been in man-to-man during the final drive, which had made it difficult for the Bengals to pick up ground easily, the way teams often do when an opponent goes to a prevent defense. That was why, even aided by two key penalties, it had taken the Bengals ten plays to get the ball just beyond midfield.

But now, needing one last defensive stop, defensive coordinator Dean Pees decided to go to a cover-two zone.

Cover-two, very simply, is a defense in which the two safeties drop deep to be sure there's no way for a receiver to get behind them for a deep touchdown. The Bengals didn't need a touchdown. They needed 12 yards.

Recognizing the defense as he took the shotgun snap, Dalton saw wide receiver Tyler Boyd running down the seam. Stepping up, Dalton threw a strike to Boyd, who had been in the slot on the right side.

Linebacker C. J. Mosley had bluffed a blitz and then dropped into coverage. The ball just cleared his fingertips, and Boyd caught it in stride at the 23-yard line. Safety Maurice Canady, who had been responsible for covering anything deep on the left side of the defense, had taken a step in the direction of LaFell, who had been split wide right and had run down the sideline. When he tried to pivot back in Boyd's direction, he was off balance and couldn't get a clean swipe at him. Neither could Weddle, desperately trying to get over to help.

The Ravens' last and only real chance to keep Boyd out of the end zone came from Carr, who flew into the play late, dove at Boyd, but could only get his left hand on the back of Boyd's uniform just before he crossed the goal line.

The Bengals' celebration was nothing compared to the party that broke out in the Bills' locker room in Miami, which was nothing short of pandemonium. It was so quiet in M&T Bank Stadium that, from the stands, you could clearly hear the sounds coming from the Bengals' sideline.

Flacco wasn't thinking about any of that. The stadium had gone almost eerily silent. His teammates were doubled over as if in physical pain. So were the coaches.

Flacco had hung his head in shock for a moment. Seconds later, he was looking at the clock. There were still forty-four seconds left. The

Ravens had all three time-outs left. "Crazier things have happened," Flacco said. "I'd just watched something completely unbelievable happen. We [the offense] had to go out there thinking there was still a chance."

There were numerous problems in all this. For one thing, the Ravens simply didn't have a big play threat. They had evolved into a dink-and-dunk offense. They had averaged 8 yards per reception on the day.

Second was the score: 31–27. Nothing short of a touchdown would do. Third, the Bengals would be in an absolute prevent defense, making certain the Ravens couldn't complete anything long.

Bullock kicked the ball short of the end zone, meaning Campanaro used up six precious seconds returning the ball to the 27.

Flacco quickly completed a short pass to Benjamin Watson, who stepped out-of-bounds after a 5-yard gain. Ball on the Baltimore 32; thirty-two seconds left.

Flacco had to try to complete something deep—or at least semi-deep. But defensive end Carlos Dunlap broke through and, before Flacco could even think to step up and throw, sacked him for a 9-yard loss. The Ravens were now 77 yards away, it was third-and-14, and the clock was down to twenty-eight seconds. Flacco took a time-out.

He tried to find Wallace over the middle, hoping the play might at least get the ball close to midfield for a first down and give Flacco a couple of Hail Mary shots. Vincent Rey broke up the pass.

It was fourth-and-14. The clock was at twenty-four seconds, but that didn't matter unless the Ravens picked up a first down. With the Bengals playing deep, Flacco threw underneath to Watson, just wanting a first down and a couple of shots at the end zone.

Rey brought Watson down a yard short of the first down.

It was 7:57 p.m. on New Year's Eve. In Baltimore, it was midnight.

25

No one was more surprised by the Ravens' last-second collapse than Alex Smith.

With the Chiefs locked into the fourth seed in the AFC regardless of the outcome in their regular season finale in Denver, Smith had been given the week off by Andy Reid.

This was done for two reasons: first, to give him some rest time to heal up a little from the various bumps and bruises of the season, and second, to get a sixty-minute look at Patrick Mahomes, even in a meaningless game.

Since Smith didn't have to do any prep for the Broncos—in the unlikely event he got in the game, he'd already seen them once—he spent a good deal of time watching tape of the Ravens, figuring they would be the Chiefs' opponent the first weekend of postseason.

"I thought, playing at home, playing well, they were pretty likely to win," he said. "When they lost, I was shocked. I was also bummed because I'd wasted a lot of time looking at their tape."

The opponent instead would be the Tennessee Titans—the first AFC wildcard. The Bills, who had become the second wildcard after the Ravens' defeat, would play at Jacksonville. The Patriots and Steelers were the AFC's top two seeds and would meet the first weekend's winners in the conference semifinals.

In the NFC, the Eagles and Vikings had both finished at 13-3, but the Eagles got the top seed based on a better conference record. The wildcard games would be between the third-seeded L.A. Rams and the Atlanta Falcons, and the fourth-seeded New Orleans Saints hosting the fifth-seeded Carolina Panthers.

Only four of the previous season's twelve playoff teams had returned: the Patriots, Steelers, Chiefs, and Falcons. Atlanta was the only NFC team to repeat, and it did so as the number six seed. Five of the eight non-repeaters had losing records, the Giants suffering the worst drop, going from 11-5 to 4-12. Three of those who were home for the playoffs—the Giants, Raiders, and Lions—fired their coaches. Jim Caldwell got the gate in Detroit after going 19-14 with a playoff appearance in two seasons.

Even though the Eagles were the number one seed in the NFC, the favorites to make the Super Bowl were the Vikings and Saints: the Vikings because of their defense and the steady play of Case Keenum; the Saints because of Drew Brees. The Eagles, even playing at home, would be underdogs to anyone they played because Nick Foles would be starting at quarterback and Carson Wentz would be cheerleading from the sideline.

The Patriots, as always, were the favorite in the AFC—especially since they would play at home if they met the Steelers in the conference title game that most people were anticipating.

Smith wasn't concerned with any of that. He just wanted to beat the Titans, knowing his team wouldn't be the least bit intimidated going to play in New England a week later after the way they had handled the Patriots in September.

The Titans' quarterback, Marcus Mariota, was in his third season in the league. He had been the number two pick in the 2015 draft coming out of Oregon after winning the Heisman Trophy. Jameis Winston, who'd won the Heisman a year earlier, was the number one pick. Mariota was, it seemed, the ideal NFL quarterback: six feet four, 222 pounds, and *fast*—he had run a 4.52 40 at the combine. He'd missed some time with injuries his first two years but had played in fifteen games in 2017.

Still, it hadn't been easy for the Titans to make postseason for the first time since 2008. They had been 8-4 before a three-game losing streak in December put them on the playoff precipice. The Jaguars, one of the NFL's surprise teams, had wrapped up the division and were 10-5 coming to Tennessee for the finale, which the Titans ended up winning, 15–10.

The tape of the game wouldn't be sent to Canton, but that didn't matter. After the Ravens' loss to the Bengals, the Titans moved up from the number six seed to the number five seed, sending them to Kansas City.

Aside from the wasted time on the Ravens tape, neither Smith nor the Chiefs minded facing the Titans. They had lost a galling game to Tennessee a year earlier, blowing an early 14–0 lead and losing at the buzzer on a 53-yard field goal by Ryan Succop—an ex-Chief.

Getting another shot at them at home—this time in postseason—was fine with Smith.

Nationally, the Chiefs and Titans weren't considered a great TV draw, so they were assigned to play the first game of the weekend—4:30 Eastern kickoff—on ESPN. The Falcons (Matt Ryan) and Rams (Jared Goff) would play the night game, and then on Sunday the Bills and Jaguars—not exactly a glamour matchup either—would play early, followed by the Saints (Drew Brees) and the Panthers (Cam Newton). The quarterbacks were always the key to ratings.

"I'm glad to play early," Smith said. "It would be nice to win, then kick back and enjoy the other games."

Smith's entire family: parents, brother, sisters—along with spouses and children—were coming to town for the game. It was, after all, the playoffs. And all were aware this might be the last game Alex played in Kansas City—regardless of the outcome.

The first half ended with the Chiefs up, 21–3. Smith had been near perfect, moving the Chiefs to three touchdowns on long drives, completing 19 of 23 passes for 231 yards and two touchdowns. The first score came on a 1-yard run by Kareem Hunt, but Smith's quick-strike passing—a pass to Tyreek Hill picked up 45 yards and a pass to Travis Kelce on the next play went for 27, putting the ball on the 2—set up the touchdown.

There were, however, some warning signs that, as rosy as things might look, this would not be the Chiefs' night.

The first came in the form of the officiating crew, led by referee Jeff Triplette.

Triplette had been an NFL referee since 1999. His most memorable moment had come that season when he threw a yellow flag in the direction of the Cleveland Browns' Orlando Brown. The flag was weighted with ball bearings and hit Brown smack in the eye.

Brown was blinded and missed the next three seasons. Even though it was clearly an accident, the NFL eventually settled a $200 million lawsuit filed by Brown for somewhere between $15 and $20 million. The weighted flags went away, along with instructions to officials to simply throw a flag at the spot, not in the direction of the player they believed had committed the infraction.

Triplette was never considered one of the league's top officials by any stretch. In fact, he hadn't worked an NFL playoff game since 2013. In the final regular season game that Triplette and his crew worked—the Bills game in Miami—there had been near chaos when a brief fight broke out and Triplette ejected a player from the wrong team and a player who didn't exist. It took ten minutes of going back through the tape in New York to straighten things out.

And yet, there was Triplette working the opening game of the NFL's postseason. Not long after the game, it was learned that Triplette was planning to retire—he made it official in March—and many wondered if Triplette had been given a going-away present by the league.

"You can't do that," said Joe Flacco, who watched only some of the game on TV because sitting through the whole thing was too painful. "There's too much at stake to be giving guys assignments like that. They should have to earn it, the same way teams have to earn it. What happened in that game shouldn't have happened."

Triplette can be difficult to understand when he opens up his mike because he has a Southern accent (born in North Carolina), but on this night a lot of what he said simply made no sense.

The most nonsensical moments of Triplette's night came late in the second quarter. The Titans had finally gotten a drive going and faced third-and-4 from the Kansas City 22. Mariota went back to pass and was sacked by a blitzing Derrick Johnson, who came from the left side of the defense untouched and slammed Mariota to the turf.

He fumbled on the way down and the Chiefs recovered, ending the Titans' threat. Except that Triplette blew his whistle as Mariota was going down and claimed that "forward progress" had been stopped.

Mariota was going backward at that moment. There was *no* forward progress. It was a clear, absolute strip sack. Because the ball had been blown dead, the Chiefs couldn't ask for replay. Instead, Ryan Succop came in and kicked a 49-yard field goal to make it 14–3.

Triplette's gaffe didn't seem all that important when Smith marched the Chiefs to a touchdown on a 14-yard pass to Demarcus Robinson with three seconds left that made it 21–3.

It was on that drive that Kelce was knocked into next week on a catch over the middle. The officials didn't call a penalty on safety Johnathan Cyprien, even though his hit on Kelce was clearly helmet-to-helmet.

That no-call was the fault of the NFL's wishy-washy rule on helmet-to-helmet hits. Because Kelce had caught the ball and was running with it, he was not deemed a "helpless receiver." Kelce was being brought down by linebacker Jayon Brown when Cyprien launched himself at Kelce.

Interestingly, in the official play-by-play of the game, Brown is listed as the only tackler.

League apologists will say that on a play like that, the helmet-to-helmet hit was caused by the fact that Kelce was going down and Cyprien couldn't stop himself. That's baloney. Cyprien launched himself, helmet first, in Kelce's direction. And yet the officials called nothing, and the league didn't fine him because the rule was so weak.

Take a bow for protecting your players, Roger Goodell. Only in 2018 was the rule amended to make any helmet-to-helmet hit a penalty.

Illegal or not, the hit knocked Kelce out of the game. He got up, clearly not knowing where he was, dizzy, and woozy. In the locker room at halftime, Smith could hear him pleading with the doctors to let him play the second half.

"There was no way that was going to happen," Smith said. "They couldn't even think about putting him back in even if he answered every question right in the concussion protocol. He'd been out on his feet. I knew he was done for the night."

Injuries are part of football, but to lose Kelce in the middle of a playoff game was devastating for the Chiefs. Hill was their most explosive receiver, but Kelce was their most reliable. He had caught 83 balls for 1,078 yards in the regular season and had already made four catches for 66 yards and a touchdown in less than a half in the playoff game.

"Kels has an innate ability to get open," Smith said. "Once he gets downfield, he is very hard to cover one-on-one. You have a tight end with that ability, it's a huge weapon."

Now that weapon was gone. Still, based on how quickly he'd recovered his faculties, it looked as if the chances Kelce could play the next week in New England were good.

Except that the second half happened.

The Titans took the kickoff and began a long, grinding drive. The time coming off the clock was in the Chiefs' favor, even as Tennessee closed in on the goal line.

The fifteenth play of the drive was a third-and-goal from the 6. There were already under seven minutes left in the third quarter. Mariota dropped, then sprinted left looking for an open receiver. Finally, desperate, he threw the ball toward the end zone.

Darrelle Revis, who had once been the most feared cornerback in the NFL, was now the Chiefs' nickelback. He got his hands on the ball and deflected it. The ball spun into the air and went directly to Mariota, whose forward momentum carried him right to the ball, which he grabbed in midair, took two steps, and fell into the end zone.

Mariota-to-Mariota: touchdown. It was only the second time in NFL history that such a play had occurred. Brad Johnson had pulled it off in a regular season game while playing for the Minnesota Vikings in 1997. It had never happened in the playoffs.

The roaring stadium went quiet—as much in shock as dismay. The extra point made it 21–10 with 6:31 left in the third.

"If you were looking for signs that it wasn't going to be our night, that one was pretty clear," Smith said, still shaking his head months later. "We weren't thinking that way then. But later, looking back . . . I mean, come on, how does that play happen?"

It looked for a while like the play would just be a historic blip. The Chiefs had to punt, but Adoree' Jackson fumbled—technically it was a muff, since he never had possession of the ball—and Keith Reaser recovered for the Chiefs at the Tennessee 28.

This was a chance to put a dagger in the Titans and get ready for the Patriots. But it didn't happen. The offense went three-and-out, and Butker's 48-yard field goal attempt hit the left upright.

Talk about not your night.

The Titans promptly drove 62 yards, capped by a 35-yard Derrick Henry touchdown run to make it 21–16 a minute into the fourth quarter.

The Chiefs' offense was now in full sputter. They picked up one first down but had to punt again. Now all the momentum was in the Titans' favor. They went 80 yards, Mariota finding Eric Decker, the ex-Jet, for the final 22 yards with 6:08 left.

Then came another questionable call. Leading 22–21, the Titans decided to go for two—wanting a three-point lead. Defensive coordinator Bob Sutton sent Daniel Sorensen on a safety blitz and Sorensen got to Mariota, spinning him around until he fumbled. Sorensen picked up the ball and sprinted toward what would have been a two-point defensive conversion—only to be stopped by Triplette—who had ruled Mariota down as Sorensen spun him around.

"That one was at least questionable," Smith said later. "It's a judgment call. When do you call the quarterback in the grasp and the play over? It could have gone either way. It just didn't go ours. Nothing did that night."

Still, there was plenty of time, and all the Chiefs needed was a field goal.

Starting at the 27, Smith completed a pass for 13 yards to Demetrius Harris, who was in the game because of Kelce's absence. Then he took off on a scramble and picked up 18 yards to the Tennessee 42. They were already closing in on field goal range.

Except there was another flag: Harris had been called for holding while trying to block for Smith downfield.

The ball came back to the Chiefs' 41. On third-and-6, Harris made up for his mistake (at least partly) by catching a 9-yard pass for a first down at the Tennessee 45.

But then the Titans' defense, playing aggressively, shut the Chiefs down. They weren't surprised by a Hunt run and stopped him for a yard. Another Smith-to-Harris pass was broken up. Third-and-9. Smith dropped. No one was open. He had to dodge and dart to get back to the line of scrimmage.

It was fourth-and-9. They weren't in Butker's range. In fact, given his earlier miss, they probably needed at least another 20 yards to feel comfortable putting their fate on his foot. The clock was at 2:15. Even with time-outs left, it was possible the offense might not get the ball back.

Reid, Nagy, and Smith decided to call a play that would normally have been for Kelce, a seam route that—they hoped—would be in front of the safeties and behind the linebackers. It was similar in concept to the play the Bengals had run to destroy the Ravens' season a week earlier.

The target, though, wouldn't be Kelce but Albert Wilson, an improving fourth-year wide receiver, who would be in the slot.

The play almost worked. Wilson got into the seam and Smith launched the ball to him. It got over the linebackers and reached Wilson with the safeties coming up to hit him.

But Smith had led Wilson by just a few inches too much. Wilson lunged, and the ball hit his fingertips and went off them, dropping to the ground. Wilson is five feet nine. Kelce is six-five. The argument could be made that the eight-inch height difference might have been the reason for the play to end in an incompletion, not a catch.

Smith shrugged when the subject came up. "It's on me, ultimately," he said. "I have to put the ball where the receiver can catch it. I didn't miss by much, but the result says I missed. Period. It's my job to get the ball there."

The Chiefs had one last gasp when Derrick Henry appeared to fumble on the first play after the Titans took over. Derrick Johnson picked the ball up and ran it in for a stunning, game-changing touchdown. This time Triplette didn't blow his whistle and rule the play dead.

But when New York looked at the replay, it was apparent he'd been wrong—again. Henry was clearly down before he fumbled. After that, the Titans picked up two first downs and ran out the clock.

Stunningly, it was over: Titans 22, Chiefs 21.

The internet and newspapers all ran the same photo the next day: Smith walking off the field wearing a Chiefs stocking cap, looking about as glum as you might expect. The headlines were virtually identical: "Did Alex Smith walk off as a Chief for the last time?"

Smith wasn't thinking about that at the time. He went through his media paces, dressed slowly, and went home to see his family.

"Mostly we talked about the calls, the Mariota-to-Mariota pass, and how many things conspired to keep us from winning," he said. "We didn't really talk much about what was next."

That would come soon enough.

26

As it turned out, the Chiefs weren't the only team to lose at home that weekend—or even that day. The Rams, the third seed in the NFC, lost to the Falcons—-not a huge upset given that the Falcons had gone to the Super Bowl a year earlier and had the more experienced quarterback: Matt Ryan in his tenth season versus Jared Goff in his second.

The next day the Jacksonville Jaguars beat the Buffalo Bills, 10–3, in about as dreary a playoff football game as anyone could remember. Then Drew Brees and the Saints outgunned Cam Newton and the Panthers.

That set up a Falcons-Eagles game in Philadelphia and a Saints-Vikings game in Minnesota in the NFC divisional games, and the Titans against the Patriots and the Steelers hosting the Jaguars in the AFC. The only home underdogs were the Eagles—most people figuring that Nick Foles simply wouldn't be able to produce enough offense to get Philadelphia past Atlanta.

Joe Flacco had watched on and off during the first playoff weekend. At some moments, it was just too hard to be a spectator for a third straight season—especially after the way the Ravens' season had crashed and burned in such shocking fashion.

At other times, he did sit down and watch. "In the end, it's still football," he said. "I love to play football and I love to watch football. Always have. I just had to keep reminding myself not to relive that last game over and over because it wouldn't do any good."

In the aftermath of the Bengals game, Flacco had jumped the line in the interview room—going in before Coach John Harbaugh, wanting to get the ordeal over with as soon as possible. Harbaugh didn't mind that at all. He was still struggling to regain his composure.

Rather than begin with a summation of the game, Flacco simply stood at the lectern and waited for questions. When he was asked about the suddenness of the defeat, he shrugged and did his best to be Cool Joe.

"It's disappointing," he said. "We didn't play well enough to win. Nothing is given to you. You have to make plays to win. We were there." He paused. "Right there. But we ended up losing."

As Harbaugh would do a few minutes later, he tried to give credit to the Bengals rather than point fingers at his own team. "They're a tough defense," he said—then repeated it. Eventually he admitted, "We had a few hiccups in the first half. We didn't pick up some first downs we should have. You give a good defense some confidence that way, it makes it tougher on you."

When he was asked if he had been aware of what was going on in the Bills-Dolphins game, he first insisted that he hadn't. "We all had blinders on," he said. "We were just trying to beat the Bengals."

But then he conceded that he'd known that the Bills had won during those final few minutes. "It was up there on the scoreboard all the time," he said. "It was impossible to miss."

It was only back in the locker room that the real emotions became evident. C. J. Mosley, who had just missed getting his hand on the final, fateful touchdown pass, sat on the floor inside his locker, staring into space. Others did the same.

Terrell Suggs, who had been with the Ravens for fifteen seasons and had taken over for Ray Lewis as the leader of the defense, kept repeating over and over, "We had it, we had it."

Finally, he quoted John F. Kennedy: "Victory has a thousand fathers," he said. "Defeat is an orphan."

Flacco sat on a chair in front of his locker, his head in his hands for at least ten minutes. Normally he would head for the shower as soon as he finished with the media, eager to get dressed and see his family. Now he just sat, unmoving, as if unable to stand up and begin taking off his uniform.

Later, he said he honestly couldn't remember much about those first few minutes of the postseason.

"It's all a blur—maybe it's better that way," he said, forcing a smile. "I know the locker room was pretty silent, and there were a lot of guys just kind of staring into space. Beyond that, I don't remember much at all. It happened so fast.

"What gets you is the realization that there's no next week. It's next *year*. That's what hits the hardest."

Ravens owner Steve Bisciotti postponed his annual postseason press conference, usually held within two or three days of the season ending, for a week. Then, instead of being joined by general manager Ozzie Newsome, as was tradition, Bisciotti arrived with only his ever-present bottle of water in hand and sat alone on the podium.

He announced that Newsome would be stepping down as general manager at the end of the 2018 season. Newsome had been the team's GM since 2002, although he had run the football operation since the Ravens moved to Baltimore in 1996. Eric DeCosta, who had been the GM in waiting for a long time, would succeed him.

The announcement was a surprise because Newsome had been one of the best and most respected GMs in the sport and was only sixty-two. But three straight non-playoff seasons had clearly gotten Bisciotti's attention, and he didn't want to lose DeCosta, who had been pursued by other teams. So Newsome would be cast in a yet to be decided role at the end of 2018.

The other surprise came when someone asked Bisciotti if he had considered firing John Harbaugh. "It was certainly a consideration but not one I was inclined to make this year," Bisciotti answered—a remarkably frank response from a team owner. He went on to say he had not given Harbaugh a "playoffs or bust" edict, but that Harbaugh clearly understood the owner expected better than 9-7 and "close" in 2018.

Clearly, Bisciotti wasn't happy. He was concerned that the empty seats he'd seen in 2017 might turn into unbought tickets in 2018. He didn't like losing. The bar had been set very high in the first seven years of the Harbaugh-Flacco era: six playoff appearances; a Super Bowl win; three conference championship games.

Then had come 8-8, 8-8, and 9-7. No postseason appearances.

Newsome stepping down and Harbaugh being given an edict to at least "do better or bust" made it clear that Bisciotti wasn't inclined to stick with the status quo. There was more to come.

—

On the weekend that the playoffs began, the coaching and scouting staffs of what was soon to be Kirk Cousins's former team in Washington sat down at length to discuss their plans for the Senior Bowl, the NFL combine, and the beginning of the March free agent signing season.

There were lots of decisions to be made, but there was no doubt what the most important one was: Who would be Washington's quarterback in 2018?

Everyone knew it wasn't going to be Cousins. They had known that throughout the season in spite of Cousins's public claims that he wanted to stay in Washington and comments that team president Bruce Allen had made about wanting to keep Cousins.

The Washington-Cousins ship had sailed long ago, and if there had been even a smattering of doubt, it had gone away long ago when Allen had started referring to Cousins in public as "Kurt."

"The problem wasn't that Kirk wasn't a good quarterback—he was a good quarterback," Doug Williams said. "Not great, not the guy who might steal you two games a year single-handed, but a good NFL quarterback. He was also a good guy.

"But regardless of what caused it, we didn't have stability at the quarterback position. The one position in football and in a locker room where you have to have stability is quarterback. The other guys have to look at the quarterback as the leader—all the time. They can't be wondering if he's going to come back the next year. If there's doubt for one year, that's not good. But when there's doubt for three years, well, that's worse."

Williams and his staff had been scouting quarterbacks all season. They had looked at the four quarterbacks who had been considered lock top-of-the-draft picks: USC's Sam Darnold; UCLA's Josh Rosen; Wyoming's Josh Allen; and Oklahoma's Baker Mayfield, the Heisman Trophy winner. Williams had been intrigued enough by Allen that he'd made the trek to Laramie, Wyoming, to see Allen in person.

Williams also liked Lamar Jackson, the Louisville quarterback who had won the Heisman a year earlier, although he looked at him a little differently than the other four.

"He needs to be somewhere where there isn't pressure on him to take over right away," he said. "He's got some technical issues—footwork especially—that he needs to work on, but those are all correctible. If he's in an offense that uses his talents, he can be a star."

There were aspects of each of the other four that Williams liked. He thought Darnold had the most upside potential; liked that Rosen had a little bit of prick in him (as he proved on the night of the draft); was impressed with Allen's arm and physical gifts; and thought Mayfield was the most ready to step in and lead a team.

"He's been through some things," Williams said about Mayfield. "He was a walk-on, he's had to prove himself, he's got edge—sometimes too much edge—to him. He's a tough guy. If you're going to play someone as a rookie, you want a tough guy."

But as the season wore on, Williams found himself focusing more and more on the intriguing possibility of a talented veteran. That guy was Alex Smith. He knew Smith had one year left on his contract with the Chiefs, which meant Kansas City would want something in return for giving him up. He also knew it was unlikely that the Chiefs were going to keep Pat Mahomes on the bench for a second year after trading up a year earlier to take him with the tenth pick.

Williams got to see Smith in action in person when Washington played the Chiefs the fourth week of the season. He liked what he saw. Then, as the season wore on, he watched tape of every one of Smith's games. He didn't watch from the normal 50-yard-line view afforded by network television cameras. He watched—over and over again—from an end zone view, so he was watching from behind Smith and the offense.

The NFL's technology is so sophisticated these days that every team has access to game tapes that show the game from several different views.

"I just press a button on my computer that says 'end zone only,' and that's the angle I see," Williams said.

Watching a quarterback from behind—with a quarterback's eye— allowed Williams to see things he might not see from the sideline view. Some of it is footwork, some of it is how he steps up in the pocket. There's more: arm angle on release—how far he has to bring his arm back to throw the ball deep.

And there's one other thing: "Is he looking for colors?" Williams said.

"Looking for colors" means reacting to the sight of an opposing uniform closing on him. A quarterback who is looking for colors is apt to throw the ball too soon, scramble rather than simply step up, and, worst of all, not hang on to the ball for that split second extra that might make the difference between a completion and an incompletion or an interception.

"It's split-second stuff," Williams said. "It's not the difference between a bad quarterback and a good one, because a bad quarterback will have other problems that aren't as subtle. But it can be the difference between a good quarterback and a very good quarterback."

The more Williams saw of Smith, the more impressed he became. He knew Smith had a reputation as one of the good guys in the league, one of the bright ones too.

"You didn't hear any negatives on him as a person—I mean none," Williams said.

When the scouts and coaches sat down in the team's war room on January 5 in Ashburn, Virginia, the meeting was co-run by Williams, Coach Jay Gruden, and team president Bruce Allen—who was there as owner Dan Snyder's eyes, ears, and mouth. Any major decision—like the quarterback position—would have to be approved by Snyder.

Williams went down the list of free agents: Cousins's name wasn't mentioned, since he was gone. Drew Brees would be a free agent, but no one in the room thought there was any chance he would leave New Orleans.

Then there was the Minnesota trio: Case Keenum, who'd had a remarkable year; Teddy Bridgewater, who had missed most of two seasons after his terrible injury; and the oft-injured Sam Bradford, who remarkably was still only thirty—but a huge risk because of his penchant for getting hurt.

Williams liked Keenum. "He'd gotten a chance to play and went out there with nothing to lose," he said. "He was like a gunslinger, not worried about anything. As the season went on and he and the team did better, you could see his confidence growing. I liked him."

Keenum was going to get paid a lot of money somewhere. He would sign, eventually, with Denver: two years, $36 million—a long way from the $2 million he had made with the Vikings.

Even though he liked Keenum, Williams didn't see him as a major upgrade from Colt McCoy, who had been Washington's backup for most of the previous four seasons. McCoy had proven he could step in when needed for a game or two and, at thirty-one, was only a year older than Keenum.

"If we decided to go with a young quarterback, then Colt would have been the starter for a year," Williams said. "That was the consensus. If we were going to go for a veteran, we needed to feel we were getting someone at least as good as Kirk."

Or even "Kurt."

Bridgewater and Bradford had both proven they could play quarterback in the NFL, but their injuries made them too big a gamble.

There was also AJ McCarron, who had been waiting his turn behind Andy Dalton in Cincinnati. McCarron was younger—he'd be twenty-eight during the 2018 season—and would be considerably cheaper given his limited playing time during his four years in Cincinnati, but the question was the same: Was he an upgrade over McCoy?

McCarron landed in Buffalo—two years, $10 million, slightly better than backup money, but not much.

Jay Cutler would be a free agent, but there wasn't much interest in him, not just because he'd already retired once but because he had been inconsistent in his best years.

And then there was Colin Kaepernick. Williams wasn't inclined to rule him out on the basis of politics, but he did rule him out because of the way Washington runs its offense. "We run the West Coast offense," he said. "Kaep isn't that kind of quarterback. It never became an issue."

Once all the names had been diced and sliced in the room, the name that stood out was Smith. Yes, he'd be thirty-four by the time the season began, but he was a "young" thirty-four. He could still run as well as almost any quarterback in the league not named Aaron Rodgers or Russell Wilson. He was coming off arguably the best year of his career—having thrown for more than 4,000 yards for the first time, even though he'd sat out the last game against Denver.

After two days—ironically on the same day the Chiefs lost to the Titans—the consensus in the room was overwhelming: Smith. The question was, how much would it take to get him?

"We all agreed Alex was the best choice," Williams said. "Bruce took it to Dan and he was on board."

Snyder had to be on board because some real money was going to have to be spent to get Smith. He had one year left on his Chiefs contract for $18 million. Washington didn't want to trade for him on a one-year rental basis.

"It was a given," Williams said, "that we'd need to sign him to an extension. That was the stability part. There was no point bringing him in for one year and then be back where we were sitting in the same place a year later. If we were going to do that, the better move was to go for one of the young guys because it was such a strong class."

That wasn't the move Williams wanted to make. Washington had the sixteenth pick in the first round. To get one of the top four quarterbacks, it would have to move up. The last time the team had done that, it had given up a king's ransom of picks to move from number six to number two to take Robert Griffin III in 2012. Most people in D.C. had forgotten how brilliant Griffin had been as a rookie. The rise was a distant memory; the fall was like an ongoing migraine.

"To get one of the young guys, we were going to have to give up some things I didn't want to give up," Williams said. "It would have made it tougher for us to fill some of the other needs we had."

So the decision was made: contact the Chiefs and see what they were looking for in return for Smith.

"I knew we'd have to give something up," Williams said. "They had Mahomes, but they didn't *have* to trade Alex."

And so, the negotiations began.

—

On the night of January 27, Alex Smith and family were on their way downstairs to have dinner in the restaurant at the Grand Cypress hotel in Orlando.

Smith had been added to the AFC's Pro Bowl roster to replace Tom Brady after the Patriots reached the Super Bowl. Ben Roethlisberger would be the starter backed up by Smith and Derek Carr, who was chosen when Philip Rivers decided not to play.

For Smith, the week in Orlando was a family vacation. Elizabeth and the kids made the trip, and a lot more time had been spent in the various theme parks than on a practice field.

"I was probably more worn-out from walking around all the parks than I would be after a normal week of practice," Smith said. "But that was fine. The week is supposed to be a bonus for playing well, not a week to grind out a game plan."

Certainly, nobody did that.

One of the highlights of the week for Smith had been a chance encounter in the hotel lobby with Mike Nolan—the man who had taken him with the first draft pick in 2005. Things had gone sideways between Nolan and Smith toward the end of Nolan's tenure as coach of the 49ers, but there had never been any serious hard feelings between the two.

Nolan was now the linebacker coach of the New Orleans Saints, and the Saints' coaching staff was coaching the NFC team in the Pro Bowl. Smith and Nolan had run into each other before—usually on the field after games—but had never really sat down and talked in the almost ten years since Nolan's firing in San Francisco.

"Even back then, when we were at odds, I never took it personally," Smith said. "I just felt as if he didn't completely understand how badly I was hurt. I honestly felt that not only would it not do me any good to play with a bad shoulder, but it wouldn't do the team any good because when I did try to play, I was awful."

Nolan had regrets about his time with Smith, but they had little to do with those final weeks.

"It's easy to look back now, but I really wish I'd let him run the same kind of offense he'd run at Utah," Nolan said. "Back then, no one thought to run what was basically a read-option offense. Alex's skills, his ability to use his legs and make decisions, were strengths that I didn't take advantage of when I could have, should have. When Jim [Harbaugh] and Andy [Reid] got him and used him that way, he became a terrific quarterback."

The two men sat and talked for an hour. Nolan told Smith that when he demanded he stand up and tell his teammates why he wasn't playing, it wasn't punitive. "I was actually hoping he'd be more afraid of doing that than trying to play hurt," Nolan said, laughing. "Got that wrong too."

In the end, Nolan realized he had only been thinking short term: he thought Smith playing was his best chance to keep his coaching job. "Alex had to think differently than that," Nolan said. "I understand that now."

Smith enjoyed the conversation because he'd always liked Nolan. There was also some catharsis and closure in it too—which was good for both parties.

By Saturday night, everyone in the Smith family was tired, which was why the easiest route was to eat in the hotel and get everyone to bed early.

On the way downstairs, Smith saw that Andy Reid had left him a message. "I figured I'd call him back after dinner," Smith said.

At that moment, there was no special reason for Reid to be calling. During Smith's exit interview with Reid the week after the season ended, there had been no discussion of the future.

"I think it was tough for Andy, to be honest," Smith said. "I knew and he knew that they had to look into making a deal. But it wasn't a sure thing, and he didn't feel like talking about it. I didn't push him on it because I didn't think there was anything he could tell me at that moment."

Smith was right.

"I guess the thought should have crossed my mind after the Tennessee game that Alex might have just played his last game for us," Reid said. "But it really didn't. Then, after we'd sat down for our postseason meetings, of course it did. But I wasn't certain we'd make a deal. We weren't going to give him up without getting something in return."

Reid had been bargaining with Bruce Allen, who was charged with trying to put a deal together after everyone agreed that Smith was the man Washington wanted.

Washington had hoped to get Smith in return for a draft pick— preferably no higher than a third, but a second could be on the table. But Reid wanted a player—specifically he wanted Kendall Fuller, a young cornerback who had shown a good deal of potential during the 2017 season.

Fuller was about to turn twenty-three and had been a third-round pick in 2016, dropping in the draft because he'd torn a meniscus late in the season at Virginia Tech and there were some questions about his health. He'd been a nickelback for most of his two seasons in Washington and had improved a good deal in his second season.

"We kept trying to put other names in front of them [the Chiefs]," Doug Williams said. "They kept coming back to the same guy. In the end, that was the only way the deal was going to get done. We talked about it over and over, and bottom line was this: you trade a cornerback to get a quarterback every time. We had to do it."

The deal had fallen into place while Smith and family were in Orlando. That's why Reid was calling. During dinner, Smith got a text from Allen Wright, the Chiefs' equipment manager and a close friend.

"Coach is trying to reach you," Wright wrote.

At that point, Smith figured something was up. He called Reid back.

"It wasn't a shock, and I really felt as if Andy had made an effort to move me to a place that would be good for me," Smith said.

Reid had done that. There had been several other teams who had expressed interest in Smith—including the Cleveland Browns—but he had wanted to try to make a deal that would be good for the Chiefs and good for Smith. When Washington agreed to put Fuller in the deal, he felt he had accomplished that.

Once the dust had settled in the wake of the Tennessee loss, Alex and Elizabeth had started discussing where he might be playing and where they might be living the following fall.

"Elizabeth is kind of big on 'what-ifs,'" Smith said. "We talked through a lot of 'what-ifs,' but my attitude was more of let's wait and see what happens. Then, just like that, it happened."

The one important detail that had to be worked out was the contract extension. Since both sides wanted it done, it was unlikely that would be an issue. Tom Condon, who had played eleven seasons for the Chiefs and had become one of the NFL's most respected agents, was Smith's agent. Within three days, the story was being leaked: Mr. Smith was going to Washington.

Predictably, the initial reaction in Washington was largely negative. There were still people buying into the notion that Cousins might return, that somehow a last-second deal would be worked out or Washington would pay $34 million to franchise-tag him again. That wasn't even on the team's radar—or Cousins's radar—and hadn't been through the entire season.

Beyond that, Kendall Fuller was suddenly seen by the Washington faithful not as a solid nickelback with the potential to be a starting cornerback, but as a cross between a young Darrelle Revis and Darrell Green—the Hall of Famer who had played his entire career in Washington.

Players tweeted angrily. Brian Mitchell, the great kick returner, who had become one of the few ex-player voices in town willing to criticize the team, did just that, blasting the trade on television.

Williams understood. Smith understood. Once the contract extension was worked out—four years, $94 million, $71 million guaranteed—both had what they wanted: stability.

Alex and Elizabeth were happy with the idea of living in suburban

Washington—they began looking for houses in the McLean, Virginia, area because they'd learned the schools in that area were excellent and it would give Alex a reverse commute to Washington's practice facility— and Williams had a quarterback who he knew would prepare well, play well, and be a natural leader.

"It's already happened," he said in May 2018, after the team had started OTAs. "You can see it in the locker room and on the practice field. There's no doubt in anyone's mind who the leader of our team is. That will only grow with time."

As soon as Smith was signed by Washington, the Kirk Cousins sweepstakes shifted into high gear. The Jets, Vikings, and Browns were the teams leading the pursuit.

Then, on March 15, the day after the 2018 NFL season "officially" opened, the sweepstakes had a winner. Cousins signed a three-year, $84 million contract with the Minnesota Vikings—every dollar of it guaranteed. It was the first fully guaranteed multimillion-dollar contract in NFL history, and it made Cousins, at that moment, the highest-paid player in NFL history—he would make $28 million a year through the 2020 season.

The Cousins signing came five weeks after the 49ers had made Jimmy Garoppolo—who had led them to five straight wins after being traded from the Patriots—the highest-paid player in history. Cousins's reign as the highest-paid player in the game lasted seven weeks.

In early May, the Falcons gave Matt Ryan a five-year extension beginning in 2019 that will pay him $150 million—$100 million guaranteed—for an average per year of $30 million.

Thomas Dimitroff, the Falcons' general manager, had once said, "Until you find your quarterback, the search for him consumes you."

That was a concise summation of the importance of the quarterback position in the NFL.

Next up was Aaron Rodgers. The consensus was that Ryan wouldn't be number one on the highest-paid list for very long.

27

On a warm spring evening in Indianapolis, after a day in which temperatures had climbed toward ninety, Andrew Luck carried two pizzas into his downtown condo, plopped down at the dining room table, and began talking rapid-fire about what the last year of his life had been like.

In a way, talking about it was easy. In another way, it was hard.

"I got to the point," he said, "where I was running away from the proverbial mirror. I didn't want to see what I was seeing. It took a while, a long while, but I can look now and feel good about what's there."

What was there was a football player who was now convinced—truly convinced—that he was going to be healthy enough to run out of the Lucas Oil Stadium tunnel as the last man introduced for the Colts' offense on September 9, shortly before one o'clock in the afternoon.

"I'll be there and I'll be playing," he said. "There isn't any doubt in my mind about that." He smiled in answer to the next question: "Yes, I've pictured what it's going to look like and thought about what it's going to feel like quite a lot."

That anticipated return would be the first time he'd set foot on an NFL field since January 1, 2017, when he'd led the Colts on a game-winning drive in the fourth quarter that allowed them to beat the Jacksonville Jaguars 24–20 and finish the 2016 season 8-8.

Seventeen days later, he'd had shoulder surgery to fix a labrum issue that had started early in the 2015 season and had lingered even as he tried to play through it.

The road to becoming the guy slamming down a pizza with a smile on his face had been long and difficult.

He still wasn't throwing footballs yet, but he was throwing weighted balls—sometimes heavier than a football—and was pain free. This was in marked contrast to the previous October, when he had returned to practice insisting he was "close" to being ready to play when his body was telling him that simply wasn't the case.

"I have to admit I still have a little bit of fear about starting to throw a football," he said. "I attach a good deal of despair, and not so pleasant memories, to the last time I tried it—because I was in pain even though I tried to deny it. I wasn't in a good place.

"It was hard for me to admit vulnerability. I'm a football player, I'm a tough guy. I can play through pain. I did it through most of 2016. So much of my self-worth was tied in to being a football player. I was confused and lost for a while.

"I'm not proud of how I handled things for a couple of years really. I put my girlfriend [Nicole] and my parents through a lot. It took me a while to understand that fear and apprehension were a part of this process. I had to let people help me. That wasn't easy. I had to be honest with myself and listen to my body. That wasn't easy either."

Luck was happy to be back in Indianapolis (back home again in Indiana?), a place he felt comfortable heading into his seventh season. He was happy to be with Nicole in the same comfortable but hardly pretentious condo he'd had since he first signed with the team, riding his bike around town, eating a takeout pizza from the box rather than sit in a fancy restaurant (although the time he has spent in Europe through the years has given him an appreciation for good food).

While he and Nicole were in the Netherlands, they finally bought something fancy: an espresso maker. Luck is quite proud of his ability to make espresso now.

At twenty-nine, he's a veteran, one of the old guys, and he's comfortable in that role. He knew things were different when he came back from his European sojourn and realized, after spending much of the winter in Palo Alto (where he still has a home), that he was glad to be back in the Colts facility; glad to be back around his teammates; even glad to interact with the media again.

"For a while I'd gotten very uncomfortable with the media," he said. "That's never been me. I've always understood that part of the job is to talk to the media, and I'd like to think I've been honest with them through the years. But not last year. I became protective and withdrawn. I avoided them. I never actually told a lie, but I felt like

I was lying because I didn't want to tell them everything—in part because I didn't *know* where I was, but also in part because the whole thing felt like it should be private.

"Now I feel like I felt in the old days with them.

"Even around the guys [teammates] it's different. I felt a lot of shame and a lot of guilt, especially when I watched the team play. I was *failing*. Maybe intellectually I understood it wasn't my fault I was hurt, but emotionally I was pretty torn up.

"I lost confidence in myself, not just as a player, but as a person. There were some rough times, bad times, after we first got to Europe, but I knew going over there was the right thing to do.

"Being around the facility didn't feel right. When you're not playing, you're not part of it. Out of sight, out of mind—even if you're not literally out of sight."

Luck has always been able to figure things out for himself. He even diagnosed himself with a concussion in 2016 after a game against the Titans. He had taken several hard hits during the game, and when it was over, he began to feel sick and nauseous. He walked into the training room and asked the doctors to give him the concussion protocol.

He was right—he had a concussion. He missed one game. One wonders what might have happened had he not asked the doctors to check him.

The nightmare and isolation that had been Luck's 2017 had shaken him to his core. "I'm not sure I understood how much of my identity was tied up in being a football player," he said. "It got to the point where when I thought of football, I associated it with pain, anguish, and failure.

"Now I'm learning again to see—and enjoy—the game the way I once saw it."

By the spring of 2018, everything about the Colts was either new or under renovation. Their practice facility, northwest of downtown, was undergoing a two-year expansion and renovation project.

The coaching staff was brand-new. The Colts had initially offered the job to Patriots offensive coordinator Josh McDaniels, and he'd accepted. The official announcement was to come right after the Super Bowl.

But two days after the Patriots' loss to the Eagles, McDaniels stunned the team and the NFL when he backed out, opting to return to the Patriots. A week later, Frank Reich, who had been the offensive coordinator for the winning team in the Super Bowl, was hired in his stead.

Reich could not have been more different from McDaniels. McDaniels had been a prodigy, becoming an NFL head coach in Denver at the age of thirty-three. He was still only forty-one and had five Super Bowl rings, courtesy of working for Belichick.

Reich was a classic grinder. He'd been a backup quarterback for most of his college career—at Maryland—and for most of a fourteen-year career in the NFL. Unlike McDaniels, he understood what it was like to play quarterback in the NFL—specifically how *hard* it was to play quarterback in the NFL. Carson Wentz and Nick Foles had both given him a great deal of credit for their success in the 2017 season.

"Sometimes getting left at the altar can be the best thing that ever happens to you," Luck said with a grin. "I'm really enjoying working with Frank and the new staff. It helps when you have a coach who has been through what you're going through and knows firsthand what it takes to succeed."

The pizza was gone. Luck was swigging water and getting ready to go to bed even though it wasn't nine o'clock yet.

"I like getting early starts these days," he said. "I feel like I have a lot to look forward to every morning."

Someday, whenever football is over for him, Luck thinks he might like to be a high school history teacher. He has no interest in becoming a talking head on TV. For now, though, his life is about becoming the football player he once was—and, he hopes, better than that football player.

"I still have a bit of road left to travel," he said. "But I've come a long, long way on the trip."

The bumpiest parts of the ride were over. He hoped.

—

For Ryan Fitzpatrick, the 2017 season hadn't been a joyride either—hardly possible with a team that finishes 5-11—but it had certainly been one of renewal. Fitzpatrick was looking for some continuity to build on in 2018.

The Tampa Bay Buccaneers' disappointing season clearly had little to do with Jameis Winston missing three-plus games. When Winston had first been injured in Arizona, Fitzpatrick had come in and almost rallied the team to a victory. Then, when Winston sat out three November games, the Bucs won the first two with Fitzpatrick starting and almost won the third. Winston returned to play well down the stretch, but the team still kept finding ways to lose.

Two days before the Bucs' final game (a victory at home against the playoff-bound Saints, bringing them to 5-11), the *Tampa Bay Times*'s Rick Stroud reported that Dirk Koetter was going to be retained as coach. Most people had thought that the eleven-loss season would doom him. Koetter had been elevated from the offensive coordinator position two years ago because—according to the Bucs' propaganda— they wanted an offensive-minded head coach to work with Winston, who was clearly the key to the team's future. Lovie Smith had been fired after the team improved from two wins to six wins in his second season. Smith was known for defense, though, not offense.

The move had seemed to work in 2016 when the Bucs went 9-7 and came up just short of making the playoffs. But the team had gone backward in 2017, even though DeSean Jackson had been signed to give Winston a deep threat, and the team had used its first draft pick to add O. J. Howard, a pass-catching tight end out of Alabama. In the twelve games Winston had started going into the finale, the Bucs were 2-10.

The working rumor the entire month of December had been that the team was going to bring back Jon Gruden to coach. Gruden had put out the word during the season that he was ready to return to coaching, and he was a legendary figure in Tampa Bay. The Bucs' only Super Bowl appearance and victory had come in his first season— 2002—when he had taken a team largely put together by Tony Dungy to the title.

The Bucs made the playoffs twice more in the next six seasons but never won another postseason game, and Gruden was fired after going 9-7 in 2008. He remade himself as a media celebrity, getting the ESPN Monday Night Football job in 2009 and then doing various other things for the network, like a series of pre-draft shows called *Jon Gruden's QB Camp,* in which he watched tape with quarterbacks who would be taken in that spring's draft and critiqued what he saw.

Gruden had grown quite wealthy as an ex-coach, and every year there were rumors that he was coming back to coaching—no doubt put out by Gruden's agent, if only to strengthen his negotiating position with ESPN.

Gruden still lived in Tampa and had been prominently featured during *Hard Knocks,* visiting the team and talking to various players and coaches on camera. He'd been inducted into the Bucs' "Ring of Honor" the previous December—during a Monday night game, naturally.

Now, after nine seasons away from the game, Gruden was apparently serious about coming back. He was still only fifty-four and, having not lost a game since 2008, was viewed as a cross between Vince Lombardi, Don Shula, and Bill Belichick.

The two places mentioned most prominently as his landing spot were the two places where Gruden had previously coached: Oakland and Tampa—both teams with coaches in trouble after disappointing seasons.

Tampa took itself out of the running two days before the season ended when Koetter was saved from Black Monday—or See-You-Later Sunday. Oakland owner Mark Davis took about five minutes that Sunday to fire Jack Del Rio once the Raiders' season was over.

Apparently, Gruden had chosen Oakland—meaning he'd be coaching eventually in Las Vegas—over Tampa. There were reports that Gruden was going to the Raiders prior to the Raiders' season-ending loss to the Chargers. Gruden had non-denied them when contacted the day before the game. "I don't want to sit here and speculate," he said. "There is no news to report."

That was technically true. The Raiders would have to go through the charade of complying with "The Rooney Rule," which requires teams to interview at least one minority candidate before filling a coaching vacancy. But by Monday morning, reports were everywhere that Gruden would be the next Oakland coach.

The minute Gruden was off the air the following Saturday night after doing the Chiefs-Titans playoff game, the Raiders announced a press conference to introduce him as their new coach.

Ryan Fitzpatrick was happy that Koetter and his staff would be returning. Generally speaking, athletes don't like change and Fitzpatrick was comfortable with Koetter and offensive coordinator Todd

Monken. He was very comfortable in the quarterback room, which also included Winston, third-stringer Ryan Griffin, and quarterbacks coach Mike Bajakian.

In his exit interview with Koetter the week after the season concluded, Koetter had told Fitzpatrick the team would like him back for the 2018 season. Since he was a free agent, nothing could happen until March.

"I feel good about my situation," Fitzpatrick said the week after the Super Bowl. "I think I showed people I can play when I got the chance this past season. A year ago, I was damaged goods after what happened in New York. I was a failed starter. Now I'm looked at as a successful backup. It changes the narrative. I feel pretty good that someone will want me. I hope it'll be the Bucs."

The game in Phoenix, when he had come off the bench and nearly rallied the team from a three-touchdown deficit, had been part catharsis, part closure, and part rebirth.

"I'd kept so many emotions relating to what happened with the Jets bottled up inside," he said. "After that game, I felt like I could release them, could look back and say, 'Yeah, that wasn't good, but it wasn't the end.' That's probably why I got emotional the next day in the quarterback room."

A longtime fan of *Seinfeld*, Fitzpatrick remembered the episode when Jerry had finally shown emotion and hadn't understood what was happening when he began to cry. "What is this salty discharge coming out of my eyes?" Jerry had said. Fitzpatrick found himself asking the same question on that Monday in October.

"I think having four girls has softened me," he said. "I'm not sure I'd have been able to do that in front of other men a few years ago. I grew up in a tough-guy environment. Now, not so much."

Remarkably, Fitzpatrick had just finished his thirteenth season in the NFL. He had thrown for 26,991 yards in his career. In 2005, he had been the fourteenth of the fourteen quarterbacks drafted.

He had hoped to get a chance to make a team coming out of Harvard and had ended up being a starter in several cities. At the end of the 2012 season in Buffalo, knowing that Chan Gailey was almost certainly going to be fired, he wondered if his career might be over.

"I knew I was finished playing for Buffalo," he said. "I brought my family onto the field after that game, and I took a good look around.

I knew the new coaching staff would clean house, and I wasn't sure if anyone else would want me."

Five years—and three teams—later, he was still playing.

At the end of the 2017 season, he was one of five quarterbacks from that draft still playing: Alex Smith, the number one pick, was a starter about to change teams; Aaron Rodgers, the number twenty-four pick in that first round, was headed for the Hall of Fame. Matt Cassel, who had also been taken in the seventh round—twenty picks ahead of Fitzpatrick at 230th—had started one game in Tennessee when Marcus Mariota was injured. Cassel had played on six NFL teams and had thrown for 17,449 yards—almost ten thousand fewer than Fitzpatrick—in his career. In March, he would match Fitzpatrick's seven teams when he signed with the Detroit Lions to back up Matthew Stafford.

The other class of 2005 quarterback still active in 2017, Derek Anderson, had been an occasional starter in Cleveland and a backup in Baltimore, Cleveland, and Carolina. And given the NFL's dearth of quality backup quarterbacks—and the fact that the thirty-two teams were apparently willing to sign someone out of a peewee league rather than give Colin Kaepernick a chance—there was good reason to believe Anderson would land a job somewhere in 2018.

Clearly, though, Fitzpatrick ranked only behind Rodgers and Smith in terms of career success.

In February, Fitzpatrick was asked to speak at opening day for the Tampa Bay Little League. As bright as he is, Fitzpatrick isn't all that comfortable as a public speaker. He had thought long and hard about what to say and—finally—it had come to him.

"You're speaking to kids as young as five and as old as twelve," he said. "The younger ones probably aren't going to be listening much, if at all. So I tried to come up with some sort of message for the older ones.

"I played everything as a kid, loved all sports; was best at football. But the only reason I got to play in the NFL was because I was a good student. I got recruited at first by one school—Eastern Washington. But I was able to go to Harvard because I had really good grades. My experience at Harvard gave me a chance to play in the NFL.

"So my message is pretty simple: no matter what it is you want to do, in sports or not in sports, your best chance to have a chance is to work in school and get good grades. I didn't want to just give one of those corny 'stay in school and work hard because your parents say so' talks. I wanted to give them a real reason to work hard. I could point to myself as an example of why it's a good idea."

That same month, Fitzpatrick flew to Buffalo to speak at a roast for Eric Wood, his former Bills teammate and good friend. Wood had played nine years in the NFL—had been a Pro Bowler—but had been told by doctors he couldn't play anymore because of a serious neck injury.

"Makes me realize all over again how lucky I've been," he said. "A quarterback in his mid-thirties can keep going for a while *if* he can stay healthy. I'm better now than at twenty-five because I have so much more experience and know the game so much better.

"I'd love a chance to be the guy one more time, but I'm realistic. I can be comfortable as a backup slash unofficial quarterback coach. I really liked working with Jameis. He *does* have a lot to say, and he's still got to work through some things. But I'm convinced he can be great."

And so, Fitzpatrick kept busy in January and February taking some of the parenting burden off Liza—"I love it all," he said—and waiting until he could hear from the Bucs about whether they were going to follow through on what Koetter had said in the exit meeting or if he was going to have to go job-hunting again.

He didn't have to wait long. During the two-day window prior to the start of full free agency on March 14, the Bucs announced that they had signed Fitzpatrick to a one-year deal, giving him a raise from 2017. If Fitzpatrick was with the team all season, he would make $3.3 million—a 10 percent raise from the $3 million he had made in 2017.

Fitzpatrick was happy to be back, to stretch his career for another year, to be in a place where he was already comfortable.

"One more year, I have a chance to get in, throw the ball around, and have some fun," he said. "Hard to ask for much more than that."

He would again get the chance to start when the 2018 season began. In late June, just before the start of training camp, the NFL suspended Winston for the first three games of the season because of a 2016 incident in which Winston had been accused of groping a female Uber driver.

Yet again, the Fitzpatrick jinx lived—once again in a manner no one would have even thought to imagine. Fitzpatrick was less than 2,000 yards from surpassing Jake Plummer, his boyhood hero, in NFL passing yards. It certainly wasn't out of the question.

And when football does end—perhaps ten years from now?—there's that Harvard degree to fall back on.

28

The case can be made that the Philadelphia Eagles' victory in Super Bowl LII (that's fifty-two in English) was the most surprising since the New York Jets shocked the world and changed football forever with their victory over the Baltimore Colts on January 12, 1969, in Super Bowl III (also known as three).

The first two Super Bowls had been one-sided routs: the Green Bay Packers of the NFL easily beating the Kansas City Chiefs and Oakland Raiders of the AFL. With the AFL due to merge with the NFL after the upcoming 1969 season, there were serious questions going into the third Super Bowl about whether the AFL's ten teams could compete with the NFL's sixteen teams.

Joe Namath and his Jets took care of that issue. A year later, Len Dawson and the Kansas City Chiefs beat the Minnesota Vikings in the last AFL-NFL Super Bowl, and there were no doubts about the ability of the AFC—which added the Baltimore Colts, Pittsburgh Steelers, and Cleveland Browns as part of the merger—to compete with the NFC.

There had been other upsets: the New York Giants had been big underdogs to the Buffalo Bills in Super Bowl XXV (twenty-five) in January 1991 and had pulled off the upset. Few people had expected the Denver Broncos to have much chance against the defending champion Green Bay Packers in Super Bowl XXXII (thirty-two) in 1998, and they had won. The New England Patriots, led by second-year quarterback Tom Brady, had stunned the seemingly unbeatable St. Louis Rams in Super Bowl XXXVI (thirty-six) in February 2002. The Giants' win in Super Bowl XLII (forty-two) in 2008 over the unbeaten Patriots had been shocking.

All but one of those upsets, dating to Namath, had involved a quarterback who was in the Hall of Fame (Namath, John Elway) or was a lock for the Hall of Fame once he retired (Brady), or would get serious Hall of Fame consideration (Eli Manning). The exception had been Jeff Hostetler, who had stepped in late in the 1990 season for the injured Phil Simms and had led the Giants to the upset of the Bills.

Most people had assumed the Eagles' chance to win the Super Bowl had disappeared when Carson Wentz had torn both the ACL and MCL joints in his left knee in the L.A. Coliseum on the afternoon of December 10.

The Eagles had brought Nick Foles back to the team the previous spring after the Kansas City Chiefs had decided not to pick up the second year option on his contract. Foles was only twenty-eight, but was well traveled. He'd been the Eagles third-round draft pick out of Arizona in 2012 and had been a backup to Michael Vick as a rookie. The quarterbacks coach that season—Andy Reid's last in Philadelphia—was Doug Pederson.

A year later, Foles won the quarterback job after Vick was injured in Chip Kelly's first season and had a remarkable year, throwing twenty-seven touchdown passes and just two interceptions. The Eagles won seven of their last eight to win the NFC East but then lost, 26–24, in the wildcard round to the Saints.

Things went in the wrong direction for Kelly, Foles, and the Eagles a year later in spite of a 6-2 start. Foles broke his collarbone in week nine (the same injury that would sideline Aaron Rodgers in 2017) and missed the rest of the season, replaced by Mark Sanchez. The team was 4-4 the second half of the season, finishing 10-6—the same record as a year earlier—but not good enough to make the playoffs.

Foles was then traded to the Rams for Sam Bradford, in a swap of quarterbacks. Things didn't go well there. Foles was benched in November in favor of Case Keenum, got his job back when Keenum missed two weeks because of a concussion, and then went back to the bench when Keenum was healthy again.

When the Rams took Jared Goff with the number one pick in the 2016 draft, Foles knew he might not make the team—with Keenum ahead of him in the rotation—and asked for his release as training camp opened. A week later, Andy Reid, the coach who had drafted him in the first place in Philadelphia, signed him as Alex Smith's backup. Foles started one game when Smith was concussed in a game against the Indianapolis Colts and had to sit for a week.

When the Chiefs decided not to pick up his option, Foles considered retiring. He even enrolled in online classes at Liberty University to study for the seminary. A devout Christian, Foles had always intended to be a high school pastor when he finished playing football.

Then the Eagles and Pederson came along and offered him a two-year contract with $7 million in guaranteed money to return to Philadelphia. Pederson wanted an experienced quarterback, one who knew his system, to back up Wentz.

Foles played sparingly—in a couple of mop-up situations—until Wentz's injury.

After Wentz went down, Foles played well in his first two starts, victories over the Giants and Raiders that wrapped up home-field advantage for the Eagles. But when he played poorly in a meaningless season finale at home against the Cowboys—a 6–0 loss—there was gloom all over Philadelphia.

Carson Wentz could take the Eagles to the Super Bowl. But Nick Foles? Nick Foles? Not happening.

Except it did. The Eagles—betting underdogs even playing at home as the number one seed—escaped 15–10 against the Falcons in the divisional round.

A week later, they were underdogs at home again, this time against the Vikings, who were being quarterbacked by Foles's former teammate in St. Louis, Case Keenum.

The Vikings had miraculously escaped from the Saints a week earlier on a final-second, 61-yard touchdown pass from Keenum to Stefon Diggs as time expired.

There were *four* lead changes in the final 3:01 of the game. The Saints, after converting a fourth-and-10 earlier in the drive, took a 21–20 lead on a Drew Brees touchdown pass with 3:01 left. Keenum then took the Vikings to the Saints' 35, where the drive stalled and Kai Forbath kicked a 53-yard field goal to make it 23–21 with 1:25 remaining. That was plenty of time for Brees, who marched his team to the Vikings' 25. When Wil Lutz's 43-yarder made it 24–23, long-suffering Minnesota fans began shaking their heads in "not again" fashion.

Older fans still remembered (vividly) the 1975 Roger Staubach–to–Drew Pearson Hail Mary that had given the Cowboys a 17–14 playoff victory on the last play of the game. Forty years later, when Staubach spoke at a luncheon in Minneapolis, he was booed.

More recently, there had been the playoff game two years earlier when the Vikings had moved down the field, trailing the Seahawks 10–9, to set up a 27-yard chip-shot field goal for Blair Walsh on the game's final play. Except Walsh somehow hooked the kick and the Vikings lost.

Now it appeared the Vikings were going to be victimized by Brees and the Saints—playing on their sparkling new home field.

The Vikings had twenty-five seconds and one time-out. After a penalty moved the ball back to the 20, Keenum found his best receiver, Diggs, for 19 yards to the 39. The Vikings spent their last time-out. Then came two incomplete passes, taking the clock to ten seconds.

The Saints had six defensive backs on the field. Any kind of completion inbounds would end the game; there would be no time for Minnesota to line up for a field goal.

Keenum dropped and, with time, threw a high pass to Diggs, who leaped to catch it. There were two defensive backs in the area: rookie safety Marcus Williams and cornerback Ken Crawley.

Williams had had an excellent rookie season with four interceptions and already had another one earlier in the game.

Now, just needing to wrap Diggs up and keep him inbounds, he *dove* at him for some inexplicable reason. Not only did he completely whiff on Diggs as he came down with the ball, but he plowed into Crawley—knocking him out of the play.

Diggs—stunned—came down on one foot, put his left hand down to balance himself, and ran the last 35 yards untouched into the end zone as the clock hit zero.

Final: Vikings 29, Saints 24.

It was one of those "Where were you when?" moments in sports. People began posting YouTube videos of Viking fans reacting, going from despondent to euphoric in an instant. The opposite, naturally, was true in New Orleans.

The front page of the *New Orleans Times-Picayune* summed up the feelings there pretty well. Over a photo of Diggs running away from the Saints' defenders, the three-deck headline said: "EXPLETIVE . . . EXPLETIVE . . . EXPLETIVE."

The euphoria lasted seven days. Then the Vikings—favored on the road to become the first team to ever host a Super Bowl in its home stadium—made the trip to Philadelphia.

The game started well for the Vikings: they took a 7–0 lead on their opening drive. Then, after an Eagles punt, Keenum made a rare—but critical—mistake. As he stepped up to throw from his own 35, he was hit by the Eagles' Chris Long, causing his pass to flutter and wobble. It was intercepted by linebacker Patrick Robinson, who set up his blockers and weaved 50 yards from the left sideline to the right sideline for a tying touchdown.

No one knew it at that moment, but the game was over. The Vikings never scored again—Keenum ended up with two interceptions and a lost fumble—and Foles pitched a near-perfect game, completing 26 of 33 passes for 352 yards and three touchdowns. The final was 38–7.

Shockingly, the Eagles were going to their third Super Bowl. Not shockingly, their opponent would be the Patriots, who were going to their eighth in the Bill Belichick–Tom Brady era. The only surprise had been how close the Jacksonville Jaguars had come to beating them in the AFC Championship game.

The Jags, after scoring all of 10 points to slip past the Bills in the wildcard round, had scored 45 (!!) to stun the Steelers in Pittsburgh, 45–42. The Jaguars led the Patriots 20–10 in the fourth quarter before Brady (surprise) led New England on two drives that culminated in touchdown passes to Danny Amendola, allowing the Patriots to escape, 24–20.

That set up David vs. Goliath—at least at the quarterback position—in the Super Bowl. It was Brady, arguably the greatest quarterback of all time, coming off perhaps his best season at the age of forty and going for a *sixth* Super Bowl ring, against Foles, the backup who had seriously considered retiring to enter the seminary less than a year earlier.

David won . . . again.

The game was a classic—at least on offense. The two teams combined for 1,151 yards, over 200 yards more than any previous Super Bowl. Brady was 28-of-48 for a staggering 505 yards. Foles was 28-of-43 for 373 yards, threw three touchdown passes, and *caught* a touchdown pass.

That came with thirty-four seconds left in the first half. Leading 15–12 and facing fourth down from the New England 1-yard line, Eagles coach Doug Pederson elected to go for the touchdown.

Foles then suggested using a play called "Philly special," and Pederson agreed.

On the play, Foles moved out of the shotgun as if to say something to his offensive linemen, but then stayed put, just behind the right side of the line, as running back Corey Clement moved over to take the snap from center Jason Kelce. Tight end Trey Burton, lined up on the left side, ran behind Clement and took what appeared to be an end-around pitch.

Instead, Burton—who had once been a quarterback—pulled up and threw a perfect pass to Foles, who was wide open in the end zone.

The stunning play gave the Eagles a 22–12 halftime lead. Brady and the Patriots rallied—of course—and took a 33–32 lead with 9:22 left in the game on a Brady–to–Rob Gronkowski 4-yard touchdown pass.

Foles and the Eagles never blinked. They drove 75 yards in eleven plays, taking 7:01 off the clock. Foles found Zach Ertz for an 11-yard score with 2:21 to go. The two-point conversion failed, and it was 38–33, Eagles.

That was an eternity when facing Brady. Except, for once, Brady turned human. On the second play of the Patriots' drive, he was sacked by defensive end Brandon Graham and fumbled. Derek Barnett jumped on the ball at the Patriots' 28. The Patriots' defense held, and Jake Elliott kicked a field goal to make it 41–33 with 1:05 still to go.

Brady had taken the Patriots on two touchdown drives that were followed by successful two-point conversions in the fourth quarter of the Super Bowl against the Falcons a year earlier. This time, though, he couldn't cross midfield. The game ended with Brady heaving a Hail Mary pass from his own 49-yard line in the direction of Gronkowski. He had to avoid a rush just to get the throw off, and when he did, Gronkowski was surrounded by five Eagles at the goal line. They all went up for the ball, which was batted around and finally hit the ground as the celebration began in Philadelphia.

Foles was voted the game's MVP—the twenty-ninth quarterback in the fifty-two Super Bowls to be the MVP. Brady has won four and no doubt would have made it five if the Patriots had pulled off another miracle.

Not this time. This time the miracle came from south Philadelphia.

—

Joe Flacco normally doesn't stay up to watch the NFL draft. He figures he'll find out soon enough and goes to bed when he feels like going to bed. Occasionally he might wait up to see whom the Ravens take in the first round, if they aren't drafting too late.

The first night of the 2018 NFL draft was a little different. Flacco was in Baltimore for off-season workouts with the team. John Harbaugh is one of those coaches who think it's very important for *everyone* to be there for the off-season workouts—not OTAs, just daily sessions of lifting, running a little, and hanging out.

Flacco would just as soon be home with his family and work out on his own, but he's now in his eleventh season with Harbaugh and he likes to keep the coach happy. "It's only about a ninety-minute drive," he said. "In the end, it's easier to be here than to be home and get a call every morning saying, 'Hey, Joe, where are you?'"

And so, Flacco was in Baltimore on the night of April 26, when the most overhyped sports event of the year began. He had a house guest, former teammate and close friend Dennis Pitta.

Pitta was in town for two reasons: he and his wife were selling their house, and he'd been asked to join a number of Ravens and ex-Ravens at the team's draft-fest, which would be held at the Inner Harbor on Saturday, the third and final day of the draft.

Because Pitta was there, Flacco didn't go to bed as early as he usually would. The two men sat and watched as four quarterbacks went in the first ten picks. They watched the Ravens trade down twice: first from sixteenth to twenty-second and then from twenty-second to twenty-fifth.

The Ravens made the moves to add picks in later rounds: they gave the Bills a fifth-round pick to swap places in the first round and got a third-round pick in return. Then they swapped back to twenty-fifth with Tennessee and got a fourth-rounder in exchange for a sixth-rounder.

It was Ozzie Newsome's last draft as the Ravens GM, and it was apparent he wasn't going gently into that good night.

When the trades were made, Flacco texted Dana Flacco, back home in New Jersey, just to keep her apprised. He knew she had her hands completely full since their fifth child—Thomas—had been born on April 6.

When the Ravens finally did pick, they chose a tight end, Hayden Hurst, from South Carolina. Having lost Pitta the previous season, the team's production at the position had dropped measurably.

"We got a tight end," Flacco texted to Dana.

"I thought, 'Oh, that's nice,' " Dana said later. "Then I went to bed."

Flacco was happy with the pick, not only because Hurst would no doubt help the offense, but because a small part of him had wondered if the team might draft a quarterback early in the quarterback-rich draft.

He had turned thirty-three in January, and it was apparent that Ryan Mallett, his backup in 2017, wasn't any sort of heir apparent. Three weeks earlier, the team had signed Robert Griffin III to a no-risk, one-year contract worth $1 million.

Griffin was still only twenty-eight, and the team was hoping he might be a reasonable backup for Flacco. He had played in five games total since 2014: none in Washington in 2015; five in Cleveland in 2016; and none in 2017.

Even after four quarterbacks were taken in the first ten picks, Flacco knew that Louisville's Lamar Jackson, who was considered a longer-term project than the so-called big four but a huge talent, was still on the board.

When the Ravens took Hurst, Flacco was ready to call it a night. Pitta wanted to watch the rest of the round. Somewhat reluctantly, Flacco agreed.

Already, the Giants were being pilloried for failing to take a successor to thirty-six-year-old Eli Manning with the number two pick, taking Penn State running back Saquon Barkley instead.

After the Patriots took running back Sony Michel from Georgia with the thirty-first pick, Flacco was eager to hear who the Eagles took, if only so he could go to bed. It was getting close to midnight. As the father of five, all under the age of six, Flacco is an early-to-bed, early-to-rise guy. He might have been half listening when Roger Goodell walked to the podium for the final time, shortly after midnight.

"The Philadelphia Eagles have traded their pick to the Baltimore Ravens," Goodell announced.

The trade had been made less than five minutes earlier, and the various networks had reported it just before Goodell walked to the podium.

After his usual pause when he announces a trade, Goodell said: "With the thirty-second pick in the 2018 NFL draft, the Baltimore Ravens select . . . Lamar Jackson, quarterback Louisville."

Jackson was the only player invited to New York still in the greenroom—wearing a green suit for the occasion. He bounded joyously onto the stage, still a little frustrated that thirty-one teams had passed on him, but relieved to be a number one pick.

"Perfect team for him," Doug Williams thought, sitting in Washington's war room. "Because he doesn't have to play right away."

As the first African American quarterback to win a Super Bowl, Williams always has an eye out for African American quarterbacks because he knows, even though things are better now than they were when he was a rookie in 1978, it is still a more difficult road for most than for white quarterbacks.

Jackson had had to deal with a number of old white men—including Bill Polian, the Hall of Fame ex-GM of many teams—insisting he should be a wide receiver. Polian had said—among other things—that Jackson was too short. Jackson is six feet three. Baker Mayfield, the number one pick in the draft, is six feet and a half-inch.

Flacco wasn't concerned with whether Jackson was white or black. He and Pitta looked at each other and started laughing, both a little shocked by what they had just heard. You could say whatever you wanted, but the Ravens had just taken someone who would be looked at as Flacco's successor.

Flacco had signed a contract extension in 2016 that could keep him in Baltimore through the 2021 season. But there was an out for both sides after 2019, meaning the Ravens could let Flacco go then (or Flacco could opt to leave). Or the team could—in theory—do what the Chiefs had done with Alex Smith: trade him with one guaranteed year left on his contract following the 2018 season.

Flacco wanted to play at least through the end of his contract. He would turn thirty-seven in January 2022. He might want to play beyond that, but he *at least* wanted to play that long—preferably in Baltimore.

Flacco and Pitta were still digesting the announcement when Flacco's phone rang. It was John Harbaugh.

"Hey, Joe, we drafted a tight end for you," Harbaugh said.

Flacco almost laughed out loud.

"John, you aren't calling me at midnight to tell me we drafted a tight end," he said.

Harbaugh dropped the act. "We all felt this was an opportunity—looking down the road a few years," he said. "I think you know that."

Flacco knew that, but it didn't fill him with confidence about what lay down that road. He decided against texting Dana again, figuring she was either struggling with the baby or trying to grab some sleep.

The next morning he called and told her the news.

"What does it mean?" Dana asked.

"I don't really know," Joe answered. "But it means that change is coming at some point."

Two days later, as requested by the team, Flacco appeared at the draft-fest in the Inner Harbor. He was there to sign autographs, take pictures, interact with the fans. But the drafting of Jackson had changed the dynamic of the day.

Flacco had spoken to Chad Steele, the Ravens' director of publicity, several times before the event. A lot of their conversations were about logistics. But knowing that circumstances had changed for Flacco with the Jackson pick, Steele told him not to worry about the media—who would inevitably show up.

"There's no need for you to talk unless you really want to," Steele said, knowing that was unlikely. "We'll have people [security] around you when you go from place to place. There will be guys [reporters] there, but you don't have to say anything. Just keep moving."

Flacco did as instructed. When *Baltimore Sun* columnist Peter Schmuck and ESPN Ravens beat reporter Jamison Hensley approached him, Flacco just said, "Not today, guys."

"It wasn't a big deal," Flacco said later. "I like both those guys. It just wasn't the time or place. I mean, what was I going to say in thirty seconds? Not much one way or the other."

Naturally, though, his "Not today, guys" stirred up the local media, creating stories about how upset Flacco was with the pick. He wasn't crazy about the idea, but he did understand.

"It's a business," he said. "I get it. I have to be realistic, though. They didn't take a guy whose skill set is similar to mine. If he's good—and I think he is—there's going to come a time when the offense will have to change if he's going to play."

Because Flacco was in Baltimore for off-season workouts Monday to Thursday (leaving to return home most weeks on Thursday afternoon) and Jackson was in town on weekends for rookie mini-camps, the two didn't cross paths until the team's first official OTAs in late May.

Much was made of Jackson saying he hadn't yet met Flacco after his first weekend in Baltimore, because clearly this was going to be an ongoing story: the veteran with a Super Bowl ring and the kid who was his successor-in-waiting.

By the time training camp rolled around, the Ravens' quarterback room had to be the most interesting in football: three first-round draft picks: Flacco (number eighteen in 2008), Griffin (number two in 2012), and Jackson (number thirty-two in 2018). One had risen to stardom, won a Super Bowl, and had ups and downs since then. One had been a runaway star as a rookie and then fallen to being a low-risk free agent signing. The third had yet to begin writing his NFL story.

All around the league, teams and their quarterbacks were starting over. There was still nothing quite like being an NFL quarterback financially. Flacco would be paid $24.25 million in 2018. Andrew Luck hoped he would earn the $24 million he was due in Indianapolis. Alex Smith would make about $23.5 million in his new home in Washington. Ryan Fitzpatrick wasn't in their league at $3.3 million, but he wasn't complaining. He knew that only a handful of the members of Harvard's class of 2005 were likely to earn as much.

Other quarterbacks had signed lucrative new contracts, among them Kirk Cousins and Case Keenum, who had gotten a $16-million-per-year raise going from Minnesota to Denver. Josh McCown, at age thirty-nine, had signed a $10 million contract with the Jets as insurance, even though they had used the number three pick to draft Sam Darnold, presumably as their franchise quarterback.

Doug Williams had become the highest-paid player in the history of his team after being named MVP of Super Bowl XXII (twenty-two) in 1988, leading Washington to a 42–10 rout of Denver after falling behind 10–0 in the first quarter.

The new contract was worth $3.5 million for three years—far less than backup money nowadays.

"It's fine with me," Williams said with a broad grin. "I can tell you from personal experience that they earn every dollar. And the best ones are worth every penny to their teams and to the league.

"Everyone takes a beating in football, but when you get hit as a quarterback, you get *hit*. You're usually helpless when some huge guy, running all out, slams into you. It hurts. Every single time, it hurts.

"But ninety-nine percent of the time, you get up and go back to the huddle and call the next play. If you can't play through pain, you can't play."

The night before his Super Bowl, Williams had to have an emergency root canal because of an abscessed tooth. No way would it keep him from starting.

Late in the first quarter, Williams twisted his ankle badly while being sacked. Because trainers came onto the field, Williams had to come out. Jay Schroeder, whom Williams had replaced as the starter for postseason, came in. He was sacked and Washington had to punt.

On the sidelines, Williams told Coach Joe Gibbs he was ready to go after his ankle had been wrapped. Gibbs was uncertain but decided to see how Williams looked for one series.

On the next *five* series—all in the second quarter—Washington scored, Williams throwing four touchdown passes. Washington led 35–10 at halftime and never looked back.

"No way was I not going back in," Williams said, years later. "It was the Super Bowl. Quarterback is an ego position. You can't play it without an absolute belief in yourself. I believed—*knew*—I was a better quarterback than Jay. I wasn't leaving that game in his hands."

The two quarterbacks had never gotten along. Once, when it appeared Schroeder was hurt during the regular season, Gibbs had sent Williams into the game. Schroeder had angrily waved him off, as if Williams didn't deserve to be on the same field with him. Williams hadn't forgotten.

And yet . . .

"Jay was a good quarterback. He was a competitor. I don't have any hard feelings directed at him.

"If you play quarterback in the NFL, you're part of a fraternity. In the grand scheme of things in sports, it's a very small fraternity. I get asked a lot, 'Tell me what it's like to play quarterback in the NFL, you did it and did it well.'

"My answer is that I can't explain it. You have to have done it, you have to have felt it—all of it. I can't explain what it feels like to walk into a huddle and have all eyes looking at you, expecting you to take control and lead."

He leaned back in his chair, one more memory flashing through his head. "December 11, 1977," he said, the date still embedded in his mind. "It was my junior year at Grambling, we played a game in Tokyo against Temple, which was a very big deal. First time two American college teams played over there. It was called 'the Mirage Bowl.' Back then Temple was a very good Division I program and we didn't get many chances to play Division I teams. We were 9-1 and down 32–28 with a little more than a minute to go, and we had the ball on our own fifteen.

"I came into the huddle and there was a lot of chatter. One of our linemen said, 'Only one voice in this huddle.' Everyone shut up. We drove the length of the field and won, 35–32.

"There's nothing like the feeling you have when you succeed playing the position and nothing like the feeling when you fail. It's always on *you*. It has to be. You have the ball in your hands on every play. No one else does.

"I've been retired almost thirty years, but I can still get chills looking back on when I played and I still get 'em when I see someone take a team eighty-five yards in a minute, knowing there's only one voice the other ten guys are hearing—huddle or no huddle.

"I still love that feeling—even vicariously. There's nothing quite like it."

Of all his Super Bowl memories, one stands out for Williams. He had received the MVP Trophy, having thrown for 340 yards and four touchdowns, and walked off the field in San Diego's Qualcomm Stadium, the trophy in his arms.

The first person he saw in the tunnel was Eddie Robinson, his old college coach at Grambling, the man who had taught him about toughness and how to be a quarterback.

"Coach Rob was standing there, waiting for me," Williams said, his normally booming voice growing soft. "He reached up and put his arm around my neck and said, 'I'm proud of you—not for the touchdowns or for that trophy.

" 'I'm proud of you because you went down, you were hurt, and you got back up and came right back into the game. They couldn't keep you down. That's what I'm proud of you for more than anything else.'"

When it's all said and done, that—more than anything—is what quarterbacks have to do. They all go down. It's the ones who get up who achieve greatness.

And all will tell you the same thing: it's not nearly as easy as it looks.

ACKNOWLEDGMENTS

A very wise man—my old pal Dave Kindred—once told me that none of us who write for a living can do our jobs very well without our sources. This is true whether writing a newspaper story, a magazine piece, or a book. It is most true when writing a book.

So let me begin with the five men who are the heart and soul of this book: Doug Williams, Alex Smith, Joe Flacco, Andrew Luck, and Ryan Fitzpatrick. Each had a very different experience during the 2017 season, and each was very generous with his time and his insights—not to mention his patience. I am truly grateful to all of them.

Although much of the reporting in this book focuses on the five men named above, there were, of course, many others who helped greatly along the way. In Baltimore, I start—as always—with Kevin Byrne and Chad Steele. Thanks also to Marisol Renner, Kevin Gleason, and Tom Valente, who took care of road credentials for me. Also: Eric DeCosta, John Harbaugh, and Ozzie Newsome—even if Ozzie never makes it easy. In Kansas City, my longtime friend Bob Sutton, Andy Reid, and Ted Crews.

Thanks also to Matt Conti in Indianapolis, old pal Pat Hanlon with the Giants, Bruce Speight with the Jets, Tony Wyllie in Washington, Allen Barrett in Tampa Bay, and Brett Strohsacker in Philadelphia. Special thanks to Will Wilson, Luck's agent, who was extremely patient dealing with me while Andrew was in Europe; and to Alex's dad, Oliver; and to Bob Kravitz, who always goes out of his way to help me when I ask.

The real driving force behind this book was my editor at Doubleday, Jason Kaufman, who probably knows far more about the NFL than I do. There were times during this process when I got very frustrated—dealing with the NFL can be very difficult—and Jason was the person who kept saying, "Keep going, you have a good book here." I think (hope) he was right. Jason and his boss, Bill Thomas, and I don't agree on everything, but they're both very patient about putting up with my various rants.

Thanks also to Jason's assistant, Carolyn Williams, who never blinks at my stupid questions and requests.

And congratulations to my agent, Esther Newberg, who has now managed to sell *forty* of my books to various publishers during the last thirty-three years. She deserves a party. Or maybe we both do. Esther's best trait as an agent through the years has been picking assistants. I should know—I married one of them. Her two most recent choices, Zoe Sandler and Alex Heimann, are excellent examples of what I'm talking about. I would also be remiss if I failed to thank John Delaney, who has lawyered my contracts on countless occasions and who I know, based on experience, never misses anything. Others at ICM who still deserve mention: Kari Stuart and the recently departed Liz Farrell.

I'm fortunate that the longest list of all is always the one that includes my friends: Keith and Barbie Drum, Steve Barr and Lexie Verdon, Jackson and Jean Halperin, David and Linda Maraniss, Bob Woodward and Elsa Walsh, Sally Jenkins, Dan Jenkins, Terry and Patti Hanson, Doug and Beth Doughty, Andy Dolich, Wes Seeley, Pete Alfano, David Teel, Gary Cohen, Pete Van Poppel, Mike Werteen, Phil Hoffmann, Joe Speed, Andrew Thompson, Omar Nelson, Frank DaVinney, Gordon Austin, Eddie Tapscott, Chris Knoche, Dean and Anne Taylor, Tim Kelly, Anthony and Kristen Noto, Derek Klein, Jim Cantelupe, and John Graves. Dicky Hall has been a great friend for more than twenty years, and I *know* he's responsible for my being made an honorary member of the Army Football Club this past summer. Everyone at Army will miss Steve (Moose) Stirling, who worked with Dicky in the equipment room forever.

Vivian Thompson-Goldstein, Bob Zurfluh, Michael Wilbon (with thanks for bringing up Alex Smith as a potential QB subject to me), Tony and Karril Kornheiser, Nancy Denlinger, Governor Harry Hughes, General Steve Sachs, Tim Maloney, Chris Ryan, Harry Kantarian, Jim Rome, Mike Purkey, Tom and Jane Goldman, Mike Gastineau, Dick and Joanie (Hoops) Weiss, Tom Brennan, Chris Spatola, Holland and Jill Mickle, Jerry Tarde, Mike O'Malley, Sam Weinman, Ryan Herrington, and Larry Dorman.

The Edwards family: Jay (in spite of his horrific politics), John Cutcher and Chris Edwards, Len and Gwyn Edwards-Dieterle, Bill Leahey, Andy North, Gary "Grits" Crandall, Drew Miceli, Paul Goydos, Steve Flesch, Billy Andrade, Brian Henninger, Olin Browne, Kevin Sutherland, and Tom and Hilary Watson. And to Tom Stathakes—again.

Thanks to former colleagues, still friends from Golf Channel: Todd Lewis, Brandel Chamblee, Frank Nobilo, David Duval, Rich Lerner, Kristi Setaro, Eric Rutledge, David Gross, Courtney Holt, Andrew Bradley, Notah Begay, Lisa Cornwell, Damon Hack, Gary Williams, Jay Coffin, Steve Burkowski, Tripp Isenhour, Justin Leonard, Billy Kratzert, Don Cross, Jon Steele, and Tony Grbac.

Others who worked like hell to try to make me look good on-camera: Julie Hoddy, Tom Forrest, Robert (Swanny) Swanson, Brian Thorne, Mike Davis, and John Feyko. Actually, Feyko never tried to make me look good, but he did make me laugh.

At CBS Sports Radio: Andrew Bogush, Max Herman, Pete Bellotti, David Mayurnik, Mark Chernoff, Anthony Pierno, Billy Giacaolone, and gone-but-not-forgotten Mike Diaz.

At *The Washington Post*: Matt Rennie, Matt Vita, Matt Bonesteel, David Larimer, Marty Weil, Mark Maske, Gene Wang, and Kathy Orton.

Others in various sports: David Fay, Mike Davis, Mary Lopuszynski, Frank and Jaymie Bussey. Others in golf: Tim West, Marty Caffey, Henry Hughes (still), Sid Wilson, Joel Schuchmann, Todd Budnick, Dave Senko, Doug Milne, Colin Murray, John Bush, Laura Hill, Tracey Veale, James Cramer, Joe Chemyz, Phil Stambaugh, Dave Lancer, Ward Clayton, and Guy Scheipers. I miss Denise Taylor.

The rules guys: Mark, Laura, and Alex Russell, who are still right but know I'm correct; same for Slugger White, Steve Rintoul, Jon Brendle (emeritus), Robbie Ware, Ken Tackett, Dillard Pruitt, John Paramour, and Stephen Cox, who I know blames me for West Brom's relegation. Sorry, Stephen.

Hoops people: Mike and Mickie Krzyzewski; Gary Williams; Roy Williams; David Stern; Tim Frank; Brian McIntyre; Seth and Brad Greenberg; Jim Calhoun; Brad Stevens; Shaka Smart, Mike Rhoades; Billy Donovan; Larry Shyatt; the Odom family—Lynne, Ryan, and Dave—pretty much in that order; Jim Larranaga; Mack McCarthy; Pat

Flannery; Nathan Davis; Ralph Willard; Fran O'Hanlon; Jim Crews; Zach Spiker; Pat Skerry; Emmett Davis; Ed DeChellis; Jimmy Allen; Bily Lange; and Tony Shaver. Frank and Susan Sullivan are as good as it gets when it comes to friends.

Others at Army and Navy: Boo Corrigan, Rich DeMarco, Dean Darling, Joe Beckerle, John Minko, Bob Beretta, Jeff Monken, John Loose, Chet Gladchuk, Scott Strasemeier, Stacy Michaux, Justin Kishefski, and, of course, Kenny Niamatulolo.

Docs—still a long list at my age: Eddie and Amy McDevitt, Bob Arciero, Gus Mazzocca, Murray Lieberman, Steve Boyce, and Joe Vassallo. Got a wake-up call this spring on my health. Trying to heed it.

The one and only Tom Konchalski. Enough said.

Swimming knuckleheads: Jeff Roddin, Jason Crist, Clay F. Britt, Wally Dicks, Mark Pugliese, Paul Doremus, Danny Pick, Erik (Dr. Post) Osbourne, John Craig, Doug Chestnut, Peter Ward, Penny Bates, Carole Kammel, Mary Dowling, Margot Pettijohn, Tom Denes, A. J. Block, Pete Lawler, and, of course, Mike (three-timer) Fell.

The China Doll/Shanghai Village gang: Aubre Jones, Stanley Copeland, Harry Huang, Geoff Kaplan, Mark Hughes, Jack Kvancz, Joe McKeown, Pete Dowling, Bob Campbell, Joe Greenberg, Morgan Wootten (who will be back any week now), Jeff Gemunder, and Lew Flashenburg. Gone but still talked about often and fondly: Red, Zang, Hymie, Rob, Arnie, and Reed.

The Rio gang: Tate Armstrong, Mark Alarie, Clay Buckley, and the completely insane Terry Chili.

The Feinstein Advisory Board: Dave Kindred, Keith Drum, Frank Mastrandrea, and, of course, Bill Brill—who must be smiling up in heaven every time Trump tweets.

The last year has often been difficult—a sad part of getting older. My brother-in-law, David Sattler, died last December after a long, brutal battle with a rare form of Alzheimer's. He was one of the best men I ever knew. My pal Jim O'Connell, who was as well liked as anyone in my profession, died in late June—he had been sick for a long time, too. David was fifty-eight. Oc was sixty-four.

And then there was John McNamara, whom I had known most of my adult life, the epitome of a *pro,* a guy who knew a story when he saw it and knew how to write it. Bright, funny, the kind of guy everyone knows and likes. John was one of the five people killed in the shooting spree in the *Annapolis Capital-Gazette* newsroom. He was fifty-six. Next time you hear the president of the United States crassly refer to the media as "the enemy of the people," please think of John and his colleagues.

Last and never least, my family: Bobby, Jennifer, Matthew, Brian, Marlynn, Cheryl, and Marcia. And Margaret, Ethan, and Ben, who have done an amazing job of carrying on without their husband and father.

Most of all the four people I thank God for every day: Christine—whose place in heaven is assured—and Danny, Brigid, and Jane, also known as the 2018 three-hole junior champion of Congressional Country Club. Not that I'm the least proud of that. Clearly, *not* a chip off the old block.

INDEX

ABC, 256
Abdullah, Husain, 105
Adams, Davante, 203, 211
Afghanistan War, 159, 181
African Americans
    draft and, 31, 88
    as general managers, 163–64, 270
    kneeling controversy and, 158–59, 171
    as quarterbacks, 10, 23–32, 61–62, 73–78, 330
Agholor, Nelson, 169
Aikman, Troy, 56, 155
Air Coryell offense, 103
Air Force Falcons, 49
Akers, David, 84
Alabama, University of, 25–26, 76, 316
Alcorn State University, 41
Allen, Brad, 241, 247
Allen, Bruce, 79, 162–64, 167, 193, 225–26, 303–6, 309
Allen, Buck, 286
Allen, George, 193, 224
Allen, Josh, 80, 213, 303
Alonso, Kiko, 252–54
Amendola, Danny, 326
American Football Conference (AFC)
    Championship, 8, 89, 93, 98–100, 108, 249, 326
    Divisions: Central, 91; East, 89, 114–15, 185; North, 1–3, 42, 93, 201, 259–60; South, 105, 96; West, 19, 105, 108, 109, 139, 200, 231, 242, 247
    playoffs, 109–10, 116, 139, 178, 292, 293, 300

Pro Bowl, 307
    wildcard, 15, 256, 259, 292
American Football League (AFL), 27, 28, 322
American Legion Tournament, 26
Amos, Adrian, 206–7
Amsterdam Admirals, 283
Anderson, Robby, 237
Andrews, Dr. James, 57–59, 73–75, 172
Appalachian State University, 41
Arena Football League, 137
Arians, Bruce, 286
Arizona, University of, 323
Arizona Cardinals, 55, 59, 118, 154, 170, 188–89, 195, 200, 215, 286, 318
    Super Bowl XLIII (2009), 90
Arizona State University, 188
Arizona Wranglers, 34
Army Rangers, 159
Atlanta Falcons, 41, 81, 101–2, 109, 187, 196, 198, 215, 223, 227, 237, 251, 266, 275, 292, 294, 300, 311, 324
    Super Bowl LI (2017), 275, 327
Auburn University, 69

Bailey, Dan, 202, 226–27
Bajakian, Mike, 318
Baker, David, 154
Baldwin, Doug, 271
Ballard, Chris, 171–73, 249
Baltimore Colts, 222, 322
    move to Indianapolis, 203–4
    Super Bowl III (1969), 322
Baltimore Ravens, 1–4, 6, 8, 23, 38–45, 51, 55, 73, 77, 84, 88–100, 118, 125, 130–34, 137–38, 151–58, 160–61,

166, 179–84, 200–210, 214–17,
    233, 251–56, 258–60, 263,
    277–80, 282–93, 298, 300–302,
    328–32
move from Cleveland, 2
Super Bowls: XXXV (2001), 39,
    90, 92; XLVII (2013), 8, 81, 87,
    100–101, 204, 279
Baltimore Sun, 331
Banks, Tony, 90
Barkley, Saquon, 329
Barnett, Derek, 327
Barr, Anthony, 210, 212
Barry, Joe, 164
Barth, Connor, 208
Batch, Charlie, 95
Battle, Arnaz, 57
Baylor University, 7, 71, 73
BCS leagues, 37, 49
Beathard, Bobby, 192
Beathard, C. J., 187, 239
Beck, John, 62, 72
Beckham, Odell, Jr., 268
Belichick, Bill, 39, 51, 99, 115–16, 134,
    144, 146, 155, 170, 179–80, 185,
    269, 315, 326
Bell, Le'Veon, 182, 218
Bellard, Emory, 86
Bennett, Martellus, 210–11
Bergstrom, Tony, 154
Berra, Yogi, 203
Berry, Eric, 105, 146
Big East, 36–37, 49
Big Ten, 30–31
Billick, Brian, 38–39, 41–42, 88, 90–91
Bisciotti, Steve, 6, 44, 90, 96, 137–38,
    158, 302
Black Monday, 286, 317
Blake, Jeff, 38
Bledsoe, Drew, 9, 31
Bloomfield Rams, 222
Blount, Jeb, 29
Boldin, Anquan, 93, 100
Boller, Kyle, 38–39, 55, 88, 91, 168
Bortles, Blake, 160, 221, 266
Boryla, Mike, 29–30
Boston College, 41–42

Boswell, Chris, 110, 260
Bouye, A. J., 160
Bowe, Dwayne, 106
Bowles, Todd, 113–14, 117–19
Bowling Green State University, 48
Boyd, Tyler, 290
Boyer, Nate, 133–34
Boyle, Nick, 207
Bradford, Sam, 9, 72, 127, 134–35, 137,
    168, 186, 204–5, 210, 215, 217, 258,
    267, 305–6, 323
Bradley, Bill, 21
Brady, Tom, 8–9, 31, 42, 63, 93, 99,
    101, 107, 115–16, 129, 134, 136,
    141, 145–46, 169–70, 179–80, 202,
    214, 259, 262, 266, 307, 322,
    326–27
Brate, Cameron, 189, 276
Bray, Tyler, 102, 141–42
Brees, Drew, 8, 63, 84, 101–2, 107,
    129–30, 136, 169, 187, 213, 266,
    293–94, 300, 305, 324–25
Bridgewater, Teddy, 76, 168, 186, 215,
    221, 305–6
Brigham Young University, 48–49
Briscoe, Marlin, 26–27
Brissett, Jacoby, 136, 168, 170, 248, 283
Brohm, Brian, 41, 63
Brooks, Derrick, 43
Brown, Antonio, 218, 260
Brown, Donald, 105
Brown, Jayon, 296
Brown, Jim, 204
Brown, Orlando, 294
Brown, Sashi, 163
Brown, Zach, 17
Bruce, Isaac, 60
Bryant, Bear, 26
Buffalo Bills, 22, 62–66, 106, 108,
    111–13, 116–20, 126, 140, 185, 190,
    198, 228, 237, 243, 245, 266–67,
    289–90, 292, 294–95, 326, 328
Super Bowl XXV (1991), 322
Bulger, Marc, 59–60
Bullock, Randy, 287, 289, 291
Burton, Trey, 327
Bush, Reggie, 20, 49

Butker, Harrison, 16, 18, 178, 196–97, 218, 241, 264–65, 297–98
Butte Junior College, 50
Byrne, Kevin, 3, 44–45, 181

Caldwell, Jim, 96, 286, 293
California, University of, Berkeley (UC-Berkeley), 48, 50–51, 168
California, University of, Los Angeles (UCLA) 80, 211, 303
Callahan, Ryan, 205
Cameron, Cam, 41–45, 88, 90, 96
Campanaro, Michael, 207, 282, 288, 291
Campbell, Earl, 26
Canady, Maurice, 290
Carolina Panthers, 7, 82, 136, 187, 190, 223, 243, 258, 266, 292, 294, 300
Carr, Brandon, 217, 286, 289–90
Carr, David, 167
Carr, Derek, 8, 109, 127, 194–96, 200, 219–21, 242, 258, 264, 307
Carroll, Pete, 271
Cass, Dick, 284
Cassel, Matt, 102, 201, 319
Castonzo, Anthony, 129
Catanzaro, Chandler, 246
Cavanaugh, Matt, 28, 37, 164
CBS, 218, 231, 282
Central Florida University, 183
Cerrato, Vinny, 52
Champions Indoor Football League, 137
Charles, Jamaal, 103–5, 108–9, 142
Chicago Bears, 1, 31, 38, 81, 86, 148, 150–51, 155, 180, 187, 203–9, 215, 227, 256, 258
  Super Bowl XLI (2007), 235
Childress, Brad, 177
Cincinnati Bengals, 1, 22, 38, 43, 60–61, 88, 96, 111, 118, 125–26, 130, 137, 151–52, 155, 180, 226, 258, 260, 277, 283–91, 293, 298, 300–301, 306
Clark, Dwight, 85
Clement, Corey, 224, 232, 327
Clemson University, 31, 40
Cleveland, Ravens' move from, 38, 204

Cleveland Browns, 1, 9, 11, 32, 39, 61, 74, 76–77, 89–90, 116, 119, 128, 152–53, 158, 163, 165, 170–71, 173, 186–87, 204, 231, 236–37, 260, 277–79, 282, 286, 294, 310, 322
Cleveland Indians, 24
Clinton, Hillary, 280
Cobb, Randall, 255
Cohen, Tarik, 206
Colby College, 39
Coleman, Tevin, 276
College of New Jersey, 36
Collins, Alex, 1, 3, 182, 255, 259, 287
Collinsworth, Cris, 56–57, 258
Colorado University, 70
Condon, Tom, 310
Conference USA, 212–13
Conley, Chris, 197
Cook, Connor, 168
Cook, Jared, 201–2, 220
Cooke, Jake Kent, 192
Cooper, Amari, 219–20
Coryell, Don, 103
Cosell, Howard, 256–57, 281–82
Couch, Tim, 32, 167
Coughlin, Tom, 224, 268–69
Cousins, Kirk, 5, 8, 63, 73–74, 76–81, 136, 164–67, 169, 187, 193–97, 223–27, 271–72, 302–3, 305–6, 310–11, 332
cover-two defense, 290
Cowher, Bill, 90
Crabtree, Michael, 86, 220–21
Crawford, Tyrone, 226
Crawley, Ken, 325
Crews, Ted, 199
Crosby, Mason, 202–3
Crowder, Jamison, 197
CTE (chronic traumatic encephalopathy), 153–54, 156–57
Culpepper, Daunte, 168
Culverhouse, Hugh, 33
Cundiff, Billy, 94
Cunningham, Bruce, 181
Cunningham, Randall, 38
Curry, Vinny, 178
Curtis, Kevin, 60

Cutler, Jay, 56, 251–52, 258, 274, 306
Cyprien, Johnathan, 17, 296

Dallas Cowboys, 52, 56, 61, 73–74, 76, 84–85, 89, 96, 109, 114, 155, 166, 168, 185, 195, 201–3, 210, 224–27, 239, 257, 270–71, 275, 324
Dalton, Andy, 151, 258, 285–86, 288–90, 306
Daniel, Chase, 102
Daniels, B. J., 113
Darkwa, Orleans, 240–41
Darnold, Sam, 80, 303, 332
David, Lavonte, 189
Davis, Knile, 105
Davis, Mark, 195, 317
Davis, Vernon, 81, 84–85
Dawson, Len, 322
Decker, Eric, 18, 116–17, 297
DeCosta, Eric, 2, 39–45, 90–91, 302
Deflategate, 8–9, 126, 134, 170, 249
Delaware, University of, Blue Hens, 1, 2, 37–41
Delaware State University, 41
Del Rio, Jack, 286, 317
Dennard, Darqueze, 287
Denver Broncos, 26, 56, 65, 91, 96–98, 103–5, 108–9, 126, 158, 168, 195, 202, 223, 230–34, 239, 266, 292, 305–6, 332
    Super Bowls: XXII (1988), 23; XXXII (1998), 322; XXXIII (1999), 263; L (2016), 109, 263
Detroit Lions, 30, 59, 61, 75, 152, 166, 185, 258–59, 293, 319
Diab, Nessa, 138
DiCaprio, Leonardo, 138
Dierdorf, Dan, 257
Diggs, Stefon, 324–25
Dilfer, Trent, 2, 38, 90–91, 110, 263
Dimitroff, Thomas, 311
Disney Company, 257
Doctson, Josh, 78, 272–73
Donahue, Terry, 51
Dorsett, Phillip, 170
Dorsey, Ken, 51

Douglas, Joe, 39, 43
Drexel University, 229
Drysdale, Don, 24
Duerson, Dave, 154
Dungy, Tony, 30–31, 316
Dunlap, Carlos, 291

Eastern Washington University, 46
Edwards, Lachlan, 245
Edwards, Trent, 62–63
Eisenhower, Dwight D., 176
Ekeler, Austin, 265
Ellerbe, Dannell, 100
Elliott, Brett, 47–48
Elliott, Ezekiel, 226–27
Elliott, Jake, 232, 327
Elway, John, 263, 322
Enemkpali, IK, 114, 268
Erickson, Dennis, 51
Ertz, Zach, 224, 233, 327
ESPN, 61–62, 112, 195, 198, 257–58, 282, 286, 294, 316–17, 331
Evans, Lee, 94
Evans, Mike, 151, 189, 191

Fassel, Jim, 39, 215
Fassel, John, 215
Favre, Brett, 56, 268–69, 275
Fewell, Perry, 63
Fiesta Bowl, 37, 49–50, 71
Fisher, Eric, 110
Fisher, Jeff, 135, 186, 215
Fitzgerald, Larry, 189
Fitzpatrick, Brady, 111, 238
Fitzpatrick, Jane, 111
Fitzpatrick, Liza Barber, 23, 111, 113–14, 148, 238, 320
Fitzpatrick, Lucy, 111, 238
Fitzpatrick, Maizy, 111
Fitzpatrick, Ryan, 10, 125, 268
    Buffalo Bills and (2009–12), 22, 62–66, 111–12
    career arc of, 19–23, 46
    Cincinnati Bengals and (2007–8), 22, 60–62
    college football at Harvard and, 20–22, 46

Fitzpatrick, Ryan (*continued*)
  contracts and salaries and, 23, 59, 64,
    111, 117–18, 332
  draft of 2005 and, 19–22, 46, 52–53
  future of, with Tampa Bay, 315–21
  Hard Knocks and, 150
  Houston Texans and (2014), 113
  injuries and, 65, 111, 113, 121, 214
  marriage and family and, 23, 111,
    113–14, 148, 238
  New York Jets and (2015–17), 22–23,
    111, 113–22, 147
  St. Louis Rams and (2005–7, rookie
    year), 22, 59–60, 111
  Tampa Bay Bucs and (2017), 22–23,
    63, 147–51, 188–92, 235–39, 243,
    273–77, 315–16, 332
  Tennessee Titans and (2013), 22, 112
  Wonderlic test and, 42, 167
Fitzpatrick, Tate, 111, 238
Fitzpatrick, Zoey, 111, 114
Flacco, Brian (brother), 36
Flacco, Dana, 132, 253–54, 328–29
Flacco, Joe, 10, 77, 125, 136, 180
  Baltimore Ravens and: (2008, rookie
    year), 88–90, 155; (2009), 90–92;
    (2011), 93–94; (2012), 94–101;
    (2016), 130; (2017), 1–3, 23,
    130–34, 137–38, 151–57, 160–61,
    179–84, 200–209, 216–17, 251–56,
    258–60, 277–80, 282–83, 285–91,
    295, 300–301
  college football and: Delaware, 37–38;
    Pittsburgh, 36–37
  contracts and salaries and, 2, 6, 94–95,
    95, 101–2, 107, 130, 330–32
  drafted by Baltimore (2008), 1–2,
    38–45
  early life of, 36
  future of, with Baltimore, 77, 327–32
  injuries and, 23, 121, 132–33, 137–38,
    252–54
  kneeling and, 157
  marriage and family and, 3, 132
  media and, 2–4, 152, 198–99, 208,
    300–301, 331
  "Mile-High Miracle" and, 98

  nickname "Cool Joe," 2, 89
  Pitta injury and, 131–32, 142
  Super Bowl and, 6, 92–93, 100–101
  Wonderlic test and, 42
Flacco, John, 36
Flacco, Karen, 36
Flacco, Mike, 36
Flacco, Steve, 36
Flacco, Thomas (son), 328
Flacco, Tom (brother), 36
Fleener, Coby, 249
Fletcher, London, 65
Florida State University, 22
Florio, Mike, 262
Foles, Nick, 9, 110, 134–37, 140, 214,
    232–33, 268, 293, 300, 315,
    323–24, 326–27
Folk, Nick, 274
Forbath, Kai, 205, 211, 217, 324
Fordham University, 274
Fouts, Dan, 103
Fox, John, 150, 204, 286
Fox News, 157–58
Fox TV, 187, 219, 282
Frankfurt Galaxy, 68
Frerotte, Gus, 60
Fuller, Kendall, 309–10
Fuller, Kyle, 205–6
Fulton, Zach, 18

Gabbert, Blaine, 134, 168, 187
Gailey, Chan, 63–65, 112–14, 318
Gaines, Phillip, 241
Garcia, Jeff, 84
Garçon, Pierre, 73, 164
Garoppolo, Jimmy, 8–9, 134–35, 170,
    180, 221, 239, 311
Gates, Antonio, 265
George, Jeff, 192–93
Georgia, University of, 43, 329
Georgia Tech, 37
Gibbs, Joe, 27–31, 34–35, 162, 192, 194,
    224, 333
Gifford, Frank, 256, 281
Gillislee, Mike, 143–44
Ginn, Ted, Jr., 85
Glennon, Mike, 148, 150–51, 155, 204

Goff, Jared, 56, 135–36, 167–68, 186–87, 215, 266–67, 294, 300, 323

Gonzalez, Zane, 277

Goodell, Roger, 72, 114, 157, 296, 329

Gore, Frank, 283

Graham, Brandon, 327

Graham, Corey, 97–98

Graham, Jimmy, 84

Graham, Otto, 204

Grambling State University, 24–28, 333–34

Grant, Ryan, 197

Grbac, Elvis, 38, 91

Green, A. J., 43, 285–86, 289

Green, Darrell, 310

Green Bay Packers, 6–7, 9, 40, 52–53, 56, 63, 75, 82, 85, 101, 109, 135–36, 166, 185, 201–3, 210–12, 225, 254–56, 258, 275
  Super Bowls: I (1967), 322; XXXII (1998), 322

Green Berets, 133–34

Grier, Chris, 163

Griffin, Robert, III, 7–8, 71–77, 80, 95, 136, 165–67, 186, 307, 329, 332

Griffin, Ryan, 148–49, 318

Gronkowski, Rob, 143, 327

Grossman, Rex, 38, 61–62, 72, 235

Gruden, Jay, 76–77, 164–66, 225, 305

Gruden, Jon, 164, 281, 316–17

Gumbel, Bryant, 134

Hackenberg, Christian, 117, 168, 237

Hall, Andy, 37

Harbaugh, Jim, 7, 68–70, 83–87, 100, 102, 308

Harbaugh, John, 3–4, 41–42, 84, 87–88, 90, 94, 98, 100, 137, 157, 159, 180, 208, 217, 251–52, 260, 278–79, 283–85, 287, 300–302, 328, 330–31

Hard Knocks (HBO series), 149–50, 214–15, 273, 317

Harris, Damon, 240

Harris, Demetrius, 16, 144, 218, 298

Harris, James, 26–27

Harris, Walt, 36–37

Harvard University Crimson, 19–22, 42, 46, 111, 147, 318–19, 321, 332

HBO, 134, 149–50

Heap, Ashley, 253

Heap, Holly, 253

Heap, Todd, 253

Hedberg, Randy, 29

Heisman Trophy, 7, 20, 22, 26–27, 49, 69–71, 76–77, 88, 149, 293, 303

Henne, Chad, 41

Henry, Derrick, 18, 297, 299

Hensley, Jamison, 331

Hill, Brian, 288

Hill, Shaun, 59, 81

Hill, Tyreek, 108, 145, 221, 243, 245–47, 265, 294, 296

Hilton, T. Y., 105, 129

Hogan, Kevin, 152

Holliday, Trindon, 97

Hollins, Mack, 224

Holloway, Condredge, 25–26

Holmgren, Mike, 102

Hopkins, Dustin, 197, 226

Hortiz, Joe, 43

Hostetler, Jeff, 263, 323

Hostler, Jim, 57–58

Houston, Justin, 197–98

Houston, University of, 135, 212–13

Houston Oilers, 41, 67, 106

Houston Sports Authority, 68

Houston Texans, 10–11, 31–32, 44, 59–60, 81–82, 93, 96, 108–9, 111, 113, 128, 135, 154–55, 163, 186, 200, 212, 214, 231, 248–51, 258, 286

Howard, Jordan, 207–8

Howard, O. J., 191, 316

Hoyer, Brian, 113, 187

Huff, Gary, 29–30

Humphrey, Marlon, 255, 289

Humphries, Adam, 275

Hundley, Brett, 211–12, 255, 258

Hunt, Clark, 159

Hunt, Kareem, 16, 142–43, 145, 177, 197, 218, 241–42, 244–45, 247, 264–65, 294, 298

Hunt, Lamar, 159
Hurst, Hayden, 328–29

Illinois University, 213
Indianapolis Colts, 7–9, 23, 39, 55–56,
  71–72, 82, 92, 96–97, 105–6,
  108–9, 113, 119, 125–28, 130, 136,
  155, 167, 169–74, 194, 248–51,
  260, 269, 277, 280, 282–83, 286,
  312–15, 332
  move from Baltimore, 203–4
  Super Bowl XLIV (2010), 96
Irsay, Jim, 251
Irsay, Robert, 203
Irving, David, 227
Ismail, Qadry, 91
Ivy League, 20–21

Jackson, Adoree', 297
Jackson, DeSean, 164, 191, 272, 275,
  316
Jackson, D'Qwell, 173
Jackson, Fred, 65
Jackson, Hue, 42–43, 77
Jackson, Lamar, 77, 80, 303, 329–32
Jackson, Samuel L., 138
Jackson, Terry, 29–30
Jacksonville Jaguars, 1, 38, 44, 71,
  89–90, 94, 154–58, 160, 179, 200,
  248, 264, 266, 284, 292–94, 300,
  312, 326
Jauron, Dick, 62, 63
Jeffery, Alshon, 177, 232, 267
Jenkins, Janoris, 241, 251
Jensen, Ryan, 252
Jeter, Gary, 30
Johnson, Brad, 192, 297
Johnson, Chad "Ochocinco,"
  285
Johnson, Derrick, 295, 299
Johnson, Lane, 267
Johnson, Mike, 82
Jones, Byron, 227
Jones, Chandler, 188
Jones, Chris, 178
Jones, Christian, 205
Jones, Jacoby, 98

Jones, Jerry, 195, 224, 227, 249
Jon Gruden's QB Camp (TV show),
  316
Joseph, Vance, 230–31
Judon, Matthew, 288
Jurgensen, Sonny, 110

Kaepernick, Colin, 86–87, 101–2, 112,
  133–34, 137–38, 141, 148–49,
  157–58, 187, 306
Kansas City Chiefs, 6, 15–23, 32, 64, 76,
  80–81, 87, 92, 102–10, 118–19, 125,
  135, 139–46, 151, 158–59, 175–79,
  183, 185, 195–200, 218–21, 223,
  230, 239–47, 261–66, 292–300,
  304, 306–11, 323–24, 330
  Super Bowls: I (1967), 322; IV (1970),
  322
Kansas City Phantoms, 137
Karras, Alex, 257
Kearse, Jermaine, 246
Keeler, K. C., 37–38
Keenum, Case, 9, 134–37, 185–86,
  205, 210–17, 258, 267, 293, 305,
  323–26, 332
Keenum, Kimberly, 215
Kelce, Travis, 17–18, 108, 178, 196,
  198, 221, 240–42, 245, 247, 264,
  294–96, 298–99, 327
Kelley, Robert, 78, 272
Kelly, Chip, 69, 135, 323
Kennedy, John F., 301
Kentucky, University of, 25
Kerrigan, Ryan, 169
Kessler, Cody, 168
Keyes, Leroy, 228
Khan, Shad, 157–58
King, Tavarres, 241
Kitna, Jon, 155
Kizer, DeShone, 152, 277–78
Koch, Sam, 208, 216, 278
Koetter, Dirk, 188, 191–92, 235–36, 238,
  274–76, 316–18, 320
Kroft, Tyler, 286–87, 289
Krueger, Paul, 98
Krueger, Phil, 33
Kubiak, Gary, 231

LaFell, Brandon, 289–90
Landry, Tom, 224
La Salle University, 229
Lattimore, Marcus, 191
Layne, Bobby, 267
Lazor, Bill, 286
Leaf, Ryan, 167, 221
Leftwich, Byron, 38, 95
Leinart, Matt, 49, 56, 168
Levy, Marv, 62
Lewis, Alex, 154
Lewis, Marvin, 285–86
Lewis, Ray, 87, 92, 96–97, 100, 138, 157, 163, 183, 204, 233, 301
Lewis, Roger, 241
Lewis, Walter, 26
Liberty Bowl, 48
Limbaugh, Rush, 61
Linehan, Scott, 60
Liske, Pete, 27
Locker, Jack, 112
Locker, Jake, 168
Logan, Bennie, 246
Long, Chris, 326
Los Angeles Chargers (*formerly* San Diego Chargers), 185, 196, 200, 231, 242–43, 247, 263–67, 317
Los Angeles Clippers, 162
Los Angeles Rams, 30, 32–33, 53, 56, 59–61, 86, 119, 130, 135, 164, 168–70, 186–87, 194, 202, 212, 214–15, 227, 266–68, 272, 294, 300, 323
  Hard Knocks and, 214–15
  move from St. Louis, 135, 168
  Super Bowl XXXIV (2000), 58
Losman, JP, 168
Louisiana State University (LSU), 25–26, 108, 230
Louisville, University of, 20, 41, 80, 186, 303, 329
Lucas, Bernard, 24–25
Luck, Andrew, 10, 63, 136, 169
  age and, 128–29
  college football at Stanford and, 68–71, 83

contracts and salaries and, 8, 126–27, 332
drafted by Indianapolis (2011), 7–8, 56, 71–72
early life of, 7, 67–68
fiancée Nicole Pechanec and, 249–50
future of, with Indianapolis, 312–15
Indianapolis Colts and: (2012, rookie year), 71–72, 97, 99, 125, 127, 155; (2013), 8, 105–6, 125, 127; (2014), 8, 126–27; (2015), 8, 126, 249; (2016), 127–28, 314; (2017), 23, 130, 169–74, 248–51, 255, 283
injuries and surgery and, 7–9, 23, 125–30, 136, 169–74, 249–50, 312–14
media and, 125, 173–74
Luck, Kathy, 67
Luck, Oliver, 7, 67–68
Lutz, Wil, 324
Lynch, John, 134, 187
Lynch, Paxton, 168, 231

MacAfee, Ken, 26
Maclin, Jeremy, 130, 151, 160, 182–83, 252, 278
Madden, John, 257–58
Mahomes, Patrick, 32, 80, 140–42, 159, 262–63, 266, 292, 304, 307
Mallett, Ryan, 113, 137–38, 214, 253–54, 329
Mamula, Mike, 42–43
Manning, Archie, 67
Manning, Eli, 39, 67, 136, 241–42, 265, 268–70, 275, 323, 329
Manning, Peyton, 7, 56, 67, 71, 92, 96–98, 101, 105–6, 109, 127, 155, 167, 204, 230–31, 263, 269, 275
Manuel, EJ, 66, 112, 200–201
Manusky, Greg, 164
Manziel, Johnny, 168, 221
Mara, John, 269–70
Maravich, Pete, 24
Marino, Dan, 110
Mariota, Marcus, 17–18, 267, 293, 295, 297–99, 319
Marrone, Doug, 65, 112

Marshall, Brandon, 117, 268
Martin, Doug, 189
Martin, Jamie, 59–60
Martz, Mike, 58–60
Maryland, University of, 40, 315
Massachusetts Institute of Technology
     (MIT), 153
Matthews, Clay, 211
Mayfield, Baker, 80, 303–4, 330
Mayle, Vince, 201
McAdoo, Ben, 239, 268–70, 275, 286
McBride, Ron, 47–48
McCarron, AJ, 285, 306
McCarthy, Mike, 55–56
McClain, Terrell, 272
McCloughan, Scot, 58–59, 79, 81,
     162–63, 166–67, 193, 225, 272
McCourty, Devin, 143
McCourty, Jason, 152
McCown, Josh, 236–37, 243, 245–46,
     332
McCown, Luke, 236–37
McCoy, Colt, 76, 165–66, 305–6
McDaniel, Josh, 314–15
McDermott, Sean, 266–67
McDonough, Sean, 198, 281
McDougald, Bradley, 272
McEvoy, Tanner, 273
McInally, Pat, 42
McKay, John, 27–30, 32
McKenzie, Reggie, 163
McKinnon, Jerick, 211
McMahon, Jim, 67
McManus, Brandon, 231
McNabb, Donovan, 32, 61–62, 72, 186
McNair, Steve, 39–41, 88, 91, 93
McNown, Cade, 168
McVay, Sean, 164, 186
Meredith, Don, 256–57, 281–82
Merriman, Shawne, 65
Meyer, Urban, 48, 49, 59
Miami Dolphins, 27, 89, 91, 114, 119,
     150, 163, 166, 176, 223, 237,
     251–52, 258, 266, 273–74, 289, 301
Miami Marlins, 176
Michaels, Al, 257–58
Michel, Sony, 329

Michigan, University of, 31, 41
Michigan State University, 73, 165
Mid-American Conference, 142
Miller, Terry, 26
Miller, Zach, 205–6
Mills, Keith, 4
Minnesota, University of, 31
Minnesota Twins, 216
Minnesota Vikings, 1, 9, 60, 71, 76,
     134–37, 168, 185–86, 204–5,
     210–13, 215–18, 227–28, 251, 253,
     258, 263, 267, 278, 283, 292–93,
     297, 300, 305, 311, 324–27, 332
   Super Bowl IV (1970), 322
Miracle on 34th Street (film), 228
Mirage Bowl, 334
Mississippi, University of, 25
Mississippi State University, 201
Mitchell, Brian, 310
Mixon, Joe, 286–87
Modell, Art, 163
Monday Night Football, 57, 256–59,
     281, 316
Monken, Todd, 317–18
Montana, Joe, 85, 90, 103, 107
Moon, Warren, 30, 67
Moore, Chris, 206–7, 217, 287
Moore, Matt, 201, 251–52, 258, 274
Moore, Sterling, 94
Mornhinweg, Marty, 160
Mortensen, Chris, 62, 112
Mosley, C. J., 290, 301
Mountain West Conference, 49
Murphy, Tim, 20–21
Murray, Eric, 220
Murray, Latavius, 217
Murray, Patrick, 237, 274

Nagy, Matt, 16–17, 142, 144–45, 244,
     263, 298
Namath, Joe, 28, 119, 257, 322
National Basketball Association (NBA),
     20, 162, 230
National College Athletic Association
     (NCAA), 7, 21, 41, 47, 69–70, 212
National Football Conference (NFC),
     185, 227

Championship, 9, 32–33, 85, 134
Divisions: Central, 32; East, 73, 166,
    203, 224, 232, 323; North, 95, 203,
    285; South, 187; West, 84, 86
playoffs, 109, 137, 201–2, 292–93,
    300
Pro Bowl, 308
National Football League (NFL)
African Americans and, 10, 23–31,
    61–62, 73–77, 88, 162–65, 236,
    270, 330
antitrust lawsuit vs., 281
attendance and, 280–82, 284–35
bye weeks and, 223, 239
collective bargaining agreement (CBA),
    127
as colossus, 5
combine, 27, 31, 38, 42–43, 50–51,
    108, 127, 141, 163, 167, 177, 213,
    293, 303
concussions and CTE and, 153–57,
    214, 253, 314
contracts and, 101
domestic violence and, 108, 131, 227
draft: (1969), 228; (1982), 67; (1995),
    41; (1998), 167; (1999), 32; (2000),
    31; (2001), 129; (2003), 38–39, 155;
    (2004), 38–39, 265; (2005), 19,
    21–22, 49–54, 239, 308; (2007),
    88, 230; (2008), 1–2, 38, 39–45;
    (2010), 72, 76, 168; (2011), 71, 72,
    285; (2012), 7, 72, 126, 165, 230,
    323; (2013), 72; (2014), 72, 160,
    221; (2015), 1, 131, 149, 211, 213,
    251, 293; (2016), 135, 167–68, 201,
    309, 323; (2017), 10, 31, 32, 80,
    139–41, 162; (2018), 140, 213, 236,
    328–32
exhibition games, 132–33
flag rules and, 282, 294–95
flex games and, 258
gambling and, 198
game tapes and, 304
halftime and, 144–45
helmet-to-helmet hits and, 296
injuries and, 6–10, 86, 120–22, 136,
    198, 210–12, 258, 281
kneeling and, 133–34, 156–59, 170–71,
    179–81, 194–95, 281, 284
lockout of 2011, 83, 132
merger with AFL, 27
Monday, Sunday, Thursday, night
    games and, 218–19, 257–58
multipurpose stadiums and, 176
overtime and, 115, 207
owners and, 195, 218–19, 249
penalties and, 212
player safety and, 17
playoffs, 7–9, 17, 22, 32–34, 39,
    55–57, 65, 71, 74, 79, 84, 89,
    91–96, 99, 104, 106–7, 109, 117–19,
    128, 130, 135–37, 139, 165, 194,
    201–2, 209, 223, 230–32, 238–39,
    249–51, 256, 260, 266, 269, 277,
    279, 283–85, 289, 293–94, 297,
    302, 316, 323
quarterback fragility and, 258
quarterback needs of, 134–38
referees and, 294
replay decision rules, 144
running backs and, 142
salary cap and, 101, 127
scouting and, 167, 201
smart quarterbacks and, 10
ticket prices and, 282
Trump and, 156–58, 281
TV ratings and, 280–82
Navy, 2, 40
NBC, 31, 218–19, 256–58, 262, 282
Nebraska, University of, 26, 213
Nelsen, Bill, 28
Nelson, Steven, 246
New England Patriots, 8, 27–28, 31, 38,
    51, 63–65, 92–95, 99–100, 104–6,
    109, 114–17, 119, 125–26, 134, 136,
    139, 143–46, 170, 175, 178–80,
    185, 187–88, 209, 214, 224, 237,
    239, 260, 263–64, 266, 274, 285,
    292–93, 300, 326, 329
Super Bowls, 214; XXXVI (2002),
    322; XLII (2008), 322; XLVI
    (2012), 96, 99; LI (2017), 187, 327;
    LII (2018), 307, 314–15, 326–27
New Mexico, University of, 47–48

New Orleans Saints, 30, 73, 84–85, 129, 186–87, 189–91, 223, 235, 266, 292–94, 300, 308, 316, 323–25
New Orleans Times-Picayune, 325
Newsome, Ozzie, 2, 23, 38–39, 41, 43–44, 91, 96, 138, 163, 183, 251, 270, 302, 328
Newton, Cam, 31, 69–70, 136, 169, 187, 258, 266, 294
New York Giants, 29–30, 35, 51, 61, 73, 85, 91, 96, 103, 114, 163, 185, 187, 194, 200–201, 215, 223–24, 226, 230, 238–45, 262–63, 268–70, 286, 293, 324, 329
   Super Bowls: XXV (1991), 263, 322–23; XXXV (2001), 39, 91; XLII (2008), 322; XLVI (2012), 96, 99
New York Jets, 22–23, 51, 63, 65, 111, 113–20, 126, 135, 147, 185, 192, 194, 215, 235–38, 243–47, 251–52, 261–66, 268, 273, 332
   Super Bowl III (1969), 322
New York Post, 117
NFL Europe, 68
NFL Films, 149
NFL Network, 138
Ngata, Haloti, 73
Nolan, Dick, 51, 58
Nolan, Mike, 51–52, 55–59, 81–82, 307–8
North Carolina, University of, 31
North Dakota State University, 167
Northern Iowa, University of, 41
Notre Dame, 69, 152
Nugent, Mike, 226–27

Oakland Raiders, 56, 64, 82, 91, 109, 112, 114, 127, 139, 158, 163, 176, 194–96, 200–201, 203–4, 219–21, 230, 239, 242, 245, 258, 263–65, 268–70, 285–86, 293, 317, 324
   move to Las Vegas, 176, 195
   Super Bowls: II (1968), 322; XI (1977), 29
O'Brien, Bill, 113, 155
O'Brien, Tom, 248
Odoms, Joey, 181

O'Donnell, Pat, 207
Ogden, Jonathan, 163
Ohio State University, 213
Oklahoma, University of, 80, 303
Oklahoma Outlaws, 34
Oklahoma State University, 71, 108
Olivo, Frank, 228–29
Olson, David, 137–38
Omalu, Dr. Bennet, 153
Orange Bowl, 69
Oregon University Ducks, 51, 69–70, 293
Organized Team Activities (OTAs; mini-camps), 1, 9, 54, 128, 131, 132, 311, 331–32
Orlovsky, Dan, 71
Orton, Kyle, 112
O'Sullivan, J. T., 59
Osweiler, Brock, 230–32
Owens, Terrell, 285

Pacific-10 and -12, 69–70
Pagano, Chuck, 170–71, 248–51, 286
Painter, Curtis, 71
Palko, Tyler, 37
Palmer, Carson, 38–39, 60–61, 155, 285
Palmer, Jordan, 61
Parcells, Bill, 103, 224
Parker, Ron, 220, 265
Paterno, Joe, 25, 213
Patterson, Cordarrelle, 220
Pearson, Drew, 324
Pechanec, Nicole, 173, 249–50, 313
Pederson, Doug, 175, 232, 267, 323–24, 326
Pees, Dean, 290
Penn State University, 117, 213, 237, 329
Pennsylvania, University of (UPenn), 21, 36, 229
Perriman, Breshad, 1, 131, 183–84, 205–6, 251, 278
Peterman, Nathan, 267
Peters, Marcus, 158–59, 241, 246, 265
Peterson, Adrian, 49, 189
Peterson, Julian, 57
Petty, Bryce, 119
Philadelphia 76ers, 229

Philadelphia Eagles, 9, 29, 32, 39, 42–43, 55–56, 60–61, 73–75, 79, 146, 135–36, 168–69, 175–78, 185, 192, 200, 223–24, 227–34, 239, 258, 263, 267–68, 292–93, 300, 323–27, 329
  Super Bowls: XXXIX (2005), 175–76; LII (2018), 9, 134, 314, 322–27
Pitta, Dennis, 1, 100, 130–32, 142, 153, 184, 205, 256, 278, 328–30
Pitta, Mataya, 132
Pittsburgh, University of, 36–38, 49
Pittsburgh Steelers, 1–4, 31, 41, 57, 61, 89–96, 108–10, 116, 127–28, 130, 139, 154, 158–59, 161, 175, 179–83, 186, 200, 203, 218, 221–22, 258–60, 263, 266, 277, 285, 292–93, 300, 322, 326
Plummer, Jake, 148, 188, 321
Polamalu, Troy, 90
Polian, Bill, 330
Ponder, Christian, 168
Pop Warner football, 68
Power Six conferences, 49
Prescott, Dak, 31, 136, 168, 201–3
Pro Bowl, 1, 29, 135, 153, 307–8
Pro Football Hall of Fame, 30, 43, 67, 81, 112, 154, 163, 222, 260, 322–23
Pro Football Talk (TV show), 262

Quick, Brian, 78, 272
Quinn, Brady, 102, 168, 230
Quinn, Dan, 186–87

Rae, Mike, 29–30, 33
Rainey, Bobby, 206
Rattay, Tim, 51, 55
Raye, Jimmy, 81–82
Raymond, Tubby, 37–38
read-option offense, 75, 80, 86, 308
Reaser, Keith, 297
Redman, Chris, 38
Reed, Ed, 93
Reed, Jordan, 194
Reese, Jerry, 163, 239, 268, 270
Reich, Frank, 315
Reid, Andy, 16, 17, 32, 80–81, 102–4,

107–8, 139–45, 158–59, 175–77, 218, 232, 239, 242, 244, 261–63, 265, 267, 292, 298, 308–10, 323
Revis, Darrelle, 17, 297, 310
Rey, Vincent, 291
Rhein Fire, 67
Rhodes, Xavier, 211
Riccio, Sonny, 37
Rice, Lance, 47
Rice, Ray, 97–98, 131
Richardson, Paul, 272
Rivers, Philip, 39, 104, 136, 265–66, 275, 307
Robinson, Demarcus, 17, 247, 295
Robinson, Eddie, 25–26, 213, 334
Robinson, Patrick, 232, 326
Robiskie, Terry, 25
Rodgers, Aaron, 5–9, 48, 50–53, 56, 63, 101, 107, 109, 135–36, 169, 201–3, 210–12, 215, 225, 227, 254–56, 258, 306, 311, 319, 323
Roethlisberger, Ben, 3, 39, 90, 92–93, 95, 110, 127, 129, 136, 182, 200, 218, 258–60, 265–66, 307
Romo, Tony, 201
Rooney Rule, 317
Rosas, Aldrick, 241
Rose, Neil, 21
Rose, Nick, 226
Rosen, Josh, 80, 303–4
Rowan University, 37
Russell, JaMarcus, 167, 230
Rutgers University, 36
Rutherford, Rob, 36
Ryan, Matt, 41–44, 101–2, 187, 266, 275–76, 294, 300, 311
Ryan, Rex, 22, 114, 116–17
Rypien, Mark, 23, 110

Saban, Lou, 26–27
Sanchez, Mark, 236
Sanders, Deion, 192
San Diego Chargers (*later* Los Angeles Chargers), 57, 77, 104, 109, 129, 167, 185
Sandusky, Gerry, 184
Sandusky, Jerry, 25, 213

San Francisco 49ers, 9, 51–59, 70, 76, 81–87, 107, 134–35, 141, 164, 173, 183, 186–87, 223, 227, 239, 308, 311
  Super Bowls: XVI (1982), 85, 103; XLVII (2013), 81, 86–87, 100–101
San Jose Mercury News, 58
Santos, Cairo, 110, 227
Sapp, Warren, 43
Savage, Phil, 39
Savage, Tom, 113, 155, 248, 258–59
Scandrick, Orlando, 226
Schefter, Adam, 112, 286
Schiano, Greg, 235
Schlichter, Art, 67
Schmuck, Peter, 331
Schottenheimer, Marty, 192
Schroeder, Jay, 35, 333
Seattle Seahawks, 7, 57–58, 74–75, 78–79, 108–9, 142, 158, 171, 271–73, 275, 325
Seau, Junior, 154
Seau, Sydney, 154
Seifert, George, 103
Selmon, Lee Roy, 32
Senior Bowl, 42–43, 50, 162–63, 303
Serby, Steve, 117
Sessions, Jeff, 156
Shanahan, Kyle, 62, 76, 165, 186, 239
Shanahan, Mike, 8, 61–62, 72–76, 103, 164–65, 186
Shaw, David, 70
Shelton, Danny, 153
Sherels, Marcus, 216
Shuler, Heath, 168
Siemian, Trevor, 230–31
Simms, Phil, 231, 263, 269, 323
Simpson, O. J., 228, 257
Sims, Charles, 237
Singletary, Mike, 59, 81–82
Slater, Matthew, 115
smashmouth offense, 103
Smith, Akili, 168
Smith, Alex, 10, 69
  career arc of, 19–20
  college football at Utah and, 20–21, 37, 46–50

contracts and salary and, 54–56, 59, 62, 81, 83–86, 107, 310–11, 319, 332
drafted by San Francisco (2005), 19–20, 46, 49–55
future of, with Washington, 80–81, 304–11, 319, 330, 332
injuries and surgery and, 57–59, 81, 86–87, 121
Kaepernick and, 86–87, 101, 141, 158
Kansas City Chiefs and: (2013), 102–7; (2014), 107–8, 180; (2015), 108; (2016), 108–11, 135, 323; (2017), 15–19, 80–81, 139–46, 158, 175–78, 185, 196–200, 218–21, 239–47, 252, 261–66, 270, 292–99, 330
kneeling and, 158–59
Mahomes mentored by, 80, 140–42
media and, 6, 198–99, 242
read-option offense and, 86
San Francisco 49ers and: 82–83, 141, 307–8; (2005, rookie year), 54–56, 59, 155; (2006), 56–57; (2007), 57–58; (2008), 58–59, 81; (2009), 81–82; (2010), 82–83; (2011), 83–86, 104, 107; (2012), 86–87, 101
  Super Bowl and, 101, 106–7, 110
  "The Grab" and, 85
  West Coast offense and, 56, 84, 102–4, 306
  Wonderlic and, 51
Smith, Bruce, 192
Smith, Elizabeth, 142, 199, 262, 307, 310–11
Smith, Geno, 113–14, 117–18, 235–36, 268–70
Smith, Harrison, 205
Smith, Jimmy, 201, 255
Smith, John (Rams player), 60
Smith, John L. (uncle of Alex), 20, 49
Smith, Lovie, 235–36, 316
Smith, Torrey, 97, 183
Smith, Troy, 82, 88
Smith, Za'Darius, 278
Smith-Schuster, JuJu, 182

Snyder, Dan, 52, 75–76, 79, 158, 162–67, 186, 192–95, 224–25, 249, 305–6

Sorensen, Daniel, 18, 298

South Carolina, University of, 328

Southeastern Conference, 25–26

Southern California, University of (USC), 20, 27, 29, 51, 69, 80, 228, 303

Southern Illinois, University of, 41

Southern Mississippi, University of, 48, 213

South Florida, University of, 36

Spagnuolo, Steve, 270

Sproles, Darren, 84, 177, 233

Stafford, Matthew, 8, 258, 319

Staggers, Harley O., Jr., 67

Stanford University, 7, 37, 68–71, 83, 126, 152, 250

Staubach, Roger, 224, 324

Steele, Chad, 331

Sterling, Donald, 162

Stills, Kenny, 251, 274

St. Joseph's University, 229

St. Louis Rams, 22, 55, 71–72, 86, 88, 111, 135, 212, 214
  move to Los Angeles, 135, 168
  Super Bowl XXXVI (2002), 322

Stokely, Brandon, 98

Stover, Matt, 90–91, 94

Strange, Luther, 156

stretch plays, 103–4

Stroud, Rick, 316

Succop, Ryan, 105–6, 294–95

Sudfeld, Nate, 233

Suggs, Terrell, 138, 301

Suh, Ndamukong, 61

Sun Bowl, 69

Sunday Night Football, 50, 257–58, 281

Super Bowls, 27–28, 39, 57, 106–7, 110, 126, 213, 224, 302, 322; I (1967), 322; II (1968), 322; III (1969), 322; IV (1970), 322; V (1971), 92; XI (1977), 29; XVI (1982), 103; XVII (1983), 35; XXII (1988), 5, 10, 23, 78, 162, 332–33; XXV (1991), 263, 322–23; XXXII (1998), 322; XXXIII (1999), 263; XXXIV (2000), 58; XXXV (2001), 2, 38–39, 58, 90–91, 204; XXXVI (2002), 322; XXXVII (2003), 192, 316; XL (2006), 90; XLI (2007), 96, 235; XLII (2008), 39, 269, 322; XLIII (2009), 90; XLIV (2010), 84, 129; XLVI (2012), 39, 96, 99, 269; XLVII (2013), 2, 6, 8, 81, 86–87, 100–101, 204, 279, 332; XLVIII (2014), 108–9; XLIX (2015), 180; L (2016), 109, 231, 263; LI (2017), 187, 275, 300; LII (2018), 9, 31, 110, 178, 210, 212, 263, 264, 293, 322–23, 326–27

Sutton, Bob, 145, 298

Swayne, Harry, 254

Syracuse, University of, 32

Tagliabue, Paul, 52

Taliaferro, Mike, 119

Tampa Bay Buccaneers, 22, 27–30, 32–34, 43, 63, 76, 81, 148–51, 164, 187–92, 223, 235–38, 243, 273–77, 315–21

Tampa Bay Little League, 319

Tampa Bay Times, 316

Tannehill, Ryan, 251, 258, 274

Tarkenton, Fran, 216

Tatham, William, Sr., 34

Tavecchio, Giorgio, 221

Taylor, Lawrence, 35

Taylor, Tyrod, 266

Tebow, Tim, 168

Tedford, Jeff, 50

Temple University, 229, 334

Tennessee, University of, 25–26

Tennessee Titans, 15–18, 22, 63, 89–91, 109, 112, 114, 126, 128, 158, 194, 201, 251, 254, 267, 292–300, 306, 314, 319, 328

Tessitore, Joe, 281

Testaverde, Vinny, 38

Texas, University of, 76, 86

Texas A&M University, 48

Texas Christian University, 285

Texas Tech University, 140, 272

Theismann, Joe, 35
Thomas, De'Anthony, 218
Thompson, Chris, 224, 227
Thornton, Rick, 68
Thursday Night Football, 56, 121, 218–19, 257–58, 281
Ticket City Bowl, 213
Toledo, University of, 142
Tolzien, Scott, 100, 169–70
Tomlin, Mike, 90
Toronto Blue Jays, 65
Toronto series, 65, 111
Treadwell, Laquon, 216–17
Trestman, Marc, 160
Trevathan, Danny, 205
Trinity College, 39
triple-option wishbone offense, 86
Triplette, Jeff, 16, 18, 294–95, 298–99
Trubisky, Mitchell, 10–11, 31–32, 151, 155, 204–8
Trump, Donald, 3, 5, 34, 78, 156–59, 170–71, 180–81, 193, 195, 224, 280–81
Tucker, Justin, 94, 98, 152, 201, 206–7, 217, 252, 278, 282–83, 287–88
Turner, Norv, 52, 56–57
Tynes, Lawrence, 85

Unitas, Johnny, 204, 221–22, 267
United States Football League (USFL), 34, 156, 281
U.S. Supreme Court, 198
Urschel, John, 153–54
Utah, University of, 20–21, 37, 46–50, 59, 70, 308
Utah State University, 48

Valvano, Jim, 98
Van Brocklin, Norm, 176, 268
Vaughan, Dustin, 137
Vermeil, Dick, 32, 224
Ver Steeg, Craig, 47
Vick, Michael, 114, 323
Villanova University, 229
Villanueva, Alejandro, 159
Vinatieri, Adam, 105, 129, 283
Virginia Tech, 69, 309

Wallace, Mike, 4, 182, 200–201, 206, 255, 278, 286, 288, 291
Walsh, Bill, 102–3
Walsh, Blair, 325
Walsh, Jimmy, 28
Walton, Bill, 20
Wannstedt, Dave, 37
Ware, Spencer, 108–9, 142
Washington, 7, 10, 23, 27–28, 34–35, 51–52, 55, 60–61, 63, 65, 72–80, 90, 95–96, 111, 132, 136, 158, 162–69, 175, 186–87, 192–98, 223–27, 268, 271–73, 302–11, 332–33
   Super Bowls: XVII (1983), 35; XXII (1988), 332–33
Washington Capitals, 230
Washington Nationals, 230
Washington Post, The, 193, 227
Washington Wizards, 230
Watson, Benjamin, 182, 277, 291
Watson, Deshaun, 10–11, 31–32, 155, 200, 248, 255, 258
Watt, J. J., 200
Weatherford, Steve, 85
Webb, Lardarius, 151
Weddle, Eric, 182, 259, 289–90
Weeden, Brandon, 113, 201
Wentz, Carson, 9, 56, 134–36, 167–69, 175, 177–78, 224, 230–34, 258, 267–68, 293, 315, 323–24
Wesleyan University, 39
West, Charcandrick, 145, 197
West Alabama, University of, 108
West Coast offense, 102–4, 165–66, 306
West Virginia, University of, 7, 67, 114
White, Jack, 49
White, Tre'Davious, 243
Whitehurst, Charlie, 112
Wilkins, Jeff, 60
Williams, Ashley, 33
Williams, Brandon, 278
Williams, Cary, 100
Williams, Doug, 10
   college football at Grambling and, 25–26

contracts and salary and, 28, 33–34, 332
death of wife Janice and, 33
drafted by Tampa Bay (1978), 27–30, 33
as early black quarterback, 5, 27–32, 78, 330
early life of, 24–25
injuries and, 30
marriage and family and, 28–29, 33
Oklahoma Outlaws and (1984–85), 34
on quarterbacks, 5, 169, 332–34
quits Tampa Bay, 33–34
Super Bowl and, 5, 23, 78, 332–34
Tampa Bay Bucs and, 81; (1978–82), 29–33
Washington and: as quarterback (1985–89), 23, 34–35, 78, 332–34; as senior VP of player personnel, 23, 78–80, 162–65, 167–69, 194, 330
Washington scouting by, and Smith trade, 78–81, 225–26, 271–73, 303–11
Williams, Janice, 33
Williams, Kyle, 85
Williams, Laura, 24
Williams, Marcus, 325
Williams, Mario, 65
Williams, Maxx, 205, 283
Williams, Robert, Jr., 24–25
Williams, Robert, Sr., 24
Williams, Tramon, 189
Willis, Jordan, 287

Willson, Luke, 271
Wilson, Albert, 17–18, 197, 298–99
Wilson, Russell, 31, 136, 169, 213, 271–73, 306
Winston, Jameis, 22, 31, 63, 148–51, 187–92, 235–36, 238, 273–74, 277, 293, 315–16, 318, 320
Wisconsin, University of, 213
Witten, Jason, 281
Wolf, Ron, 40
Wonderlic test, 42–43, 51, 60, 167
Wood, Eric, 320
Woodhead, Danny, 1, 130, 288
Woodruff, Josh, 137–38
World League of American Football, 7, 67, 283
Wright, Allen, 309
Wright, Anthony, 39
Wright, Kendall, 208
Wyoming, University of, 80, 303

Yale University, 21, 62
Yanda, Marshal, 1, 153–54, 256, 279
Yates, T. J., 248
Young, Steve, 112
Young, Vince, 56, 168
Youngblood, Jack, 30

Zachary, Louisiana, 24
Zampese, Ken, 286
Zimmer, Mike, 205, 215, 217
zone blocking, 103
Zuckerberg, Mark, 147

ABOUT THE AUTHOR

JOHN FEINSTEIN is the #1 *New York Times* bestselling author of the classic sports books *A Season on the Brink* and *A Good Walk Spoiled,* along with many other bestsellers, including *The Legends Club* and *Where Nobody Knows Your Name.* He has written twelve young adult novels, including *Last Shot,* which won the Edgar Allan Poe Award for mystery writing in the Young Adult category.

Feinstein is a member of the Naismith Basketball Hall of Fame, the National Sports Media Hall of Fame, the U.S. Basketball Writers Hall of Fame, and the Greater Washington Jewish Sports Hall of Fame.

He currently writes for *The Washington Post, Golf Digest,* and *Golf World;* does commentaries on the CBS Sports Radio Network; and appears on the Army Radio Network during football and basketball season.

He is married to Christine Bauch-Feinstein and has three children: Danny, Brigid, and Jane.